D0853353

Chicago Public Library

Form 178 rev. 1-94

TOMORROW'S ^HR^ MANAGEMENT

TOMORROW'S HR MANAGEMENT

48

THOUGHT LEADERS

CALL FOR

CHANGE

DAVE ULRICH, MICHAEL R. LOSEY, & GERRY LAKE, EDITORS

John Wiley & Sons, Inc.

New York • Chichester • Weinheim • Brisbane • Singapore • Toronto

Copyright © 1997 by Dave Ulrich, Michael R. Losey, and Gerry Lake
Published by John Wiley & Sons, Inc.

Library of Congress Cataloging-in-Publication Data:

Tomorrow's HR management : 48 thought leaders call for change / edited
   by David Ulrich, Michael Losey, Geraldine Lake.
       p.   cm.
   Includes index.
   ISBN 0-471-19714-9 (cloth : alk. paper)
   1. Personnel management. 2. Human capital. I. Ulrich, David,
1953-   . II. Losey, Michael, 1938-   III. Lake, Geraldine S.
HF5549.S84248   1997
658.3—dc21   97-11787

Printed in the United States of America

10 9 8 7 6 5 4 3 2

To the HR professionals who face a future that will be perhaps the most exciting time in the profession and to our lifetime partners, Wendy, Ann, and Dale—our best human resources

CONTENTS

INTRODUCTION

DAVE ULRICH, MICHAEL R. LOSEY, and GERRY LAKE

We recently heard the quip, "These are the good old days that someone in the future will someday look back on with nostalgia." In the future, we probably will look back on these days and see patterns of thought and action that can be woven into a sensible theory of how Human Resources (HR) has evolved. In the present, however, the future of HR practices, departments, and professionals is much less clear.

Many argue that HR issues are increasingly salient to business performance, under labels such as core competence, intellectual capital, organizational capability, high-performing work systems, process management, value-based management, empowerment, involvement, productivity, culture change, and high-performing teams. Underlying each of these labels or organizational initiatives rests an assumption that HR practices impact executive thought and action—and an organization's performance. That's why we've written the title as we have, inserting "HR" into "Tomorrow's Management." The people, the human resources, that make up a company are its key assets and in organizations where effective *human resource* management hasn't been an integral part of *management,* it will have to be inserted for optimum success.

While not all authors, executives, or students of managerial and organizational action use HR vocabulary, they generally do focus on issues and practices central to HR. For that reason, this book is not just for HR practitioners; it's for all senior managers, even for CEOs.

At the same time that HR issues are gaining prominence, traditional HR departments are under increased pressure to rethink, redefine, and reevaluate their roles. Some call for the demise of the HR function as we know it; others see it being outsourced; others see it becoming a part of the management role; and others suggest it continue on much the same path as it is presently. A number of experiments are underway that involve outsourcing, shared services, strategic partnership, line manager accountability, and other forms of governance of HR departments.

Table I.1
Current and Future State of Business Strategy

	Current		Future
Business Environment/ Strategy	What is our business environment and strategy?	gap 1	Given environmental trends, what will be the likely business strategy?
		gap 2	
Organization Capability (Culture, Core Competence)	What are our organizational capabilities?	gap 3	Given our future strategy, what capabilities will be necessary?
		gap 4	
Organization/Management/Human Resource Practices	What are our practices?	gap 5	Given our future strategy and capabilities, what will be our future HR practices?

In the midst of increased pressure for business results through HR issues and reexamination of the traditional HR department, HR professionals are also facing increased expectations. HR professionals are being asked to do more with less, to do different work, and to do work better. HR professionals, to be successful, must have a clear picture of the current and future state of business strategy, organization capability, and HR practice (see Table I.1). HR professionals who live only in the present will fail to move strategy (gap 1), organization (gap 3), and HR (gap 5) to a future state. In addition, HR professionals in the future will need to align future strategy and organization (gap 2) and organization and HR practice (gap 4). The future is likely to create change that will impact HR practices, departments, and professionals.

This book offers one approach to thinking about the future of HR. A number of other approaches can and have been used. Futurist methodologies have been applied to study the "state of the art" and the future and have through surveys of thought leaders identified likely priorities for the future.

Our approach to thinking about the future of HR parallels closely and draws heavily on a methodology used by Frances Hesselbein, Marshall Goldsmith, and Richard Beckhard. They have produced two excellent anthologies, *Leader of the Future* and *Organization of the Future* under the auspices of the Drucker Foundation. Their methodology for thinking about the future was to invite thought leaders on leadership and organization to produce original essays that laid out their views on the future of leadership and organization.

We have liberally adopted their methodology. We have tried to select thought leaders in three groups: academics who study and write about HR issues, consultants who offer advice and counsel on an array of HR issues (from HR professional search firms to professional consulting firms), and HR professionals who practice the craft of HR in leading companies. While we expected these three groups to have unique and different points of view, what we have found is that these three distinctions (academic, consultant, and practitioner) do not differentiate the messages of the authors. We have also tried to produce essays from both those who have been in the field for some time and those who are newer to the field. We know that the 37 essays we have selected are indicative, not conclusive. There are others whose ideas we value and whose insights on the future of HR would have been useful additions to this book, but size and timing forced us to limit our scope.

An early impetus for this work came from the alliance of the University of Michigan Business School, John Wiley & Sons, and the Society for Human Resource Management around the *Human Resource Management Journal*. Beginning in January 1997, these three partners, each respected in its own domain, formed an alliance to create, produce, and distribute the *Human Resource Management Journal*. Many of the essays in this book were first published in the inaugural issue of this Journal.

Each of the contributors to this book was asked to write an original ten-page essay on "the future of HR" as he or she chose to define it. We asked for personal statements more than references, bibliography, theory, and data. We wanted to document the points of view of these leaders. We wanted to feel from their words, insights, concerns, and passions how they would articulate and frame the future of HR. Our hope in this book was for a unique variety of opinion: positive, negative; broad, narrow; optimistic, pessimistic; provocative, discreet; calls for change, calls for status quo.

We are delighted with the material we have received. Without hesitation, the authors have been willing to share their ideas and feelings with clarity and candor. We are indebted to each of them for taking valuable time to prepare a thoughtful essay. In addition, we are grateful that each author has agreed that all royalties from this book will be donated to the Society of Human Resource Management Foundation and the National Academy of Human Resources Foundation to further the profession.

We have organized the essays into some general categories that may help the reader capture the message of the book. In doing so, we have identified six themes that form prescriptive actions for the HR professional of the future.

I. *Manage Human Resources Like a Business:* HR departments must become more business-focused. This means that HR departments need to have clear outcomes they deliver to the business with clear theory and foci guiding action within the department.

II. *Play New Roles:* HR professionals will have many new roles to play in the organization and competitive environment of the future. Many ways of thinking about and performing these roles are articulated.

III. *Respect History, Create a Future:* HR functions need to and have changed . . . or have they? Rather than merely live for an uncertain future, HR work needs to be grounded in its past. The discipline of human resources has a history that has both good news and bad news. The good news is that much of the history should be maintained in moving toward the future. The bad news is that some of that history needs to be changed to meet the future with competence.

IV. *Build an Infrastructure:* The HR infrastructure focuses on how the HR function itself is governed. It deals with issues such as measurement of HR practices, competencies of HR, and the changing role of HR leaders.

V. *Remember the "Human" in Human Resource:* Sometimes, in the quest to be business partners, HR professionals have focused more on the business and less on the people side of the business. Under the label of intellectual or human capital, HR professionals need to keep focusing their attention on the human side of the enterprise.

VI. *Go Global:* Technological advances in information, travel, media, and other parts of our lives have made a large world smaller. Changes in one country are quickly understood and/or adapted throughout the world.

These are not the *only* themes for the future of HR, but they do indicate issues that are not only salient, but unsolved. They will need to receive more attention over the next few years. In this work, we offer current and future thinking and ideas that may trigger innovative and exciting HR work.

SECTION I

MANAGE HUMAN RESOURCES LIKE A BUSINESS

Businesses generally are defined externally by their customers, internally by their cultures, and between the two through strategy, products, services, and structures. Line managers are often defined as individuals who work in customer or production activities. Staff managers are generally those who work in functions that support customer or production work. As business learns to compete in an increasingly complex and changing world, traditional line/staff distinctions need to be replaced with unified models of management.

To move human resources (HR) as staff to more of a line perspective, its leaders must learn to operate HR more like a business. Businesses have clear strategies, outcomes, products, services, and structures to accomplish ✓ goals and deliver the outcomes. A business plan lays out how the environment, strategy, and organization will change to create value for shareholders, customers, and employees.

To become more like a business means that HR departments need to have strategies that define specific outcomes they deliver to the business, products and services that will be delivered to accomplish the strategy, and organization processes in place to create value. HR departments need to have business plans that detail movement from current to future state of strategy, organization, and action.

Section I essays discuss how to manage HR more like a business. The essays deal with a series of questions such as:

5

- *What Is the Strategy of HR?*

  Strategy defines how a business positions itself and allocates resources to products and/or services to deliver value to customers. An HR strategy articulates the purposes of HR within the firm, the deliverables or outcomes from HR work, and the products and/or services delivered by HR departments.

- *What Are the Products and Services of HR?*

  Many typologies of HR work exist to describe types of HR processes. Emerging HR typologies will identify new HR products and services required to meet changing business needs. Many of these new products will ensure the flow of intellectual capital and knowledge within a firm; others will ensure the development of a new generation of leaders within a firm.

- *How Should HR Be Organized to Ensure That the Strategy Is Executed?*

  Increasingly, organizations are being defined less by structure and more by how capabilities are acquired and deployed. As HR functions articulate clear strategies, products, and services, they identify the organizational choices that ensure that capabilities, even across organizational boundaries, meet strategic goals.

The essays in this section provide a conceptual rationale for the strategy of an HR department, identify deliverables from an HR strategy, suggest emerging tools for ensuring intellectual capital and leadership depth, and suggest critical organizational processes for securing capital across boundaries. Through strategy, products, and services, HR departments become more like a business, and HR professionals become less staff and more line oriented.

The message from these essays is for HR professionals to think about the HR function as though it were a free-standing business that must have clear strategy, products, services, and structure.

CHAPTER 1

THE BUSINESS OF
HUMAN RESOURCES

KENNETH M. ALVARES

$\mathbf{I}$t has become increasingly clear that human resources (HR) in the future must operate strategically—not as the currently popular "partner to the business," but as a business in and of itself. There are a number of critical reasons to move in this direction, not the least of which is that it may be the only way for HR to take control of its own future.

Today's competitive business environment allows little tolerance for departments that exist solely as overhead. Many companies are downsizing their human resource operations at the same time they are placing greater demands on the function to provide better, faster, and cheaper solutions to increasingly complex business problems. Outsourcing options abound.

This means that HR functions must look for ways to leverage their resources. The number and type of shared services, for example, are already growing. Another probable trend will be using technology to provide low-cost, convenient ways for people throughout the enterprise to have direct access to previously proprietary HR information and to be able to perform transactions themselves.

So what will human resource professionals spend their time doing? As more alternatives for performing transactional activities become available, HR staffs will be able to focus on adding value to the enterprise. They will also become heavily involved in managing the business of human resources. Savvy HR professionals are already taking actions to develop the business acumen that will allow them to do so successfully, and more must follow suit.

7

The bottom-line business of human resources must be the delivery and/or development of human capital that enable the enterprise to become more competitive, to operate for maximum effectiveness, and to execute its business strategies successfully. HR professionals who understand these objectives and have the business skills to see that they are achieved will be invaluable in the future.

The HR function, as it is currently structured in most companies, will not be able to operate effectively. The traditional model in which corporate human resource groups design programs and set policies and procedures while field human resource groups execute programs is, in reality, more problematic than productive. Corporate HR often views field HR as little more than a mechanism for executing corporate directives, while field HR likes to think that corporate HR should exist solely to provide policies and programs at the field's bidding. Neither is correct, but the traditional model reinforces this mentality and contributes to a divisiveness within the function than may actually prevent it from meeting enterprise business needs.

A MARKET-BASED HR MODEL

Human resources must recreate itself as a customer-centric business with support groups that exist to meet customer needs as efficiently as possible. By becoming a virtual HR network, HR can offer its customers easier access to a greater range of products and services, freeing them (and itself) from the need to manage a hierarchy.

The delivery system shown in Figure 1.1 is analogous to that found in line organizations, where customers can and do go elsewhere if a business is unable to provide quality products or services quickly and at competitive prices.

The following discussion examines the roles and responsibilities of the four groups suggested in this new way of thinking about an HR function, the skill sets required for those who will staff them, and how they will be funded.

Account Managers

Account managers, like their counterparts in line sales, provide primary client interface. Their job includes establishing a relationship with their customers, helping them find needed products and services (either off-the-shelf

Figure 1.1
Delivery of HR Services

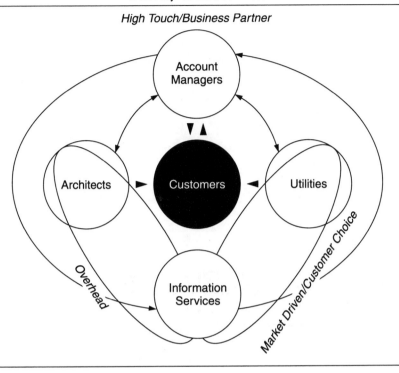

High Touch/Business Partner

or custom-designed), and managing HR-related projects on the client's behalf. Their services are funded by direct charge to the line and, just as in sales, they are held accountable for profit and loss.

The people who serve as account managers must, first and foremost, be able to understand and participate in the business. (They must understand and influence the extent to which the human capital of an organization drives business strategy.) They also, however, need to be good listeners who can diagnose problems and come up with best-practices solutions. In addition to being able to delegate and manage projects effectively, they must be service-oriented and have strong people skills.

Finally, they must be familiar with HR products and services. In fact, the most effective account managers might well come from marketing and/or line organizations rather than from inside the traditional human resource function.

Architects

This group is staffed by technical experts and specialists who create the parameters within which the function operates. They establish direction, set priorities, and create mechanisms for communicating the key elements of the corporation's strategy to the field. This group's perspective is corporate; its vision is long-term. The collective culture and values of the enterprise are the focus of this group, and its services are paid for through corporate overhead.

It is staffed by those with technical expertise in HR disciplines; specialists in compensation, benefits, and labor law are examples. In addition to being strategy-oriented, architects must have strong conceptual ability, sound planning skills, and a mastery of the business that enable them to link the activities of the function with the strategy of the company.

Information Services

This area provides data, analyses, interpretations, and systems directly to internal customers. This group operates as a self-contained business-delivery unit, providing products and services through a variety of channels including, but not limited to, centralized answer centers, internal publications, and networked communications technology. Products and services are paid for by a combination of per capita allocation and product chargebacks.

Ideally, this group is staffed by people with strong organizational and analytical skills and with the ability to focus on details. They should be productive, efficient, service-oriented, systems-knowledgeable, and capable in the field of statistics.

Utilities

These are internal vendors who develop and provide off-the-shelf and/or custom-designed products and services, such as training and recruiting, directly to customers. Their products and services are paid for by the line on a chargeback basis, and they compete for business directly with the external market. For example, HR at Sun Microsystems, Inc. is currently experimenting with the chargeback system for certain services provided by the corporate employment group, international human resources, and the "SunU" training function.

Utilities need to be staffed by people with technical expertise in relevant areas who are able to conceptualize, develop, and implement new products and services in a timely and cost-effective way. In addition to being service-oriented, they must be market-focused and entrepreneurial. They must also manage profit and loss much as the rest of the line organization.

HOW WILL THE MARKET MODEL WORK?

Suppose a field manager wants general training for a new employee. He or she can contact the utility directly for information about off-the-shelf courses that are available, or he or she can request custom-designed services directly from the utility. If an internal utility vendor has a standard new-employee orientation class that is appropriate, the manager can register the employee and pay a fee for the class in the form of a chargeback to the department. No contact with the account manager is needed, and no additional charges are incurred.

Suppose the employee needs additional training on computer programs A and B. Again, the manager contacts the utility directly to see what is available internally and learns that the utility has a course on computer program A, but not on program B.

The manager enlists the assistance of the account manager, who determines that a nearby community college offers a course covering both computer programs, but the external course does not touch on the company's internal applications of program B. The account manager consults with the internal utility to determine whether it might be able to develop a course that covers programs A, B, and the internal applications of B.

There are, however, no internal experts qualified to teach computer program B. Based on the account manager's input, utility group members agree to create a computer-based-training (CBT) course to deal with the company-specific applications of program B and to work with the information systems group to get the new CBT program online.

The solution devised by the account manager results in employees taking the community college course on programs A and B then returning to access CBT when convenient to learn company-specific applications.

As far as the cost to the manager/customer, he or she pays for the employee to take the community college course and accepts a chargeback for the account manager's services. The architects' costs are included in the operating overhead, and the manager/customer is charged on a per capita basis for any ongoing use of utility products such as other training courses.

Where do the architects fit in? Their involvement is not visible in this scenario, but they do have an impact. Any HR-related work that is conducted must be performed within the parameters set by the architects who preserve consistency across operating units and ensure that corporate values are honored. The architects' costs are included in the operating overhead.

IS THERE A DOWNSIDE?

Are any complications created by this external market model? It's possible. For the sake of discussion, consider that the above solution causes enrollment in the utility's program A course to drop by half.

The utility now needs to reevaluate (1) whether it can make program A more competitive to attract more paying customers, (2) whether it needs to redesign the course to include program B, or (3) whether it no longer makes sense to offer program A at all.

Just as with the deregulation of formerly monopolistic utilities in the real world, the ability of paying customers to obtain products and services elsewhere can have a significant impact on the internal utility's ability to stay in business.

Of course, some HR services are so intrinsically linked to the culture of the enterprise and are so critical to its ability to meet business objectives that making them optional or allowing them to be outsourced would be unwise. It is completely appropriate to fund these services through allocations based on headcount or on a percentage of payroll. As the chargeback model gains momentum, providing timely, high-quality products and services at competitive prices will take on an urgency that previously has been more familiar in the external business world than in an internal support function.

THIS IS RISKY BUSINESS

Clearly, human resources takes a risk when it adopts an external market model. For example, if products and services are not designed to meet business needs and are not delivered on time, customers will end up paying more than before for inferior quality products. There also may be a temptation to create wildly popular, highly marketable products that do not add value to the business.

Faintheartedness is also a risk. The failure to follow through with the tough decisions regarding outsourcing and staffing will be fatal. Additionally, there will doubtless be disturbing consequences for those who cannot adapt to change or develop the skill sets required by the new model.

How does the function guard against these potential risks? (Remember, human resources is now a business, and businesses are accountable for results.) In a true market-based economy, non–value-add products, no matter how initially popular, will gradually disappear. Metrics will allow for the measurement of those results and for corresponding adjustments, while accountability is offset by rewards for those who are successful.

Chief Executive Officer (CEO) involvement and support are also key, but lack of enthusiasm at the top must not preclude HR from moving in the right direction. It is ultimately the HR professional's responsibility to make a business case for the model and, in so doing, ensure senior management support.

Still, resistance from several fronts is possible. Despite the function's insistence that one-stop shopping convenience and do-it-yourself options are service enhancements, line managers may at first have difficulty believing that fewer interactions with HR personnel mean anything other than a lower level of service. Some will not want to make decisions regarding the purchase of HR products and services, and others will dislike having responsibility for performing HR-related transactions themselves.

Resistance from within the function will likely be strongest during the time in which roles and responsibilities in support of the new delivery model are being defined. During the transition period, judgments of "value" will tend to be made relative to the old, more traditional model, rather than relative to this new business oriented way of thinking. There will be a tendency for everyone to want to be an account manager, but not everyone can or should they want to occupy this position.

Top management may also be hard to convince as the new model does not automatically cost less and, in fact, may require up-front investments in the form of technology and training. Long-term market pressures, however, would drive unnecessary costs out of the system. Finally, change is generally difficult for everyone—and this is a very big change in the mindset for most HR professionals.

How, then can resistance be overcome? Gradually, by starting with a few areas and expanding. Selective hiring is useful, as is positive reinforcement for the new model through rewards for those who make it work.

The best way to overcome resistance, of course, is to prove the model's value in response to the inevitable stakeholder question of "What's in it for me?" In some cases, however, there is simply no alternative to forcing the change—gently, when possible, or not-so-gently, when necessary.

FROM PERSONNEL TO BUSINESS MANAGER

This is not the first time that the discipline of human resources has undergone significant changes. Consider the distance the profession has come already from its narrow focus as a primarily transactional personnel function to the larger perspective represented by its human resource identity.

It was not too many years ago, in fact, that "personnel" was transformed into "human resources" at most companies. At first, it was a change in name only; many of us now in "HR" continued to process paperwork, perform routine administrative transactions, and make and enforce policy in much the same way we had for years.

It was a simpler time, of course. Companies were not required to comply with so many regulations. We in HR did not have dozens of decisions to make about which benefit plans to offer. People chose careers in personnel because they liked people, but as the external business environment changed, so did organizational needs and expectations.

Human resources, a company's human assets, became an important competitive advantage, and the human resource function was required to begin acting as an integral part of the business rather than as an employee support system; this transition was not always easy. The more explosive the industry, the more radical the changes needed to meet the company's HR requirements.

HUMAN RESOURCES AT SUN MICROSYSTEMS, INC.

Sun Microsystems (Sun) is a case in point. The company is one of the world's leading suppliers of distributed computing technologies, products, and services, providing solutions that enable its enterprise customers to build and maintain open network computing environments.

Sun was founded in 1982 and has grown rapidly, not only in number of employees (currently in excess of 16,000) but also in terms of the revenues generated (this year in excess of $7 billion) and products offered. At present, a full 85 percent of Sun's product line has a shelf life of less than one year.

This dizzying product development cycle has profound implications for an HR function that must ensure Sun has the talent in place to move from its current status to the $20 billion-plus company it wants to become. Until fairly recently, however, Sun's human resource function fit into the traditional HR mold.

Because Sun faces strong global competition for human capital, its human resource function must allow swift, cost-effective responses to the enterprise's business needs throughout the world. It became obvious that traditional ways of doing business were simply not going to work. Change was made difficult, however, by the recent success of the company as a whole. It is far more difficult to argue for sweeping changes when a company is doing well than when a company is looking for ways to reverse less than exemplary performance.

The first steps taken by Sun HR toward becoming a more strategic, business-oriented function were somewhat reactive, but they got peoples' attention: The function was restructured, and the number of HR personnel was reduced by a third.

In keeping with Sun culture, the function then looked to technological solutions to fill the gap between what was desired and what could actually be accomplished with current resources. An outdated mainframe HR information system (HRIS) was phased out and a whole series of network centers, distributed applications, were developed to reflect the new way of conceptualizing the HR function. A human resource team worked with its line customers to redesign the business practices themselves. Again, in keeping with Sun's basic business model, a new series of applications was developed to support these new practices. Two principles guided all of the development: self service and universal access.

This streamlining exercise was one response to Sun's self-imposed constraint on the human resource function that would grow at half the rate of the enterprise overall. Like so many businesses, human resources at Sun would have to find ways to provide more products and services of value to its customers and do so with fewer people and for less cost.

ALIGNING HR VISION AND STRATEGIES WITH BUSINESS IMPERATIVES

In order to operate as a business, the function first needed to have a clear understanding of Sun's overall business strategy. A serious look at Sun's business imperatives revealed that a competitive Workforce, Organization, and Workplace (WOW) would be needed by the enterprise in order to maintain its leadership position in the industry. It was also clear that the new HR had an important role to play in the delivery of WOW.

Vision and mission statements articulating HR's direction in relation to Sun's business strategy were communicated to the people who would be responsible for achieving the function's objectives. Elevating the function's purpose and priorities, however, again presented the dilemma of achieving more sophisticated objectives with fewer people. In response, three HR strategies were developed to provide direction for the function's future actions.

The *first strategy* is to design innovative products and services. Within the Sun culture, this means identifying technological solutions and creating online tools to improve universal access to information and to simplify transactions both for human resources and for the line organization as a whole.

The use of technology will surely be a trend of the future for human resources even in generally nontechnological environments. The addition of self-service options for the line, where possible, will free HR staff to add value by developing new products and providing a higher level of much more strategic and business oriented service.

Sun's *second HR strategy* for achieving WOW is to develop organizational capabilities and individual competencies. Methods for strengthening both are now under development and will follow Dave Ulrich's HR skill/competency model which adds functional knowledge, leadership and change, and business understanding to the important element of personal credibility.

In the future, emphasis is likely to be placed on certification both at Sun and throughout the HR community. Although it is controversial today, certification will reinforce human resources' status as a true profession with a body of functional knowledge to be mastered and a measurable set of standards to be upheld.

Finally, Sun's *third HR strategy* for accomplishing WOW is to define uniquely new delivery mechanisms. This is the area in which the real leading-edge work will be performed to take human resources into the 21st century as represented by Sun's external market model and chargeback methodology.

This strategy presents a number of challenges in that it requires the examination of roles, responsibilities, and skill sets needed to support new ways of delivering services and products. It will have a profound impact on the human element of the profession, requiring practitioners to develop new knowledge and competencies; to achieve a paradigm shift from soft "people" skills to an intense focus on business, metrics, and the bottom line.

It won't be easy, but it is critical to becoming an HR function that can face the future successfully.

NO PAIN, NO GAIN

Despite the fact that Sun HR has not fully transformed itself into the "function of the future," there is no turning back. Is the payoff big enough to outweigh the risks and pain? Absolutely. There are too many business imperatives to do anything else.

For those who step up to the challenge, human resources as a business affords new career directions. Those who grow along with the discipline will experience unlimited opportunities to have a bottom-line impact on the enterprise not only as a key contributor to the business, but as the manager of a self-contained business within a business.

At Sun, this means developing new processes, technologies, and products that may ultimately have applications outside the internal community traditionally served by the human resource function. At the very least, by delivering human capital in the form of a competitive work force that enables the achievement of business imperatives, HR at Sun will provide true economic value to the enterprise.

SUMMARY

Human resource functions patterned on an external market model are beginning to take shape at forward-thinking companies. They will operate as customer-centric businesses with sales and product development entities. Internal customers will have ever-increasing freedom of choice as they are no longer required to purchase products and services from what was formerly a human resource monopoly.

The new human resource "business" will have a clear incentive to provide timely, high-quality products and services at competitive prices. The alternative will be to go out of business or, at best, outsource parts of the function to other HR businesses with better performance.

Technology will allow universal access to HR-related information, and self-service options will increase customer convenience. These, in turn, will free HR professionals to add value by developing new products and services in support of the enterprise.

Finally, those who choose to pursue the discipline of human resources will know the entrepreneurial challenges and joys of running a business with all its attendant risks and rewards. It's a future well worth pursuing.

CHAPTER 2

WHERE IS HUMAN RESOURCES?

RALPH N. CHRISTENSEN

Much has been and will be said about the human resource (HR) issues with which large complex organizations will have to deal in the coming decade. While I find an understanding of the specific issues to be essential, I believe that how we posture the leadership of human and organizational issues in the future is critical in and of itself. For the purpose of this paper, I will focus on the posturing of HR rather than upon the particular issues which will no doubt be dealt with in some of the other articles. I do this because I have mixed feelings about HR. On the one hand, I am delighted by the emerging awareness on the part of business leaders of the importance of the people factor in the success of the enterprise. On the other hand, I am troubled that so much of the leadership for the people issues comes from other than HR departments. Business leaders are looking, almost desperately, for guidance in the people arena and all too often are unsure where to find it. More and more I see them going to other organizational leaders since they do not find what they need in HR. Finance has taken the lead in much of the recent downsizing, with what many would say are the "to be expected" results. Quality leaders have often led in the creation of team based work design. Business leaders are looking to academics and consultants for guidance in a broad array of strategic human and organizational issues. Too many are asking, "Where is HR?"

HR POSTURING: INSIGHTS
With that backdrop, let me offer some insights into the future posturing.

1. The future of HR must include the development and acceptance of a simple, yet powerful theory base, so that the myriad HR activities can become grounded in the business and integrated with one another.

I recall being at the University of Michigan several years ago with a group of Human Resource leaders from industry. Early in the program C. K. Prahalad had been invited to speak to us. The one thing that I recall most from his comments was that in general he found the Human Resource functions in most companies to be pretty ineffective. Unlike most who come to that same conclusion and then leave the HR audience either to defend itself or slink away into some dark corner to hide, he suggested a reason for the problem. He said that HR had never identified a coherent theory base from which to operate. In the absence of a good theory base, the field had wandered without focus or direction. If his hypothesis is correct, it is no wonder that HR has become such a popular point of criticism.

Other disciplines that appear better able to relate to the core organizational purpose seem to have a simple enough theory base. Finance, for example, works off of the assumption that investors invest with the expectation of return. Nothing very complicated about that as a theory base, but it does act as a simple focus for innumerable financial systems and activities that plan for, track, and measure the financial elements of an organization.

Surely HR must also have an equally simple, yet focusing theory base. As I explored my own thoughts, I tried psychology as a potential theory base. No, too focused on the individual. Perhaps sociology could offer some help. No, not able to link closely enough to the purpose of the organization. With help from Prahalad's questioning and comments, I have stumbled across a simple theory base that has worked for me since that time at Michigan.

HUMAN COMPETENCE IS THE ENGINE BEHIND THE CREATION OF VALUE

So what is so profound about that, you may ask. Well, I don't know just how profound it is, but it has provided a starting place for me to connect HR to the purpose of the business and to integrate the various components of HR. Let me share a model which depicts the central role of competence to HR. It has emerged for me over the past 20 years work at Digital Equipment, Martin Marietta, Wyatt, and now at Hallmark Cards. It portrays the evolution of a frustrated organizational development (OD) guy who came to distrust the gap that still exists, far too often, between OD and HR. I concluded that we had to find a way to integrate good systems thinking with the broad array of human dynamics in complex organizations (Figure 2.1).

Every business exists in a given business environment which provides opportunities and challenges; it also provides the resources to capitalize on the

Figure 2.1
Integrating Human Resource Practices Vertically within the
Business and Horizontally with Each Other

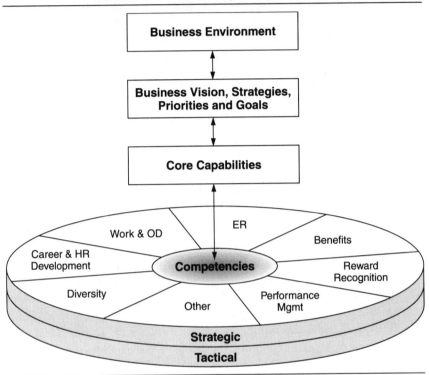

opportunities and to overcome the challenges. From that environment, leaders establish a vision of what role they want to play in that environment.
With the vision in mind, they also establish a strategy. The strategy expresses
the specific path the organization will take from the array of possible paths
available to fulfill the vision. Every strategy assumes certain organizational
capabilities—those abilities demonstrated by the system as a whole which
differentiate it from others. Building organizational capability requires very
specific talent or competencies. Now we have the connection between the
competence of people and the overall business direction. This is the *vertical
link between people and the business*. No Human Resource management effort
should be entertained without a clear understanding of the connection between it and the business needs. I tell all management groups with whom I
work that they should kick me out of the room if a proposal of mine does

not make that connection. At the same time, I tell HR folk that I will kick *them* out of the room if they bring a proposal that doesn't make that connection.

An example of this connection may help. In the very late 1980s, some at Digital acknowledged that the industry and market were going through fundamental changes. As a result of customer pressures, the industry needed to move from a vertically integrated strategy of providing the full range of information technology (silicon, hardware, software, services) to a horizontal strategy of competing head on with niche players. This transition in huge companies such as IBM and Digital requires massive people changes in terms of number of people, skills needed, and organization/management process design to better leverage work. While these changes have been executed with variable degrees of success, this example demonstrates well the connection between the business environment and the human resources systems required in the business.

Assuming that the needed talent is on board, how can the almost infinite number of HR processes be integrated to best leverage them in the creation of value? Every HR process, tool, or technology should leverage talent to fulfill the organizational vision. If any one of these doesn't, we in the firm and especially in HR shouldn't do it. We also need to ensure that the various HR initiatives are integrated, horizontally if you will, with each other. Not one HR system can be designed without it having implications upon others. For example, a compensation system or approach cannot be created without being very clear about the implications upon Employee Relations. Neither can a new work flow or organization be devised without understanding and taking into account the implications for rewards.

The final point of the model deals with defining and identifying what is strategic and what is tactical. For years, I fell into the trap that many fall into of believing that organization design and people development represent the "strategic" side of HR and that employee relations (ER) and compensation represent the tactical side. This is one of the greatest faux pas of the HR culture; it has torn apart unnumbered HR departments. The question is not to decide which elements of HR are strategic and which are not. The question is to identify both the strategic *and* the tactical elements of the entire array of HR technologies. They then should be integrated at both the strategic and at the tactical levels. Successful HR professionals of the future will do this well.

In summary, HR must develop a simple, yet powerful theory base that gives meaning to the people issues of an enterprise and integrates them with the vision of the business.

2. HR will differentiate between human resource management and the human resource department.

How often might one ask for the HR plan or strategy of a given organization, only to get a description of the upcoming activities of the HR Department? Many times these plans have little obvious connection at all to the business plan. Sometimes they are stapled to the back of the business plan to give some semblance of connection to the business or, at a minimum, to soothe the consciences of HR folk who know that they should be part of the business plan. Hogwash! The Human Resource Plan doesn't necessarily have anything *at all* to do with the HR Department. *The HR plan belongs to the business.* It is just as much the responsibility of the business leaders to develop it and to ensure its fulfillment, as it is their responsibility to have and fulfill their investment plan or technology plan. It is one key component of the overall business plan.

If an organization has chosen to invest in an HR department as part of its strategy to deal with the human issues of the enterprise, it should also expect a "business plan" of the HR department. This HR business plan sets out the vision, strategy, priorities, core capabilities, and required competencies of the HR department. Through appraisal of the plan the firm's executives can assess and measure whether or not they are getting an appropriate return from their investment in an HR department. The HR business plan should certainly be clearly supportive of the business human resources plan, but, they are two separate plans.

The above comments about planning are really only symptoms of the lack of clarity regarding who is responsible for human resource management. Managers and HR professionals of the future will understand that line managers are the "people leaders" of their organizations and as such, they are ultimately accountable for human resource management. Some line leaders seem to want an HR person who can take all of the people work off their plates so that they can get on with the truly important work of the business. They don't seem to understand that the people work is the important work; it is core work of management. If a manager doesn't want to deal with the people side of the job he or she should be moved into a technical individual contributor job, which seems to be what he or she wants to do, and let someone else lead the human resource. Leadership of people is an honor, not a bleak chore to be passed on to someone else.

Unfortunately, many HR people are more than happy to take all the people work off the manager's plate, in an apparent attempt to make sure that their own plate is full of something. In contrast, however, too many HR

Table 2.1
Contrast between HR Management and HR Department

	Human Resource Management	Human Resource Department
Focus	Implementation/application of HR tools and practices.	Development of HR tools and practices.
Owner	Line management.	HR department leadership.
Outcome	Creation of value through effective management of competencies.	Effective Human Resource Management practice.

people seem intent on giving everything having to do with people to the leaders until that leader is encumbered with such HR administrivia that he or she finally revolts and tosses it all out. The HR professional of the future will know how to walk the fine line of ensuring that managers take full responsibility for the people side of the business, while providing needed tools and coaching to ensure their success. Does this mean that HR people are not accountable for anything, as has been the lamentation of many managers? No, of course not. The question is what are they accountable for and to whom? They are accountable to management for excellent human resource management processes, tools, and coaching that work. They are responsible to energetically influence managers to effectively use the tools that have been designed. If their current tools and coaching don't work, management should find HR providers who can provide tools and coaching that do work.

The matrix (Table 2.1) depicts aspects of the contrast between Human Resource Management and the HR department.

CONCLUSION

I believe that the arena of Human Resources is the most challenging and exciting aspect of organizational success being addressed today. It is the arena most likely to provide competitive opportunities in the future. Managers are beginning to realize that behind every single business issue (or symptom) ultimately lies a human issue. For example, poor financial performance is not the problem; it is a symptom of a human system that is either unable to plan for, to execute, or to measure its financial goals. Time to market is not the problem; it is a symptom of human systems that don't work. As leaders acquire this point of view, they increasingly look about them for HR leaders who can help with real business solutions through effective people management. Business leaders who have identified a problem tend to figure out how to address it; they will find that help somewhere. *The question for HR is whether or not they will find it with us.*

While the two issues identified here do not address all that must be dealt with in the issue of "The Future of Human Resources," they do provide part of the posturing for a successful future for Human Resources.

CHAPTER 3

LEADING THE HIGH-CAPABILITY ORGANIZATION: CHALLENGES FOR THE TWENTY-FIRST CENTURY

JAMES L. HESKETT and LEONARD A. SCHLESINGER

Some would say that the high-capability organizations we have studied over the years succeed primarily because of a brilliant strategy that shields them from forces confronting their less-fortunate competitors. Others might maintain that their success depends primarily on the execution of human resource strategies defined to an unusual degree in terms of people and working cultures, but either of these is a moot point. There would be no debate without the leadership supplied by an unusual group of people.

In examining the leadership enjoyed by high-capability organizations we have studied, we assume that these people do well what all leaders are expected to do including: (1) defining the organization's mission and values, (2) insuring that a process is in place to determine and review long-term goals and strategies, (3) marshaling and allocating both financial and human resources, (4) maintaining a sense of perspective and direction in the affairs of their organizations, and (5) representing their organizations to the outside world. We will not dwell on these matters. Of greater interest to us are those extraordinary things they believe and do that set them and their organizations apart from those that are merely good.

WHO ARE THEY?

Leaders of high-capability organizations come in all shapes and sizes. Some are more profane, some more dignified, some more elegant, and some more reverent than others. By education they include lawyers, teachers, engineers, and those schooled in the liberal arts. Most are, however, people who, at least in appearance, would not stand out in a crowd.

All of the roughly thirty organizations we have considered are led by individuals who have had long associations with their organizations. They are people who have shaped cultures and been shaped by them. They understand the power of culture and how it can be used. They have selected themselves into the organizations, missions, values, and policies with which they are entrusted.

Before looking at other qualities, there is one that we believe distinguishes the leaders in this sample that deserves underlining. They have extremely high levels of self-confidence that far outweigh their egos, over which they maintain strong control. Thus, they find it easy, and even enjoyable, to listen to and attribute the source of good ideas to others.

This rare quality allows them to be self-deprecating. They can enjoy telling stories that elevate those around them. They often poke fun at themselves. In listening to John Martin of Taco Bell, David Glass of Wal-Mart, Bill Pollard of ServiceMaster, Herb Kelleher of Southwest Airlines, or others, it is easy to conclude that they use stories, many times with themselves as the object lesson, as an important management device.

WHAT DO THEY BELIEVE?

By and large, the leaders in our sample believe in a number of predictable things such as: (1) the importance of values alongside a good strategy, (2) the strategic importance of human resource management and organizational capability, (3) the need to communicate mission and values constantly, (4) the need to provide daily examples of what they believe, and (5) the need to set outrageously high goals and then do everything possible to provide the capability needed by those in their organizations to meet them. More unexpected, at least for us, was the degree to which a number of the leaders in our sample also emphasized, among other things: (1) the need to carefully walk the fine line between building organization pride and avoiding arrogance in the behaviors of themselves and their colleagues, (2) the critical nature of the basic hiring decisions in their organizations, and (3) at least on the part of several of these leaders, a firm belief that the customer is not always right. Consider how these themes are played out in four highly diverse examples that nevertheless typify the patterns of leadership we have observed in other organizations.

General Robert Herries at USAA

When one asks "What's going on here?", one finds a combination of strategy, brilliant execution, culture, and leadership executed by an organization with simple goals: the highest results and value to its clients of any company in the financial services industry.

Since 1922, USAA has carved out a niche providing low-cost, high-service financial services primarily to military officers and their families. It has succeeded so well in achieving both goals that its military officers ("members") rarely think of going outside USAA, especially for insurance products. The organization understands its customers and their needs. For example, when many of its members became involved in Operation Desert Storm, unlike other insurance companies, USAA called its members to make sure they felt they were adequately covered before going into a high risk situation.

Organizational capability at USAA is centered around, and to some extent dependent on, dealing with a select clientele comprised of disciplined, honest, reliable military officers with limited time and a great deal of mobility in their lives and work. As a result, contact between USAA and its members is solely through telephone, mail, and increasingly through personal computers, very effective and low-cost means of communication. The communications process helps explain how USAA is able to serve its members with some of the lowest costs (and lowest insurance rates) of any company in its industry.

"Remote" service to intelligent, demanding members requires a huge frontline service force with great attitudes and considerable aptitude for utilizing one of the most sophisticated information systems in business today. This, along with the military penchant for education, helps explain a human resource development strategy that calls for very high expenditures for job- and life-related education. This service has lent itself as well to the creation of an organization of more than 10,000 people located almost totally in one office building in San Antonio, Texas that quite characteristically is compared in size to the Pentagon in Washington, DC.

An unusually high proportion of USAA managers are former military officers and, therefore, members (customers) of the company. Many maintain their military titles on the job. (They are sensitive, too, to the fact that all member information systems provide for referring to members by military title.) Its military culture gives USAA strong advantages, but it has also posed a great challenge to USAA's erstwhile Chief Executive Officer (CEO), Brigadier General Robert McDermott, and his successor, General Robert

Herries, in going forward. The "natural" market for USAA's services is shrinking with cutbacks in United States military spending. This means that USAA will, if it wishes to continue to grow, have to expand its markets to include new or existing services to increasing numbers of nonmilitary people with whom it is not accustomed to dealing.

General Herries, conscious of the challenges and with a deep understanding of the culture of his organization and its primary customers, has begun the change by continuing the top-to-bottom review of process improvement started under the leadership of his predecessor, a quite natural result of his background in the development of one of the most extensive information systems in operation today in the private sector. This has required a cultural transformation from more heavily top-down command and control approaches to those centered around process improvement teams with greater latitude. On the frontline, it has involved the creation of systems to support service people being given broader latitude than before.

Herries, himself military in bearing and attitude, is leading this process with the understanding that goal-setting in the past had the equivalence of orders issued from the top. Goals were not argued; they were achieved. With this in mind, he has been reluctant to either set goals or prescribe methods for the transition that is taking place at USAA, but he has employed his knowledge of the military culture at USAA in this process. According to him:

> Ours has been a natural progression from less dramatic forms of change to more dramatic forms. We want to avoid explosive and potentially dangerous change, change which is forced on us by external conditions, by pre-empting it. We're always thinking about change, perhaps as a result of the military need for flexibility. (Heskett & Hallowell, 1993, p. 7)

General Herries has sent a strong signal to the organization of the need for change by carving out a separate four-state geographic region, in which a business process review team has been given a wide latitude in seeking new ways to do business as well as to develop new services. One of the themes that has been adopted for this effort, "service tomorrow with yesterday's traditions," fits well with the company's values and strategies. It provides a concise way of communicating effectively to this large army what the company is really about.

USAA will make its mistakes, if it has to, in a relatively small part of its business, but it will do so with a company of soldiers operating on the frontline (and ready to go all-out for its leader) rather than from division headquarters. It will do it led by someone who understands both the military culture and how to utilize it to produce change.

Frances Hesselbein at the Girl Scouts of the USA

In many ways, Frances Hesselbein's challenge when she became Executive Director of the Girl Scouts of the USA (GSUSA) parallels what General Herries is facing at USAA. The GSUSA was a huge organization with stagnant membership. It was perceived by many as harboring the values often attributed to white, suburban America, out of touch with demographic, social, and other changes taking place in the United States. It was (and is) also an organization with strong values centered around the Girl Scout Promise (On my honor, I will try: To serve God and my country, to help people at all times, and to live by the Girl Scout Law) and the Law (I will do my best: to be honest, to be fair, etc.) and the mission of helping each girl to achieve her full potential. These provide two of the three pillars of today's GSUSA, in Hesselbein's words, an organization that is "mission focused" and "values based."

Change required that Hesselbein's organization revamp its planning process to include larger numbers of the 750,000 volunteers and 7,500 paid staff members; consolidate Girl Scout Councils to build critical mass at the operating level; and institute a massive human resource development program for directors, volunteers, and staff members. It also required a huge change in the way in which volunteers viewed their own organization and its relevance for society. Long discussions produced the third pillar of the modern GSUSA, the importance of ethnic and racial diversity in the make-up of the organization's membership and volunteer corps—something that would make it, in Hesselbein's words, "demographically driven." As a result, goals that some thought were unattainable were set for increasing the proportion of members and volunteers drawn from diverse groups in the population. Symbolic of this change was a policy fostered by Hesselbein of picturing girls with diverse backgrounds in every ad and piece of literature distributed by the organization. The substance of the change was embodied in the development of programs for "latch-key" girls who were at home alone after school, projects to attract new members from Hispanic communities, and efforts to discourage teen pregnancy.

Role models are important in an organization dedicated to young people. No one understood that more than Frances Hesselbein during her 14-year tenure, which ended in 1991, at the head of the organization. This required extraordinary attention to appearance, speaking ability, and leadership bearing. It required careful, professional management as well, because implicit in much of what Hesselbein and her colleagues did was the belief that women must hold themselves to very high standards when it comes to management. At the grassroots level, it required finding young women who were good role models (such as successful businesswomen) as troop leaders.

In addition to action, Hesselbein understood the importance of symbols and language as a part of effective leadership.

> The power of language is so important in this job. People often refer to us as a traditional organization. I try to remind them that we're a contemporary organization with a great tradition. When people say Scouts, I point out that we're the Girl Scouts, not to be confused with the Boy Scouts. When people, including those in our own organization, refer to cookie sales as a business activity, somebody has to remind them that it's a girl's program activity. All of us have to constantly remind ourselves that the bottom line in this organization is changed lives. (Heskett, 1989, p. 13)

In preference to her non-official wardrobe, Hesselbein regularly wore her Girl Scout uniform. As a way of emphasizing the change in the organization and making the wearing of the uniform even more appealing, especially to adult volunteers, she had designer Bill Blass volunteer his time to completely redesign the line of Girl Scout uniforms so that they were more attractive and could be worn to a great variety of official and social functions.

One of the reasons why Hesselbein could lead with a particular sense of authority and self-confidence while delegating greater responsibility to the Councils in the field is that she was the first Executive Director in the history of the organization to be promoted with "field" experience as a troop leader, national board member, council president, and council executive director. Wearing the uniform had become a habit for her.

William Pollard at ServiceMaster

ServiceMaster, the largest provider of about $3 billion worth of custodial and other services to hospitals, schools, and homes in the United States, "wears" its values on many of its official documents, including its annual report. They are: (1) to honor God in all we do, (2) to help each person develop, (3) to serve our customers, and (4) to earn a profit. The first two goals are described by Chairman William Pollard as "ends" objectives, the third and fourth as merely "means" objectives (Heskett, 1987). At ServiceMaster, Pollard is fond of pointing out, executives not only have to ask themselves what they are doing and how they are doing it, but also why they are doing it. According to Pollard, the "why question" is the most important question facing business today, even though it is too rarely asked. Pollard refers to his organization's activities as a "ministry." This attitude hasn't stood in the way of profits; in fact, at ServiceMaster it is used as a way of explaining why the company regularly has to rank at the top of all others of its size on its return on investment in order to achieve the stewardship implied in its goals. The attitude has not stood in the way of growth. ServiceMaster's corporate goal is to double in size every five years. This is not just to satisfy shareholders; a ministry that doesn't grow doesn't fulfill its "ends" objectives.

Pollard, a former teacher of law and one in a line of ServiceMaster CEO's who regarded their primary task as building and preserving the company's values, uses actions and language as effective tools. "Servant leadership" is a term heard as often at ServiceMaster as at Wal-Mart, another organization whose leader, Sam Walton, may have coined it. It is acted out frequently at ServiceMaster when managers, from Pollard down, regularly assume the jobs of their frontline service providers, cleaning hospital operating rooms and other facilities and often suffering the indignities familiar to those performing such tasks. It is all part of an effort to continually sensitize management of the need for methods, materials, and equipment not only to help frontline employees become more productive but also to help them perform their jobs with more dignity. When asked about the most important quality that he sought in his CEO successor, Carlos Cantu, Pollard said, without hesitation, "a servant's heart."

The first of ServiceMaster's goals, "to honor God in all we do," provokes curiosity in many observers, investors, and potential employees. It is a clear signal to those self-selecting themselves into the organization and helps explain why ServiceMaster's management team is as cohesive as it is. Bill Pollard explains that the emphasis is not so much on religious preference as it is on the values that go with the belief.

The concept of the manager as "teacher/learner" is paramount at ServiceMaster, something that Pollard communicates frequently and in unique ways. He spends as much of his time teaching as any of the leaders in the group that we have observed. Walk into any ServiceMaster manager's office and you will see a bookcase full of books ranging from management to philosophy in their content, books that have been read.

At a recent two-day ServiceMaster board meeting attended also by some 80 senior managers, everyone was assigned seven books to read in advance of the meeting. At the meeting, participants were broken into small groups to discuss specific questions about each book, questions personally drafted by Chairman Pollard, who could be seen in the middle of his discussion leaders briefing them for the roles they were to play and enjoying every minute of it.

Herb Kelleher at Southwest Airlines

Southwest Airlines first flew in 1971 after several years of legal battles fought by its young lawyer and co-founder, Herb Kelleher. It was built on values that both belie its roots in Texas and its need to differentiate itself in the eyes of both its employees and passengers, including the importance of family, love, fun, and altruism. To its employees, Southwest says, "work is important . . . don't spoil it with seriousness" and "people are important . . . each one makes a difference." (Heskett & Hallowell 1993A) The concept of love (always spelled "luv" at Southwest) reflects on the way that Southwest's employees are encouraged to treat each other and the value-minded "road warrior" business travelers that make up its core market segment.

To preserve its organizational sense of humor and family, the selection of new employees is a critical leadership responsibility. Preserving the culture, even one as fun-loving as Southwest's is serious business. It is presided over by Colleen Barrett, Executive Vice President, Customers. She is assisted by about 50 managers from all parts of the organization who take part in approving plans designed to maintain values. Its work pervades everything that Southwest does, including the controlled, manageable rate of growth that it has elected in order to preserve its culture.

Southwest has delivered such high value to its customers, primarily through good service delivered at fares roughly 30 percent of its competitors, that it is in high demand among cities, usually a waiting list of 40 more, desiring its service. The organization, however, has limited its growth to three or four new markets per year. A new destination city is selected, among other things, on the ease with which Southwest's employees can preserve the "spirituality" (Kelleher's word) of the organization centered around its team-oriented culture; effect the on-time operation of the company's planes on which customers depend and employees are expected to deliver (requiring relatively little congestion, sufficient gate space and, if possible, generally good operating weather); and preserve low operating costs essential to delivering value to customers (through low landing fees and, again, low airport congestion).

The team-oriented culture is essential to achieving perhaps the most stringent operating goal that any airline sets for itself: turning two out of three of its flights around in 20 minutes or less with fewer gate attendants than its competitors, a goal that results in high aircraft utilization and the lowest capital requirements per revenue mile in the industry. This efficient turn-around requires that managers and employees alike work as teams. At Southwest it occurs both on the job and off as managers, beginning with the CEO, regularly work on the frontline in the company's facilities or at the Company's charity of choice, Ronald McDonald Houses for children.

Love, or luv, is good business at Southwest—first, because it supports teamwork and second because it extends to the way in which employees treat customers. In part, this is a result not only of the care that Southwest takes in selecting its employees but also the degree to which they select themselves into the organization. One of the most striking impressions of a visit to the company's headquarters in Dallas is how much people hug each other. The initial conclusion a visitor reaches is that this is a display being put on for his/her benefit, but the longer it goes on, the more it becomes apparent that this is a way of life at the company.

Southwest is known for the degree of latitude it gives its frontline employees to differentiate the airline's service from that of its competitors. Herb Kelleher sets an example for this by his own antics, whether arm-wrestling a potential litigant to forestall a possible lawsuit or appearing in his company's hangar at two o'clock in the morning to address his mechanics in a feathered scarf and dress. This inspires a high degree of creativity among airplane cabin attendants, for example, who make the on-board, FAA-required announcements in everything from poetry to song with impersonations of Arnold Schwartzenegger and Donald Duck thrown in. As if this were not enough, probably none of these organizations parties more than Southwest Airlines. The walls of corporate headquarters are covered with literally thousands of strikingly similar snapshots of people at parties, all of them members of the Southwest family. The senior Party Animal, of course, is Chairman and CEO Herb Kelleher. The point is that fun is infectious and doesn't cost much, of critical importance to an organization seeking to deliver maximum value to its customers.

At Southwest Airlines, fun has function. Ask any of the company's direct competitors and you hear stories of the deadly seriousness with which the organization competes to serve a growing number of travelers. Southwest repeatedly achieves the highest ratings for on-time service, fewest complaints, and fewest mishandled pieces of luggage coupled with the highest safety record. The ability to deliver such outstanding performance at low fares suggests that the combination of family, fun, and love leading to high frontline capability is serious business indeed.

RECURRING THEMES

Even though we have purposely selected organizations engaged in distinctly different businesses in both the for-profit and social sectors, it is hard to miss the similarities in how they are, as a group, led. These similarities are profoundly linked to the overtly distinct themes of their respective human resource management activities.

1. *Leader as Keeper of the Values.* The values of each, while very different, are clearly articulated, frequently communicated, and widely shared. They provide a basis for a very careful selection process in which prospects are provided with ample information with which to determine whether or not they fit. A good part of their success lies in their ability to attract a congenial cadre of managers and frontline employees who share the same concerns and beliefs. Each of the leaders outlined above considers this one of his/her most important responsibilities.

2. *Communicating the Values.* These leaders constantly live and communicate the values of their respective organizations. General Herries does it through the process improvement initiatives that he is sponsoring; Frances Hesselbein did it through her use of carefully selected language; Bill Pollard does it through his teaching; and Herb Kelleher constantly acts out values as an extension of his personality.

3. *Setting the Bar Very High.* The goals set for each of these organizations are extremely high. The organizations described here are slow to enter middle age, which has been characterized by slowing growth and profits.

4. *Insuring Wide Latitude for Frontline Employees.* These kinds of goals could not be met if it were not for the fact that frontline employees and managers are given wide latitude to act on behalf of their organization in the best interests of customers. They know what to do and how to do it because of their familiarity with, and belief in, the organization's mission and shared values.

5. *Demonstrating by Constant Examples.* Employees know that acting according to their best judgment is allowed on a daily basis, because the organization's leadership demonstrates by example the same philosophy, often side-by-side with the frontline.

6. *Building Pride while Avoiding Arrogance.* Employees of these high capability organizations are encouraged by their leadership to take pride in what they do and how they do it. At the same time, an important role of the Herrieses, Hesselbeins, Pollards, and Kellehers is to make sure

that members of their organizations do not adopt the arrogant attitudes toward customers and each other that have brought other great organizations to their knees. How do they do this? Through constant reminders of the challenges facing them, whether it's a shrinking core market at USAA or new competitors attempting to emulate what Southwest Airlines has succeeded in doing; through the creation of new challenges, from the achievement of greater diversity in the membership of the Girl Scouts to the development of new processes for increasing the productivity of ServiceMaster's front line. Through stories demonstrating the fallibility, often with good humor, of an organization's leadership . . . and, perhaps most important of all, through the constant setting of goals that would be impossible for competitors to attain.

7. *Personal Involvement in Hiring Processes.* Nearly every one of these leaders truly believes that the hiring decision is the most important one made in their organizations. The organizations they lead resemble clubs, cults, and religious orders. Each one is very different, of course, but they aren't designed for everyone; in fact, many casual candidates are repulsed by them. One of leadership's roles in these organizations is to keep it that way.

We would describe hiring as "self-selection" not selection. Only those with the qualifications, however, can self-select. It is true at ServiceMaster, where all managers must be "teachers/learners." Herb Kelleher describes the hiring process at Southwest Airlines as a "religious experience". At USAA, it helps to have a military background and firm personal discipline. We could go on.

8. *A Belief That the Customer Is Not Always Right.* These leaders understand the self-reinforcing relationship between good customers and high capability. When one is out of line, it can destroy the relationship. That's why several have told us what, in other organizations, would be considered heretical: "The customer is not always right, particularly when they abuse our employees." It is a way of providing support to highly-valued members of the organization. It is also a way of saying that the key to a high-capability organization is the proper match between customer and employee.

HOW DO THEY BEHAVE

In addition to the usual behaviors often attributed to leaders, those in our sample, to an unusual degree: (1) Act like members of the team they are trying to build and preserve, (2) speak a different language, (3) act out their beliefs and challenges, (4) have a great deal of fun, and (5) give other members of their organizations the ultimate degree of capability.

1. *Acting Like Members of a Team.* Many of these leaders do not stand out in groups of their peers. This is not just because of their appearance but also because their colleagues often treat them with the same degree of deference that they reserve for any other member of their organizations. The "star system" (or syndrome) doesn't exist in these organizations.

2. *Speaking a Different Language.* These leaders don't just talk a good game. They act it out. Compare, for example, the amount of time spent in stores and how much of it is spent listening to employees and customers (as opposed to telling) by the recent CEOs of Wal-Mart and Kmart, then compare the performances of these organizations over the past decade.

   Many of these leaders regularly spend time in the field working a shift on the frontline of their respective organizations. Managers at Southwest Airlines regularly work flights, something that reflects the company's policy of encouraging teamwork and cross-functional work. All managers at ServiceMaster work at least one day a year in the cleaning and service crews at hospitals and schools served by the company. They serve refreshments to their frontline service workers at monthly training meetings.

3. *Having Fun.* There are few leaders anywhere who are not intrinsically motivated. They can't wait to get to work, but leaders at all levels in the high-capability organizations we have observed perhaps do a better job of communicating the joy they get from being on the job. Fun and Southwest Airlines are synonymous, for example.

4. *Giving Employees the Ultimate Degree of Capability: Firing Customers.* One surprising finding from our explorations is that several of the leaders we became acquainted with do not believe that customers are always right. They back this up by allowing employees to fire customers. At Southwest Airlines, rude or abusive flyers are just not tolerated. Upon arrival at their destination they are told in as public a manner as possible, preferably in front of frontline employees, that Southwest never wants to see them again on one of its flights.

   It doesn't take many "public customer hangings" in extreme cases to communicate to an organization the amount of confidence that its leadership has in it and the amount of latitude that frontline employees have in carrying out their work. Being able to put that kind of confidence in frontline personnel is perhaps the best single indication we know of the existence of organizational capability of a high order. It requires leadership of no lesser order.

ORGANIZATIONAL LIFE AFTER LEADERSHIP

One comment we have encountered repeatedly in our study of high-capability organizations is "It won't be quite the same after (name of leader) is gone." They are right. There will be one less source of stories that contain organizational lore, one less source of inspiration for good ideas bubbling up from the frontline organization, one less coach and cheerleader.

The comment, however, is much different from the question invariably asked by observers of such leaders and their organizations, "Can (company) survive without (name of leader)?" The answer is "of course it can." The companies in most of our examples have survived quite well. The GSUSA after Frances Hesselbein, for example, is doing quite well under another long-term member of the organization, Rose Marie Main.

Anyone who asks the question, just doesn't get it. They don't understand the power of high-capability organizations (Collins & Porras, 1994), or that capability doesn't reside with the leader. It resides at all levels in the organization which means two very important things. First, it creates the very high likelihood that the quality of leadership will not materially change. Much more importantly . . . if the basic human resource policies and practices of the organization (1) support people at all levels just exercising their latitude to act, (2) insure that the organization gives primary emphasis to seeking out and hiring those who self-select themselves into the organization; (3) make sure that all employees have the appropriate resources, including technology as well as personal development opportunities; and (4) focus on evaluating, celebrating, and rewarding performance, the organization will survive very well—perhaps because the most significant quality of high capability organizations is that they often perform best in troubled times, times when no one leader is enough to turn the tide; times when frontline capability has to kick into full gear; times when those out in front really get going. The development and sustenance of such leadership is the central human resource challenge of the 21st century for large scale organizations.

REFERENCES

Collins, J.C., & Porras, J.I. (1994). *Built to Last.* New York: Harper Books, p. 7.

Heskett, J.L. (1989). Girl Scouts of the U.S.A. (A). Case No. 9-690-044. Boston: Harvard Business School Publishing Co., p. 13.

Heskett, J.L. (1987). ServiceMaster Industries, Inc. Case No. 9-388-064. Boston: Harvard Business School Publishing Co.

Heskett, J.L., & Hallowell, R. (1993). Southwest Airlines: 1993 (A). Case No. 9-694-023. Boston: Harvard Business School Publishing Co.

Heskett, J.L., & Hallowell, R. (1993). USAA: Business process review for the Great Lakes Region, Case No. 9-694-024. Boston: Harvard Business School Publishing Co., p. 7.

CHAPTER 4

CORPORATE STRATEGY AND HUMAN RESOURCES: NEW MIND SETS FOR NEW GAMES

GORDON HEWITT

The strategy profession has often viewed the human resource (HR) field with a mixture of superiority, suspicion, and indifference. Privately, I'm convinced the reason is that strategists have been looking around for a discipline they feel is even more methodologically unsound than theirs and have discovered HR; even inferiority complexes are relative.

Real strategy, after all, deals with complex issues such as industry and competitor analysis, portfolio allocation and management, cost and quality dynamics, and whether to hold the three-day annual planning conference in Las Vegas or Monte Carlo (venues with unfortunate connotations). Real strategy makes tough intellectual demands on senior executives, such as choosing a consistent logic for joint ventures, selecting IBM or EDS for Information Technology (IT) outsourcing, or enduring another presentation from marketing on the value of brand equity. When real strategy is in place the HR bit surely tumbles out, like night follows day.

What happens to HR, however, if there is a strategic vacuum at the top of the enterprise? If part of the new paradigm is that HR should focus on deliverables, be judged on impact, and add measurable corporate value (Ulrich, 1997), there is one critical assumption—the corporation has a robust concept and process of competitive strategy into which HR strategy can connect. I have reservations as to whether recent corporate evidence suggests that is a safe assumption.

Acknowledging the possibility of a corporate strategic vacuum starts with the need to confront three paradoxes, all of which have major implications for the strategic impact of HR in the future. First is the gap between strategic rhetoric and operational reality, often seen in corporations who claim to "do strategy" but who on closer examination are actually practicing little more than elongated budgeting, i.e., the extension of the one year financial plan by four more years. Second is the paradox of today's executive cohort—the best trained, most highly qualified, and widely read in history; but strategic literacy is not the same as strategic competence, and in many corporations something has gone wrong in the conversion process. Third is the lack of any systematic link between the possession of strategic planning apparatus and long term, superior competitive performance (Ashkenas, Ulrich, Jick, & Kerr, 1995). Some cynics shamelessly recommend the testing of the hypothesis that the correlation is actually negative.

If a corporation talks the language of strategy but is propelling itself into the future with a competitive compass consisting of little more than a vague mission statement and a detailed financial plan, what is poor HR to do? And anyway, how does the new HR paradigm deal with the balance between being an input into the strategy creation process and an output from it? Modern HR literature often quotes cases of the new breed of HR activist who goes to the CEO and says "Tell me what your strategy is and what it's trying to achieve and I'll make sure HR delivers," but it still potentially puts HR in reactive mode.

Yet I believe in many corporations HR fails to fulfill its potential in terms of underpinning long term competitive performance. Given the changing nature of the central competitive challenge facing corporations in the near future and the changing notions of what it means to be "strategic", most paths lead to the door of HR—if organizations are serious about competing for the future, not just in it. Perhaps it's a sign from the gods that at the very time HR professionals are debating the need to develop a new HR paradigm, influential strategists are doing the same for their own discipline (Hamel & Prahalad, 1994).

THE NEW COMPETITIVE LANDSCAPE— WHAT SHOULD WE HAVE LEARNED?

How are the dynamics of competition changing on a global basis? Perhaps the question should be phrased differently. I wonder how future historians and business school professors—with perfect hindsight, of course—will judge the performance of senior management in the 1990s, an era which so far has witnessed Richter-scale changes in the competitive landscape? It has also been an era in which the competitive strategies of so many corporations bear an awesome similarity.

Hopes were pinned on restructuring, downsizing, delayering, and reengineering, coupled with a heavy dose of customer focus, quality enhancement, and cycle time reduction. What were these a response to?—failure to forecast the length and depth of the economic recession or failure to anticipate and decode the irreversibility of industry transformation which requires new mind sets for new games? A shared mind set can actually be toxic if it is obsessed with winning the competitive battles of the past. If senior executives can't equip an enterprise to decode emerging patterns in the competitive kaleidoscope and to reengineer its own competitive mind set, will the future jury ask what they were there for?

In the emerging competitive landscape what are the new competitive realities which need to be addressed, and why do they pose challenges for traditional ideas of what competition is about, what strategy is about, and what HR should be about?

Challenge 1—"Industry" Is No Longer a Given

New market dynamics—usually driven by the combined impact of globalization, deregulation, technology convergence, and customer militancy—are radically altering the structure, boundaries, and even definition of many industries. For example, as electronic commerce takes off, how will the traditional financial services sector and the information industry overlap? What kind of competitive map will emerge from the already converging interests of players such as Citibank, GE, Visa, Mondex, Microsoft, Intuit, Hitachi, and Toshiba?

In situations such as the above, competing is becoming less about "playing the game better" and more about "defining the new game and the new rules." The intellectual heritage of strategy, however, is mostly concerned with frameworks and techniques which focus on the word "better" and implicitly take the "game" as a given. This is not very helpful if you are IBM's Lou Gerstner, Microsoft's Bill Gates, or Oracle's Larry Ellison, all trying to impose their own intellectual models of network based computing on the universe.

Challenge 2—The Tenure of Industry Leaders Is Shorter

In industries ranging from computers to communications to pharmaceuticals, reference is always made to the shortening of product life cycles.

Industry leadership life cycles, however, are also becoming compressed as companies enter the arena of Challenge #1. The strategic assets which are traditionally thought to reinforce industry leadership—conventional market share, resource depth, track record—are easily by-passed by competitors who change the rules of the game. Sadly, the corporate graveyard is littered with the bodies of companies who won the efficiency battle but lost the competitive war.

Challenge 3—The Sources and Sustainability of Competitive Advantage Need a Major Rethink

Strip away all the hype about competitive advantage and it essentially comes down to two sources. First it might work if a corporation possesses some unique resource endowment which is invisible or inaccessible to competitors. Second, in situations in which the above conditions do not hold, competitors might still face formidable obstacles in intiating the industry leader's magic formula. Both of the above sources are being eroded.

Forces such as global access to information and the analytical insights conducted by a wide range of corporate constituents have made most enterprises highly transparent. Value-laden resources, especially intellectual ones, are becoming increasingly mobile. When a whole equity trading desk can walk across the street, with the added incentive of a multimillion dollar "golden hello," where lies competitive advantage in investment banking?

Challenge 4—Global Competition Is All Pervasive

Executives may say that they face only local rivals, but over time most industries are seeing the erosion of national boundaries in some dimension of competition. Even when competitors for branded products apparently face only domestic contestants, competition for new competencies, resources, and knowledge arenas is increasingly global in scope.

In India, Bangalore has emerged as one of the world's leading centers of software development and programming. There you will see the corporate logo of most major IT companies in the world. Also, when you look at a company like Sharp which competes so well in the pocket calculator market, remember that it also controls 40 percent of the world market for liquid crystal displays which go into all kinds of instruments.

Years after academics have sorted out the terminological debate to their own satisfaction, many corporations still struggle to provide real meaning to the word "global" in strategic and organizational terms. Global organization charts often look impressive on paper but frequently behind them is a mindset that still sees the world in two polarized zones—domestic and international. Most practices, including those of HR, typically reflect that mind set.

Challenge 5—Everything Is Programmed through the Corporate Genetic Code

Over time, corporations develop robust frames of reference through which they make sense of the competitive world around them (Figure 4.1).

These powerful frames link together deeply held assumptions (or mind sets) about:

- The concept of industry and the process of competition (industry model).
- The process of value creation and nature of competitive advantage (business model).
- Resource requirements, deployment, and internal governance (organization model).

Figure 4.1
The Frame of Reference

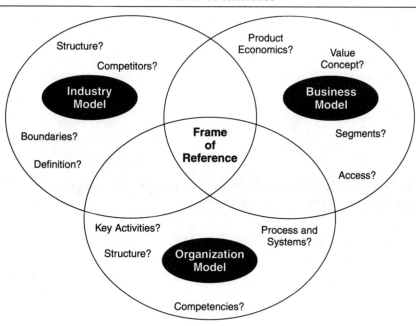

When companies find not just their products but their central frame of reference under attack, the scale of the strategic challenge rises exponentially. Microsoft's challenge to IBM and CNN's challenge to conventional broadcasting companies were three-dimensional intellectual assaults on industry leaders' frames of reference. The leaders' dilemma is how to avoid all the internal systems and processes encouraging them to develop an even better capacity to play the wrong game. To be competitive, corporations have to be more than thin and fit; they also need to remove the glaucoma and the ear wax.

Challenge 6—Corporations Are under Pressure to Rethink Their Overall Logic

There is a subtle shift taking place in the locus of strategy from business units to the corporate center. For many years the overarching logic of the enterprise was a portfolio of products and services drawing on some specialized central functions, but two concerns have emerged: *One* is whether this overarching logic depresses the value creation engine of the modern enterprise. In many well publicized cases value has actually been created simply by splitting up the parts. *The other* is that questions are raised about the role and value added of top management in a strategically decentralized organization. If their scope of strategic decisions making is focused mainly on resource allocation issues and the occasional big takeover or merger, is that enough?

The implications of this debate for HR are enormous, given that the HR organizational model has followed the decentralized strategy model, i.e., a central HR function with broad "policy" guidelines but with the real HR action taking place inside relatively autonomous business units or geographics.

A MANDATE FOR HR—ENHANCING STRATEGIC CAPABILITY

Corporations will have to devise more sophisticated platforms of strategic competence to handle these challenges. Many of the levers which HR systems control or influence could have a real impact—positive or negative—on long term corporate competitiveness. The following are implications, suggestions, and preconditions for three main arenas which flow from the above analysis.

Arena 1—HR as Architect/Protector of Core Competencies and the Resource Leverage Process

As the intellectual balance of power has shifted to the resource-based school of thinking (Collis & Montgomery, 1995), there has been tremendous interest in the concept of core competence (CC) and competence-based competition. Seen as a process by which a range of knowledge, skills, and technologies are integrated in unusual forms across conventional organizational boundaries, CCs enhance the strategic capability of an enterprise in several ways.

CCs can provide a diagnostic lens through which executives can detect industry convergence at an early stage, understand and unlock new classes of customer benefit, and provide low risk access to new market opportunities. This is a classic area, however, where in practice the hype exceeds the reality. Attempts to operationalize this attractive concept are often frustrated because the corporation lacks:

- An integrating logic that sees the possibility of linking disparate skills in new ways.
- An organizational logic that can actually blend and manage a range of skills with an agenda that goes beyond creating value for any particular business unit in the short run.
- A measurement system by which top management can judge the pay off from investment in CCs as well as businesses.

These are areas in which HR could help make decisive breakthroughs, but real progress depends on HR professionals having the capacity to develop the following:

- A competency grid which enables them to identify potential linkages and reallocation possibilities.
- A proactive input into the strategy creation process which provides a competitive logic for CC development.
- A rigorous system of intellectual capital allocation and knowledge management which can rival the all-powerful rituals of capital budgeting.
- A scorecard for the CEO which identifies processes of and pay-offs from better resource leverage as well as resource allocation.
- A power and credibility platform whose decibel factor rivals that of senior line executives, especially over issues of competence ownership and deployment.

Arena 2—HR as Architect of the "Global" Dimension of Strategic Capability

Ask HR professionals three questions:

1. Is it important for your business to have a global mind set?
2. How would you recognize it if you had it?
3. What levers would you pull to get you closer to your ideal?

It's often difficult to get past the first question, with answers varying from the need for cultural sensitivity to informing the domestically-trained CEO that London is actually quite far from Libya. Global mind set, however, even for very localized corporations, is a vital ingredient in competition to:

*   Get early insights into new patterns of global chess, and
*   Enlarge the scope of and capture a good share of emerging global opportunities.

The challenge for HR is clear. *First,* help the corporation to develop a more rigorous logic about the real meaning of global in strategic and organizational terms. Go further and develop a shared language which cuts through the persistent and unhelpful confusion between concepts such as international, transnational, multinational, etc.

Second, test all structures, systems, and processes against new global criteria. Identify all behaviors and attitudes which currently block global value-creating potential. Judged by these standards, many corporations find that existing practices encourage resource dissipation rather than resource leverage.

Third, radically reappraise the executive development concept. How does it fit a global mind set logic? Don't assume that rotating executives around different countries, diplomat style, automatically converts into global strategic experience and sophistication. People need exposure early in their careers to demanding cross-country, cross-functional, cross-business responsibility.

Arena 3—HR as Architect of New Mind Sets for New Games

In looking for ways to radically enhance strategic capability, valuable executive time can be wasted tinkering with the planning process. Deal with the real issue. Is the corporation producing enough executives with strategic brains (both left- and right-sided), and what processes will nurture this asset, dilute it, or kill it off?

Over time, the attitudes and competencies of senior executives are shaped by the interplay of three systems and processes—development, appraisal, and reward. Again, it is critical to disengage from the hype and ask "What is being grown?" If a key part of the future strategic challenge is developing new mind sets to play new games, a necessary precondition will involve creating the right development, appraisal, and reward practices to make that happen? The demise of so many industry leaders in the last few years suggests that the career development experiences of many senior executives have poorly equipped them to handle strategic challenges characterized by speed, ambiguity, complexity, and discontinuity.

CONCLUSION

Improving the process of strategy creation calls for a major contribution from HR. Apart from random stories about planning systems and action-replays of "great leaders," a robust concept of strategy creation is still lacking.

The legacy of the strategy process is hierarchical. A few top executives think and craft; everyone else executes. HR can play a pivotal role in adjusting the process to new organizational realities. How, for example, should strategy be "done" in a world in which authority doesn't necessarily mean control, in which internal networks and external alliances diffuse old balances of power, in which rank and experience don't automatically convey wisdom, and where the most valuable insights into discontinuity may be located in the least valued parts of the organization?

The challenge is to help alter both cognitive perspectives and aspiration levels in organizations trying to cope with more external uncertainty and internal insecurity. Every discipline deserves Andy Warhol's "15 minutes of fame." This could be the era for HR.

REFERENCES

Ashkensas, R., Ulrich, D., Jick, T., & Kerr, S. (1995). *The Boundaryless Organization.* San Francisco: Jossey-Bass.

Collis, D., & Montgomery, C. (1995). Competing on Resources; Strategy in the 1990s. *Harvard Business Review,* July–August.

Hamel, G., & Prahalad, C.K. (1994). *Competing for the Future.* Cambridge, MA: Harvard Business School Press.

Ulrich, D. (1997). *Tomorrow's HR Management.* New York: Wiley.

CHAPTER 5

FRAMEWORKS FOR HUMAN RESOURCE PROFESSIONALS PARTICIPATING IN BUSINESS RELATIONSHIPS

DALE G. LAKE

BUSINESS RELATIONSHIPS: NEW FACE OF COMPETITION

The race to be competitive in this decade has emerged from such trends as globalization, total quality programs, reengineering, learning organization formation, and repetitive downsizing; it now turns to competition in the form of massive industry consolidation. This consolidation in turn shifts the focus of competitiveness to all forms of business relationships, internal and external. Where once scholars tried to define and understand the firm as a legal entity, today it is best understood as a set of interfaces across a total value chain.

The purpose of developing business relationships has shifted from being mainly a survival tactic to being a new source of competitive advantage. The spectrum of business relationships has widened to include three generic types which can be characterized by degree of collaboration and added value (see Table 5.1).

The first generic type, *external relationships,* are those relationships which are simply extensions of the degree of collaboration between vendor and customer and can be ordered as follows: (a) vendor (traditional), (b) preferred supplier (usually involves certification and EDI), in-house supplier (in which full time employees work directly in the site of the customer with full access to information systems and customers), (d) one-way licensing, (e) equity investment, and (f) original-equipment manufacturer (OEM). In

Table 5.1
Spectrum of Business Relationships

Relationship	Examples	Collaboration	Value Added
External	Vendor (Traditional)	Low	Low
	Preferred supplier		
	In-house supplier		
	Licensing		
	Equity investment		
	Original equipment manufacturer		
Extended	Cross licensing		
	Strategic business partner		
	Franchise alliances		
	Equity partnerships		
	Joint ventures		
Internal	Subsidiaries		
	Acquisitions		
	Mergers	High	High

the second type, *extended,* the nature of collaboration is again increased, examples are: cross licensing, strategic business partner, franchise alliances, equity partnerships, and joint ventures. In the third type, *internal,* are mergers (i.e., the recent telecommunications industry mega merger of Bell Atlantic and Nynex), acquisitions, and subsidiaries.

The essence of business relationships as a source of competitiveness is that traditional authority conceived of as the ability to fully control the outcomes of a single entity through hierarchical position is being replaced across the spectrum. Interestingly it is being replaced by contractual (psychological and legal) arrangements and externally, large companies have had to develop strategies based on networks of relationships which link them across the entire supply chain. For example, Wal-Mart which had built a reputation for being adversarial with its suppliers now has a full time employee of Proctor and Gamble (P&G) on its purchasing council. As a member of the council, P&G has access to information systems, distribution, and logistics; *and* it can replenish its own products continuously. As Wal-Mart races to become the world's largest retailer, P&G will obviously become more than a supplier, it will become a strategic ally.

More and more, gaining competitive advantage means moving in and out of complex relationships with other entities in the industry supply chain. For instance, witness the rise of customer focused company structures such as at EDS which builds unique (virtual) organizations for each of its major customers and then destroys the organization as the customer's needs shift.

The Warren Company (Nations Business, May 1996), an alliance consulting firm in Providence, R.I., has suggested the following as essential to successful business relationships: there must be:

1. Strategic forces pushing the potential partners together;
2. Synergy of products, processes, marketing, etc.;
3. Great chemistry;
4. A win-win orientation across structures, operations, risks, etc.;
5. Operational integration (e.g., order entry, production scheduling);
6. Sharp focus (e.g., specific concrete objectives, timetables);
7. Commitment and support (key champions are behind it).

These criteria apply to the full spectrum of business relationships—external, extended, internal—however, they are of special significance in the *internal type,* especially acquisitions. Acquisitions by very large companies have become so routine that many of the acquisitor companies have created standardized processes for dealing with them, just as they have for forecasting, order entry, and quarterly reports. Even so, success with acquisitions is difficult and elusive. One such acquisitor company which has a goal of producing 7 percent of its 14 percent annual growth through acquisition still finds as many as 50 percent of the acquisitions go through major restructuring within 24 months of purchase. Gene Slowinski, (May 1996) director of strategic-alliances studies at Rutgers University, in a 10-year study found that only about 25 percent of alliances were successful; 50 percent did not meet their stated objectives; and 25 percent were disasters (Nations Business). Key reasons for failure were unequal levels of technical or business competence; clash of cultures was also reported as a significant factor in a fairly large percentage. In another study done by McKinsey examining firms between 1950–1985, 53 percent of all acquisitions were unloaded as unprofitable. (Peters, 1987).

HR's ROLE IN THE BUILDING AND MAINTENANCE OF SUCCESSFUL RELATIONSHIPS

Into this caldron of ferment called the new face of competitiveness, the HR function—in its efforts to become a strategic partner—has plunged.

In doing so a double task of learning has been created (1) to become strategic (while maintaining and improving its traditional role), and (2) to determine what HR's unique contribution is in the new face of competitiveness. Ulrich (1997) in his new book, *Human Resource Champions*, has developed a set of propositions about what it means to become strategic in HR. Similarly, companies throughout the world have been trying to define this strategic role by developing competencies required for alliance formation.

This article examines some *basic conceptual requirements for the HR function in building competitive relationships*. For purposes of illustration, acquisitions are highlighted.

DEVELOPING RELATIONSHIPS

Research developed and reported by Ulrich, Brockbank, Yeung, and Lake (1995) found that one variable which most differentiated high performing HR professionals from poorer performers was their ability *to form relationships in the context of a rapidly changing organization*. Given the growth in size and complexity described above one can argue that new competencies are now needed to extend traditional relationship building to relationships between (1) organizational units, (2) organizational functions, (3) product lines—all on the inside, and (4) suppliers and customers, (5) merging companies, (6) acquired companies, (7) joint ventures, and sometimes even competitors—on the outside. A relationship becomes central to competitiveness because positive relationships are characterized by mutual trust which means that both parties will commit to action faster than in relationships characterized by distrust. Those who act fastest to bring products to market, to develop new products, to react to a customer are those who win the competitive advantage.

DEFINING THE RULES OF ENGAGEMENT FOR HR

As has been true of other developments for HR, the first task is to determine what unique value HR might bring to the context of competitive relationships. Other functions in business organizations have expectations, which must be recognized and met, that a valuable contribution can be made by HR. A good place to begin is to provide a heuristic, a model or map which sets the conceptual foundation for contribution; many exist. Examples include: Nadler et al. (1992) who develop a basic systems model to map organizations complete with inputs, processes, and outputs. Galbraith (1995) has proposed the star model which maps the variables of people, strategy, structure, rewards, and processes onto the five points of a star. Waterman, Peters, and Phillips (1988) map McKinsey's key variables onto what is called the Seven "S" model. It contains the variables of: structure, systems, strategy, skills, style, staff, and superordinate goals (in most other models called values). Almost all such models include the following variables: focus (variously called goals, strategy, direction, etc.), structure (governance), systems (information, rewards, processes), culture (values, superordinate goals), and people (style, interpersonal competence, staffing, development). Less frequently Nadler et al.'s (1992) environmental variables are included. The point is, understanding and knowing how to use at least one such model is an excellent starting point for HR to influence the business relationship building process. It maps the playing field; it identifies key success variables; it provides a framework for diagnosis of problems and opportunities; and finally, it provides some expert leverage. Once the rules of engagement are established for the HR professional, the task becomes one of adding useful insight into each of the variables and ultimately of providing facilitation between the two parties to the relationship. The following discussion highlights these variables in light of HR's potential role in building competitive relationships.

GOALS (STRATEGY, DIRECTION, SETTING)

Potentially this is one of the more difficult areas in which to achieve congruence. A company that has just been acquired may believe that the acquiring company is indifferent to its (the acquired's) mission. For example, one acquired organization had always taken pride in its mission to produce the most flavorful jam (albeit a little more expensively) on the market (substitute the best of any product such as financial software, ready-to-eat chicken, modems, etc.). The acquiring company soon made it clear that it would not be an advocate of this fine jam; rather as with its other products, it was an advocate of return on investment, increased earnings, market position, net cash produced, etc. Further, the acquiring company made the acquisition, in part, by convincing an internal audit group that the company to be acquired would meet the acquisitor's financial goals. Can such divergence of goals be managed? The power is clearly in the hands of the acquirer, but, if that power is used to intervene in the newly acquired company without regard for what it has achieved or without regard to special nuances in its business sector, the value which has allowed it to gain a competitive advantage may be lost. In short, there is a relationship problem of goal clarity between the two companies.

HR can serve as a third party to this conflict. A simple fact finding activity involving interviews of each party listing detailed expectations the two parties have for each other, followed by a feedback and problem solving session could lead to a productive reconciliation.

STRUCTURE (GOVERNANCE)

Most organizations have experienced major erosion of the traditional concept of structure as outlined by Weber (1947), however, a continuum clearly exists as to how far organizations have moved from the early models. Even with the wide variations that exist today, organizations must find ways to specify how accountability, responsibility, and interdependence will work. The problem that arises in an alliance of any sort is that the joining parties will typically be at widely different points along this structure continuum. For example, one company may well treat the organizational chart as a rough map of how relationships are arranged, but members have learned that taking action in order to produce value for customers more often than not cuts across boundaries. The second company, however, may believe that the chart defines boundaries that are not to be taken lightly. Again, these two organizations will experience difficulty when trying to act concertedly.

The HR professional serving as a facilitator to this kind of disagreement will need to work with both parties—to obtain agreement that the form of the organization must depend on what is to be accomplished and then help both organizations to reach resolution. Often what is needed is to develop a temporary or interim organization which exists solely for the purpose of managing conflict between the two parties to the alliance; it in turn can be dissolved after the two companies have six months or so of experience and have learned, hopefully, some trust in one another. These alternatives to boundary management in organizations have been described by Ashkenas, Ulrich, Jick, and Kerr (1995).

SYSTEMS (INFORMATION, REWARDS, PROCESSES)

Each company to a new alliance (be it via acquisition, merger, joint venture, etc.) will have devoted much time and other resources to its systems of reward, information, development, succession, new product development, etc. Each may believe its systems to be superior. The temptation of the more powerful firm (i.e., the acquisitor or the one with greater equity) may be to insist that the other party *accede* to its systems. This approach will, almost always, miss opportunities for learning and will probably increase resistance.

An alternative approach is to view the new alliance as a complex change and engage the two organizations in a systematic change process. This will involve the organizations, mutually, in determining what needs to be changed, why these changes must be implemented, who the key stakeholders are to the changes, what it will take to gain their commitment, and then in designing a further process for change which will have key events, deliverables, and reflexive accomplishment cycles.

The HR facilitator must be a change agent equipped with the tools necessary for implementing change. Such tools should include at least the following: a vehicle for creating a new vision, analytic processes for identifying change targets, conflict management skills, and commitment planning and project planning capabilities. It is also extremely important in these areas to document what works and what does not so that each successive *and successful* alliance can be accelerated.

CULTURE (VALUES, SUPERORDINATE GOALS)

It is safe to assume that the new companies to an alliance will experience wide differences of culture which may be underestimated and, typically, not well articulated. I recently served as a consultant to two merging, global companies which participated as numbers one and two in three similar lines of business. While operations were quite similar, most other aspects were dramatically different. Each approached the customer (even defined who the customer was) differently; each developed different marketing approaches; one did its own distribution, the other outsourced; one focused on being low cost, the other on providing customer value; and so forth. A merger between these two organizations required conflict management of the magnitude usually reserved for achieving agreements between foreign countries.

Facilitating such divergence requires the use of a framework which will serve as a useful diagnostic and planning tool. One such tool (Cooper & Quinn, 1993) visualizes culture as the result of competing values between *flexibility and order* on one dimension and *internal and external* on the orthogonal dimension. This framework gives rise to four distinct cultures:

1. The *human relations* culture characterized by cohesion, commitment, and participation.
2. The *open systems* culture characterized by survival, insight, innovation, adaptation.

3. The *bureaucratic* culture characterized by stability, measurement, documentation.

4. The *rational* culture characterized by productivity, profits, goal setting.

Cultures one and four and cultures two and three are opposites, and an acquisition or merger bringing such cultures together would very likely fail.

The HR professional who would serve as facilitator for concomitant cultures can use such a model to diagnose potential areas of conflict and to assist participants in discovering why they are experiencing these difficulties. Blending such cultures is difficult, but the likelihood of success is greatly increased by identifying these underlying dimensions and forcing the parties to the alliance to acknowledge differences and to decide which aspects of culture will have to be changed, how they will be changed, and with what time lines.

PEOPLE (STYLE, COMPETENCE, STAFFING, DEVELOPMENT)

Finally, the way human resources itself is managed is a potentially volatile area for companies engaged in alliances. The management of staffing, training, benefits, performance, rewards, etc. will, typically, differ dramatically. It will be more difficult for the HR professional to serve as a facilitator in this area because of the substantive stakes he or she will have in the various people systems.

Ulrich (1986) has described a heuristic referred to as the "Pillars" model which can be helpful in this situation. It can serve as architecture for joint planning, discussion, and decision making between the HR departments. It will force the departments to decide what policies will be enforced regarding the HR strategy, mindset, competencies, performance management, governance, change, and leadership.

Once again, the process of alliance formation is that of assessment: What are the current similarities and differences for each of the HR systems? What problems and opportunities are presented? What decisions need to be made, by when?

SUMMARY

This chapter argues that HR can play an expanded role in competitive advantage by helping organizations to form alliances more quickly and, of course, more successfully. The importance of various frameworks to facilitate alliances is underscored.

The HR professional is challenged to engage in alliance formation by utilizing general frameworks which help to understand the core dimensions upon which organizations may differ and then to use such differences as the basis for planning, conflict management, and decisions. Such interventions will clearly increase the likelihood of success after the new alliance is formed.

Since major alliances (mergers, acquisitions, etc.), represent extreme magnitudes of risk and profit and because it estimated that so many will fail, the opportunity for increased success represents a potential major contribution that HR can make to company success and competitive advantage.

REFERENCES

Ashkenas, R., Ulrich, D., Jick, T., & Kerr, S. (1995). *The boundaryless organization.* San Francisco: Jossey-Bass.

Cooper, R., & Quinn, R. (1993). Implications of the competing values framework for management information systems. *Human Resource Management, 32*(1), 175–202.

Galbraith, J. (1995). *Designing organizations.* San Francisco: Jossey-Bass Publishers.

Nadler, D., Gerstein, M., Shaw, R., & Associates. (1992). *Organizational architecture.* San Francisco: Jossey-Bass.

Peters, T. (1987). *Thriving on chaos.* New York: Alfred A. Knopf.

Slowinski, G. (1996). Making alliances work. *Nations Business, May,* p. 24.

Ulrich, D. (1997). *Human resource champions.* Cambridge, MA: Harvard Business School Press.

Ulrich, D., Brockbank, W., Yeung, A., & Lake, D. (1995). Human resource competencies: An empirical assessment. *Human Resource Management, 34*(4), 473–496.

Waterman, R., Peters, T., & Phillips, J. (1988). Structure is not organization. In *business horizons.* Copyright by the Foundation for the School of Business at the University of Indiana.

Weber, M. (1947). *The theory of social and economic organizations.* (T. Parsons, trans.). New York: Free Press.

CHAPTER 6

HUMAN RESOURCES' ROLE IN BUILDING COMPETITIVE EDGE LEADERS

MICHAEL M. LOMBARDO and ROBERT W. EICHINGER

$\mathbf{W}$hen we were invited to present our musings on HR's role in the future for this volume, we were in the midst of analyzing our new 360° database of 6000+ raters assessing 770 executives, managers, and a few senior individual contributors. Why not, we thought, use this fresh database to pose answers to several questions about an essential and sure aspect of the future of HR—acquiring and growing the necessary talent to create a competitive edge for the organization?

Weak leadership can cripple an organization's effectiveness, while people with "the right stuff" can add to it dramatically. We used our database to look at what raters think the right stuff currently is and how current management is doing against those standards. Based on any current gaps between what's important and what people are proficient at, we wanted to know what HR will have to do to build better leaders now and load the leadership bench for the future?

WHAT'S IMPORTANT AND HOW ARE PEOPLE DOING AT IT?

In VOICES™, our 360° evaluation and feedback system, each rater is asked to rate the importance of each of 67 competencies as well as provide skill evaluations of each for each learner.

We compared current importance and current skill by dividing the 67 competencies into thirds (22 highs, 22 lows, and 23 in the middle), using the top third in importance/top third in skill as the aligned current

Table 6.1
Top Third Important for Success *and* Top Third Skill Level
(it's important and people do it well now) Listed Alphabetically

Action Oriented
Business Acumen
Comfort Around Top Management
Decision Quality
Ethics and Values
Functional/Technical Skills
Integrity and Trust
Intellectual Horsepower
Organizing Work
Problem Solving
Results

strengths and the top third in importance/lowest third in skill as the gap weaknesses. The results are listed in Tables 6.1 and 6.2.

FEEDBACK

If we were presenting these results as narrative feedback to a manager, what would we say the results mean?

The Good News

You are good at running a tactical business and dealing with today's programs:

You

- Have strong business savvy.
- Are a take charge kind of person.
- Are bright; can handle complex mental problems.
- Are resourceful, get results quickly, are action oriented.
- Manage up well.
- Get things done for customers.
- Set and have high standards.
- Put technical expertise to practical use.
- Really go after a problem until it's solved.
- Have strong character, are trusted by others.
- Are viewed as a person who makes sound business decisions.

Table 6.2
**Top Third Important for Success and Bottom Third Skill Level
(it's important and people don't do it well) Listed Alphabetically**

Building Team Spirit
Dealing with Ambiguity
Developing Direct Reports
Directing Others
Hiring and Staffing
Informing
Motivating Others
Negotiating
Strategic Agility

The Bad News

On the other hand, you are least likely to be adept at:

- Being a team builder or player.
- Celebrating success and sharing credit with others.
- Communicating effectively down or sideways.
- Developing direct reports.
- Motivating others individually.
- Negotiating win–win deals.
- Picking the right people.

You may get yourself in trouble by:

- Being rigid in the face of change.
- Being seen as excessively focused on self to build own career.
- Being too tactical; not being strategic enough.
- Doing too much yourself; a loner; not empowering others.
- Leaving others behind with not enough information.
- Being narrow in perspective.
- Trying to overwhelm others with intelligence and logic rather than listening.
- Producing poor morale and possibly high turnover.

A PICTURE OF TODAY'S MANAGEMENT?

The total 67 competencies cluster into 11 statistical factors. We have further clustered them (A–E below) for presentation here. Looking at the current strengths and weaknesses of these executives and managers against those clusters creates a fuller picture.

A. Getting the Work Out

There is apparently no shortage of skilled people who know their trade and can solve today's problems by themselves. They can overcome obstacles, take charge of a problem, and get things done (10 to 12 competencies in this cluster are rated high in skill; none is rated low).

B. Getting the Work Done with and through Others

Problems arise when these skilled people manage the work of others, and situations of conflict inevitably arise. They have problems dealing with everything from confronting to telling people what they need to know, to developing others, to dealing with ambiguous situations that don't come wrapped in clean packages (9 to 12 competencies in this cluster are rated low; none is rated high).

C. Managing Vision and Purpose

They do well technically and tactically. They are generally trusted, know their customers and the tactical business, have high quality standards, and can produce good annual plans. Anything longer term—strategy, innovation, vision—and the skill ratings are lower (4 tactical skills rated high; 4 strategic skills rated low).

D. Managing People

They do well in close or perhaps on the basics. They care, are approachable, and surprising to us, scored high in managing diversity. Anything deeper, such as what really motivates different individuals, what criteria to use to size up people accurately, or how to build a stronger team; and the scores are lower (5 competencies rated high; 6 rated low in this cluster).

E. Personal Development/Continuous Improvement

These people excel at close in task learning while falling down on listening and personal learning. They are low in self-knowledge, admitting weaknesses, and personal improvement (2 competencies rated high; 3 rated low).

What Does This Say for the Future?

If this is roughly what current management collectively looks like and if the futurists are right, and that people are needed who can think long term; deal with the problems of rapid chaotic change; build, motivate, and inspire individuals and teams; and continuously improve, organizations have a long way to go in achieving such a profile. The profile of the typical person looks like that of a nice, bright, results producing, tactical individual contributor, although the sample is overwhelmingly management!

Who Is Going to Close These Current Gaps and What Does This Mean for the Future of HR in Talent Building?

Based on these results and a combined 50 years between us of consulting time on these issues, we think the following are mandatory to build the necessary leadership organizations need to survive and prosper.

1. HR as THE Initiator and Designer of Development Experiences

There is no more scary finding from our data than that Developing Direct Reports is ranked 67th of 67 rated skills, just below Confronting Problem Direct Reports (#65) and Understanding Others (#64). With today's emphasis on more line-driven development, even more gaps will develop without the strong intervention of HR and top management. The dream (and because of downsizing and reengineering, the necessity) of transferring the responsibility for long-term talent development to the line would mean raising these very low skills, the 67th, 65th, and 64th, by 40 plus rating positions to move them into the top third! Not very likely!

Added to the low skills in developing others are weak strategic skills—Managing Vision (#58), Dealing with Ambiguity (#50), Perspective and Sizing up Others (tied at #48), Strategic Agility and Hiring and Staffing (tied at #47). It is unlikely this group of managers could build the leaders for today much less tomorrow. They don't have the time, the interest, or it turns out, the skills. Few people would trust their long-term careers to a series of bosses with this profile.

Additionally, low skill ratings for Personal Learning (#66), Personal Disclosure (#58), Self-Knowledge (#53), Self-Development (#40), and Listening (#28) coupled with the low strategic outlook skills listed above tell us that the dream of each person managing his/her own long-term development is also seriously in question.

Our data and experience tell us HR and top management must take the lead in long-term talent development and in filling the leadership bench.

Otherwise, meaningful development won't happen. Today's management and today's managers will just continue the gaps that exist today.

It's unreasonable and short-sighted to expect line management to do more than evaluate, consult, and execute well-designed development plans. They just don't have the time, the willingness, the skills, or the interest. It's equally unfair to ask people to self-develop in areas that aren't part of their current jobs and are outside their perspective or ability to greatly influence. They have the willingness and the interests but don't have the skills or the perspective.

HR must be the designers of development and provide the initiative to do it. Organizations who follow the "it's your (boss's and self's) responsibility to develop talent; HR's just here to help," will experience a significant lack of top management talent.

It will only be accomplished with a four-part harmony—the self, the boss, top management and the mission-critical heavy hand of HR.

2. HR as THE Partner of Top Management for Development

Every top management group we've worked with recently says it wants HR to become more business knowledgeable or more of a business partner. As part of that partnership, HR needs to translate current and future business needs into competencies and inform top management of what it takes to develop these competencies. Need multifunctional managers? Decentralized units won't give them to you but multifunctional projects, business switches, strategic immersion projects, or GE-Crotonville-like learning projects can. Need team builders? Courses and exhortations to build teams won't do much, but repeated development on current job assignments with requirements to motivate individuals and teams and to develop a shared mindset will. Need learners who can deal with change? Getting together to share information and ideas or brainstorm won't develop them but understanding of how people learn and change, doing competency and learning skills assessment, and developing an expanded repertoire of learning tactics will. In short, *carefully designed real life experiences will best teach these skills.*

3. Selling Top Management on Their Mission Critical Role in Talent Development

Some individuals of top management have the same strengths and weaknesses profile as presented in Tables 6.1 and 6.2. Some top managers will have to be sold on and helped with their intervention role. Top-level long-term talent building will not take place in local decentralized units; future talent belongs to the total organization, and its officers have a fiduciary responsibility to acquire and grow its talent. The data have been available for a long time on what happens to functional/unit managers whose careers are locally controlled and whose inline promotions are just a little bit more of the same—a large proportion can't handle the demands of broader general management roles. Strategic use of development councils as International Paper uses at the functional and single business unit (SBU) level and a super council that looks over corporate level talent are, we think, a must for meaningful development of talent.

4. Managing the Talent Supply

Another major partnership with top management concerns the ratio of developed to bought talent. For example, as an HR manager you need certain skills that you know start-up managers tend to have. The problem is your firm has either no or few startups, or startups are always assigned to people who have previously done them well. Your options are to develop startup-like skills through development on current jobs or to hire from the outside. Research suggests you should buy because your "development factory" will not produce a first rate product. Policies of promote from within may fail if the experiences aren't available to teach the requisite competencies.

5. HR's Unique Role in Closing the Gaps

We first grappled with this issue at the Center for Creative Leadership (CCL). One of us was a researcher, and the other was a research sponsor. Using this, as well as other research, to illuminate what experiences and developmental remedies can create growth in individuals, we developed an expert system (the CAREER ARCHITECT®) which gives, for example, a best set of remedies for building listening skills, creating strategy, or managing conflict. The remedies differ for each competency.

A bit of background. In the CCL studies, we concluded that to develop a new skill, a person must:

- Have challenging, uncomfortable tasks/assignments containing elements of the needed skill. This brought about 70 percent of reported skill development. Essentially, development is either learn to do the skill or fail at something important to you. All poor listeners have had countless opportunities to learn. They don't learn because under stress they fall back on their strength—doing it themselves without input. Tasks that develop listening, or anything else for that matter, are those in which *not learning and doing it is not a viable personal option,* for example, coaching children's sports, running a task force of computer experts when you barely know how to turn one on, or negotiating with someone who doesn't want to negotiate with you and doesn't really have to.
- Have continuous feedback on the skill against a target of success. This can take the form of a developmental partner or mentor, keeping a written summary of what's working and not working, or preferably receiving a formal assessment. Research indicates that without this further feedback, even the best development plans fail.
- Have some new/different behaviors to try—typically these come from course-work/readings and account for about 10 percent of development.
- Get out of his or her comfort zone, try many different ways to improve, and actively search for ways to make sense out of diverse experiences. These are shown in studies of personal development as behaviors of those who are best at development.

Using the above described research, we ran a prototype development plan for the gaps—the weaker but critically important competencies—to see how they are most likely developed. Not surprisingly, most of the recommendations were development remedies that are rarely used in most organizations. That's not surprising, because if they were, people would have developed these competencies!

HR'S DEVELOPMENT AGENDA

Jobs HR Must Have Input into Filling to Grow Future Talent

The jobs most likely to develop these gap skills are those involving: turnarounds, start-ups, significant long-term team building assignments, line to staff switches (for building strategic skills and perspective), and significant leaps in complexity. They are not very common job changes and are generally reserved for people who have previously done them well. Nonetheless, if our data reflect the general situation, they are what is most required in order to develop these gap competencies.

Develop-in-Place Assignments HR Must Have a Hand in Creating and Filling

Skills also can be developed by having people work on significant part-time tasks while on current full-time jobs, tasks that would prepare them for the larger full job challenges above. Tasks such as managing diverse or difficult teams on a project basis, relaunching a project/product failure, integrating diverse systems across boundaries, and creating employee involvement teams arise as critical part time assignments.

Methods of Getting People the Feedback They Need That HR Must Provide

The best methods for getting feedback were to try the skill and to learn from direct experience, from 360° feedback, and by learning from past data. These methods indicated to us that (1) providing people with many small developmental experiences; (2) targeted use of 360° processes, and (3) more careful collection and analysis of historical data (e.g., the success and failures among people hired)—how a person has done and what a person has learned from experiences that develop these gap competencies—are what will work in development.

The Best Sources of Feedback HR Needs to Facilitate

The best sources from which to receive feedback are not often accessed; the top three sources for the gap skills were HR professionals, past associates, and mentors! These sources are preferred because the gap characteristics are longer term and require the broader perspective all three bring to feedback settings. A different, more tactical list would have produced the usual sources of boss, peers, self, and direct reports. This list means that the 360° assessments of gap characteristics ought to be filled out by HR professionals, past associates, and natural mentors more than by boss, peers, and direct reports!

Assuring that Learning Takes Place

Finally, learning enhancement is needed to cement these learnings. Research tells us that just going through the right experience doesn't assure that the right learning occurs. Many "derailed people" have been through varied experiences. Here, learning from others and exploration and enhancement of one's learning skills will help people gain more from experience. HR needs to create and manage an individual learning enhancement process.

THE FUTURE TALENT BUILDING AGENDA FOR HUMAN RESOURCES

In Summary:

1. Become better business partners and competency futurists.
2. Determine the current and future gap competencies for the organization.
3. Determine which developmental experiences (jobs, learning from others, feedback methods and sources, and self-development) best develop those competencies.
4. Along with top management, intervene strongly to build a strong talent base.

SECTION II

PLAY NEW ROLES

The metaphor of roles comes from the theater where actors play roles to communicate a message or purpose. Roles have become relevant in organizations as employees, like actors, assume a part in order to communicate or accomplish a message or purpose. Organizational roles may be defined by three elements: deliverables, metaphors, and actions.

Deliverables specify what happens as a result of an individual engaging in a set of actions. At a broad level, engineers deliver designs, manufacturers deliver products, marketing delivers customer segmentation, and sales delivers customers. The debate over deliverables has begun to gain more attention. Historically, human resource professionals were asked to deliver operational outcomes such as administrative efficiency and employee commitment through the human resource practices they crafted. More recently, HR professionals have been asked to deliver more strategic organizational outcomes, such as organizational diagnosis, customer engagement, globalization, and capacity for change. In the future, HR professionals will likely be asked to deliver *both* operational and strategic outcomes as well as emerging outcomes such as globalization, intellectual and human capital, culture change, inventive leadership bench, and boundaryless organizations.

Metaphors provide images or identities that capture a role. In theater metaphors for roles abound—producer, director, lead actor, chorus, and so on. In HR multiple metaphors have been used to describe HR professionals—strategic partners, business partners, employee advocates, change agents, administrative experts, and so forth. Each metaphor provides an identity or image for which the HR professional is known. The future of HR identifies new and emerging metaphors to describe the work of HR professionals.

Actions reflect what is done to bring the role to life. In theater, actions are found in the script, stage production, and physical gestures that make a play come to life. For HR professionals, actions are often embedded in how people spend time, how they think about their work, who they meet with, questions they ask, and how they attempt to respond to those questions. As a pattern of actions emerges, HR professionals define their roles in the organization. In the future, a number of new actions for HR professionals will likely emerge around what they do, who they do it with, how they do it, and how they think about what they do. HR professionals will need to learn, experience, and master new roles. In so doing, they will need to respond to some of the following questions:

- *What are the future deliverables from HR work?*
  As HR professionals participate more actively in the management of complex organizations, they will need to identify new deliverables from their work. They will need to play a clear role in operationalizing what value they create and deliver to an enterprise. By focusing on new deliverables, they are forced into new roles.
- *What are the metaphors of the HR professional of the future?*
  As words like partner become commonplace, new steps along the HR progression need to occur. HR professionals as players, pioneers, motivators, stewards, and architects are some of the metaphors that might be considered. These metaphors provide an identity for thinking about and conceptualizing HR work.
- *What are the actions for future HR professionals?*
  Imagine a time log for a typical week of an HR professional today and again 5, 10, 15 years in the future. What would be different? With whom would he or she be meeting? Where would she be spending time? What questions would he be asking? Operationalizing the new role of HR into present and future time logs offers a concrete illustration of what might be different.

The essays in this section address these questions cleverly and insightfully. Collectively, they suggest that the future role of HR, while built on the present, will evolve to a new state. Embedded in the new roles are competencies of the HR professional of the future which also will need to evolve. Armed with new roles and competencies, HR professionals will create unique value in the future.

The message from these essays is for HR professionals to think about deliverables, metaphors, and actions on which to base future, not past, roles. When these evolving roles are adopted, HR professionals become more credible and relevant to business behavior.

CHAPTER 7

NEW HUMAN RESOURCE ROLES TO IMPACT ORGANIZATIONAL PERFORMANCE: FROM "PARTNERS" TO "PLAYERS"

RICHARD W. BEATTY and CRAIG ERIC SCHNEIER

Few would argue that human resources (HR) must adapt during times of rapid organizational change. HR has always played multiple roles (e.g., employee advocate, management conscience), but the last decade has witnessed the advocacy of new roles—the most popular of which promotes HR as a business partner. Although the business partner role is important, it carries potentially problematic implications because it focuses HR on being *part* of the team supporting the business strategy (Ulrich, 1994, 1997). The stakes are high for HR since in contemporary organizations any *part* that does not add real value to the organization can be excised through downsizing, delayering, and especially through outsourcing (Stewart, 1996).

HR must now be judged on whether it enhances the firm's competitive advantage by adding *real,* measurable economic value (e.g., shortened training cycle time), not merely on its perceived value (e.g., "training builds skills"). Above all, competitive advantage implies *customer* value: Whatever HR does must not only add value to its internal clients, but also (and more importantly) add economic value to the organization's external customers and investors. This follows from an axiom that applies as equally to HR processes as it does to all functional processes. If the external customer is unwilling to pay for the work, the organization should no longer provide it.

This value-based focus will require HR to add value to external customers in unique ways that enable firms to create unfair fights with

69

competitors in the marketplace and to deliver economic value to the ultimate customer. Thus, it is not enough to say that the HR function should have a part or merely add value to the organization (i.e., employees and managers): HR must *deliver* economic value for which the organization's constituencies are willing to pay. Ideally, such value could be *captured* as a premium paid for the product or service delivered. This is a tall order for HR, which has historically served roles such as the "people people," the personnel "police" (i.e., enforcing organizational and government policies), and, more recently, the business partner.

HR AS STRATEGIC PLAYER

The HR function (and its processes) now must become a strategic *player*. To continue the analogy, a player adds value (as do some partners); more importantly, a player *scores*. HR's focus must, therefore, be on scoring—on making things happen for customers—rather than merely being a *part* of the team. HR must be "on the field," in the game, and positioned to score. HR may not be the lead scorer, but it cannot be on the sidelines coaching, in the training room prepping, or, least of all, outside the stadium gates taking head count. If HR can evolve to a role that adds significant economic value to the firm, its security is likely to be substantially enhanced, and many comments, such as by *Fortune's* Stewart, signaling doom for HR or calls to eliminate the function will be seen as relics of the 1990s.

This chapter provides an overview of how HR can, and is, scoring points. First, we discuss the score-keeping process—measuring HR's impact on organizational performance as well as alternative HR roles in the scoring process. HR's value in executing strategy is then demonstrated via the example of mergers and acquisitions, an opportunity for HR to add demonstrable economic value that is typically unrealized.

CLARIFYING HR'S IMPACT ON ORGANIZATIONAL PERFORMANCE

The HR Scorecard

To understand how HR can score involves recognizing how the scorecard is kept. Most discussions of organizational scorecards (Kaplan & Norton, 1992) focus primarily on financial and operational measures. Financial scorecards, both short-term and long-term, involve such measures as earnings per share, equity appreciation, return on assets, with economic value added (EVA) a recent favorite. Short-term measures also include quarterly earnings and revenue growth. Operational outcomes might include customer satisfaction/success, product or service quality, speed of delivery, and productivity ("doing more with less"). There is an assumed relationship between operational outcomes and financial results. That is, if the strategy of the organization is appropriately architected, the key operational goals, often described via a small set of critical success factors, should positively impact the organization's financial results. AT&T has demonstrated this, as its customer-value-added (CVA) measure is shown to link directly to EVA.

HR's role in influencing work force behaviors to achieve operational and financial outcomes can add value by helping to ensure that the work force engages in the "right" behaviors, which produce the "right" operational outcomes, enabling the organization to achieve its intended financial results. Influencing work force behaviors to achieve a desired result ought to be a major HR role; however, HR's focus is often on activities (e.g., number of people trained), not on results (e.g., new sales). Hence, the relationship of behaviors to outcomes had not until recently (Huselid, 1995) been empirically demonstrated using a large sample of firms. Within a single firm this relationship is much more difficult to demonstrate. Indeed, AT&T has yet to demonstrate the relationship of its people-value-added (PVA) measures, for example, to CVA. Thus, specifically how a firm may add economic value through its HR function has yet to be adequately demonstrated.

One reason HR has not been asked to prove its economic value may be the many roles it has been asked to play. HR roles focus away from economic value added. Ulrich (1996) explains HR historically as an emphasis on people over processes and operations over strategy. One of Ulrich's HR roles has a long tradition: Focusing on people and HR processes to create operational systems that serve employees. In this *employee advocate* role, HR's major contribution is serving the work force by providing the many services employees expect, such as work schedule flexibility, benefits flexibility, career growth and development counseling, as well as employee assistance programs. Few would argue that such a service role is not useful, only that its strategic value is less than other HR roles Ulrich (1996) articulates. Because the employee advocate role is more a partner than a player role, HR is not credited with scoring (i.e., delivering economic value), even though State Farm Insurance, Chick-fil-A (Reicheld, 1996), and others maintain that the employee advocate role manifests itself in employee (and thus customer) loyalty (Jones & Sasser, 1995).

One important and relatively new way in which HR can score in this domain is through facilitating the *care and feeding of the core competency work-force*, that component of the work force that staffs the organization's core competencies (Prahalad & Hamel, 1994). These positions are the high-leverage positions where obtaining, building, and retaining essential talent directly impact the organization's competitive advantage (for example, software engineers in Microsoft or traders in Salomon Brothers). In many respects, this new HR role may be likened to a very sophisticated employee relations function for which the primary constituency is the core competency work force, the cadre charged with adding economic value. The implication for HR here is that investment in the work force may vary based on the ability/inability to leverage the organization's competitive advantage. Obviously, this role may become more prominent as many traditional parts of the employee advocacy role are severed from organizations (Koch & McGrath, 1996).

Another role receiving considerable attention is *HR's management of operational processes*. Organizations are asking the HR personnel function to become administrative experts, taking costs out of HR systems while improving the quality of services (Yeung, Brockbank, & Ulrich, 1994). The result has led to the reengineering of HR processes, to shared services, to centers of excellence, to organization design (Ulrich, 1994), and to considerable movement toward outsourcing or eliminating low-value-added HR work, as well as exporting some HR work back to line management (e.g., staffing and discipline). Administrative efficiency (i.e., cost effectiveness), although critical to organizational survival, is often subsumed under the business partner rubric. Because this role primarily impacts the cost side of an organization's economy, it has less to do with strategic leverage than HR roles that directly impact the revenue side. HR here is more of an implementor than a strategic partner.

The third HR role Ulrich describes, *executing the business's strategy* (see also Schneier, Shaw, & Beatty, 1991), is at the heart of HR becoming more of a value-added player. In this role, HR's central responsibility becomes aligning the HR "tool kit" to deliver the behaviors needed to realize the business strategy. This is accomplished by improving the focus of work force behaviors, especially toward the operational objectives of the firm. HR's tool kit consists of, for example, designing work and organizations, measuring performance, selecting, developing, and rewarding a work force, as well as communicating and clarifying strategic objectives (see Table 7.1). How the HR tool kit should be designed, aligned or integrated, and implemented is based on the organization's primary strategic choice.

Table 7.1
Strategic Choices and Traditional HR Alignment

	Work Design	Performance Measures	Selection	Development	Rewards	Communication

Operational Excellence	• Right Work
	• Key Processes
	• Job Design
	• Organizational Design
	
	• Centralized/controlled
	• Strict policies/procedures
		• Culture
		• Expectations
		• Feedback
		• Levels
		
		• Total cost productivity
		• Errors
		• Waste
		• Abandoned calls
		• Lost customers/accounts
		• New sales + head count
		• Times/deadlines met
			• Hire
			• Move
			• Exit
			
			• Strong basic education:
			Quantitative
			Verbal
			  *Written
			  *Oral
			• Process competencies
				• Orientation
				• Current Job
				• Career Level
				
				• Strong orientation on expectations, rules
				• Predictable career ladder
					• Behavior
					• Consequences
					• Reward Levels
					
					• Team productivity awards
					• Profit sharing tied to performance criteria
					• Skill-based pay
						• Strategy
						• Mindset
						• Status
						
						• Teamwork
						• Encourage process improvement
						• Productivity improvement feedback

(Continued)

Table 7.1 (Continued)

	Work Design	Performance Measures	Selection	Development	Rewards	Communication
Product Leadership	• Coordinated Teams (cross functional)	• Percent Sales from new products (e.g., last 3 years) • Margin • Sales growth • Customer growth • Industry accolades/recognition • Copyrights • Patents	• Technical/ research competencies • Outside-the-box thinkers	• Employees responsible for learning • Mandatory competency growth • Feedback on professional competency growth	• Team innovation awards • Competency-based pay	• Antibureaucratic • Candor • Humble • Encourage ideas/problem-solving • Let employees know what a winner "looks like" • Feedback on new product sales
Customer Intimacy	• Autonomy • Know the customers' needs	• Customer guarantees • Customer retention rate • No. referrals from current customers	• Active learners • Networking competencies • Resourcefulness	• Oriented toward long-term focus with customer • Not a lot of ladders • Acts as a consultant to customer/ partner	• Individual awards • System awards • Nonfinancial awards • "Fee for Service" awards	• Customer advocates • Know customers' needs

Implications: What must we do? First? Second?

74

How HR Executes Different Company Strategies: Operational Excellence, Product Leadership, or Customer Intimacy

How the choice of business strategy relates to HR work force issues can be examined in terms of Treacy and Wiersema's (1995) model of three basic paths to competitive advantage: operational excellence, product leadership, and/or customer intimacy. An organization following an *operational excellence strategy* attempts to be the low price provider. Thus, it must build operational systems that continually reduce cost/price, while offering a quality product that consistently adds greater value to its customers than do competitors' products. A performance measure that could energize a work force to attain operational excellence might include total cost productivity, whereby the work force would be constantly reminded it must do more with less in order to achieve strategic success in the marketplace. The message may be reinforced by rewarding productivity improvements through programs such as gainsharing (Stack, 1992). In gainsharing, the power of the "HR tools" of reward and measurement has been clearly demonstrated to impact the bottom line (Becker & Huselid, 1997). Another HR tool or lever for change, work force selection and development, could also be aligned with the low-price strategy by recognizing that most operational excellence firms require employees who are trainable and flexible. They can fit in and follow the "battle plan," because the work design is explicit and does not permit variation. In a low-cost environment, few customers can have it their own particular way. Economic efficiencies come through standardization; variation must be driven out. A firm (or business unit) with an operational excellence strategy would seek to create a core work force "mind set" which focuses on shorter-term production objectives, avoids waste, and is concerned about quantity; it would certainly avoid free spirits and ostentatious behavior (see Table 7.2). Examples of operational excellence companies would be Federal Express, Dell, and Nucor.

In contrast, a firm competing on a *product leadership strategy* requires innovation in products and/or services to create its competitive advantage and would likely seek a core work force (e.g., R&D employees) with an antibureaucratic, entrepreneurial mind-set, individuals who are highly versatile; possess a longer-term focus; have a very high concern for results over processes; have a high tolerance for ambiguity; and enjoy challenging one another, cross-functional collaboration, a high degree of creative behavior, and risk taking. Because the value added is in the product or service itself (as opposed to price), firms such as 3M, which are pursuing a

Table 7.2
The Value Disciplines and Human Behavior

Operational Excellence —Cost—	Product Leadership —Innovation—	Customer Intimacy —Solutions—
Core Workforce Mind-Set		
• Identifies with process • Trainable/can learn • Follow the Battle Plan • Dedicated to organization • Shorter-term focus • Avoid waste and cost • Driven by incremental improvement • High concern for output quantity • High concern for process • High comfort with stability • Lower level of risk-taking	• Identifies with, values, and is humbled by the discovery process • Challenges the possible/ the status quo • Antibureaucratic • Longer-term focus • Versatile • Driven by learning • Higher concern for outcomes • High tolerance for ambiguity • Greater degree of risk-taking	• Identifies with customers • Shares "secrets" readily, easily • Seeks customer intelligence • Adaptable/flexible • Makes customer results happen • Quick study • Driven by customer success • Anticipates customer needs • High tolerance for ambiguity
• *NOT:* Free spirits/ostentatious	• *NOT:* Structured/ streamlined	• *NOT:* Clones
Typical Behaviors		
• Teamwork • Working to fit in/find a role • Relatively repetitive and predictable behaviors • Primarily autonomous or individual activity as part of process	• Problem solving • Challenging one another • Cross-functional collaboration • High degree of creative behavior	• Share ideas and solutions • Thinks/works across boundaries • Develops broad-based skills • Networks effectively • Customer management
Examples		
Federal Express, Dell, Nucor	Sony, Glaxo, Merck, 3M, Intel	Four Seasons, Airborne, Roadway, Home Depot, Cott

product leadership strategy have developed employee incentives based on sales of new products developed during the prior three years to reward employees (especially those who constitute the core competency work force).

Firms following a *customer intimacy strategy* offer unique solutions that enable their products or services to be readily customized at the lowest level of customer interface. Since unique customer solutions are essentially what provide the competitive advantage for such organizations, the selection and development system would seek and develop active learners, customer advocates, and employees who demonstrate a willingness to share and enhance learning in the organization. Overriding measures of performance might include delivering on customer guarantees/warranties and going beyond them to retain profitable customers. Rewards would focus on those in primary contact with customers to reinforce employee networking, communication, and relationship-building with the customer, so that customization would be continually enhanced and delivering on promises to customers would be continually improved. Thus HR's use of its tool kit in strategy execution would afford the HR function an opportunity for an impact on near-term economic value.

HR's Culture and Transformation Role

Besides HR's role in executing the business's strategy, Ulrich describes another potential source of considerable long-term economic value to the organization: *HR's role in transforming a culture*. The transformation role is more complex than creating or improving a culture (Schneier & Beatty, 1995). The latter may be accomplished by aligning the HR tool kit to deliver improvements in operational outcomes to achieve the business strategy (as discussed above). The point about transformation is made in *Competitive Advantage Through People* (Pfeffer, 1994). His book cites five firms with the highest equity return from 1972 to 1992: Southwest Airlines, Wal-Mart, Tyson Foods, Circuit City, and Plenum Publishing. All enjoyed equity appreciation of over 14,000 percent during that 20-year period. What the "Pfeffer Five" share in common, besides a uniquely focused operational excellence strategy, is a firm culture created after 1945. In contrast, the cultures of many of America's business pantheon were created well before then (e.g., General Electric, General Motors, DuPont, Sears, and IBM, to name a few) and had to change (or adjust) their cultures compared to the Pfeffer Five. Such venerable organizations undoubtedly built systems and work forces with an HR tool kit well suited to a time when HR's role as employee advocate for the entire work force was appropriate. When these organizations began to experience global competition, deregulation, new entrants into their markets, and enhanced competitive pressures, however, traditional HR solutions did not serve the organizations' needs for a strategic player to execute strategy *and* to transform cultures. All five pre–World War II firms mentioned above engaged in transformations, and in those companies in which HR played a significant role (e.g., Sears), HR's role was not the role it had traditionally taken (see Ulrich, 1997).

Culture change may offer the highest potential leverage for HR to impact the organization's economic performance. Typically, survival is at stake; however, many major organizational transformations have been made largely without HR's initial, intensive involvement (e.g., ABB Asea, Brown, Boveri; British Petroleum; GE; IBM; and SAS). If HR is to be involved, it must assume substantially different responsibilities; it can no longer sit on the sidelines brokering consulting services or facilitating meetings. (HR has traditionally played an important role in supporting cultures.) HR must become a leader in managing a cultural transformation by shaping the mind set and behaviors that impact the firm's operational and financial outcomes, thus enabling the organization to survive and thrive.

Cultural transformation requires HR to be in the game and scoring on a regular basis. Even HR's significant role in organizational transformation however, may lead to difficulty demonstrating HR's economic impact on a firm. More work is needed on measuring the impact of HR on the behavioral, operational, and financial success of organizations. One new HR role may offer insight into this process—the role of HR in mergers and acquisitions.

A HIGH-LEVERAGE PLAY FOR HR: MERGERS AND ACQUISITIONS

Mergers and acquisitions (M and A) are legendary for their impact on culture (and performance). For example, RCA's merger (and subsequent demerger) with Whirlpool was followed by RCA's purchase and absorption within the GE culture. Once inside GE, RCA ceased to be an independent operating entity. (The RCA building, a New York landmark, is now known as the GE building.) Many acquisitive corporations' cultures are also noteworthy, such as the effect upon ITT when Harold Geneen was operating well over one hundred companies. The performance of acquisition strategies has been questioned (e.g., Porter, 1987), however, and the recent strategic emphasis is on "focus, focus, focus."

The "financial play" for portfolio management is out; focus and operational earnings are in.

Many M&A failures have been attributed to executive egos needing a trophy acquisition to impress shareholders (or their peers). The evidence is that such marriages seldom succeed (*BusinessWeek,* 1995). Often there is a lack of compelling strategic rationale for the merger/acquisition, and there are unrealistic expectations of "synergy" and/or excessive compensation for the acquisition.

M&A Failures: Inadequate HR Due Diligence

Likely causes of M&A failure, besides excessive compensation or CEO ego, include inadequate due diligence on the part of the acquirer or merging partner, conflicting corporate cultures, or a failure to move quickly to meld the two companies. These have implications for the *people* competencies in organizations and hence the HR function in particular. While the HR function may not be able to greatly influence failures related to flawed strategic analysis, HR may increase the probability of successful M&A strategies by playing a significant role in due diligence of the "soft assets" (e.g., intellectual capital; see Quinn, Anderson, & Finkelstein, 1996). Such a due diligence would include, for example, how the work gets done in each operating entity, an assessment of the work force which supports corporate core competencies, and an analysis of the target's culture, as well designing methods to integrate rapidly once the transaction is completed (especially important in an unfriendly acquisition). Financial assessments of a target firm's intellectual capital may be a "deal maker or breaker," as we are beginning to witness (Beatty, 1996).

The Role of Intellectual Capital Assessments in M&A Work

Intellectual capital varies widely, even among firms in the same industry, and is crudely assessed in the marketplace's financial valuation by assigning an estimated value over and above that which is obtained via traditional due diligence (the assessment of bricks and mortar). The point is best illustrated in diversified firms. Some firms, such as General Electric, seek synergy, although they are considerably diversified. Others do not. PepsiCo, for example, is far less diversified. PepsiCo's managers and work force are aligned within a particular product line, and there is little corporate cross-fertilization, except at the top. Enhanced learnings, competencies, and operational efficiencies are not captured, communicated, or utilized across the various units. Each business unit at PepsiCo is relatively independent. The strategy is more of a financial play rather than that of creating value through synergy. Thus most of PepsiCo's growth has been a function of its acquisitions; it has relied less on building businesses via the development of intellectual capital at the corporate level (although it certainly possesses intellectual capital within its business units) to solve business problems.

HR's Role in Preacquisition

HR can begin to demonstrate (and measure) its economic value added prior to an acquisition, by considering categories of analysis which provide data on targeted acquisitions. Top-level executives usually understand the target company's strategy and product lines, but perhaps not its core competencies, intellectual capital, culture, HR focus and strengths, and work force strengths. These all should be assessed systematically to determine the extent to which the target firm must be changed to create the appropriate synergy or whether the target should be managed independently (a relatively pure financial play). While such an investigation may seem onerous, it is much easier in today's information age, because much of the data needed to determine a firm's core competencies and work force capabilities are available in the public press.

Once a soft-asset due-diligence model has been constructed, it can be used to prioritize potential targets. A firm might seek a partner that provides a uniqueness that strengthens a current organizational weakness. For example, a firm in the financial services industry may conclude that it has been unsuccessful in remedying inadequate client-servicing information technology because the intellectual capital required has not been developed. It may thus seek a partner and work force competencies that can provide such capability (Beatty, in press).

Once the target's strategy is identified, the next step is to access intellectual capital. The analytical focus would depend on strategic choice: For product leaders (e.g., Sony, 3M), the focus is on the R&D work force; for operational excellence firms, such as a mass merchandiser (e.g., Wal-Mart), it is on the operational systems' work force of its logistics and distribution network; for customer intimacy firms (e.g., Airborne Express, Buckman Labs) it is on the strength of point-of-purchase interface.

The intellectual capital imperatives described here would lead prudent firms active in mergers and acquisitions to develop an excess capacity in

deployment-ready executive resources to quickly export and replace existing executive teams in target companies. The new team would be charged
with "awakening" and then aligning the acquisition in a new strategic direction, for example, by communicating the new future and rearchitecting
the organization's processes and systems (e.g., measures, rewards, selection,
budgets). The organization's culture is thus changed (over time), and the
new strategy better realized. It may also be important to have an HR function with excess capacity which also can be exported to utilize the "HR
tool kit" to elicit the behaviors essential to strategic success and to create
a new culture aligned with the business strategy.

HR's Role in Postacquisition

After the acquisition, HR should verify the quality of the intellectual
capital acquired by assessing the work force relative to the core competencies. If the verification process occurs rapidly, some of the target's executives
might be asked to remain to facilitate the transition. The executive team
should include a senior HR person charged with realignment of the target's
HR function.

CONCLUSION

The challenges for HR of becoming a player are much more difficult than
those of a business partner. Some forms of partnership can take place "below
the line" (i.e., through reengineering and serving as the employee advocate),
but becoming a full-fledged player starts with above-the-line activities in
which the HR tool kit (e.g., measurement, rewards, etc.) is actually aligned
with strategy to create a culture that supports the strategic direction. This
can provide a more measurable economic impact. To begin this process, *the
strategic value of all HR work must be assessed in terms of impact on the financial
and operational outcomes of the firm.* HR's *core* work must be retained, that work
which truly creates economic value and contributes to the organization's
reasons for existence. For example, HR must look beyond the added value
of processing benefits for employees (or even the broader employee advocate
role), because the value added may not be captured in the marketplace.

The second assessment is synergy, defined as the *congruency or strategic fit.*
Many HR practices should not be aligned, rather they must be excised—
eliminated, outsourced, or exported back to line managers. Synergy means
not only aligning the HR tool kit with the *desired* culture but also ensuring consistency between short-term (e.g., through HR service centers)

and long-term objectives (e.g., through building work force competency which creates significant new technology). This is a substantial challenge for the HR function. In meeting this challenge, the business partner role can be seen as a transitional stage on what may be the only road to survival of the HR function: Becoming a player that adds measurable economic value to the firm's major constituencies.

REFERENCES

Beatty, R.W. (1996). HR's role in mergers and acquisitions: Soft asset due diligence. Manuscript under review.

Beatty, R.W. (in press). HR's next challenge: Acquiring, building and retaining intellectual capital. In H. Risher and C. Fay (eds.), *Rethinking the HR function*. San Francisco: Jossey-Bass.

Becker, B.E., & Huselid, M.A. (in press). Managerial compensation systems and firm performance. *Academy of Management Journal,* special issue on Managerial Compensation and Firm Performance.

BusinessWeek. (October 30, 1995). The case against mergers.

Jones, T.O., & Sasser, W.E. (1995). Why satisfied customers depart. *Harvard Business Review,* Nov.–Dec.

Kaplan, R.S., & Norton, D.P. (1992). The balanced scorecard—measures that drive performance. *Harvard Business Review,* Jan.–Feb. 1992, 71–79.

Koch, M.J., & McGrath, R.G. (1996). Improving labor productivity: Human resource management policies do matter. *Strategic Management Journal, 17,* 335–354.

Pfeffer, J. (1994). *Competitive advantage through people.* Boston: Harvard Business Press.

Porter, M.E. (1987). From competitive advantage to corporate strategy. *Harvard Business Review,* May–June.

Prahalad, G.K., & Hamel, G. (1994). *Competing for the future.* Boston: Harvard Business Press.

Quinn, J.B., Anderson, P., & Finkelstein, S. (1996). Managing professional intellect: Making the most of the best. *Harvard Business Review,* Mar.–Apr.

Reicheld, F. (1996). *The loyalty effect: The hidden force behind growth, profits and lasting value.* Boston: Harvard Business Press.

Schneier, C.E., Shaw, D.G., & Beatty, R.W. (1991). Performance measurement and management: A tool for strategy execution. *Human Resource Management, 30*(3), 279–301.

Schneier, C.E., & Beatty, R.W. (1995). Making culture change happen and making it last: Using structure, systems and skills as change levers. In L. A. Berger (ed.), *Handbook of culture change*. Burr Ridge, IL: Business One/Irwin.

Stack, J. (1992). *The great game of business*. New York: Doubleday/Currency.

Stewart, T. (April 1996). Taking on the last bureaucracy. *Fortune,* p. 105.

Treacy, M., & Wiersema, F. (1995). *The discipline of market leaders,* Reading, MA: Addison-Wesley.

Ulrich, D. (1997). *Human resource champions: The next agenda for adding value and delivering results.* Cambridge, MA: Harvard Business Press.

Ulrich, D. (1997). Human Resource: From rhetoric to reality. *Strategic Partners for High Performance* (Work in America).

Yeung, A., Brockbank, W., & Ulrich, D. (1994). Lower cost, higher value: Human resource function in transformation. *Human Resource Planning Journal, 18*(2), 25–37.

CHAPTER 8

THE TRANSFORMATION OF THE HUMAN RESOURCE FUNCTION: RESOLVING THE TENSION BETWEEN A TRADITIONAL ADMINISTRATIVE AND A NEW STRATEGIC ROLE

MICHAEL BEER

$\mathbf{T}$here is little question that human resource management is undergoing profound change as the twentieth century draws to a close. What are the forces for change? Where are human resource management and the human resource (HR) function going? What are the obstacles to getting there? These are the questions I will discuss.

FORCES FOR CHANGE

Competition, globalization, and continuous change in markets and technology are the principal reasons for the transformation of human resource management. Additionally, a revolution in capital markets has given shareholders a more powerful voice and has made it possible for them to claim a larger share of the corporation's resources.

As a consequence of these forces, corporations are finding themselves in the midst of a revolution in organizing and managing people that will continue well into the twenty-first century. A flatter, less bureaucratic, less hierarchical, faster and more responsive organization is emerging as the model for the future. In such an organization people will be employed in a more *cost effective* manner. More importantly, organizations will have to enhance a number of capabilities and make these the source of their competitive advantage (Beer & Eisenstat, 1996b; Hamel & Prahalad, 1994; Ulrich & Lake, 1990). Far higher levels of (1) *coordination* across functions, business units, and borders; (2) employee *commitment* to continuous improvement; (3) general management and leadership *competence;* (4) *creativity* and entrepreneurship; and (5) open *communication* will have to be developed. To acquire these capabilities corporations are struggling to realign their organizations and their human resource policies and practices with new competitive realities. Nothing less than a cultural revolution is underway.

In the United States at least, *the first wave of change focused on cost effectiveness.* In the past decade tens of thousands of jobs have been lost as downsizing has swept the corporate landscape. That wave is now spreading to the rest of the world, where the need to attend more closely to shareholder value is just beginning to make itself felt. Even Japan may not be exempt from these pressures, though clearly change there will occur in ways that are consistent with that country's traditions and norms. Pressures for cost reduction not only demand a different corporate organization, they place pressure on the human resource function to be cost effective. Reengineering of the HR function is occurring in many corporations and with it a search for a new role and organizational form.

Though the cost-effectiveness wave has not yet run its course in the United States many companies are discovering that downsizing is not enough. The implementation of new strategies requires fundamental changes in organizational behavior. Leaner organizations are not necessarily more effective. In fact recent research suggests that when cost reduction is the principal thrust of change, company performance is not enhanced in the long run (Nohria, unpublished).

Chief Executive Officers (CEO) are the second major force for change. As the need for strategic change in organizing and managing people began to be felt, CEOs looked to their HR functions for help and discovered that they were not up to the task. Consider the dilemma faced in 1988 by Ray Gilmartin, the CEO of Becton Dickson, a medical technology company. To support its global strategy the company had introduced a Transnational Organization; its main feature was ten worldwide business teams. The company, however, lacked the culture and managerial skills to implement the structure. Turning to his HR function for help, Gilmartin found that it lacked the capability or credibility to help the company with the needed organizational transformation. This was particularly surprising in light of the fact that the company had brought in a new vice president for human resources several years earlier, and he had built what many considered a state of the art function. A new education and training initiative was launched, a new performance appraisal and compensation system installed, and an innovative cafeteria approach to benefits established. Despite these initiatives and an Award for Professional Excellence from the American Society for Personnel Administration, line executives in the company saw an expensive HR function making a negligible contribution to their business. Gilmartin's responded by asking his vice president of strategy to take responsibility for HR. The merger of HR and the Strategy function led to a new conception of HR as a strategic function; it also led to a core process by which HR would partner with general managers and employees throughout the company in aligning their organization and behavior with strategy and aspirational values, a development to which I will return later in the chapter.

A third major force for change is the development of new knowledge about the potential for organizations and their people to be a source of competitive advantage. In the last decade several books have been published which establish, more firmly than did previous research, the relationship between organization effectiveness, corporate culture, and financial performance (Collins & Porras, 1994; Denison, 1990; Kotter & Heskett, 1992; Pfeffer, 1994). Effectiveness, these studies showed, is much more than the aggregate talent of the firm's employees. It is a function of the coordination around business processes the organization is able to develop (Beer, Eisenstat, & Biggadike, 1996; Ulrich & Lake, 1990). That coordination is in turn a function of the company's cultural context (Beer & Eisenstat, 1996b).

The fact that many of these books on this new knowledge were written for managers has helped to establish human resources as a key to competitive advantage. The claim that organizational behavior and business success are linked also gained credibility due to CEOs such as Jack Welch of General Electric and Jan Carlzon of Scandinavian Airlines who received attention from the business press in the late 1980s and early 1990s for leading major transformations in their companies' cultural context. These books also point to a redefinition of HR from a traditional focus on attracting, selecting, and developing talented individuals to a new focus on developing an organizational context which will attract and develop leaders as well as facilitate team work.

Simultaneously, research on corporate change revealed what many employees already knew. Programmatic change driven by the human resource function does not lead to an effective corporate transformation (Beer, Eisenstat, & Spector, 1990; Shaffer, 1988). Education programs, changes in compensation systems, culture programs, changes in structure, and total quality programs, for example, do not lead to a transformation in the management of human resources or in the organization's culture. Successful corporate change, according to recent research, occurs unit by unit (Beer, Eisenstat, & Spector, 1990). A few organizational units (business units, stores, or manufacturing plants), often at the periphery of the corporation, developed innovative approaches to organizing and managing people—team-based management, high employee involvement and communication, and new approaches to decision making. When top management recognized that these innovations resulted in superior performance and employee relations they encouraged innovation in other units. They initiated conferences, visits to innovative units, and the transfer of successful change leaders from innovative units into lagging units. Top management's active development of an ever larger circle of innovative organizational units and leaders was the most important factor differentiating corporations that were successful in transforming their culture from those that were not. Importantly, leaders of innovative units succeeded in changing culture by focusing on the task, not on human resource programs. They involved their top team in defining the competitive threat and agreeing on the strategic task, and then organized people in teams to improve quality, to introduce products more quickly, or to develop and implement a world-wide business strategy.

In summary, *new research has established firmly that the organization and management of people can make a difference in the bottom line.* Collins and Porras (1994) demonstrated, for example, that visionary companies, such as Hewlett-Packard, returned an average of $6,356.00 in 1992 for $1.00 invested in 1960 as compared to $955.00 for comparison companies in the same industry and $415.00 for the general market. Research on successful and less successful cultural transformations shows that such transformations are far from easy to implement and cannot be achieved with bigger and better human resource programs and functions. No matter how innovative these programs are, they do not make the organization more effective nor do they transform its culture. In the companies that were most successful in transforming their cultures, a change-oriented human resource function, in partnership with top management, played an important role (Beer, Eisenstat, & Spector, 1990).

Unfortunately, until the mid-1980s the administration of HR programs was the main activity of most human resource professionals, and their power came from ensuring compliance. But, given the demands of the competitive environment, the increasing awareness of CEOs that organizational effectiveness is critical to competitiveness, and CEOs' growing realization that their HR function is expensive and ill equipped to help them build a competitive organization, the stage is set for a major transformation of HR.

A VISION OF THE NEW HUMAN RESOURCE FUNCTION

To make a successful transformation, the HR function will have to shed its traditional administrative, compliance, and service role and adopt a new strategic role concerned with developing the organization and the capabilities of its managers. Bill Hewlett, co-founder of Hewlett-Packard, expressed this view some years ago. He said, "The role of Personnel is to enhance the quality of management."

Unfortunately, the track record of companies who have tried to introduce this new role into their HR function has not been good. The rise and fall of organization development departments in the 1960s and 1970s, even those whose practice was focused on strategic business issues rather than interpersonal relations, suggest an inherent tension between the outlook required for a strategic human resource role and the outlook of human resource specialists in a traditional HR role. These roles attract and require people with very different professional outlooks, skills, and identity. Moreover, HR executives who have been able to integrate both roles have found that there is simply not enough time to do both. The urgent demand for service delivery drives out the more important, ambiguous, and longer term task of assisting line management with an organizational and cultural transformation. Furthermore, HR professionals who have somehow been able to perform both roles, often find their inclination to perform the traditional role diminishes. In short, the administrative and strategic roles do not easily coexist in the same function or the same person.

The older administrative, compliance, and service-oriented human resource activities will have to become more differentiated from the new strategic HR activities. This process is already underway. Companies are creating geographically decentralized human resource service centers responsible for providing traditional administrative services. Unlike the strategic human resource professionals, typically called human resource partners, HR specialists in these centers are not affiliated with a particular business unit, branch, or plant. Enabled by information technology and telephone eight hundred numbers, these centers provide services to geographically dispersed subunits of the corporation. Administrative service centers do not have to reside within the HR function, however; a more radical, and probably superior solution is to transfer these centers to a corporate service organization that will provide HR services for a fee. Increasingly HR services are being outsourced to external vendors. Moving administrative and service functions out of HR is *essential* if a new strategic role is to emerge.

Still another way the HR function will transform itself is by eliminating human resource systems and practices long held to be central pillars of effective human resource management. For example, should the practice of requiring all managers in the company to complete annual performance appraisals continue? Evidence has been accumulating for years that performance appraisal systems, no matter how well designed, do not differentiate employees sufficiently to make valid and reliable compensation, promotion, and layoff decisions. They do not necessarily even lead to better coaching. Instead these systems have become bureaucratic nightmares and have put human resource professionals in the role of "cop." At Alcatel Network Systems, in Richardson, Texas, for example, the corporate performance appraisal system has been discontinued at the urging of Terry Latham, the senior human resource executive. This move is consistent with evidence that effective individual performance evaluation and development are fostered not by a performance appraisal system, but by a high involvement organization, performance-oriented managers, and a culture that tolerates mistakes, encourages letting consistently poor performers go, and recognizes outstanding performers.

Similarly, does it make sense for a company to ask its HR and line management executives to devote considerable valuable time and energy to administering tightly coupled contingent pay for performance compensation systems? Despite the rhetoric, these systems probably do not contribute much to the effectiveness of organizations. Systems that differentiate only at the extremes and payout on a variable ratio schedule for outstanding performances are effective—and far easier and less costly to administer. This chapter is not the place for an in-depth discussion of this issue; suffice it to say that some of the most successful companies in the world do not have executive bonus or commission systems, for example. They have thick team-based cultures. A recent survey of senior executives from around the world found that they do not perceive that their executive compensation system has much motivational value. Moreover, executives in companies with a thick team-based culture saw more dysfunctional effects from such pay systems (Beer, unpublished). It appears that complex compensation schemes may not only take a lot of time, they also do not motivate and may actually be injurious to building the very team-based culture companies are aspiring to develop. Human resource executives should spend more of their time helping corporations develop these cultures.

The same logic—shed traditional HR practices and focus on aligning the organization and its culture with emerging competitive realities—applies to other areas as well. Human Resource functions spend enormous amounts of time and money in educational programs intended to develop management and leadership skills when the evidence has long been available that these programs do not readily translate into changed behavior on the job (Fleishman, Harris, & Burtt, 1955). Even the most motivated and skillful individuals coming out of these programs are too weak to overcome "the system," bosses, and organizational norms that oppose the new pattern of management. Individual development occurs most powerfully when the person becomes aware of the need to change and develops needed skills while participating in an organizational change process connected to business imperatives (Beer, Eisenstat, & Spector, 1990).

Human Resource executives also spend extensive time as principals in recruitment and selection when these decisions should be made by managers. Once again, focusing on aligning the organization's cultural context with competitive realities will stimulate changes in the lens that managers apply to selection and promotion decisions. As a result of an organizational change process executives either change their perspectives or are themselves changed. The organization is left with many more managers who are competent in identifying people who "fit" the emergent pattern of management.

I have described what should be eliminated from the human resource function, but what will the new HR function look like? It will be much smaller but more high powered; its key role will be strategic. At the business unit level, human resource partners will work closely with the general manager and her or his team to assess, diagnose, and develop the alignment of the organization with strategy and aspirational values. This role will demand of the human resource specialist a deep understanding of the business, plus expertise in organization design, organization change, and intervention methods. Analytic and interpersonal skills needed to facilitate change will also be essential.

The corporate human resource staff will be composed of a few key subject matter experts in disciplines such as compensation, management development, diversity, and organization effectiveness. They will support general managers and their human resource partners. A small organizational effectiveness group will take responsibility for developing systems, methods, and skills needed to facilitate organization development at the unit level. One of the most important responsibilities of the corporate human resource staff will be to promote an organizational learning process by facilitating the diffusion of innovations from one part of the company to another (Eisenstat, 1966). Since the principal means of aligning the corporation with its strategy and values is the transfer and promotion of managers, the corporate HR staff will play an important role in promoting an effective succession planning process which supports the company's efforts to align its organization with its strategy and values.

This vision for HR assumes that continuous strategic and cultural change will be required as the pace of change speeds in the twenty-first century. Consistent with the research discussed above, my vision of HR assumes that the process of organization development, while motivated by top management, cannot be led from the corporate level, particularly in multibusiness corporations. It must be led by unit managers throughout the company. The CEO's role is to create a corporate context that supports an *action learning* process in each subunit *and* to lead a process of strategic change in the top management unit. In the main, action learning, not educational programs, consultants, or research by academics, will be the principal means by which an organization produces new approaches to organizing and managing that are implementable (Argyris, 1994). Best practices in other companies do not necessarily align with the strategy or culture of one's own company and innovative systems and practices developed by outside experts do not necessarily incorporate important tacit knowledge in the organization. The result is failure in implementation.

How might a corporation institutionalize an action-learning process for strategic alignment and what will be the role of the human resource function? Consider, Strategic Human Resource Management Profiling developed at Becton Dickson in response to the concerns of its CEO, Ray Gilmartin, about the capability of the company's HR function described earlier (Beer, Eisenstat, & Biggadike, 1996; Beer & Eisenstat, 1996c). Strategic Human Resource Profiling is a high involvement process by which a general manager and his or her immediate reports can inquire into the alignment of their organization with its strategy and values in partnership with employees at lower levels. It is facilitated by a "profiler" from human resources or the strategic planning department. The process begins with the leadership team defining its strategic task and its values. An employee task force of eight high potential employees, one or two levels below the top team, is appointed to interview 100 employees and customers about what barriers to strategy implementation they perceive and about the extent to which management's behavior is aligned with its stated values. Data collected by the task force is fed back to top management and processed in a three-day profiling meeting. The first day of the meeting is devoted to feedback with the task force using a fishbowl method to facilitate open communication. The second day is devoted to rigorous diagnosis using a diagnostic model. The third day is devoted to developing a vision as to how the organization and its management processes must be redesigned and to the creation of a number of design teams which will be engaged in the actual redesign activity. To create accountability it is intended that the general manager will report task force findings and action plans to the next level after reviewing them with the employee task force.

An analysis of issues identified by Strategic Human Resource Management Profiling in several corporations revealed six core barriers to strategy implementation and reformulation: (1) poor coordination and teamwork, (2) unclear strategy and priorities, (3) an ineffective top team, (4) top-down or laissez faire management, (5) poor vertical communication (particularly upward communication), and (6) inadequate management and management development throughout the organization (Beer & Eisenstat, 1996b). These findings suggest that strategic HRM involves fundamental management issues. These issues must be a major part of the change process if changes in structure, systems, and HRM policies are to create fundamental change. Evaluation of Strategic Human Resource Management Profiling reveals that the process helps HR professionals play an important role in stimulating important change in systems, structure, and behavior though the extent of the changes is dependent on the leader (Beer and Eisenstat, 1996b). Strategic HRM Profiling also provides managers with the opportunity to develop as leaders.

For an HR function to develop a strategic role it will have to develop and institutionalize a core action learning process such as the Strategic Human Management Process described above. Without such a process, the HR partner will have difficulty developing commitment to behavior change. She or he will be put in a position of having to personally provide feedback that is potentially threatening and embarrassing. First of all HR executives find this difficult, given organizational politics. Second, even if they find it possible to provide honest feedback, management can deny its validity. It is possible that the HR professional's fear of providing honest feedback and/or management's desire to avoid it is responsible for many less threatening but less effective human resource programs.

OBSTACLES TO THE TRANSFORMATION OF THE HUMAN RESOURCE FUNCTION

The transformation of the human resource function faces many obstacles. These obstacles are related and mutually reinforcing making them hard to overcome.

Perhaps the most formidable of the obstacles, is the capability of most human resource professionals. To play a strategic role they will have to have analytic and interpersonal skills equal to the best consultants corporations now use to assist them with organization effectiveness and change issues. Many HR professionals lack these professionals skills. In most companies, the traditional HR role and the rewards that typically go with that role make it hard to attract professionals with required talent. One alternative is to transfer into the HR function line executives who have shown success in leading organizational change; they already possess business knowledge and have demonstrated skills in managing organizational change. If augmented with professionals in organization effectiveness and change within the function they can enhance HR's credibility. Yet another alternative is to train HR professionals in the skills for organizational analysis, design, and change they will need. In one company, studied by Beer, Eisenstat, and Spector (1990), the corporate organization development group constructed a training program for HR professionals throughout the company in which cases, lectures, and actual intervention projects were used to enhance those skills.

Guided processes, such as Strategic Human Resource Management Profiling, operationalize the organizational alignment and cultural transformation process thereby providing a consistent approach for strategic human resource management within a company. Consistency will increase the quality of professional HR work and will lead to institutionalization. Consistency in approach also enables higher management to hold line management accountable for developing an effective organization without having to rely on HR executives to provide information that may be seen by general managers as potentially threatening to their careers.

A second major obstacle to the transformation of the HR function is top management itself. CEOs say they want a more strategic HR function, but often do not understand what this entails. Many still judge the function by its effectiveness in delivering administrative services and keeping the company out of trouble with regulatory agencies. They are, therefore, unreceptive to radical ideas such as splitting off administrative and service functions and placing them within other administratively oriented corporate departments. CEOs further frustrate a transformation in the human resource function when they expect HR executives to be their agents. This is often accompanied by an ambivalence about giving the HR function the freedom and power to confront deep cultural issues, particularly when these issues are connected to top management's own assumptions, values, and behavior. Yet, as the research cited above has demonstrated, these issues are precisely the ones that must be confronted for a transformation in human resource management to take place. Once again, a well established action learning process such as Strategic Human Resource Management Profiling developed at Becton Dickinson may help overcome this problem (Beer, Eisenstat, & Biggadike, 1996). Along with consolidating HR and the Strategic Management Department under the Vice President of Strategy, it was Ray Gilmartin's principle means for transforming the concept of human resource management. It enabled a far deeper and more comprehensive analysis of organizational and human resource issues and their link to strategy at the corporate and division level. It also shifted the definition of HR in the eyes of many. Illustrative of this shift is the response of a manager at Becton Dickinson to a case discussion intended to show managers how Strategic Human Resource Management Profiling would help managers analyze their organization and transform them. "I thought this session was supposed to be about human resource management. What we are talking about here is management," said a puzzled participant. The Profiling process also stimulated a collaboration between HR and the Strategy Department. It involved HR professionals in strategy, organizational analysis, and organization redesign thereby changing their role and creating an opportunity for the learning of new skills. It taught members of the Strategic Management Department that the implementation of strategy depended heavily on human and cultural dimensions of the organization.

Overcoming these obstacles to the transformation of the human resource function will not be easy. To do so HR professionals will have to shed their ambivalence about the new role. They will have to be comfortable with the uncertainty and ambiguity associated with all change. Nothing short of a bold approach will suffice. Nor will these efforts succeed unless HR executives take the initiative. They must impart to top managers a new vision of HR and propose frame breaking changes in its organization. Top managers do not yet understand the activist change agent role the HR function personnel can and must play if they are to transform human resources in their company into a source of sustainable competitive advantage.

REFERENCES

Argyris, C. (1994). *Knowledge for action.* San Francisco: Jossey-Bass.

Beer, M. (1996). A survey about executive compensation. Harvard Business School, unpublished.

Beer, M., Eisenstat, A.R., & Spector, B. (1990). *The critical path to corporate renewal.* Boston: Harvard Business School Press.

Beer, M., Eisenstat, R.A., & Biggadike, R. (1996). "Developing an organization capable of strategy implementation and reformulation: A preliminary test." In B. Moingeon, & A. Edmondson (Eds.), *Organization learning for competitive advantage,* London: Sage Publications.

Beer, M., & Eisenstat, R.A. (1996a). Developing an organization capable of implementing strategy and learning, *Human Relations, 49*(5).

Beer, M., & Eisenstat, R.A. (1996b). The silent killers: Overcoming the hidden barriers to organizational fitness. Working Paper 97-004. Harvard Business School, Division of Research, Boston.

Beer, M., & Eisenstat, R.A. (1996c). American Medical Technologies Inc.: Learning the capabilities needed to implement strategic change. In J. Storey (Ed.), *Blackwell cases in human resource and change management.* Oxford, UK: Blackwell Publishers Ltd.

Collins, C., & Porras, J.I. (1994). *Built to last: Successful habits of visionary companies.* New York: Harper Business.

Denison, D.R. (1990). *Corporate culture and organizational effectiveness.* New York: Wiley.

Eisenstat, R.A. (1996). What corporate human resources brings to the picnic: Four models for functional management, *Organizational Dynamics,* Autumn.

Fleishman, E.A., Harris, E.F., & Burtt, H.E. (1955). *Leadership and supervision in industry.* Columbus: Ohio State University, Bureau of Educational Research.

Hamel, G., & Prahalad, C.K. (1994). *Competing for the future.* Boston: Harvard Business School Press.

Kotter, J.P., & Heskett, J.L. (1992). *Corporate culture and performance.* New York: Free Press.

Nohria, N. (1996). Unpublished paper. Harvard Business School.

Pfeffer, J. (1994) *Competitive advantage through people.* Boston: Harvard Business School Press.

Schaffer, R.H. (1988). *The Breakthrough Strategy.* Boston: Ballinger.

Ulrich, D., & Lake, D. (1990). *Organizational capability: Competing from the inside out.* New York: Wiley.

CHAPTER 9

WHAT HUMAN RESOURCE PRACTITIONERS NEED TO KNOW FOR THE TWENTY-FIRST CENTURY

W. WARNER BURKE

It may be that *learning* is now in the process of replacing *leadership* as the organizational management term of the day. If so, look for a spate of books in the near future on organizational learning, life-long learning, adult learning, nontraditional learning, un-learning, learning dissemination, and so on. But *what* do we need to learn, to know? The purpose of this paper is to provide a brief list of "need to knows" for the human resource (HR) practitioner over the remainder of the decade and into the next century. The list of definitions and explanations are by necessity brief, but for more depth numerous references are included for further perusal, if not *learning*. Beyond piquing your interest with this list, it is my hope that you will find the references a valuable addition.

This list of "need to knows" is *in addition* to the basics of HR practice— employee relations, compensation and benefits, selection and placement, training and development, succession planning, and so on.

The nine need-to-knows are presented in an approximate order moving from the more obvious to perhaps the not so obvious. We begin, therefore, with performance improvement, an obvious need-to-know, and conclude with power shifts, a more subtle and complex need-to-know, that is not so obvious.

Note that whenever the term employees is used, I mean any and all organizational members, nonmanagement and management.

Each of the nine sections concludes with an implications statement for the HR practitioner.

1. PERFORMANCE IMPROVEMENT

Improving performance is a lot like the weather. We do a lot of talking about it. Two kinds of actions are needed. First, we need to understand more about and expand our measurements of performance; and second, we need to learn more about the critical antecedents of performance, that is, what are the direct and indirect enhancers and inhibitors of high performance?

Measurement

For too long we have been driven by the bottom line—narrowly defined. There is far more to performance than profit and loss. Again, we talk a great deal about important matters such as customer service, but if we do not measure it, incorporate customer service into our definition of performance, and do not reward people accordingly, then it is merely talk. Kaplan and Norton (1996, 1993, 1992) have provided significant help. Their "balanced scorecard" of performance includes (as expected) financial measures, but they include three additional perspectives that balance what may ultimately be defined as organizational performance—customer satisfaction, internal business competencies, and innovation and learning, which mean essentially continuous improvement and creating value. Kaplan and Norton further provide ways of quantitatively measuring these softer, more qualitative domains, and they give numerous corporate examples.

Antecedents

Does pay, for example, enhance performance? Rarely, if ever, and at best only temporarily. There are many other more important enhancers, especially those associated with intrinsic motivation, the work itself, that in turn contribute to high performance. It seems clear that high congruence between job requirements and an individual's skills and abilities directly enhances motivation and, in turn, performance. It also seems clear that individual commitment to the mission of the organization enhances motivation and, in turn, performance, but probably more indirectly. These are examples of what we need to learn more about to understand as thoroughly as possible the complexities of performance improvement. Key sources for recent findings on performance enhancers include Huselid (1995); Kleiner, Block, Roomkin, and Salsberg (1987); and Lawler, Mohrman, and Ledford (1995).

Implications

The prudent HR practitioner will be deeply involved in matters of individual and organizational performance. Besides, how much closer can one get to the core of a business than to be involved in performance measurement and enhancement? Thus, it behooves the HR practitioner to learn as much as possible about (1) broader ways of defining and measuring performance and (2) what in the human equation contributes to high performance.

2. RESTRUCTURING

It is obvious that the restructuring of corporations in America continues to take the country by storm. Activities such as downsizing, reengineering, and business process redesign proceed unabated. Unbelievable as it may seem, restructuring has even reached the university. We at Teachers College are in the midst of a significant restructuring. What is not so obvious is the effect, the long-term impact and consequences of these activities. There is widespread reporting that downsizing, for example, continues in spite of considerable uncertainty regarding its effects on the bottom line (McKinley, Sanchez, & Schick, 1995) and the negative impact on people (*New York Times, 1996*). Harder evidence confirms much of what has been cited in the popular press; see, for example, Cameron, Freeman, and Mishra (1991).

Yet there is some indication that the way downsizing is implemented can make a difference. If it is systemic and part of a larger strategic effort, negative effects can be minimized (Cameron et al., 1991).

Although minimal at this stage, what documentation (beyond anecdotes) of reengineering that does exist shows negative to mixed results (Cameron, 1996). The point about restructuring is that much of what is known shows more negative than positive outcomes.

Implications

The HR practitioner must go beyond the popular press to understand the consequences of restructuring. These are early days, thus the evidence is only beginning to accumulate. There is help, nevertheless. Brockner's (1992) work provides guidance, particularly regarding those who remain at the organization after downsizing; a recent article by Feldman (1996) is also quite useful; and for an up-to-date assessment of the effectiveness of TQM, downsizing, and reengineering, see Cameron (1996).

3. ORGANIZATION CHANGE

Based on a huge data set, Ulrich, Brockbank, Yeung, and Lake (1995) have highlighted the importance of understanding and being competent in the practice of managing organizational change for HR practitioners. In fact the competence category in their study, management of change, resulted in the highest proportion (41.2%) of the critical competencies for HR practitioners to be effective in their jobs. The other two critical competence categories, but less proportionally, were HR functional expertise (23.3%) and knowledge of business (18.8%). As Ulrich et al. state, "The high [proportion] in managing change suggests that this competence is the most important predictor for overall competence of HR professionals" (pp. 482–483).

Implications

With change now being equated with death and taxes, the HR practitioner must establish a reasonable base of understanding of and competence in organization change and the management thereof. It is only natural that organizational executives and managers should turn to their HR person for help in change management; if not to the HR practitioner, then to whom? If not to the HR practitioner, then executives and managers must look externally. For external consultants, this mode of seeking help is fine, but the growing expectation is that the organization's HR practitioner *should be* a main resource.

In addition to a few basic books on organization development (Block, 1981; Burke, 1994; French & Bell, 1995) some current useful sources for learning more about change management include Berger and Sikora (1994); Carr, Hard, and Trahant (1996); Howard and Associates (1994); Hurst (1995); Litwin, Bray, and Brooke (1996); Nadler, Shaw, Walton, and Associates (1995); Nevis, Lancourt, and Vasallo (1996); Nolan and Croson (1995); Tichy and Sherman (1994); and the annual series by Pasmore and Woodman.

4. GLOBALIZATION

Not every corporation in America is "going global"; it just seems that way with all the hype and admonitions about being expansive in thinking and being other-culture sensitive. We should bear in mind that 90 percent or more of businesses in America are family-owned, employing a small number of people. Many of these small businesses, however, serve big ones as suppliers and service providers, and the big corporations are indeed being

pressed to go global. Thus, even many smaller businesses are being influenced by the globalization movement. Moreover, as Henry Wendt, former
Chairman of a large global corporation, put it,

> Indeed, it is fair to say that through the remainder of this century and well
> into the next, [global corporations] are likely to be decisive not only for the
> way individuals live and work, but for the way in which the politics and
> economies are bound together. (Wendt, 1993, p. 3)

Wendt is not the only one sending this message. Globalization is with us
now and is likely to progress geometrically into the twenty-first century.

Implications

A leading expert on globalization, particularly from the corporate perspective, is Stephen Rhinesmith. In addition to emphasizing the importance of
understanding change management (see above), he stresses that "It is impossible to develop a free-flowing, competitive global organization with structured, inhibited people. So globalization is largely the business of mindset and
behavior change" (Rhinesmith, 1996). In other words, it is the human factor, and therefore the HR practitioner is central to any organization's "going
global." Rhinesmith's book is helpful to the HR practitioner in that he focuses on six key skills for developing the global mindset—managing competitiveness, complexity, organizational alignment, change, multicultural
teams, and learning. The book edited by Pucik, Tichy, and Barnett (1992)
is also useful.

5. GROUPS AND TEAMS

At the present time, there are at least three clear and definite trends concerning group dynamics. *First* is the distinguishing of group from team.
Previously we tended to use group and team interchangeably, much as we
did with leader and manager. Today, however, we are at least more cog-
nizant that a group may be nothing much more than an assemblage, whereas
a team is a group with a common and challenging goal, and members behave interdependently. Two recent sources have provided clarity, one from
the world of practice (Katzenbach & Smith, 1993) and the other from acad-
emia (Guzzo, Salas, & Associates, 1995). As Katzenbach and Smith point
out, a real team is derived predominantly from a group of people with a
highly challenging goal, not from the designation "team" or from team
building activities. The Guzzo et al. book provides useful knowledge regarding team research, especially the chapter by McIntrye and Salas (1995).

Second, self-directed groups are becoming more prevalent. This trend is a result of organizational structures becoming flatter with the consequent outcome of wider spans of control and therefore greater reliance on at least semi-autonomous work groups. Downsizing is also contributing to more reliance on groups. Another contributor is at least some managers' attempts to empower their direct reports by providing more autonomy to them as a group. There are, no doubt, other reasons for this trend; in any case, the movement toward self-directed groups is here to stay and will accelerate. Arguably the best source for understanding this form of group dynamics is the work of Hackman (1992).

Third is the trend toward the use of large group interventions. This kind of organizational intervention involves the meeting of an entire system, or relatively autonomous subsystem, in a singular space usually for one to three days to tackle a significant issue or problem(s) facing the organization. The limit of the size of the group, which may range from 50 to 500 people (and sometimes even larger), is often a function of available and appropriate space. Reasons for this trend include management's desire for widespread participation and involvement, the potential for speed of decision making and action, and the attraction of having the entire organization in one space together, face-to-face, in so-called real time to solve big problems.

Bunker and Alban have assembled a useful array (1992) and an in-depth discussion (in press) of different approaches to large group interventions.

Implications

Even though culturally it is not exactly the American way, organizational leaders and managers are relying more and more on groups and not as much on individuals, at least when compared with the past. The astute HR practitioner will become an expert on group dynamics and teamwork. Learning more about how to (a) select people for group- and teamwork, (b) use groups for specific purposes, and (c) reward people in a more collective sense should be the goal of every HR practitioner today.

6. ACTION LEARNING

As argued earlier (Burke, 1995), I believe we are in the early stages of a third wave of innovation in the domain of training and development. The first wave was the T Group, beginning in the late 1940s. The second wave was "structured feedback" beginning in the late 1950s, becoming stronger in the 1970s and particularly now. Accomplishing many of the same objectives as the T-group, feedback on one's behavior (especially interpersonally, structured feedback) today takes the so-called 360° form, yet differs from the first wave in that the structured process, typically, is not face-to-face. In the early stages of use and not yet fully understood, the third wave of innovation is action learning. A working definition:

> In essence, action learning is combining the solving of actual problems in real time in the organization with learning about how to work together better, how to solve problems more effectively, and how to improve the learning process in general—that is, learning about learning. (Burke, 1995, p. 166)

For additional explanation, see Froiland (1994) and for applications toward organization change, see Tichy and Sherman (1994).

Implications

The HR practitioner needs to learn about this third wave because action learning:

- Reduces significantly the time between learning and application,
- Is based on sound knowledge about and experience with group behavior and experiential learning,
- Concentrates both on results or outcomes and process,
- Focuses on the present and the future,
- Can reduce costs,
- Provides useful feedback to organizational members on their behavior and performance,
- Can deliver innovative solutions to tough if not heretofore irresolvable problems,
- Can increase organizational commitment, and
- Can enhance organizational learning (Burke, 1995).

7. INTER-

The cryptic title for this section means that this need-to-know domain covers a number of "inters"—interpersonal, intergroup, and interorganizational. Despite the fact of so many people staring at computer terminals much of their working day, there appears to be as strong, or perhaps even stronger, a need as ever (maybe in part *because* of the isolation of sitting before a screen) to interact with others both for work and social reasons. Furthermore, rather than growing more adept (perhaps it is my narrow viewpoint), people today seem to be *less* skillful than ever in interpersonal skills. For some pessimistic evidence supporting this view, see Goleman (1995).

In any case, with fewer people having *the* answer, with greater reliance on groups and teams, with more emphasis on cross-group activities (i.e., attempts to attenuate the problems of "silos" that result from hierarchy as well as functional and business center territoriality in most organizational structures), and with the burgeoning of interorganizational relations (e.g., mergers and acquisitions), there is a strong trend toward interaction of all kinds in the workplace. If enrollment in our courses and workshops at the University are indicative, people are expressing an ever greater interest in gaining knowledge and skill in conflict management and resolution, in co-operation, and in negotiation in the workplace.

So, it is a matter of *relationships,* relating with others to get work done, to get complicated problems solved, and with the increasingly chaotic conditions of work these days, to check periodically with colleagues to see if we are relatively sane.

Implications

To use the term that Argyris (1970) wrote about, HR practitioners need to see themselves as interventionists, to be *in between* people, groups, and organizations to facilitate relationships. There is a great need. For example, when it comes to making a strategic alliance or merger (read acquisition) work, the due diligence that managers conduct prior to the eventual relationship typically goes well. Evidence shows, however, that most of these interorganizational relationships rarely reach the potential that is touted by both parties beforehand. The devil is in the details of the relationships and corporate culture. For a current summary and evaluation of interorganizational relationships, see Burke and Biggart (1996). For some new thinking on interpersonal relations, see Senge (1990) on the concept and skill of dialogue, and Barrett (1995) and Cooperrider and Srivastva (1987) on appreciative inquiry. For more learning about conflict, cooperation, and distributive justice and intergroup relationships, see Deutsch (1985) and Bunker, Rubin, and Associates (1995).

8. TIMESHIFT

More than ever, employees talk these days about how much harder and longer they work. It also seems that people try to cram more activity into the time they have. Another related trend is the blurring of time on the job and off the job—people work more at home, on airplanes, and trains—as well as the mixing of personal activities, for example, mailing a gift in time for Mother's Day, with regular work activities (Crispell, 1996). We are a nation of very busy people (Burns, 1993), and seemingly we complain more about being tired. Yet a recent study showed that "employed Americans are no more likely than they were 20 years ago to say that work wears them out . . ."— 24 percent in 1975 compared with 23 percent in 1995 (Robinson & Godbey, 1996, p. 48). We obviously have a conundrum here.

One explanation is the point made above about the blurring of the boundary between work and personal life, although we as individual workers may be getting slightly better at this balance (Robinson & Godbey, 1996). The fact that many today are taking care of certain personal needs during work hours and that more take work home (since we have at our disposal laptops, e-mail, voice mail, and fax machines), we stretch our work day and our personal time. It appears that fewer of us leave our work at the office, thus with the blurred stretching of our day in both work and personal life, we perhaps are able to take care of both more adequately.

Another explanation is that many of us who report that we are very busy seek recognition for our hard work. As Robinson and Godbey (1996) point out, "Stress is prestigious."

Implications

First, supervisors and HR practitioners need to be tolerant of the blurring of work and personal life. Provided productivity and quality of performance do not suffer, we should have little if any problem with this blurry boundary situation.

Second, while we as employees like to be recognized for the results we achieve, we have an even stronger need to be recognized for our *efforts* not to mention our unique talents) in achieving the results. (See, for example, Chen & Church, 1993; Deutsch, 1985; and Kanfer, 1990). Supervisors and HR practitioners would be wise to emphasize effort in their recognition processes. Stronger motivation and subsequent performance are likely to follow.

9. POWERSHIFTS

We can consider the shifts of power at two broad levels—*micro* or organizational, and *macro,* meaning multiorganizational, societal, and global.

Micro

I remember Chris Argyris during a National Training Laboratories' summer session at Bethel, Maine in 1967 saying that the computer would force more openness in organizations because so many employees would have access to information about the organization and its performance. Almost 30 years later in a meeting I attended recently, Stan Davis stated that the Internet represented a significant shift of power to the people. Technology is obviously making a difference regarding shifts of power; so are changes in organizational structure to flatter hierarchies as well as trends toward the virtual (Davidow & Malone, 1992) and the knowledge-based organization (Davis & Botkin, 1994). Moreover, even though there are strong needs for job security in the present, it is nevertheless unlikely, when compared with past behavior, that people will be as patient and tolerant of abusive bosses (Hornstein, 1996).

Macro

At a much broader level, power is gradually but clearly shifting from the nation state to global corporations (Korten, 1995). One (if not *the*) issue in this regard is that as the economy in developed and in developing countries grows, so does the divide between rich and poor. While there is no conspiracy involved, it does seem, as Estes (1996) dramatically highlights, that "the tyranny of the bottom line" has uncontrolled and unconcerned power over the public. He argues that corporate power has gone awry. And as Korten (1995) points out, corporations, particularly those operating globally, do not have the checks and balances of government organizations.

Implications

At the microlevel it is essential that the HR practitioner be discerning about the use of power and its consequences, such as, distinguishing between mere compliance on the part of employees and intrinsic motivation and commitment. Understanding this distinction has implications for job placement and the reward process. In addition to being aware of abusive bosses and taking appropriate action, being clear about the differences between leadership and management helps in the understanding of the different forms, bases, and uses of power.

At the macrolevel, the HR practitioner may feel rather powerless. Yet being sensitive to the issues touched on above can encourage the HR practitioner to speak out on matters such as downsizing in the exclusive service

Table 9.1
Summary of Nine "Need to Knows"

The Nine	What HR Practitioners Need to Know
Performance Improvement	Broadened measurement; determine key performance enhancers
Restructuring	What are the long-term consequences?
Organization Change	How to manage change; HR practitioner's role
Globalization	Understanding the impact cross-culturally and on small and medium size business
Groups and Team	Differentiation; self-directed groups/teams; large group interventions
Action Learning	"Third Wave" of training and development
Inter-	Relationships at multiple levels
Timeshift	Blurring of work and personal time; "stress is prestigious"
Powershifts	More dispersion individually and organizationally, yet more toward the global corporation

of the bottom line, of potential harm to the environment merely to save costs, and other matters related to corporate responsibility.

By way of an overall summary, refer to Table 9.1.

CONCLUSION

These nine need-to-knows are not by any means exhaustive. Space does not allow for further coverage. We could have covered much more on the changing nature of organizational design and structure. We could have covered leadership in more depth, the kind likely to be required in the twenty-first century. We could have covered the changing nature of the psychological contract between employer and employee. And even for the nine need-to-knows that were covered, we barely skimmed the surface. But if you, the reader, and especially if you are an HR practitioner, agree in large measure with these nine and see a need to learn more, then your plate is quite full for the time being. Nine is quite enough for now.

So you learn more about these "need to knows"—then what? Are these just nice to know? There are at least three primary and overlapping benefits: (1) a broadened repertoire and therefore an avoidance of overspecialization, (2) the advantage of anticipation, and (3) the power of diagnosis. First, organizational executives are *not* looking for their HR practitioners to know more and more about less and less. The HR generalist inside the organization is more valuable; continuing to broaden one's repertoire is therefore critical. Second, executives need HR practitioners who can tell them what to expect in the future and then to help them plan and take action. Continuing to expand one's need-to-know list puts the HR practitioner in an anticipatory and therefore preventive position. Finally, learning these need-to-knows, especially in more depth than this paper provides, helps the HR practitioner to *understand* and diagnose organizational issues and problems both more accurately and comprehensively. This enhanced understanding increases the HR practitioner's value as an adviser and as a staff executive in the organization.

REFERENCES

Argyris, C. (1970). *Intervention theory and method*. Reading, MA: Addison-Wesley.

Barrett, F.J. (1995). Creating appreciative learning cultures. *Organizational Dynamics, 24*(2), 36–49.

Berger, L.A., & Sikora, M.J. (Eds.). (1994). *The change management handbook: A roadmap to corporate transformation*. Burr Ridge, IL: Irwin.

Block, P. (1981). *Flawless consulting*. Erlanger, KY: Pfeiffer & Co.

Brockner, J. (1992). Managing the effects of layoffs on survivors. *California Management Review, 34*(2), 9–28.

Bunker, B.B., & Alban, B.T. (1992). *Large group interventions*. Special issue, *Journal of Applied Behavioral Science, 28*(4), 473–591.

Bunker, B.B., & Alban, B.T. (in press). *The new way to change organizations: Large group interventions,* (working title). San Francisco: Jossey-Bass.

Bunker, B.B., Rubin, J.Z., & Associates. (1995). *Conflict, cooperation, and justice.* San Francisco: Jossey-Bass.

Burke, W.W. (1995). Organization change: What we know, what we need to know. *Journal of Management Inquiry, 4,* 158–171.

Burke, W.W. (1994). *Organization development: A process of learning and changing* (2nd ed.). Reading, MA: Addison-Wesley.

Burke, W.W., & Biggart, N.W. (1996). Interorganizational relations. In D. Druckman, J.E. Singer, & H. Van Cott (Eds.), *Enhancing organizational performance*. Washington, DC: National Academy Press.

Burns, L.S. (1993). *Busy bodies*. New York: W. W. Norton.

Cameron, K.S. (1996). Techniques for making organizations effective: Some popular approaches. In D. Druckman, J.E. Singer, & H. Van Cott (Eds.), *Enhancing organizational performance*. Washington, DC: National Academy Press.

Cameron, K.S., Freeman, S.J., & Mishra, A.K. (1991). Best practices in white-collar downsizing: Managing contradictions. *Academy of Management Executive, 5*(3), 57–73.

Carr, D.K., Hard, K.J., & Trahant, W.J. (1996). *Managing the change process: A field book for change agents, consultants, team leaders, and reengineering managers.* New York: McGraw-Hill.

Chen, Y.R., & Church, A.H. (1993). Reward allocation preferences in groups and organizations. *International Journal of Conflict Management, 4,* 25–49.

Cooperrider, D.L., & Srivastva, S. (1987). Appreciative inquiry into organizational life. In R.W. Woodman & W.A. Pasmore (Eds.), *Research in organization change and development, 1,* (pp. 129–169). Greenwich, CT: JAI Press.

Crispell, D. (1996). Chaotic workplace. *American Demographics, 18*(6), 50–52.

Davidow, W.H., & Malone, M.S. (1992). *The virtual corporation.* New York: Harper Business.

Davis, S., & Botkin, J. (1994). *The monster under the bed: How business is mastering the opportunity of knowledge for profit.* New York: Simon & Schuster.

Deutsch, M. (1985). *Distributive justice, a social-psychological perspective.* New Haven, CT: Yale University Press.

Estes, R. (1996). *Tyranny of the bottom line: Why corporations make good people do bad things.* San Francisco: Berrett-Kohler Publishing, Inc.

Feldman, D.C. (1996). Managing careers in downsizing firms. *Human Resource Management, 35*(2), 145–161.

French, W.L., & Bell, C.H. Jr. (1995). *Organization development: Behavioral science interventions for organization improvement,* 5th ed., Englewood Cliffs, NJ: Prentice-Hall.

Froiland, P. (1994). Action learning: Taming real problems in real time, *Training,* January 27.

Goleman, D. (1995). *Emotional intelligence.* New York: Bantam.

Guzzo, R.A., Salas, E., & Associates. (1995). *Team effectiveness and decision making in organizations.* San Francisco: Jossey-Bass.

Hackman, J.R. (1992). The psychology of self-management in organizations. In R. Glaser (Ed.), *Classic readings in self-managing teamwork* (pp. 142–193). King of Prussia, PA: Organization Design and Development.

Hornstein, H.A. (1996). *Brutal bosses and their prey.* New York: Riverhead Books.

Howard, A., & Associates. (1994). *Diagnosis for organizational change: Methods and models.* New York: Guilford.

Hurst, D.K. (1995). *Crisis and renewal: Meeting the challenge of organizational change.* Boston: Harvard Business School Press.

Huselid, M.A. (1995). The impact of human resource management practices on turnover, productivity, and corporate financial planning. *Academy of Management Journal, 38,* 635–672.

Kanfer, R. (1990). Motivation theory and industrial and organizational psychology. In M.D. Dunnette & L.M. Hough (Eds.), *Handbook of industrial and organizational psychology* (2nd ed.), 1, (pp. 75–170). Palo Alto, CA: Consulting Psychologists Press.

Kaplan, R.S., & Norton, D.P. (1996). Using the balanced scorecard as a strategic management system. *Harvard Business Review, 74*(1), 75–85.

Kaplan, R.S., & Norton, D.P. (1993). Putting the balanced scorecard to work. *Harvard Business Review, 71*(5), 134–147.

Kaplan, R.S., & Norton, D.P. (1992). The balanced scorecard—measures that drive performance. *Harvard Business Review, 70*(1), 71–79.

Katzenbach, J.R., & Smith, D.K. (1993). *The wisdom of teams: Creating the high-performance organization.* Boston: Harvard Business School Press.

Kleiner, M.M., Block, R.N., Roomkin, M., & Salsberg, S.W. (Eds.). (1987). *Human resources and the performance of the firm.* Washington, DC: BNA Press.

Korten, D.C. (1995). *When corporations rule the world.* West Hartford, CT: Kumarian Press: San Francisco: Berrett-Koehler.

Lawler, E.E. III, Mohrman, S.A., & Ledford, G.E. Jr. (1995). *Creating high performance organizations: Survey of practices and results of employee involvement and TQM in Fortune 1000 companies.* San Francisco: Jossey-Bass.

Litwin, G.H., Bray, J., & Brooke, K.L. (1996). *Mobilizing the organization: Bringing strategy to life.* London: Prentice-Hall.

McIntrye, R.M., & Salas, E. (1995). Measuring and managing team performance: Lessons from complex environments. In Guzzo, R.A., Salas, E., & Associates, *Team effectiveness and decision making in organizations* (pp. 9–45). San Francisco: Jossey-Bass.

McKinley, W., Sanchez, C.M., & Schick, A.G. (1995). Organizational downsizing: Constraining, cloning, learning. *Academy of Management Executives, 9*(3), 32–41.

Nadler, D.A., Shaw, R.B., Walton, A.E., & Associates. (1995). *Discontinuous change: Leading organizational transformation.* San Francisco: Jossey-Bass.

Nevis, E.C., Lancourt, J., & Vassallo, H.G. (1996). *Intentional revolutions: A seven-point strategy for transforming organizations.* San Francisco: Jossey-Bass.

New York Times. (1996). *The downsizing of America.* New York: Times Books.

Nolan, R.L., & Croson, D.C. (1995). *Creative destruction: A six-stage process for transforming the organization.* Boston: Harvard Business School Press.

Pasmore, W.A., & Woodman, R.W. (Annual series beginning in 1988). *Research in organizational change and development.* Greenwich, CT: JAI Press.

Pucik, V., Tichy, N.M., & Barnett, C.K. (Eds.). (1992). *Globalizing management: Creating and leading the competitive organization.* New York: Wiley.

Rhinesmith, S.H. (1996). *A manager's guide to globalization: Six skills for success in a changing world,* 2nd ed., Alexandria, VA: American Society for Training and Development and Chicago: Irwin.

Robinson, J.P., & Godbey, G. (1996). The great American slowdown. *American Demographics, 18*(6), 42–48.

Senge, P. (1990). *The fifth discipline: The art and practice of the learning corporation.* New York: Doubleday Currency.

Tichy, N.M., & Sherman, S. (1994). *Control your destiny or someone else will.* New York: Harper Business.

Ulrich, D., Brockbank, W., Yeung, A.K., & Lake, D.G. (1995). Human resource competencies: An empirical assessment. *Human Resource Management, 34*(4), 473–495.

Wendt, H. (1993). *Global embrace: Corporate challenges in a transnational world.* New York: Harper Business.

CHAPTER 10

THE FUTURE OF HUMAN RESOURCES: SUPERHUMAN RESOURCE LEADERSHIP IN THE TWENTY-FIRST CENTURY

HOWARD V. KNICELY

Thinking about the future of human resources (HR) brings to mind a quote attributed to Yogi Berra, the former star catcher of baseball's New York Yankees, who said, "The future ain't what it used to be."

The evolution of HR reflects what is happening everywhere—issues that affect people, organizations, and sociopolitical environments all over the world. It is exciting to note that the HR function has increasingly positioned itself at the center of so many of the major changes and recent trends affecting business organizations today. These issues have become the "organizationspeak" of the late twentieth century.

Acquisitions—Benchmarking—Core competencies and culture change—Diversity—Employee involvement and empowerment—Family-friendly practices—Globalization—Health care costs—ISO and QS 9000—Job (in)security—Knowledge work and learning organizations—Layoffs and more layoffs—Merger mania—New contract with employees—Organization capabilities—Professional and career development—Quality and continuous improvement—Reorganizations and restructuring—Seamlessness and sharing best practices—The trust gap—Unrelenting cost/price pressures—Vision and values—Workforce demographics—The XYZs of change vs. The ABCs of HR. Who will win the war?

These challenges are firmly in place for the forseeable future. Most HR people will continue to find themselves leading the way on, or at least in

111

the middle of, many of these ongoing trends. What then will distinguish the HR professional of the 1990s from the superhuman resource leader of the twenty-first century?

There are at least seven skills that top-notch HR leaders of the future must be able to demonstrate better than anyone else:

1. See around corners.
2. Venture out.
3. Captivate the MTV generation.
4. Practice brutal optimism.
5. Steal (and share) shamelessly.
6. Balance the scorecard.
7. Model the 3 Cs.

1. SEE AROUND CORNERS

HR professionals have been making the transition over the years from administrators to business partners to leaders of change. The next logical step in the transformation of the HR function will involve the ability to see around corners. This skill encompasses the vision and foresight to anticipate future trends globally and the business savvy, credibility, and leadership skills to influence and shape these trends on a global basis.

HR people will focus increasingly on turning human resource and organization capability into a strategic competitive advantage for the business. Line executives and HR practitioners alike are beginning to acknowledge that both technology and capital can be easily copied by competitors. The quality of people and people-related practices is, however, exceedingly difficult to copy. Accordingly, the ability to see around corners reflects the increasing importance of integrating business and HR strategies.

Human resource professionals will continue to experience the growing linkage between business and HR strategic planning and can anticipate a marked change in the relationship between the HR and planning functions within organizations. Historically, HR types and planners ignored one another then later saw each other as necessary evils. More recently, the HR and planning functions have learned to coexist peacefully. Examples of such cooperation include acquisitions, mergers, or joint ventures in which the planners are charged with focusing on issues such as financial impact, effect on earnings per share and stock price, competition/customer/government regulator reactions, or market share implications.

HR people are usually involved (too little and too late) in dimensions such as integrating cultures, assimilating people, creating organization structures, building teams representing people from both organizations, and merging policies and practices appropriate to the new combined organization. Watching HR and planning people discuss these issues is much like watching the dynamics between well-intentioned sets of parents planning a young couple's wedding. HR and planning, like the bride's and groom's parents, mean well but are not on the same wavelength and are too often operating from different frames of reference.

The future holds numerous exciting opportunities: *first,* working toward seamlessness between the HR and planning functions on strategic planning and development processes, including better integration of strategic HR issues into strategic business plans; *second,* more developmental moves and assignments will be seen that cause HR and planning people to move between the two functions and to collaborate more on initiatives of strategic importance to the company. HR people who learn to master the new relationship between the HR and planning functions will indeed be able to see around corners.

2. VENTURE OUT

HR people have tended to spend the vast majority of their time concentrating on the inside stuff—internally oriented policies, practices, and problems. The external issues have most often been handled by others, including sales and marketing, engineering, purchasing, planning, and law. These distinctions will blur at an accelerating pace.

HR people will partner with customers more than ever before on joint HR initiatives, such as training and moving people across company boundaries for temporary developmental and service-oriented assignments. This trend will apply to relationships with key suppliers and joint venture partners as well and will likely involve assisting some to upgrade their HR practices.

To further solidify relationships with key customers, HR people will follow the example set by sales and engineering professionals who spend a lot of energy determining customer requirements regarding product and process capabilities. HR professionals will be similarly charged with determining and meeting customer expectations of organization capabilities—the capacity to respond to customer concerns and act on their behalf. As part of this process, customers will be more directly involved in issues such as the selection and assessment of individuals in key assignments. This kind of interaction with customers and other external influences will cause HR people to venture out beyond traditional organizational boundaries.

3. CAPTIVATE THE MTV GENERATION

Predictions about the future of HR are futile without understanding what employees of the future might be like. One reasonable predictor is to make observations about the prevailing values and attitudes of today's 18-to-35-year-olds around the world: a balance between work and personal life—flexibility—entrepreneurialism and ownership of ideas, achievements, and results—involvement in decisions—increasing loyalty to values, ideals, causes, networks, and freedom of choice—decreasing loyalty to large companies, organizations, governments or other formal institutions—willingness to change jobs, companies, professions, and careers by choice—much less willingness to change almost anything if pushed to do so by "authority" —diverse interests—high thirst for knowledge—increasing empowerment through direct access to information and technology such as the Internet.

Members of the MTV generation expect stimulation, options, and the power of choice; they need to be captivated. If they are not, they can be expected to change companies or careers almost as quickly as they would change television channels. The MTV generation is holding the remote control.

Implications for HR professionals are clear. We in the profession are moving out of the era characterized by "workforce assimilation to the changing workplace." The future will require increasing "workplace assimilation to the changing workforce." Three trends in particular will characterize this transition.

First, organizations must continuously create a more flexible workforce. The traditional notions of job security, lifetime employment, and loyalty to one company have already given way to a new kind of employer/employee contract—employability. Professional development initiatives will become the norm, including major commitments to training, global developmental assignments, and modern-day apprenticeship programs to keep pace with changing technology. Pay for skills and knowledge, as well as variable pay incentive plans, stock options, and portable pensions for all employees will support these steps. Employees will expect these commitments as tradeoffs for limited job security. The rapid rise in company-run learning centers and chief learning officer positions is only the beginning of this growing trend toward a more flexible, multiskilled workforce supported by the workplace as school.

Second, organizations will more fully promote and deploy flexible, family-friendly workplace practices: flexible work schedules and time off–family/personal leaves and sabbaticals–job sharing, telecommuting, and remote work locations–employee assistance counseling, child and elder care, financial consulting, and on-site convenience services–casual dress. None of these concepts are new, but few are commonly available on a consistent or global basis. They will be, by necessity.

Third, a more open workplace through access to information—exchanged seamlessly across organizational, functional, and geographic boundaries—will become increasingly commonplace. This kind of open exchange will be facilitated not only by information technology but also by a shift in organization cultures to support more networking, listening, and sharing of information and best practices.

Employees will increasingly demand help in building their skills and employability, on balancing their work and personal lives, and in networking openly. It is our job as HR professionals to meet and exceed these expectations—to captivate the MTV generation.

4. Practice Brutal Optimism

Unfortunately, over the years fewer noble leaders have been produced than attempts to define leadership. Most of the notable quotables about leadership tend to mask the less glamorous but essential roles leaders must play.

Max DePree, author of *Leadership Is an Art,* may have said it best when he said, "The first responsibility of a leader is to define reality . . ." (1989, p. 9). Credible leaders do what they say they will do, but they also talk about things as they really are. Employees expect leaders to be brutally honest, to define the realities of the business and how employees can help. They do not always like the message, but they do not prefer fiction. HR people have a major responsibility to convince leaders in their own organizations of this principle.

The future role of HR will be to create organizational cultures that unambiguously confront these realities and make the inner workings of the organization much more transparent to the typical employee. For example, some people in finance and planning may say they cannot openly talk about financial performance or strategies because competitors will find out and use that information to their advantage. Competitors knowing a company's strategy is not nearly as dangerous as that company's employees not knowing. It is the HR function's job to convince others of this truth.

In the face of brutal reality, HR people must also help to provide the counterbalance through hope and optimism. To the extent reality is intimidating, leaders are responsible for instilling in their people self-confidence that they have the requisite strategy, skills, resources, and culture to meet the challenge.

It has been said that organizational competence is a function of individual confidence. HR leaders of the future will have the savvy and credibility to instill that confidence in employees by practicing brutal optimism—defining reality for people while simultaneously convincing them that extraordinary things are possible.

5. STEAL (AND SHARE) SHAMELESSLY

Sharing best practices–benchmarking–doing more with less–getting lean–acting with speed–these trends have become reality, and they are here to stay. In the future, HR people can expect more of the same with a few twists.

As organizations strive to become seamless, the emphasis on collaboration across business units, functions, countries, cultures, and companies will likely increase significantly. Today many companies are talking about collaboration and sharing, but precious few are doing so well enough to create competitive advantage. The transition to a collaborative culture has as much to do with overcoming human nature and learned behaviors as it does with doing what makes sense for the business. A recent article, "Toddler Property Laws", *Cleveland Magazine,* Sept., 1996), humorously illustrates this point:

1. If it's in my hand, it's mine.
2. If I like it, it's mine.
3. If I can take it from you, it's mine.
4. If I had it a little while ago, it's mine.
5. If it's mine, it must never appear to be yours in ANY WAY!!!
6. If I'm building something, ALL the pieces are mine!
7. If it looks just like mine, IT IS MINE!

Those of us with children or grandchildren understand why sharing can be a difficult concept to sell in organizations!

HR professionals have a major role to play in making seamlessness a competitive weapon. *First,* it is our job in HR to define the kinds of sharing behaviors we expect of people. *Second,* we must take the lead in convincing people that collaborating, sharing ideas, and "stealing" others' best practices—openly and with integrity—are not ideals reserved for organizational wimps. *Third,* we must begin to reshape the definition of innovation by legitimizing achievements that are based on studying others' practices and quickly implementing them in our own organizations. Only those modifications that truly add value or uniqueness should be celebrated. *Fourth,* organizations need to reward the "stealers" and "sharers" more than they reward the "reinventors." In essence, HR people will have to help create new kinds of heroes.

Organizations that develop the capability to share and steal practices faster and less expensively than do their competitors will hold a real advantage. There is an important caveat, however. As professor and author Jeffrey Pfeffer says, "If you do what everybody else does, by definition you are average." The implication is that benchmarking and sharing practices are not enough. Real value comes from implementing these practices more fully and quickly than everyone else and building on them to create a unique advantage. HR people will increasingly be at the center of helping organizations to steal (and share) shamelessly.

6. Balance the Scorecard

The relentless pressure for improved organizational financial performance and reduced costs has been a major trend and will not subside anytime soon. Organizations will, therefore, continue to struggle with striking a balance between shorter term, financially driven objectives and longer term more qualitative goals. In the future, balancing the scorecard will involve more than a mere reconciliation of these competing priorities.

This debate will increasingly involve the issue of accountability for employee satisfaction and organization capability, and of measuring these priorities with nearly the same degree of rigor used to measure financial performance. If we in HR believe in the adage, "What gets measured gets done," then HR people will be responsible for working with leaders from planning, finance, and general management to embrace the importance of holding managers as accountable for leadership style, organization culture, customer satisfaction, employee satisfaction, and living the organization's core values as we now do for "making the numbers." Someday HR and organization capability audits may even be as commonly accepted as are financial audits.

While a small percentage of companies have demonstrated leadership in this area, most have a long way to go. The HR community must ensure that goal-setting, performance management, compensation, promotion, and consequence systems are designed with balancing the scorecard in mind.

7. MODEL THE 3 Cs

Some excellent work has been done over the past few years to study and document critical competencies and success profiles for HR professionals. In general, these competencies tend to fall into categories such as leading and managing change, business skills, HR technical skills, and leadership of the HR function.

Human relations people have plenty of room to grow before fully living up to the expectations created by these models. The best way for HR professionals to be successful in the future is to first focus on the 3 Cs—credibility, competence, and courage.

- *Credibility* involves doing what we say we will do—in everything, maintaining a level of integrity beyond reproach, and keeping confidences.
- *Competence* includes constantly upgrading business and HR skills, broadening the professional tool kit to address changing organizational needs, being aware of shortcomings, using good judgment to search out best practices and help from others.
- *Courage* is characterized by challenging the process of how things are done, pushing for continuous improvement, and demonstrating the willingness to take risks.

HR professionals who successfully model the 3 Cs will not only be tremendous assets to their organizations, but will also be superhuman resource leaders in the twenty-first century.

For new HR people entering the field today, as well as for seasoned practitioners, the opportunities to make a difference for individual and organizational success are screaming out. Perhaps the best way to characterize the endless possibilities for HR people is with a favorite old quote from an unknown but wise source, "Do not follow where the path may lead. Go instead where there is no path, and leave a trail."

REFERENCES

DePree, M. (1989). *Leadership Is an Art*. New York: Doubleday.

Pfeffer, J. (1995). Presentation at TRW HR Worldwide Conference, May 2.

Toddler Property Laws. (1996, September). *Cleveland Magazine*.

CHAPTER 11

REBALANCING THE ROLE OF HUMAN RESOURCES

THOMAS A. KOCHAN

Over the long run, the influence of human resources (HR) rises and falls depending on how well professionals in this field anticipate and respond to changing external and internal forces that shape the employment relationship. The key external labor market forces affecting the role of human resources historically have been the tightness of labor markets, the influence of government policies regulating employment relations, and the strength or threat of unionization or other forms of worker unrest (Baron, Dobbins, & Jennings, 1986; Jacoby, 1985; Kochan & Cappelli, 1984). In recent years, these forces have taken a back seat to the product market competitiveness pressures and the increased activity and power of shareholders and financial institutions. Chief executive officers (CEOs) and line managers were the first to feel these pressures and they in turn demanded significant changes in employment practices that would increase productivity, quality, customer responsiveness, and adaptability while simultaneously controlling compensation costs, restructuring, downsizing, and outsourcing work not deemed to fall within the organization's main mission or core competencies. As a result, the human resource profession has been preoccupied with efforts to become a more strategic resource to senior and line management. This has led the profession to turn somewhat inward and, in the view of one leading professional, to behave as "perfect agents" of top management (Doyle, 1993). The major question facing the profession

Funds for this work are provided by the Alfred P. Sloan Foundation. The views expressed are solely those of the author.

today is whether this internal orientation has now become myopic and
disconnected from the changing realities of today's workplace and tomorrow's employment problems and challenges.

I believe it has and that the profession either will undergo dramatic shifts
in the years ahead or will lose even more influence both within the managerial community and in the broader society it is expected to serve. I will
lay out the reasons for this view and then propose the shifts in perspective
and approach that will be needed for human resources to play a more influential and constructive role in the future.

PROFESSIONAL MYOPIA

Table 11.1 illustrates the current myopia among opinion leaders in the
human resource profession. It lists the seven most significant business challenges facing organizations today compiled from a survey of top HR professionals (executives, consultants, and academics) in 1994 (Eichinger &
Ulrich, 1995). Table 11.2 then reports the seven top priorities these opinion leaders say HR executives should be addressing today. Both lists validate Doyle's basic point: HR executives see their job largely as focusing on
making their individual enterprises more competitive. These are laudable
and important objectives but, unfortunately, reflect only the internal roles
of the HR profession.

Contrast this perspective to the goals for the future that come from examining the employment relationship from a public policy point of view.

Table 11.1
The Seven Most Significant Business Challenges
Facing Organizations Today

1. Building and operating an effective customer responsive organization

2. Gearing up for becoming an effective global competitor

3. Competing profitably with low cost (product and service) providers

4. Transitioning from a profit through cost cutting to a revenue growth environment

5. Effectively taking advantage of new information technology

6. Attracting, developing, and retaining top talent

7. Operating internationally with the lack of a competitive, probusiness industrial
   policy matching those of foreign competitors

Source: Bob Eichinger and Dave Ulrich, *Human Resource Challenges,* The Human Resource Planning Society, 317 Madison Avenue, Suite 1509, New York, NY 10017, Phone: (212) 490-6387,
Fax: (212) 682-6851. Reprinted with permission.

Table 11.2
The Seven Top Priorities HR Executives Should Be Addressing Today

1. Helping their organization reinvent/redesign itself to compete more effectively

2. Reinventing the HR function to be a more customer focused, cost justified organization

3. Attracting and developing the next generation—21st century leaders and executives

4. Contributing to the continuing cost containment/management effort

5. Continuing to work on becoming a more effective business partner with their line customers

6. Rejecting fads, quick fixes and other HR fads; sticking to the basics that work

7. Addressing the diversity challenge

Source: Bob Eichinger and Dave Ulrich, *Human Resource Challenges,* The Human Resource Planning Society, 317 Madison Avenue, Suite 1509, New York, NY 10017, Phone: (212) 490-6387, Fax: (212) 682-6851. Reprinted with permission.

Table 11.3 reports the "Goals for the 21st Century Workplace" contained in the final report of the Commission on the Future of Worker Management Relations. Or consider the comments of a mixed group of HR executives and other employment experts expressed in the 1996 Human Resource Outlook (Freedman & Associates, 1996). The excerpts from this report, summarized in Table 11.4, depict a group that is concerned about the

Table 11.3
Goals for the Twenty-First Century Workplace

1. Expand coverage of employee participation and labor-management partnerships to more workers and more workplaces and to a broader array of decisions

2. Provide workers an uncoerced opportunity to choose, or not to choose, a bargaining representative and to engage in collective bargaining

3. Improve resolution of violations of workplace rights

4. Decentralize and internalize responsibility for workplace regulations

5. Improve workplace safety and health

6. Enhance the growth of productivity in the economy as a whole

7. Increase training and learning at the workplace and related institutions

8. Reduce inequality by raising the earnings and benefits of workers in the lower part of the wage distribution

9. Upgrade the economic position of contingent workers

10. Increase dialogue and learning at the national and local levels

Source: Report and Recommendations: Executive Summary, Commission on the Future of Worker–Management Relations, Washington, DC, December 1994.

Table 11.4
Views of the Human Resource Outlook Panel

A recession is not on the horizon—but there are many signs of trouble of a softer sort. The rich are clearly getting richer and the poor falling deeper into poverty. Job insecurity is undermining confidence in the U.S. economy, even as it has become the most efficient, flexible, and competitive in the industrial world. Job growth is occurring at both ends of the wage spectrum, but there are net employment reductions in the middle pay ranges. More important, it seems that all jobs are at risk: everyone worries about being forced to "start looking" again, sooner or later. This threat is demoralizing to employees at a time when the median search period is two months (and the average is over four months)—but it is disastrous for the low-paid or poorly-skilled.

Under these circumstances, business must become concerned that the general tension can easily pollute the working environment as well. The tone of working and public life seems to have acquired the unpleasant sound of hard individualism; you can't rely on government, or extended family and social groups—or depend on career employers. When politicians' rhetoric is focused on cutting entitlements, even in private employment there is talk of reducing "the expectations" that grew from employer paternalism during the post-World War II era. The message to the public and to employees now seems to be: Expect only that you must make your own way.

Source: Human Resource Forecast 1996. New York: Audrey Freedman and Associates, 1995, pp. 8–9.

growing anxiety and tension in the workplace and a declining confidence in all employment institutions—firms, government, and unions, and a growing divisiveness among interest groups in society. The bottom line of this group is that the world in which positive employee relations and organizational performance could be bought with job security is over; however, how to achieve these objectives in today's economy is yet to be determined.

This latter group agrees with those who argue that the implicit social contract that governed employment relations over the three decades following World War II and that allowed the work force, economy, and industry to prosper is now broken. That contract essentially had two components. First, hourly employees could expect to exchange a fair eight hours of work for eight hours pay, and white-collar workers and managers who performed well and remained loyal to the firm were rewarded with long term employment security. Second, gradual improvements in productivity of the economy and profitability of individual enterprises produced improvements in real earnings. We all know the trends of the past two decades. Real earnings of the majority of the work force have stagnated and failed to rebound even in the 1990s in manufacturing industries where productivity and profitability growth have been relatively good. Income inequality has increased. Restructuring has broken the loyalty for security commitment between white collar workers and managers and large employers. Hourly workers can no longer expect to be paid well simply for eight hours of physical work. To do well in *today's* labor market they need to bring similar levels of psychological commitment, technical skill, and analytical ability to their work as do managers and other professionals. Together, these changes have produced what many believe is a growing anxiety in the work force and a decline in confidence in employers, government, unions, and other labor market institutions.

Politicians have been quicker to see and act on these perceptions than have HR professionals or other business (or labor) leaders. The Republican primaries of early 1996 demonstrated the appeal of a new form of populism and perhaps even nationalism about jobs, trade, and economic security. Democrats responded with a new emphasis on corporate social responsibility that stressed the importance of family-friendly policies, training and education, benefit portability, partnerships with employees, and partnerships with the government to improve workplace safety and health. A bipartisan coalition in Congress led by Senators Kassenbaum and Kennedy took up the issue with a modest bill that would provide laid off employees an option of continuing their health insurance coverage (at the worker's expense). Other bills and administrative actions have been proposed that would either provide tax incentives or require firms to adopt "socially responsible" or "worker friendly" employment practices. At the same time other bills have been introduced into Congress that would significantly weaken enforcement of several regulatory agencies including the Occupational Safety and Health Administration (OSHA) and the National Labor Relations Board; these bills would also make it harder for workers to form independent unions or professional associations.

The political climate for human resources is thus polarized, uncertain, and searching for ways to respond to the undercurrent of anxiety, insecurity, and perhaps even suppressed anger in the work force. If these pressures are real, and if human resource professionals fail to respond to them, they will once again find themselves in a reactive and catch-up rather than a leadership position in responding to changing product and labor market cues.

OVERCOMING THE INWARD FOCUS

Human resource professionals will continue to be buffeted by both internal and external pressures. All the forces leading HR professionals to try to become more knowledgeable and skilled in managing change, contributing to strategic planning and decision-making, and updating their technical skills and knowledge will be as important in the future as they are today.

This is, however, only part of the challenge. These skills will need to be complemented by the ability to negotiate, to build coalitions, and to solve problems with multiple internal and external interests and organizations including professionals in other firms, government, educational institutions, labor unions, and professional associations. The primary reason for this shift in focus is that solving many of today's most critical workplace problems lies beyond the capabilities of any single firm. Indeed, acting in isolation may even put an individual firm at a cost disadvantage in the short run if its actions are not matched by its competitors. This is the type of classic market failure situation that requires coordinated efforts among all key actors and institutions affecting employment policies and practices. A look at the critical challenges facing employment relationships today will illustrate why I believe this shift in perspective and approach is necessary.

Reversing Trends in Earnings and Inequality

From 1973 to 1994 real earnings of nonsupervisory workers declined by approximately one percent per year. American workers are now (hopefully) ending the longest period of stagnant real earnings ever recorded (Thurow, 1996). Family earnings have not fallen as far because of the increased labor force participation of women; however, this cannot continue to grow indefinitely. Earning differentials increased primarily because of the declining earnings of those without college or technical education and skills and because of the escalation in earnings of very high level executives and professionals. While researchers do not fully agree on the relative weights to assign to causal factors such as changes in technology, international trade, declining union coverage, and so forth, there is general consensus that reversing these trends will require both increased investments in education and training and changes in compensation structures to reward more people for increasing their skills, contributing to improved productivity and profitability, and being willing and able to move and adapt to where the new job opportunities are found (Freeman & Katz, 1994). Market failure problems, however, limit the incentives for any individual firm to invest in the training and related organizational innovations needed to provide workers (especially low-wage workers) with the general human capital needed to reverse these trends. Thus, a more coordinated effort among employers, unions, and government will be needed. To play a constructive leadership role in this effort, HR professionals will need to become more active in local, state, and national bodies and strategies to promote broad diffusion of training and new compensation structures.

Designing Portable Benefits

If employment security is no longer part of the implicit contract, portability of benefits will become increasingly important to the long-term employment and income security of both the work force and the overall population. In recent years no issue has generated more bipartisan support more quickly than the call for greater portability of pensions and health insurance. Many companies are also acting quickly by, among other things, shifting from defined benefit to defined contribution, cash balance, and 401(k) saving and pension plans and including health care coverage as part of severance and early retirement packages. The biggest problems in the benefits area lie with workers employed in small and medium-sized firms and those in the contingent or otherwise high-turnover segment of the work force. These labor force participants have a much lower probability of being covered by a pension or a health insurance plan than do those employed in larger enterprises. Proposals have been advanced in Congress and within the executive branch to make it easier for small enterprises to adopt 401(k) plans and to increase vesting and portability of pensions and to allow workers to continue their health coverage (by purchasing it) when laid off. These policy proposals and private company actions all appear sensible on the surface but may have significant second-order effects on existing pension and health insurance plans and on the incentives and costs facing employers. HR professionals need to analyze the costs and benefits of these and other proposals to *all the interests at stake* and continue to search for the most efficient way to attend to the long-term income and health security arrangements for their individual employees and for the overall labor force.

Treating Employees as Stakeholders

Historically, workers have turned to the labor movement, and society has endorsed collective bargaining as the preferred means for providing workers a voice in decisions that affect their interests; it has also provided a strategy for balancing the power of employers and distributing profits between shareholders and the labor force. As is well known, however, unionization continues its forty-year decline and now has reached the same level in the private sector (approximately 10%) as it was prior to the Great Depression and the sudden explosion and rise of industrial unionism. Yet there is no evidence that workers have lost their desire for a voice on their job or for effective forms of independent representation. Consistently, one-third of the nonrepresented labor force expresses a desire to join a union if given the chance (Farber & Krueger, 1993; Freeman & Rogers, 1995; Kochan,

1979). An even larger number—over 70 to 80 percent of the work force—express a desire for a more direct opportunity to participate in decisions affecting their work, their employment rights, and their long-term economic and employment security (Freeman & Rogers, 1995). Yet our prevailing labor laws fail workers (and employers) on both accounts (Commission on the Future of Worker Management Relations, 1994); and business, labor, and government leaders remain locked in a twenty-year stalemate over how to modernize labor laws and institutions to fix the problem.

There is no single, quick fix to this problem. The diversity of worker preferences and employment settings demands that our law, institutions, and management practices allow and support a variety of options for employee participation and representation including traditional unions and collective bargaining, broad based labor–management partnerships, employee stock ownership plans, direct employee participation on workplace and production/quality issues, and employee representation in corporate governance structures and processes. All of these have a place in a modern, diverse economy, yet most of these are discouraged or blocked by an outdated labor law. HR professionals face a choice as to how to respond to this stalemate. They can continue to oppose efforts to update labor law in a comprehensive fashion and support only those changes that would relax the provisions limiting direct employee participation, or they can look at the full set of facts and support a comprehensive overhaul and modernization of labor law. Maintaining the prevailing political and ideological positions means that the HR profession will once again be in a reactive mode if (I believe it is actually when) pressures mount sufficiently to break this political stalemate.

Managing Diversity and Resolving Workplace Conflicts

The majority of employment conflicts no longer conform to the labor versus management dichotomy anticipated by labor and employment law. Instead, conflict takes a variety of subtle, suppressed, and overt forms that, if not managed and resolved effectively, imposes significant personal and organizational costs on those involved. Globalization increases diversity of the work force along a number of personal dimensions and thereby further raises the potential for workplace conflict. In response, there is a growth in interest and experimentation with diversity programs and in various alternative dispute resolution (ADR) techniques and procedures both within individual firms (Bencivenga, 1996) and in regulatory agencies (*Dispute*

Resolution Journal, 1995). Agencies such as OSHA are experimenting with partnership plans that offer workplaces that have comprehensive safety and health management systems (that include employee and where present union participation), lower exposures to inspections and fines, and more of an opportunity to internalize responsibility for enforcing government regulations. These efforts have yet, however, to gain the confidence of the work force necessary for their long run effectiveness. Women's, labor, and civil rights' organizations remain skeptical, fearing ADR will reinforce rather than overcome the power imbalances experienced by individual workers who challenge their employers. To make these systems credible and effective, HR professionals will need to work cooperatively and negotiate effectively with professionals in government, labor, and in this case women's and civil rights organizations. Once again, a more external orientation will be called for in this substantive arena.

LEARNING FROM PAST EXPERIENCE

How might the HR profession go about taking up these challenges in a constructive way without losing the support of the other stakeholders to whom HR professionals must also remain accountable—senior executives, customers, shareholders? A few examples from the past might help show the way. During what Strauss and Feuille (1978) referred to as the "Golden Age of Industrial Relations," that is, from the 1940s to the early 1970s, HR professionals had to be more externally oriented and involved in a more diverse professional community. They had to develop constructive dialogue with both union leaders and government policy makers since both groups were initiating changes (e.g., Title VII of the Civil Rights Act, employment and training policies, the Occupational Safety and Health Act) through collective bargaining and active government policy making on employment issues. Labor relations and human resource professionals were active in a wide range of public and quasi-public bodies such as the National Manpower Policy Task Force; The National Commission on Employment Policy; the National Labor-Management Advisory Committees established by Presidents Kennedy, Johnson, and Nixon; state level Committees and Task Force established to shape recommendations for Public Sector Labor Relations Statutes; state level Human Rights and/or Discrimination Commissions, and so on. Through their involvement in these groups HR professionals provided well-grounded practical input needed to translate the goals of public policy into administrative practices and rules that reflected the needs and realities of the modern workplace. More recently, reflecting the increased polarization of national politics, policy development and legislation have become more partisan and polarized, with little room for or interest in professional dialogue, analysis, or compromise.

Changing this state of affairs will require leadership from many quarters, including the HR profession. For example, the new welfare legislation will place significant demands on employers to absorb an influx of relatively low-wage workers in need of training, flexible work schedules, and practices that allow them to balance their work roles with diverse family responsibilities. A multitude of state-level experiments is about to unfold providing opportunities to learn from different experiences. While no single HR professional or single employer has a big self-interest in working with government agencies and welfare advocates, collectively the self and societal interests are clear. The leadership must come from and through HR professional associations and groups. Local, state, and national HR professional groups such as the Society for Human Resource Management, the Human Resource Planning Society, or the Industrial Relations Research Association might therefore do well to mobilize and bring together the diverse professional talent needed to make these new policies work for *all* stakeholders involved.

ACHIEVING THE RIGHT BALANCE

I believe the workplace tensions discussed above will, one way or another, occupy increasingly prominent positions on the future agenda of HR professionals. How the profession responds to these tensions will affect its influence and stature both inside the corporation and in society. In responding to these external pressures, however, HR professionals must be careful not to lose the support of top management. Tilting too far in the direction of becoming an advocate for employee concerns would do little other than remarginalize the HR function within the management structure. This was the ultimate fate of the labor relations professionals who failed to respond in the latter 1970s and 1980s to growing market pressures to improve productivity and break out of the rigid patterns of work organization and traditional collective bargaining that they had become accustomed to and successful at managing. The underlying challenge facing human resource professionals in the coming years lies in finding the right balance between building coalitions with other professionals who share responsibility and influence over employment relations and deepening efforts to make human resources a strategic asset for their firms.

REFERENCES

Baron, J., Dobbins, F.R., & Jennings, P.D. (Sept., 1986). War and peace: The evolution of modern personnel administration in U.S. industry. *American Journal of Sociology, 92,* 350–383.

Benivenga, D. (1996). Fair play in the ADR arena. *HR Magazine,* January, 50–56.

Commission on the Future of Worker Management Relations. (June, 1994). *Fact finding report.* Washington, DC: U.S. Departments of Commerce and Labor.

Dispute Resolution Journal. (1995). The future of employment ADR. October–December, entire issue.

Doyle, F. (March, 1993). GE's Doyle urges HR to embrace a world of change. *Work in America Report, 18,* 3.

Eichinger, R., & Ulrich, D. (1995). *Human resource challenges.* New York: The Human Resource Planning Society.

Farber, H., & Krueger, A.B. (1993). Union membership in the United States: The decline continues. In B.E. Kaufman and M. M. Kleiner (Eds.), *Employee representation: Alternatives and future directions* (pp. 135–168). Madison, WI: Industrial Relations Research Association.

Freedman, A., & Associates. (1996). *Human resources forecast 1996.* Los Angeles: The Anderson Graduate School of Management at UCLA and the Society for Human Resource Management.

Freeman, R.B., & Katz, L.F. (1994). Rising wage inequality: The United States. In R. B. Freeman (Ed.), *Working under different rules* (pp. 29–63). New York: Russell Sage.

Freeman, R.B., and Rogers, J. (1995). The worker participation and representation survey. Princeton, NJ: Princeton Survey Research Center.

Jacoby, S. (1985). *Employing bureaucracies.* New York: Columbia University Press.

Kochan, T.A. (1979). How American workers view labor unions. *Monthly Labor Review, 102,* 13–22.

Kochan, T.A., & Cappelli, P. (1984). The transformation of the industrial relations and personnel function. In P. Osterman (Ed.), *Internal labor markets* (pp. 133–162). Cambridge, MA: MIT Press.

Strauss, G., & Feuille, P. (1978). IR research: A critical analysis. *Industrial Relations, 17,* 258–277.

Thurow, L. (1996). *The future of capitalism.* New York: W.W. Norton.

CHAPTER 12

"DON'T SEND ME ONE OF THOSE TYPICAL HUMAN RESOURCE PEOPLE": A TRUE LIFE ADVENTURE STORY

HAROLD E. JOHNSON

This story begins with the fact that, after years of "buying" executive search while the head of human resources (HR) for three very large American corporations, I moved to the "sell side" of the search business about six or seven years ago. A large part of my practice is in human resources where I have worked closely with some of HR's most imaginative, creative, cynical, visionary, and capable thinkers— including Chief Executive Officers (CEOs), academics, consultants, and pracitioners. The assignments I have completed are diverse and range from the senior VP positions at IBM and Xerox, to the head of HR for Major League Baseball, to the head of staffing for Starbucks. In addition to the United States and Canada, I have filled HR jobs in Australia, Switzerland, China, and the United Kingdom.

The story starts to get a little scary when one considers the fact that in *almost every meeting* I have with a CEO about a search for a new head of HR, the conversation starts with:

> I don't want a typical HR type. I don't even think I want someone from HR. I want this person to be the brightest, smartest, bravest, most strategic, and highest potential individual on this management team. That's probably not going to be somebody from HR.

I have heard those words at least two dozen times. It's an amazingly uniform script. I suppose a reader could take some comfort in the fact that those

CEOs usually don't mean exactly what they say because they generally pick someone from HR. They believe the people they pick are truly unique and, if I am doing my job, they probably are.

The story gets scarier when I start interviewing candidates for those positions. Uniformly, almost every one of the HR people I interview, within the first five minutes of our conversation, says something like:

> By the way, I'm not the typical HR person. I'm really different from the rest of the people in the field. I'm a business partner. I'm strategic. I am a change agent!

Those two chapters from the same book imply a lot about the status of the HR function, where it has been, where it is going, and the opportunities for those who decide to get into it. Isn't it odd that the function is viewed as somehow tainted or second class both by the people in it and by its most important clients? What is going on here?

Based on what I hear many of my clients (the CEOs and the new-breed HR executives I deal with) asking of the function, it is clear that HR may ultimately be the most exciting game in town. It is finally being recognized as integral to the company's success by some of the people whose attention those in HR have striven so long to attract. The question is whether HR people will be doing the work in the years ahead.

There are some outstanding people leading and developing HR at some of the United States' great companies, and I am convinced that the correlation is not accidental. The standards they set for themselves and for those who work for them are extraordinary and clearly on the leading edge. HR, in these situations, has transformed itself from an administrative backwater, engrossed in manuals and inspections, into a pivotal new role. Unfortunately, while the demand for new-breed, value-added, and business-focused HR people is growing, in too many companies the next generation of HR is sparsely populated with the kind of people who will be truly "ready" to assume the roles they'll be asked to fulfill.

As an example of those new roles, the CEO at one of America's best known and highly respected corporations started our recent conversation by saying:

> I want someone who understands business. I want someone who understands what it is like to have to meet the payroll and make a buck. The job to be done is enormous! This company is known for the excellence of its products that are driven by a series of chemical, electrical, and mechanical processes that have made us among the best in the world. The fact is that I

have 150,000 people walking down a path that is driven by that historical structure and technology and, as I see it, our future is *entirely* digital! That fact will change everything about us. It represents fundamental change to the competencies and mindsets of our people, our customers, our suppliers, and the people who service our products. It changes every element of our business, and I don't know how to accomplish that change. I don't know how to move this organization to the new digital path. Find me someone who does. I really don't care much about compensation and benefits and labor relations. I figure I can outsource a lot of that. I need leadership help.

This CEO got what he was looking for—and it was someone with considerable experience in HR. The question I ponder is whether enough of the people in the function are ready for the kind of challenge he described and are ahead of the curve in this kind of new responsibility. Based on the dozens and dozens of HR people I see every month, the answer is clearly, sadly, "No!" Everything I see tells me that, as never before, HR is being invited to the party and asked to make a contribution to the direction and focus of the company, to play a direct strategic role, to be involved in the most fundamental issues facing the company. Too few practitioners are prepared to play this emerging role.

One reason stems from the fact that there have been few people from whom to learn. Too many of HR's role models along the way have been caught up in the pointless self-appraisal that has dogged HR for years. In my past life, I attended scores of meetings of HR people where much of the day was devoted to questions such as "Why don't I get any respect?" "Why don't they like me?" "Why is my contribution not sought out?" "Why am I not a full member of the team?" For years, HR people have railed at their lack of status, which both tainted the outlook of too many of the people growing up in HR and which forced those who hated being "second class" out of the function, thus negatively influencing those who stayed behind. I worked in Teheran for a year and remember the demonstrations of thousands of religious zealots arranged in long, chanting lines, winding through the streets of the city. These were half-naked fanatics who were flogging themselves with chains, barbed wire, and thorns to proclaim the glory of martyrdom. Too many meetings of too many HR people have reminded me of those masochistic dancers. *For a number of HR executives, I think it is true that their managements didn't understand and respect them. The problem, however, was with the HR executives, not with their clients, and the solutions were within their reach.*

Looking ahead to changing the equation and being "ready when invited," effective human resources leaders of the future will have taken the time and made the effort to truly understand the historical comments of their line critics. I've always thought that too few people in HR know far too little about their clients' needs, and yet, we in HR expect them to know all about ours—and have empathy for our roles—and to buy into our propositions—and to give us respect. In too many places, the situation is as it is because too many HR leaders, who were supposed to be nurturing the next generation of leaders, have too little to talk about that had any relevancy to their line managements' most visceral problems and concerns. The fact is, not enough people in HR have had the foggiest notion about the things that keep their clients awake at night, that scare the living hell out of them, that drive them to 70-hour weeks and away from their homes and families and health. Without being really connected to the people who run the business, or to the emerging science concerning people in organizations, how can HR be integral? For years, it was primarily the heads of HR who resisted the transition of the historical "soft side" of HR (organization development, organization effectiveness, training and development, etc.) to its current "hard side" status. Too many people clung too long to compensation and benefits and labor, while neglecting to understand how their customers' needs were changing. The "gatekeeper" title was an earned one. If there is a lesson for HR people for the future, it is to be *relevant* in what we do.

To be successful in the years ahead, effective HR people will know, *really know,* about the economics of the business and how the firm prospers, and how people can be mobilized and motivated to achieve common goals. Future HR people must understand the balance sheet, cash flow, the income statement, and where profits come from. Without those skills, is there any question that the boss will still be looking for something different?

Sometimes, in describing the spectrum of human resource people to a prospective client, in trying to get at what he or she is looking for in a new head of HR, I have divided the community into two segments. One larger (but happily shrinking) part of the human resources world is the supply side which represents about 80 percent of HR. Supply side HR people have carved out honorable, credible places in the world and are, when viewed as effective, the first place to call when people in the organization need help—when they need jobs evaluated, training programs established, college graduates recruited, organizations downsized, and so on. The best supply side HR people fill those orders and do it quickly, imaginatively, and with credible and effective products. They do important tactical "stuff."

The other 20 percent of the people in HR (and I think this percentage is growing), are those who could be called the "demand side" people. That is, they handle the tactical work but *understand that their fundamental role does not involve waiting for an order or for the phone to ring.* The best praciitioners are ahead of their line clients and are deeply involved with their companies' most fundamental and strategic planning. They have thought through the implications of the strategies and business plans and in anticipation have begun to formulate and test solutions and programs to deal with anticipated issues. They are people who understand what committed human resources can do and that their role includes the responsibility and right to go to the company's general managers and say such things as, "I've been thinking about your business plan, what it is that you want to do, and I've been thinking about the global initiatives we have started, and I see what the competition is doing, and I don't believe we will get there unless you and I partner-up, starting today, to do the following four things that will have a measurable impact on your plans for our future." This approach will astound line management and will guarantee a whole new outlook—or point of view about the relevancy of the HR function by those outside the function.

Demand side HR executives are anticipatory, visionary, brave, relevant, and highly driven by the businesses they serve in the context of a rapidly changing, real time, complex, global business village. They weave themselves into the fabric of the decision-making process and are as relevant as *any* other member on the management team. As one of my placements said:

> These senior HR jobs are really different and, when attained, they are hard to describe to the people who support you. There are weeks in which I spend two or three entire days in meetings where I may only speak ten sentences, or nod my head, or raise an eyebrow at the right time. In fact, those acts sometimes change the course of the company. No one bestows the ability to make that impact on you. You have to earn it.

Consider the impact that these demand side HR leaders are having on their organizations and the HR people working for them! They are having the times of their lives. They matter! Unfortunately, when clients describe the ideal HR executive they seek in a "demand side" way, I don't have many places to look and am hard pressed to deliver more than a handful of candidates who are truly different than "the typical HR professional."

I suspect that one reason HR people have historically been viewed as less than full partners is that very few people in the function have ever had to play "Bet your job." Yet, those kind of stakes are a fact of life for most internal clients. Successful HR people of the future will have taken the time to be well-prepared and have the confidence that comes from relevant, creative expertise. They'll have to be willing to take the same kinds of risk that their clients face every week. It's like the case of a good friend of mine who wanted to see if he had the courage to make a parachute jump. He agonized over the decision for two or three years and finally decided to do it. He jumped and said that it was the most thrilling thing he could imagine, but he will never do it again. Nevertheless, he says he now has an entirely new appreciation for others who have taken the long first step out of an airplane door, even once. It has been a unique bonding experience that he never anticipated. I suppose it is like the camaraderie that exists among those who have been together in the Marine Corps. For me, the lesson is that when our clients see us as willing to step out of the door with them, human resources will be more fully functional, and truly appreciated.

Almost every company I know of expresses a need to change to be better. Every general manager I know wants *real* help. Human resources people are the most logical people to lead that change and provide that help, but they have to "walk the talk." HR ought also to be the role model for the entire organization when it comes to change. It also ought to be the best at growing people, instituting "quality," understanding the business, hiring the best, and weeding out the mediocre in everything it does. HR ought to exude talent and aim to be the place that other departments of the organization look to when trying to find the brightest, smartest, most energetic, highest potential people in the organization. For the most part, it is simply a matter of deciding to do it.

Not long ago, I checked a reference on one of my successful HR candidates who exemplifies what I think most of my clients are seeking; it might be helpful as a template for those who intend to rise in the function in the future. A division CEO provided me with extensive information about the candidate I had recruited from his company, and it included the following:

> Summing up, in the crustiest of terms, Bob has a very low B.S. threshold which I view as one of his most endearing charms. Most HR people try to make you happy and spend a lot of time snuggling up to the line managers but without much substance. I always liked this guy because he pressed for change and was never bound by the way things were always done, without being overbearing and dogmatic. When we were both in a division together, we were allowed a lot of freedom in the terms of new management ideas and structures and he talked us into trying a lot of things without being faddish. We were willing to be experimental and Bob always pushed the people he supported to be better, even when it wasn't always safe to do so. This guy has as much courage as anybody I have ever worked with. He assumed he was there to add value and didn't wait to be asked. When we

were doing something he thought was wrong, he told us, but in a way that gave us options to fix ourselves before we got into trouble. We were recognized as having done a lot of innovative things and Bob gets a lot of credit for that. We did things when the HR people back at Corporate, to whom he had a functional responsibility, would get goosy as hell, but it didn't hold him back. The line people like to work with him because he understands almost as much about their business as they do, and he gets things done in that context. Anyone who spends 15 minutes with him will be impressed with the fact that he is a leader and has a good head on his shoulders. This guy does his homework unbelievably well and works like a damned robot. He will be in the office at 7 AM after leaving his house at 6 and will give you 12 to 14 hours on top of it, just like the rest of us. His only flat side is that he is impatient with people who are timid and lack character but no one ever loses their dignity with Bob around. If your client hires this guy, it is a significant loss for us. I wish I could keep him. There are not many HR people I worked with that I thought were integral to this business, but Bob is one of them. He never tried to dictate and have things his own way and he was never an administrative gatekeeper or bureaucrat. He spent his time understanding the needs of the business and then delivering products, ideas, and solutions, often outside of HR, that made us good. I don't know how you found him because he is so unlike most of the HR people I have known.

I think it is true that HR will provide the most exciting, impactful jobs in U.S. business life. I am encouraged by the fact that new HR leadership is emerging and that the percentage of the demand side vs. supply side professionals is changing. The question is, will enough of the brightest people around be attracted to HR and make the commitment needed to be the kind of contributor described in the vignettes above? It is a matter of will.

SECTION III

RESPECT HISTORY, CREATE A FUTURE

HR functions need to and have changed . . . or have they? Rather than merely live for an uncertain future, HR work needs to be grounded in its past. The discipline of human resources has a history that has both good news and bad news. The good news is that much of the history should be maintained while moving into the future. The bad news is that some of that history needs to be changed to meet the future with competence and confidence.

Without an understanding of history, humans often are doomed to repeat it. Without understanding the history of HR, its practitioners may end up like a neverending pendulum swinging from one set of practices to another (e.g., from centralized to decentralized operations and back again). With a historical perspective, we are able to see that much current work in HR is based on historical work and should not be changed for the sake of change. To remove this swinging pendulum, human relations might be better served by seeing HR work evolve like steps in a staircase. Each step of the staircase is important to getting to the top, but moving from one step to another does not mean the earlier steps were not equally important. In fact, without early steps, later steps don't occur.

The early steps can now be recognized from the history of HR; they were the practices and philosophies that drove HR work. They were and are important to understanding the present work required of HR professionals. Relying exclusively on the past, however, may mean failing to adapt for the future. HR professionals must also create a future and in doing so they must learn to anticipate and respond to events both seen and unseen. They must innovate new practices for new problems. They must not be shackled with solutions that reflected different contexts. Change is one of the most constant facts of current organizational life. Creating new HR processes to deal with change becomes a major challenge for HR professionals preparing for the future.

To manage the conundrum of learning from the past while adapting to the future, HR professionals must consider the following questions:

- *What is the history of HR?*

   It is often surprising how little new entrants coming into the HR field know of the heritage of the profession. They often are not aware of the work done by HR professionals in sociotechnical systems, t-groups, personality tests, labor relations, and group dynamics.
- *What of the past should be left in the past, and what should be adapted for the future?*

   People can easily get lost in their past and fail to live in the present or future. They become consumed with sorting out history more than living for the present. HR professionals should be aware of how to differentiate history as intellectual artifacts of a past era and history as a source of lessons for the present.
- *What set of conditions will create a new future?*

   Guessing about a future is less useful than predicting it. Prediction often comes from educated guesses based on a logical sequence of events. For example, if HR professionals can make the linkage from customer requirements for new products to the need for new technologies to produce the product, to the need for new work processes to generate the new technologies, to the ways in which HR practices shape processes to the specific investments in time and energy to create new practices; then HR professionals can begin to see linkages from one set of activities to another. They can then begin to see how a change in their focus (time and attention) may create a future set of products and services.

The essays in this section boldly suggest that all the denouncing, denigrating, and critiquing of HR may be unjustified. In fact, some of the past is necessary for getting to the future. These essays reveal that the future of HR may be ever-changing and that new frameworks, models, and actions will be required to make the future successful. Collectively, they suggest HR is at a crossroads where decisions need to be made about moving forward or staying static. HR professionals with a sense of history are more likely to make thoughtful forward moves into unchartered territory with confidence that the history will support the evolution.

CHAPTER 13

JUDGE ME MORE BY MY FUTURE THAN BY MY PAST

DAVE ULRICH

Premature death rites have occurred before. Truman was prematurely declared the loser before he won the 1948 election. Mark Twain, said "Rumors of my death have been seriously exaggerated." Huck Finn attended his own funeral. The 1969 New York Mets were deemed vanished prior to their miraculous comeback and World Series victory. Churchill changed political parties but continued to rebound. Phil Nieckro, the great knuckleball pitcher, was continually counted out but kept returning for another year. John Travolta's career seemed moribund before he reemerged with the leading roles in *Pulp Fiction* and *Phenomenon*. Premature deaths occur not only in lifestyles, but in professions.

In the field of human resources (HR), death rites have been proclaimed, eulogies written, and funerals prepared for the demise of the HR function. These eulogies are premature. While HR as we know it (with images of policy police, regulators, and administrative guardians) has passed, a new HR is emerging. If HR is to play the more significant role many advocate, then the future will have to be characterized by understanding and mastering nine challenges.

1. HR MATTERS: FOCUSING ON DELIVERABLES MORE THAN DOABLES

On my shelf are 40 years of HR textbooks, each distilling research and synthesizing knowledge. While the content within each chapter has evolved with new research and insight, the basic paradigm has remained the same.

The chapter titles continue to be what HR people do, for example, staffing, training, compensation, benefits, appraisal, etc. My view of HR in the future is that we need a new paradigm which focuses less on what HR does and more on what HR delivers. The chapter headings need to be topics such as globalization, customer intimacy, operational excellence, operating margin, and other business strategies. Each chapter can discuss and discover how HR activities accomplish these business goals. *The focus, however, should be on the deliverables not the doables.*

A similar logic can be applied not only to textbooks but to HR plans. Recently, I visited a world-class company where HR leaders had spent months creating their next year HR plan. They were excited by the new initiatives—competence-based staffing, action learning workshops, leadership development seminars, pay for performance, team-based pay, and employee communications. When asked for an opinion about the quality of this plan, I ventured to ask *why*—Why were they doing these new initiatives? Why would the business benefit from accomplishing these initiatives? The deliverables were never articulated, so the doables dominated thinking. If other functions used this approach, marketing would allocate its time running focus groups, doing surveys, and segmenting customers rather than on gaining market share and selling products.

As HR focuses on deliverables more than on doables, the paradigm shifts toward creating value more than running programs.

2. HR THEORY: SEARCHING FOR WHY

Theory explains why things happen the way they do. HR needs theories which explain why HR delivers what it does. For example, in working to reengage employees, HR professionals could draw on intellectual capital theory to specify the value created by each employee to the enterprise and the loss generated when an employee's intellectual capital is either underutilized or underinvested. When discussing why HR practices create results, HR professionals could draw on cognitive theory to describe the importance of a shared mindset which comes from integrated HR practices, they could then demonstrate how shared mindset reduces transaction costs (economic theory), increases ownership (agency theory), and leads to productive communities of employees (community ecology theory).

More pragmatically, HR theory serves two immediate purposes. First, it stops mindless benchmarking or best practice studies by providing an "if . . . then" logic to benchmarking. Most benchmarking focuses on the "then" or the practices engaged by the best practice company without paying any attention to the "if" or context under which the best practice occurs. As a result, firms copy a training, staffing, compensation, or other program which worked in the best practice firm because of series of conditions (the "if"). Theory focuses on why and forces clarity around the if of the "if . . . then" benchmark equation.

Second, theory sets expectations. Theory enables HR to become a profession with a set of standards of what is expected in terms of performance of HR work. Theory leads to respect because a set of standards is articulated and accomplished. Physicians have a theory which leads to standards for medical practice; architects have theories of construction standards; accountants have theories which set standards for the profession. HR needs theory which defines standards.

3. HR COMMUNITY: REALIZING THAT HR IS NOT JUST FOR HR

The community of HR needs expansion. The HR community generally includes corporate, field, service center, and center of expertise HR professions—all of whom are within the HR function. In the future, HR will not be accomplished just by those within the HR function but also by line managers, other staff managers, and strategic partnerships with outside vendors.

The HR community needs to create governance mechanisms whereby HR work is done by individuals inside and outside the formal HR function, all dedicated to common outcomes and acting within professional standards. Early outposts of HR communities exist today where HR work is done by line managers (e.g., General Electric is using line managers to teach their executive programs), staff professionals (e.g., Finance and HR have teamed at Fidelity Investments to offer services to business units), and strategic partners (e.g., Many firms have outsourced the administrative, routine, transaction work of HR). The ultimate challenge of HR as a community rather than as a function is to articulate when each member of the community adds value to an external customer.

4. HR TOOLS: MASTERING HR PRACTICES NOT YET DEFINED

The HR function has evolved over the last 40 years, each decade including a new set of HR tools: labor relations and staffing (1940s); training (1950s);

regulatory issues, compensation, benefits, appraisal (1960s and 1970s); health care, cost containment, organization design, teamwork, and communication (1980s); mergers, acquisitions, downsizing, diversity (1990s). New tools for HR will be forthcoming. These tools will focus on such areas as: global HR (learning to manage HR issues in global competition), culture change (defining tools for crafting and changing a corporate culture), technology (adapting HR to the ever-changing information highway), leader of the future (defining the competencies of the future, not past, leader), and knowledge transfer (understanding how to generate and generalize knowledge).

These new HR tools will emerge. In the next decade HR professionals will be able to be as explicit about culture change as they are today about the requirements for a successful training program or hiring strategy. Since it is easier to learn than to forget, mastering these new tools will require that old HR tools be more automated, be completed by others in the HR community, and/or be discontinued.

5. HR VALUE CHAIN: DISCOVERING THE REAL CUSTOMER OF HR WORK

HR work has generally occurred within the boundaries of the firm. As these boundaries become more permeable, HR work must shift to working across boundaries. For example, traditional programs of staffing, training, and compensation will increasingly include involvement of and focus on suppliers and customers in the firm's value chain. Today, Motorola University attendees are 50 percent suppliers and customers of Motorola. In the future, HR work will focus on the value chain as suppliers and customers participate in the design and delivery of HR practices.

These HR value chains may begin slowly; for example, McDonalds, Coca-Cola, and Disney are beginning to share information about HR practices. Over time, these chains will likely pick up speed as firms in a value chain collaborate on staffing, training, teamwork, and administrative processes. It might be possible that McDonalds, Coke, and Disney share a training center, a staffing center, an administrative processing center, and career development programs.

6. HR VALUE PROPOSITION: MEASURING THE IMPACT

If HR matters, it must be measured. Measuring the impact of HR must be built on breakeven analyses of specific HR programs (e.g., the cost/benefit of a competency based staffing program) to begin to answer such questions as:

- How do HR practices affect the market value of a firm?
- How do HR practices impact the intellectual capital of a firm?
- How can investments in HR practices be directly related to growth, cost, or other financial variables?
- What is the economic impact of using HR practices to create a shared mindset, more efficient transactions, or committed employees?
- What is the economic impact of not investing in HR practices?

In a simple way, efforts to answer these questions will connect investments in HR practices and business results. So far, HR investments have not been tied clearly to business results, leaving HR with the legacy of being soft, anecdotal, and non-business critical.

7. HR Careers: Moving from Stages to Mosaics

A career in HR will not be linear, but will be a mosaic of experiences. Linear models of careers talk about stages for HR professionals; mosaic career models build on diverse experiences inside and outside the function, in field and corporate positions, as generalists and specialists, and in working with strategy and operations. Mosaic careers focus more on what the HR professional knows and is able to do than on title and position. Mosaic careers are more the responsibility of the individual than of the firm. Mosaic careers are expanded when employees take risks and try new things. Mosaic careers prepare HR professionals as business partners more than as functional experts.

8. HR Competencies: Getting Prepped

Many in-company studies of the competencies of HR have been done. In addition, some extensive cross-company studies of HR competencies have been performed. As these studies begin to coalesce, four common clusters of competencies of HR professionals are emerging:

- *Business knowledge:* HR professionals must know the business which includes a mastery of finance, strategy, marketing, and operations.

- *HR state of the art:* HR professionals must know the theory of leading edge practices for HR tools.
- *Change and process:* HR professionals need a model of change and the ability to apply the model to a specific situation.
- *Credibility:* HR professionals must become personally credible through the accuracy of their work and the intimacy of their relationships.

As these four competencies are turned into behaviors, HR professionals can begin to identify the development and training they require to succeed in the future.

9. HR and Intellectual Capital: Investing in the Scarce Resource

Intellectual capital could be seen as another tool area awaiting HR insight, however, I believe it is more than that. Intellectual capital represents the collective insights, knowledge, and commitments of employees within a firm. It can be an asset for investment or a liability for depreciation. Investing in intellectual capital means making sure that employees who are hired with 100 units of competence add to this base annually so that ten years after employment, the original 100 units is now 200, and the 200 are significantly different than the original 100. Depreciating intellectual capital occurs when firms burnout, stress, or demoralize employees.

In many firms today, downsizing and global competition have left employees feeling more like depreciable than appreciable assets; employees often feel less loyalty, commitment, and engagement. In firms of tomorrow, intellectual capital must become an ongoing investment where employees are constantly learning, changing, challenging, and reinventing both themselves and their firms.

HR in the future should play a central role in acquiring, nurturing, and investing in intellectual capital.

Conclusions

The HR of the 1980s is dead; long live the new HR. This essay ends with optimism because these nine challenges are not insurmountable. They can be debated and defined, and they can be overcome. By so doing, they will frame the HR of the next century. The next-century HR vocabulary will include words such as: deliverables, HR community, HR value chain, HR value proposition, HR governance, culture change, global HR, knowledge transfer, mosaic careers, intellectual capital, creating value. When these words become more than ideas and ideals, then the next generation of HR will have emerged. I hope we can judge HR more by this future than by the past.

CHAPTER 14

THE FUTURE OF HUMAN RESOURCES: FORGING AHEAD OR FALLING BEHIND?

R. WAYNE ANDERSON

$\mathbf{A}$t a time when corporations are re-examining literally everything they do, the Human Resource function is undergoing the most intense scrutiny I have seen in the 31 years I've been in the HR business.

We see it everywhere. Our HR trade publications are filled with doom-and-gloom articles. Our function has not escaped the downsizing and restructuring that, in many cases, we ourselves have helped engineer and handle for our organizations. As a result, many in HR share the same job and career anxieties that affect workers throughout corporate America.

Although some of this ill wind can't be avoided, I feel strongly that the capabilities our function brings to the management of many successful companies are highly valued now and will be even more so in the future. In my view, the outlook is bright for HR leaders who use HR strategies as a multiplier to enhance the performance of their companies.

Personally, I welcome the current scrutiny as an opportunity to showcase our bottom-line contributions to the success of our organizations.

HR HISTORY

In assessing the future of the HR function, it helps to remember just how far we've come. Remember the days when so-and-so, who couldn't make it in a real job, was put into personnel because he or she was a "people" person? We've come a long way since those days.

146

Many are not aware that in a great number of organizations HR came out of the Purchasing Department. People were seen as a commodity to be "obtained," and it was Purchasing's job to find these commodities to do the work. Over time, the job skills required to "obtain" people grew because an increasingly more complex set of specialized HR roles emerged.

The rest is history, much of it relatively recent. We developed a "professional status" and a defined role. Universities began offering an HR curriculum. The rise of unions gave rise to the need for "professionals" with labor relations skills. People issues—compensation, benefits design and administration, federal regulatory compliance, affirmative action, and labor relations—became so complicated and so important that effective HR practices and competencies were seen by enlightened managements as necessary.

THE FOUNDATIONS OF HR COMPETENCY

Today the best of HR professionals have evolved to positions of influence few of our predecessors could have imagined. The best in our function today are doing three things and doing them superbly.

First, the basics of recruiting, hiring, paying, developing, motivating, utilizing, and even terminating people are fundamental requirements for any organization. These are the tasks that got us in the door, and we can't ever forget that.

Next, there will always be a need for someone in the ombudsman role. This role has changed over the years as HR has become a key part of the management team. HR can work with the employees and the management of the organization to fulfill the ombudsman role in reviewing, counseling, conducting confidential discussions, or working on any other people issues, but we should never forget that HR's primary role is to support management in successfully executing the business strategy.

Last, and most important, enlightened general managers are beginning to understand that it's the integration of finance, operations, *and* people, as part of an overall business strategy, that enables one organization to perform better than another. It's the skills and competencies provided by people executing business strategies that make the difference and ultimately make strategies come to life.

THE DIFFERENCE BETWEEN SURVIVING AND LEARNING

In considering the future, we anticipate that HR people will survive because someone has to do the basics. We in HR will also be recognized business leaders and strategic partners as we "help" management recognize that people issues must be an integrated part of successful business strategies. It is at this level that we add the most value to our organizations.

Viewed through management's eyes, the perfect world would include employees who have a strategic focus, understand the business, behave like adults, and work with integrated processes for the good of the organization.

Some would suggest delivering all, or even most, of the perfect world is impossible. Nevertheless, our sights should always focus on adding value in executing business strategies.

While we're getting the basics done (contrary to some experts, everything shouldn't be outsourced), a critical part of our role will continue to be the ability to recommend the "right" employees for the organization based on the skill sets and competencies needed. Once the right people are on board, HR can add value by assisting management in guiding these employees through the right jobs throughout their careers. HR can determine where, when, and how to fully utilize and integrate all the skills, training, and competencies available to achieve corporate objectives; but this has to be done in partnership with management.

This process, which sets up a consultative role with the management team, must be focused on all the business strategies established for the corporation to ensure they are integrated. More specifically, this means HR needs to be a partner in strategic planning and decision making. As opposed to our former role of being brought in *after* the decision was made and then being expected simply to implement that decision, HR must also be accountable in helping implement and execute business strategies.

Easy to say, but hard to do. How can we establish that partnership?

I offer seven tried and tested steps for establishing an HR partnership with management:

1. We must understand business strategies, goals, tactics, and financial performance and connect that knowledge to the skills, competencies, practices, and people that are available to execute the business strategy.
2. We must set performance goals for ourselves that relate directly to business strategies.
3. We must provide credible follow-up to management on our effectiveness in supporting the business strategy. This follow-up must cover both the good and the bad news.
4. We must know the value of the HR skills, competencies, practices, and business knowledge available to execute the business strategies. We must aggressively market these competencies to our management

because in too many cases they're not aware of what we can do to support them.

5. We must be seen as problem solvers rather than "controllers" of policy, while at the same time realizing we must solve people problems within the parameters established by the organization.

6. We must provide management with more than it asks for. This will help establish a perception of adding value that is critical to building long-term relationships. We should give back more data or counsel than initially requested or reframe the request to help management make a better decision.

7. We must feel a need for speed. Our processes must be faster so all of our customers aren't waiting for HR to "finally do something." For example, few things get support groups into management's dog house faster than not providing timely information and counsel.

THE BASIC HR PREMISE

In helping to secure our own future and implement these steps, everything we do must directly support the organization's business objectives and strategy. In fact, if we can't articulate a specific strategy or objective for every HR practice, principle, program, or process, we should stop doing it immediately. As we build these linkages, it is imperative that we ensure that the organization understands the connection to strategy. We must understand that the ultimate test of our contribution will be the successful execution of the business strategy itself.

We are not in this alone. While we're improving our own capabilities, we must continue to work with line management to develop strategies that focus on people issues and recommend HR tactics that support the business strategies. At that point management—our partners—must approve, take ownership of, and decide when and how to implement these people strategies to add full value to the business. It's at this point that we are accountable for providing the right tools and tactics to execute those strategies.

ANTICIPATING THE HR FUTURE

Looking ahead, two fundamental and specific processes can be used by HR people to help management realize full value from the HR function in support of business objectives. These processes have been tested successfully at Amoco Corporation.

The first is linking people strategies to the company's strategic management process. The second, and the one I want to explain in some detail, is

Figure 14.1
HR Strategic Planning Process Linked Business Strategy, Organization Capabilities and People Strategies

developing the Human Resources strategy to support the corporation's strategies (Figure 14.1).

STRATEGIC MANAGEMENT PROCESS

HR and the corporation's management group should engage in a strategic management process which links business strategy, organizational capability, *AND* people strategies.

A complete business strategy has three key components: an operating strategy, a financial strategy, and a people strategy. A well-developed business strategy identifies the need for specific organizational capabilities and reinforces the building of these capabilities as the primary focus of the people strategy.

The operating groups in most companies have business strategies and organizational capability requirements against which a people strategy framework can be developed. Such a framework will contain those elements that the business unit or department needs to better manage its people and to develop critical organizational capabilities, thereby improving business performance.

An important and sensitive point must be inserted here: Whatever people programs and practices are used in an organization, they must be aligned with business strategies and—here's the sensitive part—must be supported by management as value-added activities, not perceived as extra work or as HR initiatives.

At Amoco, the HR function was responsible for developing the "Renewal Star" (Figure 14.2), which became the key focus for a corporate-wide change process, but, more importantly, served as the model that tied everything together so that managers and supervisors did not see the variety of activities as being unrelated and not adding value. The star reflects the integration of each key process with the center focusing on the overall theme—improving business performance. By integrating all points on the star, we were able to make the connection as to how and why each piece was an integral part of the overall concept of integrating the business plan and processes to improve the corporation's performance.

HR STRATEGY

At Amoco, the HR strategy sets the overarching themes for all people, processes, practices, and programs for the organization. We established three

Figure 14.2
Amoco Renewal Star: Integrating Activities

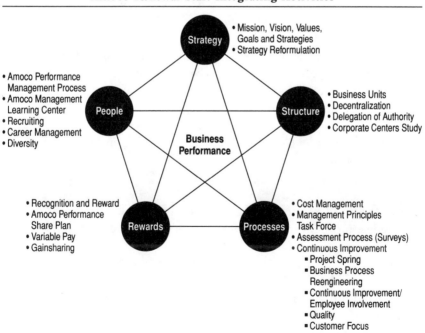

HR strategies, with supporting tactics, that will enable our management to achieve the corporation's business objectives in the future.

Our first strategy is to improve Amoco's capability *to act quickly and decisively.* Tactics to support that strategy include: increasing the organization's accountability for operating results; redesigning processes to improve productivity, speed, and agility; developing processes for rapidly handling information and making decisions; strengthening strategic-management processes focused on the external marketplace; and helping delegate authority to the lowest reasonable level.

The second strategic thrust is *to build and deploy those critical people competencies* that are needed to execute business strategies. This means defining core and business-specific competencies and utilizing people processes, programs, and practices to help shape the organization and close capability gaps.

Third, we want *to increase the return on our investment in people.* To accomplish this, we must redesign pay, benefit programs, and personnel policies to maximize the value received for each dollar spent; redesign organizations and work processes to improve productivity; and establish and maintain a work environment that enhances a productive and empowered workforce.

The HR strategic planning process also clarifies HR's goals and milestones, addresses structural and process issues, links rewards to performance, and positions us to be more productive.

But we aren't through yet. The strategy study clearly showed us that HR's role needed to be redefined. Figure 14.3, for example, shows the dramatic shift we expect in something as basic as how we spend our time.

The challenge to make this shift in time allocation (more strategic, consultative, developmental *versus* execution orientation/administrative) is critically dependent upon also changing the skill sets and competencies of the HR staff. In order to do this, we will be focusing on very specific areas of HR responsibility.

HR AREAS OF RESPONSIBILITY
Our people processes focus on four areas of primary responsibility.

Strategic People Planning

This includes organization capability and gaps identification; external and internal work climate assessment; and people strategy formulation and implementation.

Figure 14.3
HR Function's Roles Clarified

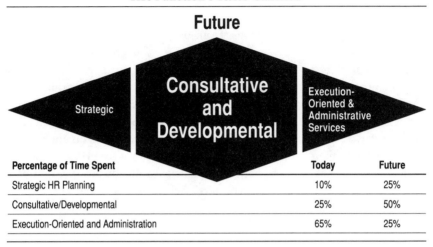

Percentage of Time Spent	Today	Future
Strategic HR Planning	10%	25%
Consultative/Developmental	25%	50%
Execution-Oriented and Administration	65%	25%

People Acquisition and Development

This comprises competency definition and development; strategic staffing planning; education and training; individual performance management and coaching; and succession planning.

Organization Design and Development

In this area we are involved with organization design and change process management; shaping the work environment to encourage desired behaviors; and designing and managing pay, benefits, and policies.

Administration of People Policies, Programs, and Practices

This covers personnel administration, staffing support, compensation and benefits administration, and HR information services.

HR'S ROLE AS CONFIDANT AND ADVISOR

I want to close with an issue that's sensitive to everyone in our profession: the role of being the confidant and senior advisor to the senior executive you support. If we're tying the value of HR to the accomplishment of business objectives, our relationship with senior management—and particularly the senior executive—is an absolute requirement and a source of strength for the organization.

There is no question that people from other functions can and do assist in advising senior executives on a wide range of people issues, including specific assignments; but it is critical that the experience, knowledge, and thought processes used by HR professionals in making key personnel recommendations be perceived by management *as adding value*. This delicate and often personal role is neither readily quantifiable nor highly visible, but it clearly has a significant impact on the performance of the organization.

The true competency in this role is knowing not only HR *and* the organization's business strategy, but being able to skillfully advance and balance the interests of HR's "customers" while maintaining the ethical requirements of the profession.

WHO WANTS JUST TO SURVIVE?

As for the future, it is possible that some HR functions will survive if for no other reason than to do the HR basics I listed earlier.

But who wants just to survive?

It is my strong belief that our corporate organizational entities need and deserve so much more from our function, and that a well-run and focused HR shop offers considerable value in achieving business goals. The bottom line for our function is to make a direct contribution to the profitability of the corporation. That's exactly what an effective HR group will help our organizations do—now and well into the future!

CHAPTER 15

HUMAN RESOURCES' FUTURE ON THE WAY TO A PRESENCE

WAYNE BROCKBANK

The business context within which human resource (HR) departments function is mandating new agendas, activities, and results. Emerging contextual factors such as information technology and globalization require that HR assume new agendas and practices. In this chapter, these contextual factors will be examined; the emerging focal agendas of HR will be discussed; and the emerging list of HR practices will be briefly reviewed.

EMERGING CONTEXTS

The radical changes in the environment context have been well documented (Drucker, 1995; Goldman, Nagel, & Preiss, 1995; Hamel & Prahalad, 1994; Stacey, 1992). The future context of business will be characterized by greater numbers of competitors, customer consolidation, consolidation of stock ownership, undersupply of skilled labor, increasingly interdependent process technologies, multifunctional product technologies, a large service sector, and lower customer-based switching costs. Each of these will have implications for future HR agendas and practices. The two emerging contextual factors which will have the greatest influence on the conceptualization and execution of HR agendas, however, are information technology and globalization.

Information Technology

Rapidly emerging information technology has enabled the gathering, consolidating, and disseminating of information as never before, thereby making possible the involvement in decision making of individuals who are closest to the work itself (D'Aveni, 1994). To obtain the benefits of such information, dispersion companies must train individuals in utilizing information in decision making, provide incentives for their involvement in decision making, and formally authorize their involvement in decision making. Well-informed, well-trained, and properly motivated workers allow spans of control to be expanded and layers of management to be reduced. Companies may thus reap the benefits of lower management costs and more responsive and informed decision making.

Globalization

As a function of reduced transportation and information costs and of the removal of social and political barriers, the globalization of business is proceeding at unprecedented and unexpected rates. The opening up of markets and competitors in countries such as China, Russia, and India places competitive pressures on virtually every major industry. Four implications for HR may be delineated. *First,* both the criteria and intensiveness of competition are changing as a result of globalization. Cost pressures increase along with demands for greater speed, quality, and innovation. Faced with this competitive environment, companies are asking their employees for more time, more commitment, and greater intensity. *Second,* as the labor force becomes increasingly global, pressures mount for greater adaptation to and accommodation for local conditions. Concurrently, many employees in the emerging competitive countries are accustomed to considerable government protection and to locally defined competitive criteria. HR must tailor its policies and practices to local conditions while at the same time modifying the mindset and technical skills of local employees to world class standards. *Third,* the identification and development of leaders who are capable of functioning on a global scale and with a global perspective become a critical issue. While the dimensions of effective global leadership may reflect those of effective domestic leadership, their relative importance and operational application vary substantially. Knowledge of effective global leadership pales in comparison to knowledge of effective domestic leadership. The depth of a firm's global leadership capability is emerging as a major enabler of global growth (Prahalad & Doz, 1987). *Fourth,* one important criterion for the functioning of global leaders is achieving optimal organizational synergy. In the same vein, it is also HR's responsibility to design HR processes which encourage the organizational functioning so that the "global whole" is greater than the sum of the parts (Egelhoff, 1988). HR is in the early phases of its ability to conceptualize and impact this agenda.

Emerging Agendas

The emerging contextual conditions of business will create pressures for HR to add greater strategic value. Emerging HR agendas embody the strategic intent for the HR function and differ from HR practices in several important ways. Agendas are long term, have broad impact, and set the criteria for practices; HR practices, on the other hand, tend to be short-term, relatively narrow, and designed within the conceptual logic of the HR agenda. Several of the emerging agendas which will reflect a more strategic perspective of HR are as follow.

Earning a Place at the Table

Before strategic HR agendas can be brought to the strategy table, senior management has to perceive that HR has "earned a place at the table." Earning that place at the table is a function of many factors including the following: knowing the strategy, culture, vocabulary, and operating issues of the business; having passion for issues which add greatest value to external customers and shareholders; and focusing on financial results. Earning a place at the table also requires a track record of keeping the HR house in order. As HR assumes the more strategic role of creating sustained competitive advantage, it must first ensure that tactical HR activities are fully aligned with the short-term business strategies and that the tactical activities are completed with fewer resources but at higher quality levels. In providing short term tactical support, HR must ensure that: (1) the right people are being hired, promoted, transferred, and fired; (2) measures and rewards are aligned with short term business results; and (3) individual employees have the technical knowledge to achieve short term objectives.

Conceptualizing the Value of People

HR must ensure that senior management has grasped the idea that people are the critical and ultimate source of competitive advantage. In a competitive, changing market environment, executives are quickly learning that the human side of the business can be their best friend or their worst enemy—depending on how the human and organizational issues are managed. We live in an era in which technologies and strategies can be imminently replicated; infrastructure capacity can be transferred; and switching costs are continually decreasing. Under such conditions, competitive advantage resides in a human organization which can (1) develop new technologies; (2) implement strategies more quickly, more efficiently, and more accurately; (3) improve operating technologies; and (4) constantly adjust to customers changing buying habits. Some companies are just now discovering and formalizing the value of the human asset. These companies are probably a generation behind in their management, though, as leading companies have already embraced the centrality of people as competitive advantage and are aggressively utilizing the management and HR partnership in identifying and creating the technical and cultural capabilities which their people must have to win in the marketplace.

Framing HR Strategy

In the future, HR departments will have to have an explicit, well-framed, and well-argued point of view; that is, they will have addressed the fundamental question of "What is the purpose of HR?" As rudimentary as this question may seem, most HR departments do not have an answer and, as a result, often lack a clear definition of what the members of the department are jointly trying to do. One exercise which may underscore the importance of this issue is to pose this question at the next HR staff meeting— "What is the purpose of HR?" Have each individual write down her/his answer. Compare the answers and discuss the implications. Each functional area within HR will probably have its respective individual purposes, but the department as a whole will not. If HR as a whole is unclear about its purpose, what can be expected from the rest of the company about the purpose of HR?

In developing a departmental point of view, the following criteria should be met. (1) Is it formally stated or is it ad hoc and assumed? (2) Does it create the short term technical knowledge and skills as well as the culture which is necessary to win over the long run? (3) Does it comprehensively cover the whole organization thereby encouraging the corporate whole to be greater than the sum of the parts? (4) Does it serve to integrate the various subfunctions within HR around commonly accepted principles or purposes? (5) Is it clearly linked to issues which are critical to long term corporate success including the present and future concerns of external customers and major shareholders? (6) Does it create explicit and measurable results?

Framing Business Strategy

Over the past few years, a dominant paradigm in strategic thinking has been the concept of core competence (Hamel & Prahalad, 1994). The core competence of the firm is what the firm does best (given that what the firm does best is consistent with what customers want most). As an example, Hamel and Prahalad cite the ability of Honda to design and manufacture internal combustion engines. The problem with framing core competence in terms of what the firm does best is that it condemns a firm's strategic thinking to a short term time perspective. The logic for this conclusion is as follows. What a firm does is based on what a firm knows. By framing core competence in terms of what a firm does, and what a firm does is based on what it knows, and given that the life-span of knowledge is shrinking, core competence logic might channel strategic thinking into short time frames. Nevertheless, core competence framework is robustly useful. The key core competence, however, is not what a firm does based on what is known but is, rather, a firm having a culture which encourages flexibility, change, learning, creativity, and adaptability to customers. When reframed in this manner, the key issue is *not core technical competencies* but rather *core cultural competencies*. Given that a major responsibility of HR is defining and creating a competitive business culture, HR is at the heart of the leading paradigm in strategic thinking (Brockbank, 1995). The conclusion of this logic is that HR has an important role to play in the formulation of business strategy. To the strategy planning table, finance brings the available financial resources; the engineering department brings the available technological options; information systems folks bring internal information resources; and marketing brings customer information resources. To the strategy planning table, HR should bring the inventory of technical knowledge and skills and, perhaps more important, an inventory of the firm's cultural strengths and weaknesses. HR should also bring a method for identifying the culture that the company needs to optimize market opportunities and a logic for creating the required competitive culture.

These two agendas are finding their way into the management paradigm of several well-managed firms such as American Express, Levi-Strauss, Disney, and Texas Instruments. Senior executives are recognizing that the managing by culture agenda has two directions of causality. They recognize that a culture must be created which is consistent with the business strategy, but they also recognize the value of creating a broadly and powerfully defined culture which is (1) strongly customer focused and (2) capable of leap-frogging the competition through continual and radical innovation. Having such a culture at their disposal creates strategic alternatives which would not otherwise be available. Thus HR becomes a major contributor to maximizing the firm's available strategic options.

Promoting Growth

During the past decade, many HR departments became highly skilled at downsizing and at other expressions of cost cutting. Undoubtedly these skills will continue to be required as HR fine-tunes its ability to create more strategically aligned work forces and as economic downturns again occur. The challenge which many companies are now embracing is top line growth. This poses new challenges for which many HR departments are less prepared.

The first step is to identify what is meant by growth: top line, bottom line, or market share. Most companies tend to define growth as some or all of the foregoing. Once growth is clearly defined, then the avenues of growth can be identified with accompanying cultural characteristics and avenues for creating these characteristics.

Four general avenues of growth may be delineated (Gertz & Baptista, 1995). *First,* firms may grow within existing markets and with existing products either by buying the competition or by taking revenues away from the competition. Revenues may be taken from the competition by lowering costs, improving service or convenience, shortening delivery times, or improving product quality. HR's capacity to create business cultures through which these revenue-enhancing strategies are implemented can be a major source of competitive advantage. If a firm purchases a competitor, the HR challenge is to identify the culture which is required for both the acquiring firm and the acquired firm to be successful and to create unity in and between both firms on the basis of the culture in which both need to succeed. The *second* avenue of growth is through existing products but within new markets (including global markets). The role of HR facilitating growth through this avenue, especially on a global scale is essential. Selecting the right local leadership, balancing local and corporate demands, and integrating the local units into a global entity—all are critical for success. *Third,* firms may also grow through new products within existing markets. The key to success in this avenue of growth is the creation of a business culture which emphasizes radical innovation as well as disciplined continuous improvement. The *fourth* avenue for growth is through new products and new markets. The HR role in this growth avenue is a combination of the above second and third categories.

Responding to the Shareholders and Board Members

An emerging HR agenda will be the responsibility of senior HR executives in building and maintaining credible relationships with key shareholders and board members. Since 1986 there has been a marked trend toward consolidation of stock ownership in publicly traded firms. This trend is the result of substantial growth in baby boomers' investments through pension funds and mutual funds (*BusinessWeek*, March 15, 1993). Since baby boomers generally will not be taking money out of the financial markets until they begin to retire, the traditional short term focus of investment fund managers is changing so that they are not interested only in short term returns but also in long term performance. These "relational investors" are asking a new set of questions of senior management including the senior HR executive. What is the logic and process of your succession planning? Are incentive packages of senior executives linked to long term performance? What is the depth of the management team? Do you have the technological and cultural infrastructures which will allow the firm to compete over the long run? As a result of these directions of inquiry, HR executives find that they are spending more time with the senior line executive, with the board of directors, and occasionally with key shareholders discussing these and related questions.

EMERGING PRACTICES

As can be seen from the above discussion, the major component of the emerging HR agendas is the creation of the cultural mindset and technical competencies which are capable of winning in market place. A key challenge for HR is, therefore, to ensure that all of the practices which influence the technical and cultural capabilities of the firm are functioning in an integrated, focused, and mutually reinforcing manner. This challenge clearly expands the set of traditional HR practices. As these practices are reviewed, it will be clear that some are directly controlled by HR whereas others are only indirectly influenced by HR.

Those practices which generally are under the direct control of HR include the following: staffing practices including recruitment, promotions, transfers, and outplacement; performance management including measurement, and monetary and non-monetary rewards; and individual learning including formalized classroom training, on-the-job training, and ancillary developmental activities.

In addition to these traditional areas of HR involvement, other practices may have important influence on the human organization which HR may only indirectly influence. These areas include the following: structural concerns such as organization design, reengineering, job design, and the physical setting; practices which influence institution level learning such as external benchmarking, comprehensive customer contact programs, systemic internal communications, and information system design; and leadership decisions and actions which are held up to self-generated standards of consistency and integrity. It is HR's responsibility to ensure that *all* of these practices are integrated and aligned as they influence the creation of the ideal human organization. It is beyond the scope of this chapter to describe the developments in each of these areas of present and future HR practices. Suffice it to say that compelling and powerful developments are occurring in the design and delivery of these broadly defined HR practices. This is especially compelling as these practices are designed within the perspective of the emerging HR agendas.

CONCLUSION

In summary, the challenge for the HR professional is threefold: *first,* examine and understand the context which drives business realities; *second,* design critical, high value-added agendas; and *third,* ensure that broadly defined HR practices are exactly aligned and unified around these agendas. As these develop, HR will contribute a more strategic and high value-added presence as firms compete in increasingly complex and changing contextual conditions.

REFERENCES

Brockbank, W. (1995). *Logic and conflict in corporate values.* Paper presented at the Third International Conference on Social Values. Oxford University. Oxford, England.

BusinessWeek. (1993). Relationship investing. March 15.

D'Aveni, R.A. (1994). Hyper-competition. New York: Free Press.

Drucker, P. (1995). *Managing in a time of change.* New York: Penguin Books.

Egelhoff, W.G. (1988). *Organizing the multinational enterprise.* Cambridge, MA: Ballinger.

Gertz, D.L., & Baptista, J. (1995). *Grow to be great: Breaking the downsizing cycle.* New York: Free Press.

Goldman, S.L., Nagel, R.N., & Preiss, K. (1995). *Agile competitors and virtual organizations.* New York: Van Nostrand Reinhold.

Hamel, G., & Prahalad, C.K. (1994). *Competing for the future.* Boston: Harvard Business School Press.

Prahalad, C.K., & Doz, Y.L. (1987). *The multi-national mission.* New York: Free Press.

Stacey, R.D. (1992). *Managing the unknowable.* San Francisco: Jossey-Bass.

CHAPTER 16

HUMAN RESOURCE MANAGEMENT: A CHANGING SCRIPT FOR A CHANGING WORLD

CLIFFORD J. EHRLICH

$\mathbf{W}$e in human resources have been called by a variety of names over the years, including personnel, industrial relations, and now human resource management. To draw a bead on where our function might be headed, it is instructive to look at the factors that have shaped it, how it has evolved, and where it is today.

For purposes of this chapter, references made to "employee management" and "effective management of employees" are intended to encompass the type of leadership that inspires people, draws on their talents, encourages their participation in business decisions, and recognizes their needs.

THE CHANGING IMPORTANCE OF EMPLOYEES IN THE EYES OF MANAGEMENT

It is apparent from examining business history that the most significant influence on the role of HR has been the degree of importance business leaders have attributed to employee management in seeing their companies succeed. HR has both influenced and reflected their views, and their perception has changed substantially over time.

The great contribution of America's earliest industrial leaders was the efficient system of mass production they created. Employee muscle made those systems work, and employees were expected to adapt to how those systems were designed. In fact, employees generally were seen and treated as extensions of the assembly lines on which they worked.

This view of employees as labor persisted for decades. Since it was the experience of business that the proper use of financial resources and the creation of attractive products were the primary ingredients of success, employee considerations easily could be pushed into the background; labor was an abundant resource. If a company managed its employees poorly, the worst thing likely to occur was that they were unhappy, joined unions, were marginally efficient, or turned over at a higher-than-normal rate. Such an environment might be unpleasant, but it didn't endanger a company's existence.

It is against this backdrop that a series of influences began to elevate the importance placed on the effective management of employees.

One influence was behavioral research done by companies such as Western Electric at its Hawthorne Plant and by academics such as Douglas McGregor (1960) with Theory X and Theory Y and Abraham Maslow (1943) with the hierarchy of needs. Their work challenged many assumptions about people in a work environment, and the theories of human motivation that evolved provided management with new insights on how to tap human potential and manage people more skillfully.

A second influence has been the rise of the service industry. The founders of companies that emphasized service—people like J. Willard Marriott and Thomas Watson—realized that it was difficult for customers to distinguish an intangible service product from the employees who provided it. These founders understood the importance of creating a different relationship with their employees than the more impersonal one that existed in manufacturing operations. They held the opinion that business success depended on employees being treated well, feeling appreciated, and conveying that appreciation to the customers they served. Their outlook challenged the historical view that the interests of labor and capital had to conflict with one another.

A third influence has been global competition that caused the quality expectations of customers to skyrocket and gave rise to the principle of continuous improvement. As employers responded to the challenge, it became apparent to them that the people who actually produced their products and services were well qualified to redesign and improve them. Work teams and other methods of collaboration gained popularity from the outstanding results they achieved in company after company.

A fourth influence has been the rise in importance of knowledge workers whose intellectual capital makes it relatively easy for them to move their value-creating capacity from employer to employer. Their freedom of movement makes them far less likely to remain in a work environment that is not employee-friendly; employers needing their services have had to respond.

A fifth influence has been the proliferation of legislation that regulates so many facets of the employment relationship. When these laws are combined with the erosion that has taken place in the doctrine of "employment at will," employers who deal callously with employees find they do so at their financial peril.

The effect of these influences has been to elevate the importance placed on employee management in creating world-class companies. Writing in the *Wall Street Journal* on June 21, 1994, Jack Welch of General Electric said:

> . . . The best companies now know without a doubt where productivity— real and limitless productivity—comes from. It comes from challenged, empowered, excited, rewarded teams of people. It comes from engaging every single mind in the organization, making everyone part of the action, and allowing everyone to have a voice—a role—in the success of the enterprise. Doing so raises productivity not incrementally but by multiples. . . . (p. A22)

As the value of inspired employees has become more clear, the long-standing notion that employees must adapt to the workplace is being replaced by the belief that the workplace should begin to adapt to employees. The increasing popularity of work-life programs during the past five years is a testament to this new emphasis and demonstrates that a genuine transformation is underway in the attitudes of business leaders toward employees and their work environment.

REWRITING THE SCRIPT FOR HUMAN RESOURCE MANAGEMENT

Given this evolution in the importance placed on employee management in achieving business success, what has been happening to the human resource (HR) function? It, too, has evolved.

Originally created as an employment function, the responsibilities of HR have grown in response to employment legislation and the requirements of effective employee management.

Throughout much of its existence, however, management's expectation of Human Resources has been primarily administrative. HR contributions could be described as providing control, compliance, and consistency. What resulted was a tendency for HR to be valued for what it *prevented* from happening—union drives, strikes, staffing vacancies, discrimination charges, Fair Labor Standards Act violations—rather than for what it *caused* to happen.

The increased importance placed on the effective management of employees in world-class companies, however, has redefined that role. It continues to be necessary for HR to provide control, compliance, and consistency when they are appropriate, but they are no longer the extent of HR's role. The challenges faced by employers also require HR to be flexible, resourceful, and creative. On some occasions, all these qualities may be required simultaneously.

An example of this involves Marriott's job grading system. For years, each of the five strategic business units (SBUs) in that company's Lodging Group maintained separate practices and policies that fit its individual needs. In an effort to deal more effectively with customers and to reduce escalating administrative costs, Lodging adopted a market management-brand management matrix organization and eliminated the SBUs.

The new Market Managers became responsible for all the brands (e.g., Marriott Hotels, Courtyard, Residence Inn, Fairfield Inn) within their geographic area. Soon after the change, a number of new issues began to emerge. One was the resistance of unit managers to transferring from a job in one brand to a job having a lower salary grade in another brand. The appearance of being demoted discouraged people from accepting the transfer even though it did not involve a reduction in pay and the developmental benefits were obvious. It was apparent that a new way of assigning pay levels to jobs had to be created.

A team of line managers and Human Resource staff was created to deal with this issue. This group eventually was attracted to the idea of career banding, an evolving concept where jobs are assigned to broad bands rather than to narrow grades. This approach enabled jobs to be assigned pay levels in a manner that facilitated the movement of managers from brand to brand.

The new system was possible because both line managers and the HR staff were willing to jettison a well-established job grading system that imposed an artificial hurdle to the objective of developing managers with multibrand experience. While their approach demonstrated flexibility and creativity, the new system still had to be administered and controlled in an orderly and consistent manner. In other words, the HR organization had to be versatile enough to demonstrate the characteristics of both its new role and its old role in addressing this issue.

PRINCIPLES FOR CREATING VALUE IN HUMAN RESOURCE MANAGEMENT

The trajectory of change facing all businesses represents a challenge to the Human Resource Management function. Based on my experience and what I anticipate the future holds for my profession, I believe the ability of HR

Table 16.1
Principles for Building the Future

#1 Human resource strategy must be anchored to the business strategy.

#2 Human resource management is not about programs; it's about relationships.

#3 The Human Resource Department must be known as an organization that antici-
pates change and understands what is necessary to implement it.

#4 Human Resources should be an outspoken advocate of employee interests, yet it
must understand that business decisions have to balance a range of factors that often
conflict with one another.

#5 The effectiveness of HR depends on its staying focused on issues rather than
personalities.

#6 Human resource executives must accept that constant learning and skill enhance-
ment are essential to their being a contributor to the business.

---

leaders to adapt and contribute will be enhanced if they focus on six principles (see Table 16.1).

Principle 1: Human Resource Strategy Must Be Anchored to the Business Strategy

The HR organization must understand the strategy and economic realities
of the business it supports. It must be regarded as an essential contributor
to the business mission. Human resource people must speak the language
of the business and their activities must reflect the priorities of the business.

Nothing contributes more to the credibility of the Human Resource
Department than for it to be focused on matters of genuine concern to the
business. If it is not, it creates the opportunity for its opinion to be disre-
garded and its contribution to be minimized or even eliminated.

Wanting to ensure its alignment with business strategy, the corporate
human resources department in Marriott recently undertook the unique
approach of producing a comprehensive list of the products it produces. In
doing so, its challenge was to think beyond day-to-day activities to the finished products its customers receive, such as settled discrimination charges
or relocated employees. The production of this list required the staff to
view its work in nontraditional ways and to develop a greater awareness of
the costs associated with each product.

When it was completed, the list was presented to each of the company's
business units for review and evaluation. After making a few minor adjustments, an agreement was reached that the products supported the business

strategy. The result was the reassurance of knowing that HR activities in Marriott were valued and were anchored to the priorities of the company.

Principle 2: Human Resource Management Is Not about Programs; It's about Relationships

The primary HR role is to create an environment in which employees are committed to the success of the enterprise that employs them. It's about developing forms of attachment with people that make them want to work there and contribute willingly.

It involves using work teams and establishing peer review systems that provide employees with a meaningful voice in decisions that affect them. It involves engaging employees in the change process and giving them a voice in shaping their future since experience shows that people support what they help create.

Creating effective relationships includes providing employees with opportunities to acquire new skills which increase their capacity to contribute. It means providing the reward and recognition that convey the importance of their contributions and an appreciation of their efforts. It also means building the sense of community that arises when people work with others they admire and respect.

Principle 3: The Human Resource Department Must Be Known as an Organization That Anticipates Change and Understands What Is Necessary to Implement It

The HR function must understand the process of change. It must work closely with managers who are leading change and assist those who must implement change but seem reluctant to do so.

HR can help managers appreciate that people do not resist change as much as they resist both *being* changed and the top-down approach often used to introduce change. HR should help managers understand that involving employees in the change process energizes them, draws on their know-how, and helps produce a sound result. HR people should be viewed as thoughtful and enthusiastic advocates of the changes and new ideas that contribute to the success of the business.

A trap to be avoided is the one of being a self-appointed change agent. Individuals in HR who attempt to impose their ideas of how an organization should change undermine themselves as well as the organization they are attempting to serve. They may be well-intentioned, but they are traveling a risky and divisive path. On the other hand, an essential role of the HR executive is to work with top executives to help them determine what changes are needed and how they can be implemented effectively. Leaders need the collaboration of someone having no personal agenda as they sort out the change priorities of their business. The role of the HR executive is well suited to make that contribution.

Principle 4: Human Resource People Should Be an Outspoken Advocate of Employee Interests, Yet They Must Understand That Business Decisions Have to Balance a Range of Factors That Often Conflict with One Another

HR must provide a thoughtful, objective, and realistic assessment of the human resource aspects of pending decisions to help ensure that the best conclusion is reached. Since sound business decisions balance a series of factors that typically conflict with one another, the HR role is not to win arguments but to ensure that human resource issues are given the attention they deserve.

The impact of decisions on employees almost certainly will be overlooked unless HR puts a spotlight on it. A failure to provide this perspective does a serious disservice to decision makers as well as to the people who will be affected by the decision. It is an uncomfortable role in situations where the decision-making process is moving rapidly, but the willingness of HR to do it even under hostile circumstances helps establish the valuable reputation that it is principled rather than partisan.

Principle 5: The Effectiveness of HR Depends on Its Staying Focused on Issues Rather than on Personalities

Much rancor and hard feeling can be avoided by keeping issues rather than individuals the topic of discussion. Regardless of how one may feel, it is less argumentative to say "We would have been a more effective team if Finance had explained before the meeting it was opposed to the salary proposal" than "When Finance torpedoed my salary proposal, it really drew a line in the sand."

Similarly, it's valuable to learn to disagree without being disagreeable. A recommendation made by a colleague that has negative human resource consequences can simply be opposed or it can be acknowledged and countered with other recommendations which accomplish the same objective but don't have the negative aftermath. In addition, if ideas presented during a discussion are not labelled as to their source (e.g., What do you think of Bill's idea?), they can be discussed more objectively and evaluated more easily in reaching the best solution. During this process, it's particularly important to stay open-minded because invariably there's more than one good solution to a business issue.

Principle 6: Human Resource Executives Must Accept That Constant Learning and Skill Enhancement Are Essential to Their Being a Contributor to the Business

The speed of change makes the half-life of much business knowledge so short that constant learning and skill enhancement are necessary. The competencies required of effective human resource executives include not only functional expertise (compensation, management development, etc.), but also business knowledge, financial understanding, consulting skills, and interpersonal skills. People in HR positions must continuously expand their know-how and avoid the mistake of carrying old skills, notions, and styles nostalgically forward.

HR must lead the discovery of new ways for mobilizing the talents and energies of employees so they are able to contribute more. HR must promote the idea that for people to be effective as employees, they have to be managed effectively as people.

CONCLUSION

It seems apparent that the management of employees has made its way onto the list of issues that are vital to the success of any company. The opportunity exists for the Human Resource organization to demonstrate beyond a doubt that it is equipped to take the lead in integrating this reality into how the organization behaves.

REFERENCES

Maslow, A. (1943). A theory of human motivation. *Psychological Review,* July, 370–397.

McGregor, D. (1960). *The human side of enterprise.* New York: McGraw-Hill.

Welch, J. (1994). A look at productivity. *Wall Street Journal,* June 21.

CHAPTER 17

LEADERSHIP DEVELOPMENT IN THE FUTURE: THE IMPACT OF NEW TECHNOLOGY

MARSHALL GOLDSMITH

The danger of writing on the impact of new technology is that the information will be obsolete before it is published. Having had the opportunity to work with many leaders in the field of applying technology in training and development, I can provide educated speculation based on current projections of technological advancement. The real breakthroughs will probably occur in ways that no one has yet imagined. Please accept this chapter as an "educated guess" based on input from the experts of today. As with most writing about the future, it will be amusing to review this piece in 10 to 20 years to see how closely it parallels the new reality.

Before the year 2000, massively available, "instant download" audiovisual programs of television quality (in terms of both picture and sound) will be available over the Internet (or Intranet). This technological advancement will change the world. Most leading hardware, software, telecommunications, and cable companies clearly understand the importance of this advancement and will invest billions of dollars in the attempt to "get there first."

The advent of massively available, "instant download," television quality, audiovisual will result in a *technological plateau*. For most people in the world, television quality audio and video are "good enough." For example, my television is eight years old. Since I am connected to the cable, the reception seems fine. The additional quality produced by a new television (if there is any) is not worth the investment to me. The huge majority of television owners feel the same way. A *technological plateau* lasts until a major breakthrough occurs that produces a superior product at a reasonable price.

When instant download Internet television is massively available, there will be a major shift in focus. Instead of investing billions in technology to improve download time or reception quality, companies will invest billions to acquire and develop *content*. Investors with foresight (such as Ted Turner and Bill Gates) have already begun to make huge acquisitions of content to meet the projected demand. The level of interest in all kinds of training and development content will soar.

This new technology and content boom will radically change leadership development. As much as we all like to pretend to be "literate," most leaders do not spend much time reading. Both Peter Drucker and Peter Senge have speculated that only a small percentage of the people who buy books actually *read* their books, however, we almost all understand television. The average person in the "developed" world has spent literally thousands of hours in front of a television. (This is especially true in the United States.) We have acquired a near addiction to high-impact video and sound. The Internet (or Intranet) will provide the medium to make interesting, high-impact audiovisual leadership development available on demand.

How might the new leadership development technology work? Let's assume that Kelly Jones is an executive in the XYZ Corporation in the year 2017. What are some options that Kelly might have available?

To begin with, Kelly will have on-line access to a Leadership Inventory that lists the desired attitudes, behaviors, and competencies for an executive in her position in the XYZ Corporation. She will be able to complete a self-assessment on-line and then record the names of all key stakeholders who will be in a position to provide her with 360° feedback. A confidentiality-coded Leadership Inventory will appear on each stakeholder's computer. After stakeholders complete their feedback for Kelly, she will instantly receive a complete 360°, on-line summary report. An analysis will be made of her perceived strengths and areas for improvement. Let's say Kelly learns that she needs to be a better listener and do a more effective job in providing performance feedback. A menu of video suggestions will appear. Kelly will punch a button, and the world's expert on listening will provide a brief audiovisual tutorial. Text-based suggestions on listening and a reading list will be available. Books on the topic can be ordered instantly on-line. She will push a second button and receive guidance on providing feedback. Since the feedback process may involve company-specific performance appraisals, she will push a third button and see an internally-developed video clip review on how to make the XYZ system work most effectively.

Kelly has greatly appreciated her Leadership Inventory feedback and the efficiently designed audiovisual suggestions, but she still wants some more help. She has some specific questions to ask and wants to interact with a real human being. She pushes another button. A menu appears with the names and biographies of coaches who specialize in various aspects of leadership development. She studies the backgrounds of potential coaches and makes a decision. The coach's schedule appears on-line. After reviewing her calendar, she automatically schedules an on-line appointment. The coach (through two-way video) appears on-line at the appointed time. Kelly and the coach have an hour-long discussion. She develops a very specific action plan for improvement and agrees to respond to her feedback with key stakeholders.

Kelly's key stakeholders live in a variety of locations around the world. Some are members of the XYZ Corporation but many are external customers, suppliers, and business partners. All are connected on-line. Kelly has the clearance to access calendars and schedule on-line appointments. She schedules brief on-line, two-way video appointments with each stakeholder to discuss the results of her leadership inventory feedback and her plans for personal improvement. She has a series of very positive dialogues with each key stakeholder and picks up some more specific ideas for change. Within four months, she will automatically receive a progress report from each key stakeholder describing her increase in effectiveness in her two areas for improvement.

One of the four global project teams that Kelly is leading is almost finished with its assignment. Kelly reviews an on-line menu describing potential projects that could be available in the near future. She reviews her previous assignments and concludes that more experience on a marketing project is critical to her future development as an XYZ executive. She makes on-line contact with her mentor (who lives in another country). Kelly's mentor provides input, and Kelly's next project is selected. Kelly would like some guidance on managing a global marketing project in her industry. She calls up a menu and selects a custom tape made by the world's authority on the topic. She also schedules video appointments with two associates who have a great track record in this area.

One of Kelly's greatest challenges is continuous education. The world in 2017 is changing so rapidly that Kelly must devote at least 25 percent of her time to learning. Since the Internet is now providing more educational opportunities than she can ever use, Kelly has an intelligent personalized editor to help her find out which educational opportunities are most likely to fit her unique needs. Each morning her editor makes an on-line report of the most interesting potential learning opportunities that are available on the Internet. She has the opportunity to review an edited analysis of the latest information impacting her company, suppliers, customers, and business partners.

Action learning (which began to be widely used in the late 1990s) is now a major tool for both individual and organizational learning. Kelly has a weekly on-line video meeting with her action-learning team. The team has eight members and includes representatives from various functions and geographies. The team is sponsored by an executive vice president who helps ensure that the action-learning projects are beneficial for both: (1) addressing major corporate issues and (2) providing developmental opportunities for all team members. Action-learning team recommendations are written and edited on-line. The team gets on-going on-line feedback from key executives on the viability of their suggestions.

As part of her ongoing leadership development, Kelly likes to combine business with pleasure. She connects with friends on-line and participates in business simulation competitions. The simulations are fun and exciting and also help prepare her for real-life situations that she may have to face in the future.

One day, while studying corporate history on the Internet, Kelly reviewed the history of leadership development. She was amused to learn about the incredibly inefficient way that things were done near the end of the twentieth century. Companies actually went to the expense of flying leaders from around the world to sit in classrooms (sometimes for days on end)! The poor leaders had to stay awake while speaker after speaker gave them more information than anyone could possibly remember. Participants were given large, "clunky" binders filled with paper to drag home. No one ever even measured whether anyone even changed as a result of the process!

Kelly was amazed. No wonder the leaders of the past seemed so backward! She probably learned more relevant information at her desk in a week than they picked up in a year.

Will the example of Kelly in 2017 prove to be accurate? I hope not! I believe, however, that it is eminently possible that the "Kelly story" will become more fact than fiction in the next ten years. Organizations that lead the way in the implementation of new technology for leadership development may well have a huge competitive advantage in the twenty-first century.

CHAPTER 18

THE FUTURE OF HUMAN RESOURCES: PLUS CA CHANGE, PLUS C'EST LA MEME CHOSE[1]

STEVEN KERR and MARY ANN VON GLINOW

$\mathbf{P}$robably in counterpoint to most of the other chapters, we predict that the future of human resources (HR) will, to a surprising degree, resemble its past. We discuss a number of activities that were historically part of HR but in recent years have been outsourced, insourced, or just ignored. In fact, the *need* for these tasks to be done well continues unabated, and we predict that as this becomes more obvious, and as it becomes clear that many organizations are not accomplishing these tasks via other means, HR will once again be asked to perform them.

As a starting point, consider the following topics, taken from a bestselling book on HR administration. Included in its Table of Contents are:

- Employee motivation; personal vs. organizational goals.
- Organizational careers.
- Job fatigue; "pathological" organizational behavior.
- The changing role of the working supervisor.
- Sharing decision making with subordinates.
- Sharing management authority with unions, customers, suppliers, and other external organizations.
- Job and institutional consequences of technological change.
- Cross-cultural comparisons.
- The need for organizational social responsibility.

You probably find this selection of topics unsurprising, possibly reflecting your own sense of mainstream issues and acute current problems. However, the HR in the title stands for human relations, not human resources, and the book was published *thirty-five years ago!*

Our point is that, whatever the justification for predicting a future for HR that is very different from its past, it mustn't rest on the assumption that the roles traditionally assigned to HR no longer need to be performed. Most of them *do* need to be performed, if not by HR then by someone, because the costs of not performing them are significant.

EMPHASIS ON EMPLOYEE LOYALTY

Organizations once depended greatly upon employee loyalty. This construct has been defined in various ways but, for our purposes, may be thought of as productive efforts (employee contributions) that go beyond what the organization has the right to expect for what it is paying (including both financial and nonfinancial inducements). In prosperous times, organizations have the resources to create a balance between inducements and contributions, and employee loyalty may not be required. Because times are not always prosperous, however, one of the most important functions of HR/Personnel departments has always been to help devise reward systems and work environments that foster, recognize, and reward employee loyalty. Starting in the 1950s, a host of tools—including management by objectives (MBO), job enrichment, transactional analysis, sensitivity training, and the Managerial Grid, to name but a few—have been employed by HR for this purpose.

Today the attitude toward loyalty in many firms is different, as exemplified by the (highly publicized, possibly apocryphal) remark attributed to one senior executive: "If you want loyalty, buy a dog." Today, although many organizations have taken to calling their employees "internal customers," their mission statements and employment practices clearly signify that they consider their true customers to be external, with payments to employees considered as little more than costs of doing business. Although the *intent* of such cost-reducing initiatives as delayering and downsizing may not be to reduce the loyalty, commitment, and identification with the firm of those who remain, it is clear that these qualities often suffer as a result.

This is especially likely when cost reduction initiatives are driven by brawn rather than brains. An example of a brainy approach stems from the work of Hammer and Champy (cf., 1993), whereby organizations are first reengineered according to what makes sense for the business, then savings in headcount and other resources often follow. Rather than taking this approach however, many organizations begin the change process by taking out some arbitrary number of heads and only then begin to wonder how they can continue to do business without sacrificing customer service or quality.

Sometimes, when downsizing follows a thoughtful process of reengineering, the resultant improvement in systems and processes enables employees to "work smarter, not harder." Even in such cases, however, and nearly always when downsizing is by brawn rather than brains, remaining employees soon realize that they are expected to work many more hours than they did previously, with little, if any, increase in their level of compensation.

Paradoxically, at the same time many organizations are claiming to be less and less in need of employee loyalty, initiatives are being undertaken that make them *more* dependent upon loyalty—employee contributions in excess of inducements—than before. As this paradox becomes more evident, *we predict that HR will once again be asked to take on the responsibility for devising reward systems and working environments that foster and encourage employee loyalty.*

OUTSOURCING AND CONTRACT WORKERS

Once employee loyalty is officially designated as not worth caring about, more and more organizations are concluding from their cost-benefit equation that outsourcing of work makes considerable sense. It is not by accident that America's largest employer of new high school graduates is not, as many people might suppose, IBM, GM, or GE, but Manpower Inc.; however, organizations might do well to include in their calculations some lessons already learned—often the hard way—about the limitations of parcelling out one's problems to others. For example, a business unit that is not now part of a company, but which committed some impropriety while it was, often remains that company's responsibility with respect to the consequences of that action. Similarly, selling off a polluted piece of land does not usually absolve a firm of its responsibility for the pollution, either in law or the court of public opinion.

In the same vein, as more and more work is outsourced, it is becoming increasingly unclear that organizations are actually solving the underlying problems that lead them to resort to this practice. For example, one of the most common reasons for outsourcing is to reduce headcount. This result almost always occurs, but in many cases generates mere paper savings rather than true reductions in cost of labor, since the "non-headcount" workers may be more expensive—may, in fact, be the *same employees,* rehired as consultants at greater compensation (but with lower dedication to the firm) than when they were on the headcount.

Another common reason for outsourcing is to reduce manufacturing costs and improve quality. Faced with intensified global competition, certification requirements such as ISO 9000, and a variety of other factors, organizations find themselves heavily reliant on suppliers for high-quality inputs. Whether they actually get such inputs, however, depends largely on why quality was poor and costs high before the work was outsourced. If job requirements are unknown, key processes poorly understood, or specs and drawings not current, outside suppliers are unlikely to deliver either efficiency or quality. In general, putting people on contracts—converting employees into suppliers, locating them outside the building, and substituting impersonal contractual relationships for whatever normative commitments previously existed—merely places these people outside the firm's sphere of direct influence, making them less accessible to improvement.

Therefore, we predict that the experiences of many organizations with outsourcing will make them question their underlying logic and cause them to realize that outsourcing not only doesn't diminish the *need* for low cost, high-quality inputs, it sometimes reduces the likelihood of securing them. *To the extent that current trends toward outsourcing are diminished and possibly even reversed, we predict that HR will be asked to play a key role in bringing this work back inside the organization.*

INSOURCING

Whereas outsourcing transfers work to outsiders, insourcing is the shifting of tasks and responsibilities to others within the organization. Insourcing of HR responsibilities is very much in vogue these days, with work presumably being transferred to line managers or to some "shared services" organization within the company. Typical examples include performance appraisal and feedback (formerly HR's responsibility, now, using 360-degree appraisal, everyone's); compensation (from hierarchical to peer recognition and rewards); employee counseling and career planning (now described as each employee's responsibility for him/herself); and global assignments, for example, expatriation and repatriation processes.

The reasons we say "presumably being transferred" is that in many organizations much more effort has gone into stopping HR from doing this work than into ensuring that anyone else is doing it instead. Even in those cases where others *are* officially assigned this work, these people are seldom given the time and the training to perform it well.

Consequently, *we again predict that, as the evidence accumulates and the costs mount, HR will be asked to reassume responsibilities for some of its traditional functions and responsibilities.*

LABOR RELATIONS

Years ago, organizations in many industries were forced to deal with strong, active, well-financed, sometimes adversarial labor unions; a critically important part of HR's workload was to administer the collective bargaining contracts and participate in the grievance process, if the firm was unionized, or undertake a variety of activities concerned with "union avoidance" if it wasn't.

In recent years, however, the power of many labor unions has been seriously eroded. Whether measured by financial assets, enrolled members, or degree of political/legislative support, it is clear that organized labor has constituted much less a threat to corporate America—which has responded by reducing dedicated resources and deemphasizing HR's role.

Until today! Today, as a result of union mergers, consolidations, massive fundraising efforts, and other factors, many labor unions are far healthier than they have been for a long time. Moreover, organized labor today operates in an unusually favorable climate of political support and public opinion as the press and politicians from both major parties rail against "corporate welfare" and "corporate greed." Recent corporate announcements of plans to downsize have generated particularly hostile reactions from government, the media, and the public at large. Inevitably, this atmosphere will add considerable ammunition to the labor union cause. Thus, *we predict that in the not too distant future, organizations will begin to pay far closer attention to both collective bargaining and union avoidance, with HR once again being asked to play a pivotal role.*

GLOBAL COMPETITION

Although this chapter has focused primarily on some of HR's traditional roles, *we predict that HR will also be asked to assume some new roles as well. One of the most important of these new roles pertains to globalization.* As organizations globalize their products and processes and derive greater revenues from off-shore operations, HR will increasingly be asked to help prepare people for international assignments and will be called upon to provide country-specific knowledge of union and labor policies, legal and regulatory requirements, compensation and benefits practices, and many other aspects of doing business outside the home country.

HR will also be asked to assume considerable responsibility for the successful assimilation of expatriates, inpatriates, host and third country nationals. Inevitably, as off-shore global operations increase, so too does the need for the "softer skills" such as: cultural awareness training; coaching and mentoring; language training; spousal adjustments; and predeparture, postarrival, and reentry adaptation planning for employees and their families. Many U.S. expatriates today have had little if any opportunity to benefit from these activities and have failed in their assignment and/or departed prematurely.

Even when American employees do acquire the necessary competencies and knowledge to operate successfully outside their home country, upon repatriation back to the United States, their skills and experiences rarely are utilized effectively to mentor and educate new expatriates-in-waiting. (Research evidence shows that the United States does far less well in this regard than do Japan and most European countries.) It is clear that numerous opportunities exist for HR to make a huge contribution in these areas.

HR is also uniquely positioned to modify what is known about giving feedback, doing 360-degree appraisals, and designing career-sensitive reward systems for international locations. For example, the American prescription to "praise in public, punish in private" is inappropriate in countries such as Indonesia and Malaysia, where public praise causes the recipient loss of "face," the implication being that the manager was surprised that the employee was able to perform the task. With respect to 360-degree appraisal, cultures such as Mexico are very reluctant to offer any upward feedback, and many customers would be offended by being asked about an employee's performance. A further example is that in countries such as Sweden financial rewards are not particularly effective, because the marginal tax rates are so high that employees would rather be given additional time off and be granted access to vacation villages. However, when such benefits as vacation villages are assigned imputed income and taxed accordingly, these rewards are less attractive. In other countries, pay for performance is opposed not because of tax consequences, but because it is seen as violating the norm that employees should work hard as a duty to their firm, not because they are "bribed" to do so. HR professionals need to be aware of these, and many other, factors.

CONCLUSION

As we think back to the practices HR typically performed during the 1950s and 1960s, we might ask: How many of these practices have been rendered obsolete, in that they are either no longer important or have been "solved?" We think, very few. Outsourcing, insourcing, downsizing, and using contract workers have neither consistently achieved nor rendered unnecessary, such desirable qualities as lower costs, higher product quality, and improved employee morale and customer satisfaction.

While results have always been mixed, the best HR departments have had considerable success at devising strategies and policies that have increased employee morale, commitment, satisfaction, and loyalty. These are valuable attributes and ought to be pursued and preserved. Unfortunately, they have often been pursued for their own sake, without seeking to connect them to shareholder returns and customer satisfaction. The solution, therefore, is *not* to divorce HR from its traditional responsibilities by casually handing them to someone else or neglecting them altogether. Rather, the solution is to challenge HR to continue to assume responsibility for these things and do these things well, but in ways that integrate them with broader business objectives.

NOTE

1. The more things change, the more they stay the same.

REFERENCES

Dubin, R. (1961). *Human relations in administration* (2nd ed.). Englewood Cliffs, NJ: Prentice-Hall.

Hammer, M., & Champy, J. (1993). *Reengineering the corporation: A manifest for business revolution*. New York: Harper Business.

CHAPTER 19

THE HUMAN RESOURCE PROFESSION: INSURRECTION OR RESURRECTION?

KATHRYN D. McKEE, SPHR

$\mathbf{J}$ac Fitz-enz is right! In *HR Magazine,* Fitz-enz (1995) states that in "many companies, management does not see the value added by human resources (HR) in effectively managing the human assets of the enterprise" (p. 85). Add to this the provocative column by Thomas Stewart in *Fortune* (January, 1996), and we, as HR professionals, have a terrible indictment of the HR function, and more importantly, the profession we practice.

With the rush to cut costs, organizations are taking a very hard look at "support" functions, and they do not like what they perceive:

- Large staffs who appear to do nothing related to either core competencies or added value.
- Unresponsive, bureaucratic HR "experts" who insist on a command and control approach to problem resolution as opposed to a partnership with the line, playing the role of an internal consultant with a mission to problem-solve.

Companies have been downsizing and outsourcing the HR function, and many times, the head of HR is not running that show. He or she is acting as a pawn rather than an origin. Why is that? Why do we behave the way we do? Rather than take the bull by the horns, we assume a passive (spelled resistive) role and let it happen to us.

WHY WE DO THE THINGS WE DO

A fuller understanding of why some HR executives may be passive in their reactions to what is going on around them may be gained by (1) examining the history of the HR function, and (2) understanding the impact of the past on the profession today and projecting to what it might portend for the future. In looking back over the past six decades in business life in the United States, four major periods emerge that may have influenced the way human resource professionals perceive their role in organizations, and may consequently have influenced their behavior:

- *1940s and 1950s: Mechanistic Period:* This was a period wherein manufacturing was the driver of American industry, and there appeared to be a mechanical, that is, a rote way of performing HR tasks.
- *1960s and 1970s: Legalistic Period:* These two decades saw an unprecedented amount of social and employment legislation that began the trend toward regulation of the workplace beyond union contract/plant rules.
- *1980s: Organistic Period:* Corporations in the 1980s underwent tremendous organization change through mergers, divestitures, restructuring, reengineering, downsizing, and bankruptcy, throwing the workplace into chaos and creating an environment wherein the HR function should have flourished.
- *1990s: Strategic Period:* At this time in American corporate life, strategic thinking and planning have allowed for a more orderly approach to the continual change in corporate organization and growth plans.

In analyzing how the HR practitioners of those periods spent their time, six dimensions emerged that allowed for the development and comparison of what practitioners were dealing with and how they spent their time (Table 19.1):

1. *Demographics:* Who comes to work in America.
2. *Employee Relations:* Union, management, and relations with employees.
3. *Pay/Jobs:* What pay and benefits practices were and are.
4. *Organization Development:* Organizational process and content issues; management and employee development.
5. *The Profession:* What was/is happening to the profession: the role HR staffs play in their organizations.
6. *The Law:* What laws and regulations bind the workplace.

TABLE 19.1
Evolution of Human Resources

Dimensions	1940s–50s Mechanistic	1960s–70s Legalistic	1980s Organistic	1990s Strategic	2000 Catalytic
Demographics	White males Racism Sexism—Rosie the Riveter No upward mobility	White male dominated Blacks hired in offices; women start to move up; other minorities invisible	White male/ female competition for jobs More Blacks and Asians in high places; more Hispanics	A Salad Bowl White males threatened Women in powerful places Baby Busters not committed Waves of immigration	Women as CEOs Beauty, Obesity, Sexual preference as diversity issues Increase in racial tensions Impact of Baby Boomers
Employee Relations	Labor-management adversarial Unions powerful	UAW/Teamsters supreme; steel union strikes	Employee involvement Beginning of decline of Union power Boomers/Yuppies bring kids to work	Teams, contingent workers Roles vs. Jobs Stress-EAPs Diversity	Loyalty to one's profession Just-in-time workforce Psychiatry at work Borderless employment Unions increase
Pay/Jobs	Fair day's work for a fair day's pay Bonuses; profit-sharing Pensions Beginnings of health insurance	Sales and mgmt. incentives 401(k); STD/LTD Stock Options An experiment with Cafeteria Benefits	Differentiated pay Rewards systems Cafeteria Compensation commonplace "Greed is Good"	Team pay Rewards and recognition Options in lieu of high base Executive pay caps	Pay for competencies Variable pay at all levels CEO pay regulated Portable benefits
Organization Development	Little employee /mgmt development Hierarchical; dehumanized assembly lines	Beginnings of Mgmt Science: Odiorne/Drucker T-Groups Hierarchical	M&A; downsizing Emergence of leadership Management process entrenched	Restructuring Androgenous Mgmt styles Learning organizations Virtual corporation Powerful leaders	Continue M&A Webs/networks Telecommuting Continued restructuring Employee self-development
The Profession	Labor Relations powerful Records; benefits admin.; recruiting	Labor Relations still powerful Compensation/Benefits/EEO emerge as specialties	HR Director powerful Continued specialization of HR disciplines	Full strategic partnership Relationship managers are generalists HR Back Office or outsourcing	"Staff-less" HR function Organization Development as king The Internet as a staff member
Law	Social Security NLRA Taft-Hartley NLRB	ERISA Civil Rights Act OSHA EEO-AAP ADEA Equal Pay Veterans Huge court settlements	OBRA/COBRA Sec 89 DEFRA/TEFRA 1986 Tax Act Wrongful dismissal; rise of Tort law in the workplace	FMLA WARN NAFTA A.D.A. OWBPA Privacy/monitoring Striker replacement	Fewer federal laws New Social Security law Revised Medicare Revised FLSA Continued tax reform

MECHANISTIC PERIOD

The Mechanistic Period saw the birth of the human resources profession. Personnel/industrial relations, as it was then known, came about prior to World War II. It was an administrative function, interpreting union contracts, keeping records, hiring people. Labor became king, and adversarial relations were the order of the day. There was little innovation in pay practices; benefit programs were just emerging; and they were dominated in their design by insurance companies. There was little organization development, and employee and management development was rare. Personnel/industrial relations managers were not considered part of the senior management team in most organizations, and with the exception of negotiating union contracts, were not participants in setting the strategic direction of organizations. There was little, if any, impact to the bottom line with the exception of labor contracts, strikes, lockouts, and boycotts. The human asset, predominantly white male, was viewed as a commodity.

Perhaps there are HR practitioners today stuck in this time warp, frozen into inactivity, not hearing messages sent from their management or from the leaders of the HR profession, not moving their organizations forward.

LEGALISTIC PERIOD

This was a period of profound change in the workplace and in the roles and responsibilities assumed by HR professionals. The demographics began to shift; people of color were admitted to jobs other than field hand, laborer, janitor, and assembler. Women were considered for positions without typewriters, and they began to move up into managerial roles.

Labor was still king, but the kingdom was changing. Whereas in the Mechanistic Period, labor law focused on union-management issues, the Legalistic Period gave rise to a plethora of employee relations laws having to do with the workplace and with the treatment of the human asset: Title VII, Equal Pay Act, Age Discrimination, ERISA, Executive Orders, Occupational Safety & Health Act, to name a few.

Civil rights litigants began testing the authority of the laws, and significant financial judgments were rendered against major corporations. Senior Management and boards of directors awoke to the fact that the "human commodity" coming to work each day was costing/could cost more than just the salary and benefits line of the Profit and Loss Statement.

The federal government, through the Equal Employment Opportunity Commission and Office of Federal Contract Compliance Programs began to question the commitment of government contractors—basically most

HR practitioners—regarding affirmative efforts and actions to create a diverse work force. Inordinate and expensive management time was spent negotiating conciliation and settlement agreements.

Management also began paying attention to the art of managing, recognizing the need for the development of managerial and organizational skills, hence the training and development function and organizational development roles began to emerge. Thus, in 20 to 30 years, HR had moved from planning picnics and keeping attendance records to a complex, impactful, "Keep us out of trouble" role. In some cases, HR managers began to report to the chief executive officer (CEO) and to participate on executive committees, playing a strategic role in their organizations.

Perhaps some HR practitioners remain in this period, more progressive than the Mechanistic, skilled in command and control behaviors, but nevertheless not moving forward in vision, thought, or action.

ORGANISTIC PERIOD

The 1980s brought a time of rapid and constant change, replete with stunning hostile takeovers, leveraged buyouts, mergers and acquisition, and divestitures. Early into these endeavors, HR was not necessarily asked to join in strategy setting or due diligence. In my own experience, Twentieth Century-Fox acquired Aspen Ski Corp. only to find out far into the integration process that the Teamsters had attempted to organize the Ski Run operators. The due diligence team—accountants, auditors, and investment bankers—had neither thought about nor investigated any HR issues other than the CEO's compensation. We were immediately dispatched to "fix it" and fix it we did.

The 1980s also brought an increasingly diverse work force; the rise of awareness of work and family issues, the demise of labor as king, another plethora of tax laws impacting benefits design, and the rise of "Wrongful Dismissal." Now HR was in the thick of it, putting out fires, staving off lawsuits, implementing more command and control policies and procedures, all to save the organization from itself. At the same time, however, on the opposite end of the spectrum, organizations were changing dramatically, removing layers, reorganizing work, and alienating more and more employees. Enlightened organizations became concerned with preserving the dignity of the individual, hence another important consultative role for human resources came into play.

Many HR professionals are stuck in the 1980s—involved, playing a tactical role, carrying out directives, but not being a strategic partner. We, in

HR, renamed ourselves, but many HR professionals to this day do not understand the difference: *Human resources is strategic; personnel is operational.*

STRATEGIC PERIOD

What have the 1990s wrought? This is a period of constant change in all dimensions of the workplace:

- The world has shrunk, and we are residents of the Global Village, conducting our transnational business electronically, heedless of time differences.
- The work force is a "salad bowl," all ethnicities working together, not necessarily harmoniously.
- An aging work force of Baby Boomers who will once again change workplace programs and attitudes toward the "older worker."
- The potential rise of white/pink collar unionism.
- The rise of diversity as a state of both mind and program which considers disability, marital status, occupational, gender preference, and weight, as well as age, race, sex, national origin, religion, and so on.

Organizations are in flux: Are they webs, networks, or matrices? Are they restructured, reengineered, or rightsized? Are they teams? Are they hierarchies? How are they rewarded? And, what about the human asset? Employees are expected to be "resilient," to plan their own careers and develop themselves, to be insecure in their tenure, but to be loyal "while you are here." What does all of this portend for the human resources professional today?

First, HR can gain a place at the leadership table with full membership: a true strategic partner—reporting to the CEO, and interacting with the board of directors. It is virtually impossible for an organization to achieve any organizational torquing without involving HR in the strategizing, plan development, and execution. If HR is not involved up front, when asked to fix it, it is too late. The horse is miles away from the barn.

Second, HR has the opportunity to throw off the mantle of command and control, leave that to the chief financial officer (CFO). HR can be a shaper of destiny, providing ideas that are efficient and cost-effective. HR can be profit oriented, and through expert program design, its goal to retain every profit dollar possible can be achievable, spending few if any on litigation, compliance reviews, or unnecessary staffing expense.

Third, HR can lead by example. It can blaze the trail by reengineering itself to be lean and mean, outsourcing functions that are cheaper to buy and then only when they are needed, such as executive search, incentive plan design, training and development, and benefits administration. It can simplify policies and delegate as much as possible to the Line.

Do it first; do not be guilty of the dancing school syndrome, waiting in the corner to be asked. HR can do more with less, and by leading the way force other functions to follow suit.

All of this is made easier if the HR executive is a strong leader, one who challenges the status quo, has a vision of where he or she wants to go, inspires others to follow where they *did not know* they wanted to go, practices and recognizes small wins, and encourages others—a tall order, but one necessary to venture into the millennium.

THE CATALYTIC PERIOD

What of the future—for the year 2000, consider the following:

- Employment will be cross-border; corporations will increase their international exposure and will want a work force comfortable in and with other cultures.
- Organizations will continue to evolve, and there will be fewer of them. Mergers and acquisitions will continue as corporations within industries look for survival by joining together.
- Staffing will be fluid and contingent; the use of "just-in-time" professional workers will become common and concomitant to outsourcing of administrative and other line support functions that are not considered core competencies of the organization.
- Unions will be growling. Time will tell if the AFL-CIO's ongoing attempts to increase union membership will work. This is not a time for complacency on the part of management as union organizers are much more professional in their approach.
- The work force at all levels will be more diverse. Continuing immigration into the United States will ensure that talent will be multicultural. There will be many more female CEOs of major corporations as they move through or remove the "glass ceiling." Sexual preferences, beauty, and obesity will be issues du jour.
- Compensation practices will be innovative. More organizations will be willing to break free of the rigid pay practices of the past to find those that fit the needs of the new approaches to planning and managing performance.

- Employees will take charge of their destinies and will be more selective in their career choices, their career moves, and their loyalty to their profession.
- Telecommuting and other forms of flexible work will be commonplace.
- Benefits will be portable. Congress will deal with the issues of Social Security and Medicare.
- Teams will be a way of life. New organization structures will emerge in reality as webs, networks, and cross-functional teams become a way of life.
- Members of the human resources profession, in order to flourish in the Catalytic Period, will need the ability to vision, to be comfortable with change, to use a consultative approach, to understand the business of the business, and to have very strong people skills. In addition, it will be critical to have global, strategic, and business perspectives to understand the power and use of technology, to be focused on the customer, and to understand the impact of market changes on the business and the profession.

In order to survive as a function and a profession, HR must take charge of its destiny and its change—to cause an *insurrection* so that we in the profession, *resurrect* ourselves as dynamic, innovative business partners. We must fill the demand for those services desired by our customers, not what we think they want or the latest flavor of the month. Their agenda must be our agenda, no more command and control. It is imperative that those professionals capable of the moving to the Catalytic Period, the "Superstars" defined by Fitz-enz, pull their colleagues stuck in the Mechanistic, Legalistic, or Organistic Periods into the Strategic, or help them exit the profession. HR cannot resurrect itself if burdened by the weight of those who cannot or will not move to a strategic partnership.

If we can't change, if we can't make this transition, we will be written off, the partnership door closed, and we will be back to picnics and attendance records.

REFERENCES

Fitz-enz, J. (1995). On the edge of oblivion. *HR Magazine, 41,* 84–90.

Stewart, T. (1996). Taking on the last bureaucracy. *Fortune,* January 15, 105–108.

CHAPTER 20

DOES HUMAN RESOURCES
HAVE A FUTURE?

JEFFREY PFEFFER

With the growing interest in implementing high performance work practices, with accumulating evidence on the effects of human resource management practices on organizational performance, with increasing attention to national competitiveness and its relationship to human resource (HR) policies on topics such as training and a stakeholder, as contrasted with a shareholder model of management, and with the proliferation of books and journals on issues related to human resource management, one might be tempted to say that the future of human resources as an organizational function is bright. My advice is to resist the temptation to believe that HR managers and staff in organizations have a rosy future or, for that matter, any future at all, because there are some profound problems facing human resources as a function within organizations, as contrasted with the study of human resources as a topic area, that make its viability and continued survival problematic.

There is evidence to support the spread of the various trends just enumerated. There is much more implementation of high performance or high commitment work practices.[1] One can debate the speed of their diffusion or even its extensiveness, but the general direction is clear, propelled by both organizational change and a process of natural selection in which establishments that don't manage their workforce for competitive advantage disappear. There is a growing number of sophisticated studies that demonstrate the connection between the effective management of people and measures of organizational performance ranging from quality and efficiency to profits and stock price and even the survival rate of initial public offerings.[2] There is a proliferation of journals and books treating the topic of human resource management. There is also increasing debate and discussion about national policies on issues such as taxes to encourage training, regulations that encourage or inhibit labor market flexibility and the use of contingent employment arrangements, and the reform of laws governing industrial relations and labor unions.

Where is the human resource function in all of this? A tentative answer is, "largely absent." To the extent it has a presence, HR is frequently an accomplice in a number of trends such as downsizing and contingent work arrangements that promise to actually undo much of the progress made in managing the employment relationship in the past several decades. Organizational HR managers have not taken the lead in assessing the consequences of various HR practices on organizational performance, that has been done by academics mostly out of an industrial relations tradition funded largely by foundations and the government. Indeed, many HR professionals are unaware of the empirical business case for managing people effectively. As debates rage about public policy on employment issues, the extent to which HR professionals have participated has largely been through the labor policy association and its efforts to weaken the labor union movement. When high commitment work practices have been implemented, this has mostly been because of initiatives taken by line managers or senior-level general managers; the human resource advocacy (as contrasted with support) role is often limited. Human resources, as a function in organizations, could have a future, but to assure that future, HR professionals will have to make some profound changes in their role and skills and how they go about adding value to the organizations in which they work.

Two examples illustrate the possible irrelevancy of human resources as a function. The examples are striking because both come from organizations that have very people-oriented management policies. The first is fairly well known. Hewlett-Packard was founded by William Hewlett and David Packard in 1939. From the beginning, it was a company with a strong set of values—the HP way—that emphasized trusting employees and building an organization whose competitive success was importantly premised on its workforce and a set of policies that, to this day, serve to attract, retain, and motivate talent in a very competitive labor market. This company did not have a personnel department until almost twenty years after it was founded, and there was much debate and discussion within the organization about starting such a department. Some executives in the company believed that human resource management was every line manager's job and that setting up a specialized department would cause line managers to pay less attention to people management issues and policies. This philosophical debate continues within Hewlett-Packard to this day—not that anyone wants to eliminate the personnel department, but it is a function that has gone through successive waves of downsizing in part because of the concern about its role in the organization.

Second, consider AES Corporation, a successful developer and operator of electric power plants. It is a company that last year had about 2,000 employees, $500 million in revenues, a market capitalization of over $2.5 billion, a strong set of corporate values including fun and a belief in teamwork—and no personnel or human resources function at all. There is a person in the finance department who oversees the company's 401(k) plan and the firm at one time had one human resources person. Today, decisions about what to pay people, how to do recruiting, what training and educational experiences employees should receive, and even the negotiation of contracts with benefits providers such as health insurance companies are left entirely to the employees, frequently operating in ad hoc task forces. If AES can operate very successfully today without any human resources staff, one wonders indeed, whether, human resources has a future.

A PROBLEMATIC HISTORY

More than a century ago, there was no human resource function. In organizations of any size, the foreman reigned supreme, often exercising despotic power, receiving bribes from people who wanted a job, and administering arbitrary and capricious discipline (Jacoby, 1985). Unfortunately, this exercise of power was despised not only by the workforce, who frequently unionized as a result, but also was not very beneficial to the interests of the organization's owners. Richard Edwards (1979) has described the replacement of this individually based control by a system of bureaucratic control, a process also described by Sanford Jacoby (1985). Bureaucratic control was premised on the idea that the arbitrary exercise of authority was to be supplanted by due process, rules, and procedures that ensured fair treatment to all employees.

The professionalization of the personnel function occurred around developing and implementing policies that today frequently are taken for granted—job evaluations and the writing of job descriptions to guide recruiting and to help administer salaries; policies on vacations, discipline, performance evaluations, and similar things that were implemented to ensure that employees were treated equitably and fairly; developing training and career progression and succession policies to ensure that there would be replacements in cases of turnover; and keeping administrative records.

The role of human resources in organizations was substantially expanded by state action, including regulation and the imposition of reporting requirements. Thus, for instance, World War II with its requirements for documenting allowable pay raises and monitoring the supply of the nation's manpower resulted in a substantial expansion in the scope and influence of human resource activities and the spread of a system of bureaucratic control (Baron, Dolben, & Jennings, 1986). Subsequent expansion of government oversight of workforce welfare, for instance, in the antidiscrimination laws of the 1960s, further enlarged the scope of HR's responsibility for rule enforcement within the organization.

Out of this history, human resources became the keeper (and occasionally the developer) of the rules and the data that documented rule compliance—the people who prescribed what salaries could be paid to what positions, how discipline was to be carried out to avoid wrongful termination lawsuits, how hiring should be done to comply with civil rights legislation, and the keeper of the records required by government policies such as affirmative action. Litigation, such as class action lawsuits on the basis of age or gender discrimination, became an opportunity for human resources to ally itself with the lawyers and to attain more power, for the function now could demonstrate substantial economic consequences from not following proper rules and practices.

The various governmental rules and regulations also seemed (and were) complex—rules on pensions, wage and hour regulations that prescribed minimum wages and who would be subject to overtime, rules on when someone could be considered an independent contractor, and so forth. Issues of test validation (required by equal employment regulations) and job analysis also had complex, technical components. Human resource professionals developed expertise in each of these areas but tended to have careers that spanned organizations rather than functions within organizations. A human resource generalist was someone who understood compensation, benefits, and industrial relations. Few organizations moved line managers into the human resource function as part of a normal career rotation (Procter & Gamble being one notable exception), and very few human resource professionals moved into line management positions. This left the HR function increasingly isolated from the business it was supposed to be serving and made the idea of human resources professionals as business partners difficult to implement in practice.

Goal displacement occurred. The rules and policies, initially a means to reasonable ends (limiting the power of arbitrary and venal foremen, providing administrative records, helping comply with government edicts) became ends in themselves. Most organizations have examples of stories such as the following told to me by a senior executive at AES to help explain why that organization did not have human resources:

> Prior to coming here, I worked at Diamond Shamrock in their chemicals business. I had a person working for me in traffic—arranging the transportation of our products. The person had been doing the job for years and was wonderful not only in meeting delivery schedules but in saving the company a lot of money. He knew the rules and regulations that governed shippers, was an excellent negotiator, and did a sensational job controlling our transportation costs. I wanted to give him a large raise based on the outstanding performance he had demonstrated. But I was told by human resources that I couldn't. He had been in the company and in his present position quite a long time, and was up against the top of the prescribed salary range for his present job. "What could I do," I inquired, "so I can pay him more money?" I was told that if he had supervisory responsibility, his prescribed pay range would increase. So I requested two clerk positions to report to him. But I didn't fill them. But think about it. The only way to give this exceptional performer a raise was to waste money by hiring people we didn't need so he would have someone to supervise, we could reclassify his job, and we could pay him more. That's why we don't have human resources at AES.

This is a story not from the distant past but from not that long ago, and it is a tale repeated time and again in many organizations. It helps one to understand why at Southwest Airlines, Charles O'Rully and I were told in 1994 that of about 100 people in the People Department, virtually all of them came from marketing and few had HR backgrounds. The department needed to market the company to potential job applicants and to market its services and how it could be helpful to the rest of the organization. This is why Southwest's People Department at that time had a "three strikes and you're out policy"—if a human resource person told line managers "no" three times, that HR person was fired. As the vice president for People said, "Our job is to help line managers do their jobs, not get in their way."

Human resources also faces another serious problem. Human resources was, and largely still is, the ultimate staff function. It is not a very highly valued staff function if one assesses value by the salary paid to its practitioners. The senior human resource executive in a company typically is the lowest paid functional manager, earning much less than the head of finance or even manufacturing, market and sales, and research and development. As a relatively less powerful unit, many of its practitioners, although certainly not all, have decided that the road to survival is to do what they are told as well as they can and to make sure the function is as inexpensively operated as possible. I go to conferences of human resource professionals in which they brag about how they have helped the CEO downsize the organization as a whole, and how they are making their own function increasingly lean and less costly, often talking about the number of human resource professionals per 100 (or 1,000) organizational employees. This seems sensible only until you compare it to other functions, whose members take a more proactive stance toward influencing organizational policies and practices in ways consistent with their knowledge and values and who do not take it as a mark of their success that they are shrinking in the organization—a trend, by the way, that has one obvious conclusion, namely, to disappear completely.

WHAT HUMAN RESOURCES NEEDS TO BE

If human resources is to have a future inside organizations, it is not by playing police person and enforcer of rules and policies, nor is it likely to be ensured by playing handmaiden to finance. Rather, its role needs to be as a provider of information about and advocate for the connection between people and profits and as a counterbalance to the financial hegemony and its associated short-termism that increasingly reign supreme, particularly in U.S. corporations, even though their economic values are open to question.

In accounting circles, there is growing interest in the concept of the "balanced scorecard," in the recognition that traditional financial measures do not do a completely adequate job of measuring how the organization is doing. Traditional accounting measures need to be supplemented with measures of operational performance, customer acceptance, and how the organization is preparing for the future. It is not only the *measurement* systems that need to be balanced, however, it is also the *decision-making process* that ultimately produces those measures. If, as organizations so frequently claim, "people are our most important asset," someone within the organization must take the lead in bringing the development of a workforce and culture that provides competitive advantage into actual choices.

This advocacy role for the connection between people and profits is potentially an important one for human resources. Unfortunately, some people went into human resources in a vain attempt to avoid the power and influence activities that such a role requires. If human resources is not to serve as an advocate for the importance of people and their effective management for the long term, who will? In many organizations, the answer is line managers in operations or senior executives with people-centered vision and values. One element of being a "business partner," however, is being a real participant in the inevitable debates about the sources of strategic leverage and competitive success. Bringing data and considerations of how to manage the employment relationship to enhance organizational effectiveness to the table is a critical task for human resource professionals inside organizations.

More than occasionally I hear human resource executives say, "We know what the organization needs to do, but it seems to be doing the opposite." When I ask what they are doing about this, they will sheepishly provide details that add up to, "not much." It is no doubt difficult to be a forceful advocate for doing things differently and to keep bringing to the organization's attention, information and analysis that it may not want to hear. That, however, is what human resources must do if it is to be taken seriously and, more fundamentally, if it is to influence organizational decisions in ways that will truly create business value.

NOTES

1. See, for instance, Paul Osterman, "How Common is Workplace Transformation and Who Adopts It?" *Industrial and Labor Relations Review, 47,* 173–188.

2. Examples include Mark A. Huselid, "The Impact of Human Resource Management Practices on Turnover, Productivity, and Corporate Financial Performance," *Academy of Management Journal, 38* (1995), 635–672; John Paul MacDuffie, "Human Resource Bundles and Manufacturing Performance: Flexible Production Systems in the World Auto Industry," *Industrial and Labor Relations Review, 48* (1995), 197–221; and Jeffrey B. Arthur, "Effects of Human Resource Systems on Manufacturing Performance and Turnover," *Academy of Management Journal, 37* (1994), 670–687.

REFERENCES

Baron, J.N., Dobbin, F.R., & Jennings, P.D. (1986). "War and peace: The evolution of modern personnel administration in U.S. industry." *American Journal of Sociology, 92,* 350–383.

Edwards, R.C. (1979). *Contested terrain: The transformation of the workplace in the twentieth century.* New York: Basic Books.

Jacoby, S.M. (1985). *Employing bureaucracy.* New York: Columbia University Press.

CHAPTER 21

SHOULD HUMAN RESOURCES SURVIVE? A PROFESSION AT THE CROSSROADS

ANTHONY J. RUCCI

Much has been written and heralded over the past few years regarding the human resource (HR) profession having achieved strategic partner status in major organizations. If one presses the issue with objective practitioners off-the-record, however, most will admit that the profession is at a perilous crossroads—that the next ten years will spell either the demise or ascendancy of the profession. The formula for demise typically involves a failure to understand business clients, failing to adapt approaches to the new global competitive demands or pursuing an HR agenda rather than an organizational effectiveness agenda. Ascendancy forecasts suggest that HR will not only survive, but will increase its influence by advancing the progress HR has begun to make in many organizations toward creating a competitive advantage through innovative people practices.

"Will HR survive?" It's the wrong question to ask. The more appropriate strategic question is, "Should HR survive?" HR's focus should not be on surviving or strengthening its status. Instead, HR should begin today to take actions which will eventually eliminate itself in major organizations. The issue to consider is not demise versus ascendancy, but rather demise under what circumstances. HR has spent far too much time worrying about how to strengthen itself instead of how to strengthen organizational effectiveness. The clearest illustration is the often repeated reference by HR practitioners on the "need for a strategic plan for HR." The more appropriate focus should be on the "need for a strategic HR plan for the organization."

ELIMINATION OF HR—TWO SCENARIOS

I suggest two scenarios, both leading to the eventual elimination of the HR profession inside organizations over the next ten years. One scenario eliminates HR's role because we as a profession have failed. The second scenario eliminates HR's role because we have been successful in inculcating the profession's skill-set and, more importantly, mindset into our organizations and managers. Under one scenario, HR loses control and influence; under the other scenario HR makes itself obsolete in the best interest of the organization.

The worst-case scenario is obsolescence caused by failure. This scenario involves HR's being dismantled by management because the profession is ineffective in adding real value. The predictors of the worst-case scenario involve a profession and practitioners who:

- Don't promote change.
- Don't identify leaders.
- Don't understand business.
- Don't know customers.
- Don't drive costs.
- Don't emphasize values.

The best-case scenario leading to HR's planned obsolescence involves HR professionals who:

- Create change.
- Develop principled leaders.
- Promote economic literacy.
- Center on the customer.
- Maximize services and maximize staff.
- Steward values.

Again, the milestone of HR's effectiveness will not be its ability to survive and do these things for the organization, but rather its ability to transfer these into the responsibilities and accountabilities of managers at all levels.

Create Change

The greatest competitive challenge faced by U.S. organizations today is speed. The very survival of entire industries and seemingly solid companies becomes challenged, sometimes overnight, by the introduction of a new technology or a virulent new competitor. Only those organizations who have stayed close to the customer and are constantly vigilant to competitive challenges have weathered a difficult twenty-year period in which most U.S. industries have seen their share of world markets decline.

Even this characterization implies an after-the-fact strategy—wait to see what the customer says or wait to see what the competition does and then react quickly and change appropriately. Organizations in the United States have been sporadically effective in reacting with speed and even less effective in initiating change and introducing it with speed. There is an increasing competitive premium on creating change, not just managing change.

What are the implications to the HR profession of the need for organizational speed and creating change? First of all, organizations have historically been based on a management model built as the antithesis of speed. The control and standardization emphasis in manufacturing, which became the competitive hallmark of the U.S. post-Industrial Revolution period of the early 1900s, crept its way into the people and organizational management practices of organizations. The organizational model of "Plan, Organize, Motivate, and Control" was a management-science mantra as recently as ten years ago. HR was unfortunately too effective in adapting to this model; job descriptions, job grades, policy manuals, and a host of other examples speak to a compliance mentality adopted to promote standardization. Worse still, the one-size-fits-all emphasis in the profession spilled over into the advice and counsel HR provided line management. The standardization of HR prevented the development of an organizational capability of flexibility, speed, and risk-taking.

HR's survival will be threatened to the extent that it insists on retaining the vestiges of the manufacturing era, rather than on meeting the new requirements of a service era. Eventually, HR will be forced to do so by its management and its customers. More proactively, HR should voluntarily reassess its infrastructure and eliminate unnecessary rules and systems, thereby emphasizing the need for individual judgment and accountability by managers. This reassessment can be a powerful catalyst toward enabling organizational speed, creating change, and encouraging risk taking.

HR can provide a constructive influence by creating policy architecture and designs which are consistent with and supportive of the organization's strategic goals, but not being so prescriptive in those designs as to inhibit creativity and business flexibility.

HR can help create powerful change by providing opportunities for the organization to identify its weaknesses, and then facilitate organizational efforts to improve in those areas. Even more proactively, HR can provide leadership in facilitating efforts to help the organization envision a world class future state and organize efforts and measures designed to achieve that standard.

Develop Principled Leaders

A true limitation in major organizations today is the scarcity of leadership talent. Rarer still are the leaders who ground themselves in a base of moral or ethical principles that are nonnegotiable and which do not "flex" to each new situation. The operative word here is "principled." Principled leaders are those who are role models in behavioral ethics and who demonstrate a courage of conviction regarding values as well as business performance. Such individuals can and do exist at all levels in organizations, not just at top management levels. In fact, depth of principled leadership at all levels is a hallmark of excellent organizations and suggests that senior management has made principled behavior a requirement for selection and promotion decisions.

HR has a key role to play here. Selection, promotion, and performance management techniques must result in the advancement of individuals who display courage of conviction, a willingness to listen and be influenced, and an unwillingness to compromise their principles. To the extent that the profession is successful in identifying these leaders today, they will select in their own likeness in the future. HR's most proactive role here will be to help the organization identify the leadership qualities necessary for success and to create simple, user-friendly ways for managers to implement those criteria in decision making.

Promote Economic Literacy

As a direct effect of the emphasis on organizational standardization, specialization of functions and professionals has evolved. Accompanying specialization, however, has been a narrowness of focus. As a result, the typical U.S. employee, manager, and executive all too often do not possess a broad understanding of business, their company's competitive environment, or their company's competitive position. This is not an indictment of the U.S. workforce; it's an indictment of managers who have failed to provide information openly to their employees; they are constricted by their own specialization.

HR must be a leader in educating the U.S. work force. Education and literacy are not training and development, the historic purview of HR functions. Animals are trained, but people are educated.

While HR must play a leadership role in the education process, this is yet another area where we should seek to greatly reduce the profession's direct accountability for coaching and teaching. Skills training can be designed by HR but should be delivered by subject matter experts in an area.

Management education can be designed by HR but should be delivered by subject matter experts as well. Those subject matter experts are other managers or outside experts, not HR professionals. HR must think of itself as the administration of an educational institution, the deans and provosts, but not the faculty. HR should proactively move toward minimizing its role in conducting training and development and focus on creating the necessary conditions and initiatives for self-renewing, learning organizations.

Center on the Customer

The service era of today could just as accurately be labeled the era of the customer. Consumers of goods and services are more discriminating, more knowledgeable, and more demanding than ever before. Competitive price and quality have become the cost-of-entry into business. It is those companies who wrap a total customer focus around their products and services who are winning in the market place. A consumer can purchase the same brand product from a myriad of distributors at a comparable price. How convenient, reliable, quick, friendly, and knowledgeable a distributor's service is has become the measure of competitive advantage.

The implication of the era of the customer is that organizations must focus on their target customers and design their infrastructures to help the organizations meet the customer's requirements. HR must help create boundaryless organizations that permit information about and from customers to influence the work of every associate in the enterprise. HR's focus here need not be on eliminating its role, since it historically has not played a pivotal role. HR should, instead, eliminate policies and practices which prevent an external focus on the customer. In addition, HR can introduce the primacy of the customer into every aspect of management practices, by including customer orientation and customer service in performance reviews, promotion criteria, and incentive compensation plans, for example.

Maximize Services/Minimize Staff

Just as organizations must focus on their customers, HR must focus on its customers. HR's internal customers have also become more discriminating purchasers of HR services. As evidence, note the trend toward internal shared service environments and complete outsourcing of functions and subfunctions.

Rather than viewing this trend as a threat to survival, we in HR must actively adopt a continuous justify-our-existence mentality. HR must identify where we do add value and eliminate those areas where we do not. We must continually look for ways to drive down costs, just as any business must, and eliminate features for which the customer is unwilling to pay. In those HR areas where our skill sets do not represent a core competency of the enterprise, we should also agressively move those activities outside.

An explicit goal of HR organizations over the next five years should be to eliminate as much of its staffing as possible. A key measure of HR's success should be how few HR professionals are on the payroll of major companies ten years from now as well as the strategic character of those HR roles which remain.

Steward the Values

Companies that have excelled over the past twenty years and longer are those with strong cultures, grounded in a common understanding of a few, simple, shared beliefs. Those shared beliefs need not be formal, moralistic statements of value and ethics but rather a simple, shared understanding of what the enterprise views as inviolable principles. Given a choice between earning an expedient profit or sustaining their shared beliefs, premier organizations will safeguard their beliefs. Being profitable can indeed be a legitimate shared belief, so long as it is balanced with the other beliefs of the enterprise.

Too often HR functions and senior management have delegated to HR the role of surrogate values guardian, or worse still, the role of conscience of the organization. HR and HR professionals do not have a corner on the "values market." HR should not be the values police in our organizations nor should we seek out that role to solidify our job security. If managers require a third party such as HR to remind them of the organization's shared beliefs then they aren't "shared" beliefs anyway.

So, what is HR's role in stewarding values? Consistent with the adage of "what gets measured gets done," HR must develop measurement systems that reflect both the values goals and the financial goals of an enterprise. To the extent that HR can create measures, incentives, and rewards on nonfinancial measures we can further eliminate the need to police those values.

TO THE FUTURE

The implications of the organizational challenges discussed are indeed profound and are equally so for HR. To summarize, we in HR must do the following:

- *Create Change.* Eliminate HR systems and policies which inhibit speed in organizations. In the process, eliminate the HR staff necessary to administrate and audit those systems and policies. More proactively, create an opportunity for the organization to envision a world class future state and help mobilize teams to initiate actions to achieve that vision.
- *Develop Principled Leaders.* Provide leadership in helping organizations define the necessary qualities to ensure the selection and development of principled leaders at all levels of the organization, but HR should not be the decision maker in selection.
- *Promote Economic Literacy.* Eliminate HR's role in delivering training and education to employees, relinquishing that responsibility to subject experts and line managers. HR's contribution and professional skills should be applied to the design of effective educational techniques and to the creation of virtual universities where coaching and teaching are expected components of each manager's job.
- *Center on the Customer.* Eliminate HR policies and practices which inhibit boundaryless organizations and open communication or which promote an internal focus versus a customer-centered culture. Introduce measures into performance reviews, promotion and selection standards, and compensation incentives which evaluate and reward managers on their customer focus.
- *Maximize Services/Minimize Staff.* Eliminate nonvalue-added HR activities and outsource those HR activities which are not core competencies of the enterprise. Retain those roles which are essential to imparting cultural norms and shared beliefs. Staff HR with people interested in facilitating organizational change, not in perfecting HR competencies.
- *Steward the Values.* Extricate HR from the "values police" role and replace itself with measurement systems that incent and reward both nonfinancial and financial measures.

The goal of eliminating HR in organizations may appear harsh or critical but is actually quite a strategic objective. It is only by taking that perspective that the HR profession can stay ahead of the competitive pressures facing organizations today. If we in HR establish a goal to eliminate our function, our attention will turn toward ways to infuse what the profession has tried to achieve into the daily jobs of leaders and line managers. It's hard to disagree with that as being a healthy outcome for organizations.

Will the goal lead to the literal elimination of HR and its practitioners inside major organizations? Perhaps not completely, but it will certainly lead to more effective HR organizations, and it will at least prevent the eventual elimination of HR due to management frustration with its ineffectiveness.

Some HR professionals may feel threatened by the goal of eliminating or minimizing the role of HR in organizations. The greater threat is not in choosing that course of action. The profession will almost certainly come under continued challenge to its existence unless it changes to meet the new organizational needs.

If we're successful at eliminating the need for HR, what will happen to those in the profession? The business-literate, customer-focused, principled leaders among the profession should find their new roles in line management quite exciting as an opportunity to practice what the profession has preached. Those individuals who were not business-literate, customer-focused, principled leaders probably weren't effective HR professionals and change agents anyway. We in HR should be held to no lesser standard than we require of any other area in our organizations.

Ironically, eliminating the need for the HR profession and its roles may be the most effective way of demonstrating HR's value. On a visit to an outside company recently, I struck up an informal conversation with an administrative employee. She told me what she was doing in her job in checking invoice accuracy and then added that the shareholders of the company shouldn't have to pay for a job to do that function. Her goal, as she stated, was to figure out a way to eliminate the need for her job. In this era of job insecurity you can imagine my surprise at that comment. I asked her if she wasn't a little worried about the possibility of eliminating her own job. She replied quickly, "Not at all. I figure that if I'm creative enough to eliminate the need for my job, then I'm exactly the kind of employee this company will want to find another more important role for."

Should HR survive? No—at least not in its current configuration, but it should cease to exist where appropriate, for the right reasons, not the wrong ones.

SECTION IV

BUILD AN INFRASTRUCTURE

In a recent service project for their church, ten youths went to rake leaves off a lawn. With unbridled enthusiasm, they drove up to the lawn, grabbed their rakes, and started putting leaves into piles. Within about 30 minutes, ten large piles of leaves were created around the large yard. Then, they found a tarp to put the piles in and, *while seven watched,* three put the leaves in a pile and took it to the street, then they did the next pile, then the next. An hour later, they were done. The group had energy and enthusiasm, but they lacked infrastructure. Instead of everyone quickly starting to rake, someone should have realized that the sooner you can get some leaves onto the tarp, the quicker you can get the overall job done. Some simple reengineering of how the work was done would have cut the 90-minute job into about 45 minutes.

HR departments often do equally creative and inventive work that is sometimes disconnected because of a lack of infrastructure and governance. For example, one firm spent enormous resources creating a competence model that was used for staffing, but an entirely different needs assessment was used to design training, another for performance management, and yet another for succession planning. Ensuring consistency between/among HR practices comes from creating an infrastructure by which to manage and control HR work.

Infrastructure includes governance issues about how work is allocated. In recent years, for example, outsourcing has become a "hot" phenomenon and a number of outsourcing firms have been spawned in everything from benefits to training to compensation. Coming to grips with which work should be done where (inside vs. outside; corporate vs. field; line vs. staff; senior vs. junior staff, etc.) continues to impact the HR function.

Infrastructure also deals with issues of measurement. Without measurement systems, no one can know for sure the impact of an activity. Measurement is critical in benchmarking what should be done as well as in assessing the impact of what has been done. In the future, measurement of HR will need to become more precise and at the same time more elegant. Precision will come when HR professionals can align specific HR work with equally specific outcomes. Elegance will emerge as the overall impact of HR work becomes clear.

Infrastructure also deals with how the HR department needs to adapt to the changing work environment. As the nature of work changes, so must the way work is delivered. For example, knowledge workers may require more flexibility in how they work than do traditional manufacturing workers.

In thinking about the future infrastructure of HR, a series of questions should be addressed:

- *Where Should HR Work Be Done?*

   HR work traditionally has been done by HR professionals. Now, with pressures for cost reductions as well as increased specialization the boundaryless organization is emerging in which HR work may be contracted to an outside partner who brings specific knowledge to a particular problem. Current experiments in outsourcing or partnering, however, are just that; it is not yet clear how much to outsource, to whom to outsource, or how to govern a positive outsourcing relationship.

- *How Do We Measure HR Work?*

   Measurement requires models which show the impact of activity x on outcome y. As such models are created, tested, revised, and tested again, firms can begin to find how different HR practices produce different results. Innovations in measurement are necessary for HR to become more a discipline rather than a fragmented set of practices loosely clustered under the banner of human resources.

- *How Do HR Executives Align HR Work Both Inside and Outside?*

   External alignment means that HR work should be creating value to those outside the firm, for example, suppliers, customers, or communities. HR in the future needs to consider these external alignments more carefully. Internal alignment means that everyone within an HR department focuses attention on similar issues. This means that HR executives and new hires should be concerned about and working on similar issues. Creating such alignment is neither fully understood nor appreciated by all HR professionals.

These essays offer insights into infrastructure, the processes used to govern HR work within an enterprise. They offer an HR professional the array of choices and alternatives by which to make decisions about how to create internal processes that adapt to future demands. The infrastructure should also ensure connected and integrated HR practices—that which is done for one practice affects another. Had the leaf-rakers had more infrastructure, they would have had more clearly assigned roles (e.g., tarp carrier, leaf raker), and time would have been saved in completing the task.

CHAPTER 22

HUMAN RESOURCE LEADERSHIP IN KNOWLEDGE-BASED ENTITIES: SHAPING THE CONTEXT OF WORK

HOMA BAHRAMI and STUART EVANS

Knowledge-based entities are fast becoming the engines of economic growth as we evolve from the industrial era to the information age where knowledge and intellectual capabilities are the critical competitive differentiators. Technology is transforming the work place in ways which were unimaginable ten years ago—posing novel challenges. The emerging trends toward "forward-deployment," "anytime/anyplace" work, remote management, horizontal relationships, contingent workers, and virtual offices are rapidly diffusing in business entities around the world. Many emerging and traditional firms are rapidly becoming populated with knowledge workers.

Shaping the context of work is one of the most critical challenges facing knowledge-based entities. Context refers to the physical, technological, symbolic (visual reinforcers of cultural norms), and organizational environment within which knowledge workers operate. Our research indicates that human resource professionals have a pivotal role to play in designing, shaping, and reinventing the work context. The remainder of this article explores the context-shaping role of human resource professionals. It is based largely on our field research in leading high tech enterprises in Silicon Valley and elsewhere.[1]

THE WORK CONTEXT

Work in many knowledge-based companies is characterized by intensity, novelty, and collaborative teamwork. Many knowledge workers are especially motivated by belonging to socially cohesive communities, working on challenging assignments, and having "fun" in the process. Since the boundaries between personal and work life are increasingly blurred, the work context provides an anchor of stability and "friendship" opportunities, nurtures a spirit of belonging, and can facilitate teamwork and cooperation.

As technological sophistication makes remote work more feasible, the physical workplace is becoming more significant. Silicon Valley firms are active advocates of remote work and flexible work practices but also invest in creating campus-like physical structures which can nurture creativity and innovation and create a spirit of community. As shown in Table 22.1, the work context has to balance the creation of (1) an infrastructure for remote communication and information exchange, (2) a physical environment which can transmit the cultural norms and reinforce the desired interaction patterns, and (3) an organizational design which can align responsibility, authority, and accountability.

From an organizational vantage point, knowledge-based high-tech companies face three simultaneous challenges: how to continuously innovate, operate with speed and agility in view of short product and service life cycles, and create an organization geared for flexibility to deal with unexpected changes. These challenges demand a work context which can balance the need for physical as well as virtual colocation, can create alignment, and can be organized for creativity and agility. The HR team is positioned ideally to address these challenges and place itself in a pivotal leadership role.[2]

Table 22.1
Shapers of Work Context

Physical Infrastructure	Organizational Infrastructure	Information Technology Infrastructure
General look and feel	Organizational design	Nomadic work tools: remote office enablers
Informal interaction patterns	Flexible work arrangements	Digital filing systems
Formal interaction modes	Decision norms; communication protocols	HR Systems
		On-line learning tools Internet, electronic, and voice mail protocols

THE LEADERSHIP ROLE OF HR

There is no single task associated with shaping the context of work. Instead, HR leaders and pracitioners need to consider four interrelated roles of: "orgitecht," "vendor," "hub," and "glue"—each addressing a critical component of the work context. Figure 22.1 depicts these roles and some of the activities associated with each category.

The "Orgitecht"

Creating, shaping, and updating the context of work requires formulating a strategic vision which can blend together the three dimensions of the work context: the physical facilities, the Information Technology (IT) infrastructure, and the organizational design—turning the HR leader into what may be called an "orgitecht" (a hybrid term, blending organization, technology, and architect).

Figure 22.1
The Emerging Role of HR Teams

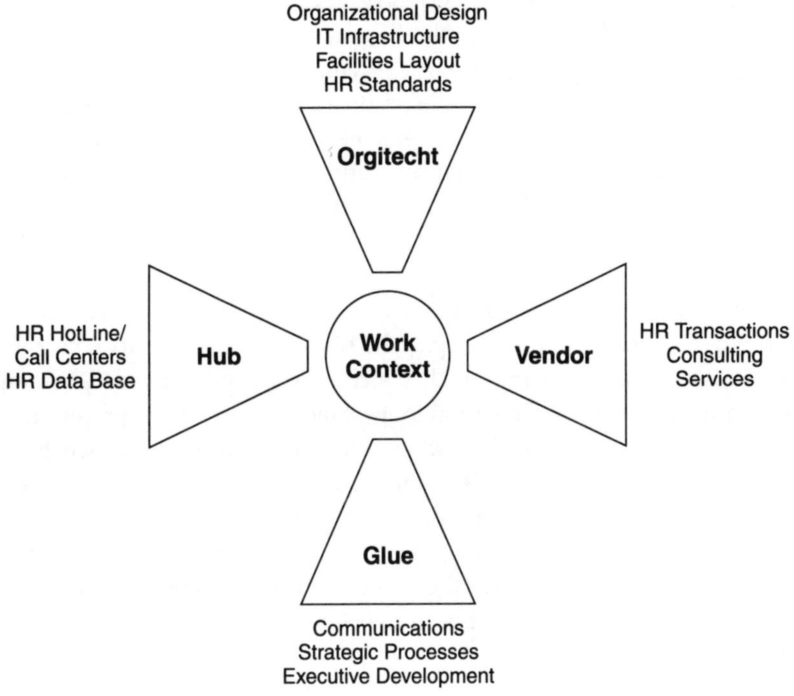

Organizational Design
IT Infrastructure
Facilities Layout
HR Standards

Orgitecht

HR HotLine/
Call Centers   **Hub**   **Work
Context**   **Vendor**   HR Transactions
Consulting
HR Data Base   Services

Glue

Communications
Strategic Processes
Executive Development

The first dimension involves the design, use, and allocation of the physical facilities which impact formal and informal communication and interaction patterns, the physical symbols which visually reinforce underlying cultural norms, and the overall image of the organization to the outside communities and stakeholders.

For example, the facilities of Sun Micro-systems in Menlo Park, California, are deliberately designed to create a campuslike ambiance. A feature of the architectural design is a central thoroughfare, analogous to a downtown or a main street, with various office complexes around it. People "bump" into each other, almost as a matter of course, as they go from one meeting to another. The stairways were deliberately designed to be wider than normal, to allow work teams or clusters of people to walk down together and continue their conversation in the process.[3]

The continuous development and refinement of the IT infrastructure is another dimension of HR's leadership role as an "orgitecht." The Information Technology (IT) infrastructure poses a special challenge due to its complexity, rapid pace of change, introduction of new products and services, and the "learning curve" impact on the users. Despite the challenges, it is crucial for collaborative teamwork, remote interaction, sharing information, and creating organizational flexibility and agility.

HR professionals can address the IT challenge in novel and innovative ways. One case in point is a current experiment initiated by the HR team at VeriFone, a global leader in transaction automation. Its organization is described as a "blueberry pancake"—the blueberries refer to its many work sites around the world. The IT infrastructure is a crucial component of its organizational design enabling product development teams, for example, to work collaboratively 24 hours a day despite their lack of physical and geographic proximity.

A number of customized software applications facilitate connectivity and information exchange—for example, the travel itineraries of its senior executives are available on-line so that meetings can be scheduled without going through endless coordination loops. Since many of their professionals travel extensively as part of their work, and may be away from their families for periods of time, the HR team is currently undertaking a pilot experiment to enable the children of its employees to be logged on to the company's internal mail system and have access to a variety of information sources. The expectation is that the program may create greater awareness, alignment, and connectivity between the employees and their families even when they are on the road.

The third dimension of a knowledge-based orgitechture is the organizational design component including alignment between structure, culture, reward, and evaluation criteria, areas which historically have been associated with HR, albeit in a more tactical capacity. The challenge facing HR teams is to strike a balance between the macroconsiderations, such as structural groupings and cultural norms, and microconsiderations including a whole range of people practices and standards. These include recruiting, evaluation, development, reward systems, promotion policies, succession planning, career tracks, and so on. In addition, given the fast pace of change, these design considerations have to be continuously updated and recalibrated as new realities unfold.[4] The entire area of change management is therefore an integral component of this role.

While HR leaders and professionals do not necessarily have to "own" all three areas of orgitechtural design—in terms of reporting relationships and allocation of authority, they do need to view themselves as the integrators, the catalysts, and the hubs, pulling together the different constituencies and creating a shared vision for the organization. A number of high-tech companies have fused all three areas under the leadership of the HR team.

A good illustration is that of 3Com, a leading data networking company, where "Corporate Services" encompasses HR, facilities, and IT and has been represented, as a cluster, on the "Corporate Executive Committee," the most senior policy-making group. Its HR team is in the process of creating what is called an "adult community," where people can work flexibly, leverage their limited time by having "life" services (such as dry cleaning) on site, and develop a spirit of community, albeit in the context of an adult-to-adult rather than the traditional parent–child relationship.

The "Vendor"

This is the area associated with the traditional HR function. It comprises the set of transactions and administrative processes which address the implementation of a portfolio of people management practices including recruiting, compensation and benefits, and evaluation and appraisal. An important issue for knowledge-based entities is the extent to which such transactions should be automated to enable all employees to undertake the tasks, leaving HR to manage the IT infrastructure, update on-line information, and act as a consultant on an "as-needed" basis.

A second issue is the extent to which these services should be outsourced, allowing HR teams to focus on setting people "standards," screening potential outsourcers, and managing outsourced relationships. Many high-tech companies tend to outsource the nonproprietary activities such as identifying and screening the first pool of potential recruits, while retaining the proprietary or unique aspects in-house. Additionally, HR-related administrative transactions are being consolidated in order to reduce costs, leverage synergies, and create simplicity by setting up single points of contact for the end-users.

A good case in point is the HR infrastructure at Hewlett-Packard. Organized on the basis of focused, self-contained divisions, it had historically provided the divisional support functions including HR. In recent years, however, the HR organization has evolved to create consolidated units for key HR transactions such as compensation and benefits. While divisions still retain certain HR liaison activities, they focus mainly on customized consulting and organizational development activities, rather than on transaction processing.

"The Hub"

A third role associated with HR teams in high-tech companies is one which can be best referred to as the "hub"—*providing an integrated, single point of contact for the provision of a variety of HR information to the end-user.* The rationale is that as IT is replacing the administrative role of HR, all employees need to have access to updated HR information and services on an as-needed basis. Delivery mechanisms include hotlines and call centers.

A number of companies in Silicon Valley—such as Apple Computer— were early pioneers of the HR Hotline, designed to provide efficiency, fast service, and supplement their IT-based, HR infrastructure. These capabilities are used extensively in many companies and are typically staffed by highly experienced and knowledgeable HR professionals.

In a sense, the hub role and the internal consultant role go hand in hand. Line managers want up-to-date information and a responsive service, but they also want the information delivered in ways which are relevant and customized. This places the call center or the hotline respondents in a highly influential position since they have to customize the information and in the process build credibility with the line users.

"The Glue"

In view of the recent trends toward network organizations, remote management, and globally dispersed units in many knowledge-based entities, *there is a critical need for some kind of a "glue" to align knowledge workers behind a common purpose and set of values.* This is where the "glue" dimension of the HR professionals' role comes into its own. In contrast to the hard glue provided by the finance and the IT teams, the HR team has to create and manage the soft glue which not only binds and aligns but also motivates.

A variety of mechanisms is used to create this soft glue. Many involve some form of interactive discussion, typically between the generals and the troops. The most common delivery mechanisms include executive and management conferences and workshops, typically designed by HR teams in response to changing priorities and business realities.

By way of illustration, the HR team at Cable & Wireless, a telecommunications company, took the lead role in organizing a series of management conferences among the top 100 executives from various parts of the world in order to brainstorm suitable options for evolving the strategy and the organization. A series of conferences was organized to bring together senior executives, key line managers, a cross section of customers and alliance partners, and external thought leaders. Designed as action learning sessions, the discussions culminated in a new strategic and organizational blueprint for the future.

Such trends are compatible with a seeming paradox in many knowledge-based companies: While there is continuous emphasis on development and training instead of classroom based events separate from the work context, in the words of one HR leader "development is opportunity-driven, real time, embedded in the work, and available to all."[5]

THE CURRENT STATUS: SCHIZOPHRENIA OR TRANSITIONAL LEARNING?

These roles provide exciting opportunities for HR leaders to create, shape, and transform the context of work in knowledge-based entities.

Not surprising, however, what we most commonly observe today, can be best characterized as a sense of "schizophrenia": one foot in the old camp, viewing HR in terms of the traditional administrative transactions, and one foot in the new environment where HR teams have the opportunity to shape the work context of the future.

Traditional firms face a three-fold challenge during this transitional phase as they become populated increasingly with knowledge workers. First, HR leaders have to be preemptive in seeding new initiatives and focused experiments which can help shape a stimulating work context. Second, HR teams need to hone their competencies in order to become true partners, driven by business issues, fluent in business parlance, and confident in their leadership abilities. Finally, as knowledge workers cannot be managed within the command and control paradigm, HR teams have to undertake these roles by exercising influence without authority, building bridges to other functions, and viewing themselves as synthesizers and catalysts. This three-fold challenge may be initially daunting, yet it presents the HR community with the opportunity to migrate to the center stage of the organization at a time when intellectual and people assets are becoming the most significant source of competitive advantage.

NOTES

1. Some of the research findings have been reported in a number of articles; See Bahrami, H., & Evans, S., "Flexible re-cycling and high technology entrepreneurship," *California Management Review,* Vol. 37, No. 3, Spring 1995; Bahrami, H. "The emerging flexible enterprise: Perspectives from Silicon Valley," *California Management Review,* Vol. 34, No. 4, Summer 1992; Bahrami, H., & Evans, S., "Emerging organizational regimes in high technology firms: The bi-modal form," *Human Resource Management* Spring 1989; Bahrami, H., & Evans, S., "Stratocracy in high technology firms," *California Management Review,* Vol. 30, No. 1, Fall 1987; (Reprinted in G. Carroll & D. Vogel (eds.) *"Organizational Approaches to Strategy,"* Ballinger, 1988); Evans, S., "Strategic flexibility for high technology manœuvres: A conceptual framework," *Journal of Management Studies,* Vol. 28 (1), pp. 69–89, 1991.

2. The term "HR team" is used here to refer to the group of HR specialists and generalists brought together to address a specific HR challenge. While the HR professionals may comprise the core team, line managers and individual contributors from other functions typically are included, in a flexible mode, depending on the nature of the project.

3. The term "orgitecht" evolved out of an informal discussion with Eric Richert, Director of Work Effectiveness at Sun Microsystems.

4. See Bahrami, H., & S. Evans "Strategy-making in high technology firms: The empiricist mode," *California Management Review,* Vol. 31, No. 2, Winter 1989.

5. Comments by Debra Engel—Vice President of Corporate Services—at 3Com, California Strategic Human Resource Partnership, May 1996.

CHAPTER 23

THE TRUTH ABOUT BEST PRACTICES: WHAT THEY ARE AND HOW TO APPLY THEM

JAC FITZ-ENZ

Russia is a riddle, wrapped in a mystery, inside an enigma.
Winston Churchill
1938 Radio Broadcast

Just as Churchill described the inherent contradictions within Russia, the search for best practices has been hindered by several self-imposed paradoxes. As a result, many believe that some publicized process is an example of a best practice. In actuality, it is only the visible result of something much more fundamental within the organization, which is itself the true best practice.

Today's more effective human resource (HR) managers are looked to for information and ideas on best practices in human asset management. This is a growing expectation which, in the future, will further separate the professional from the administrator. The objective of this paper is to provide human resource managers with a validated model of best human asset management practices.

THE PARADOX MASK

Three paradoxes mask the truth about best practice. The *first* is the search for the magic wand. We, as business people, expect to find simple solutions to today's complex organizational management problems. When we do latch onto our imagined magic wand in the form of another company's practice all we have done is deluded ourselves. The paradox within this paradox is that we know and even admit it. Recently, a client came seeking metrics to which she could compare her operation. In the course of our discussion, I pointed out that I could give her norms that matched her demographics, but she should not make staffing and budgeting decisions based on them. Her issues were much more complex and unique. She replied, "I know it, but I want to use them anyway." In short, she was willing to conduct a function on a simplistic foundation.

The *second paradox* is that the visible program that someone touts in a journal as a generalizeable best practice is neither generalizeable nor a best practice. Follow-up interviews with authors, reporters, and employees involved in those reports most often showed them to be exaggerations or even misstatements of the facts. Even when the report was more or less accurate the Saratoga staff found that the practice was not repeatable with the same or better results. In short, it was a tale of fanciful proportions that was not applicable to any other situation. A generous estimate is that the staff found this to be "a tale" in about 70 percent of the stories reported in professional journals over a three-year period in the early 1990s.

The *final paradox* is the irony of seeking enlightenment about the future from studying the past, that is, articles detailing what someone did a year or two ago. While it is true that one who fails to learn from history is condemned to relive it, in this case what is being sought from the past are practices that the future would recognize as anachronisms. Many have written about the shift from industrial to information or knowledge economy. The organizational structures of the future are already being reformed around information technology. The concept of a "job" as we have known it is rapidly being replaced by portable skills. As a result of these two forces, the knowledge economy and changing concept of jobs, we at Saratoga see people metaphorically rearranging chairs for an organization of the future in which no one will be sitting down.

With evolutionary level change coming at revolutionary speed the only hope one has of preparing for the future is to find practices that are so fundamental, so near bedrock, that they will play as effectively fifty years from now as they do today. The question is, "Is that possible, or is it in itself another paradox?" The result of our research at Saratoga into the nature of best practice yielded a positive answer.

BEST PRACTICE'S SECRET

We as businesspeople have been snorkeling in our search for the pearls of best practice when we should have been scuba diving. Best practice is not

a surface program, process, or policy. It is something more basic. Best
practice is better described as:

> An enduring commitment to a set of basic beliefs, traits, and operating
> stratagems. These are the constant context of the organization: the driving
> forces that distinguish it from all others.

Best practices in management are found deep inside the organization.
Only their progeny appear on the surface. In 1990, Saratoga Institute began
a formal, ongoing research program dedicated to answering clients' constant
question, "Who is good at _____ ?" Over the course of the next three years
we uncovered and verified eight factors that appear to be the common traits
of the best human asset management companies. The seminal point is that
none of the factors have anything to do with administrative or operational
programs.

THE METHODOLOGY

The research began within our human resource financial report database
(1991–1994). This database was launched by Saratoga in 1985 under the
sponsorship of the Society for Human Resource Management. The first
report was published in 1986 and has been updated every year since. The
database contains cost, time, and quantity data, and discussions of qualitative implications and applications for employee productivity, staffing,
pay and benefits, absence and turnover, and training from about 600 companies in more than 20 industries. The Saratoga process goes into the
database and pulls out the top 25 percent of the performers in each function. That is, we at Saratoga look for the lowest costs, fastest cycle times,
largest volumes, and highest quality data in staffing, compensation, benefits, retention, and human productivity. These identify the companies
who are top performers on an objective basis. No panel of experts is consulted, and no nominations are accepted. Objective performance is the
only qualifying mechanism. The first round companies are then subjected
to a screening process that includes detailed questions in the following
categories:

1. What was the business (not human resource) problem that you focused on last year and in which your results were better than three
   out of four participating companies?
2. Was there something unique about what you did to obtain your results, rather than that circumstances merely favored you last year?

3. Can you provide detailed data on the who, what, where, when, why, how, and how much of your activity and the outcomes?
4. Can you describe quantitatively as well as qualitatively the effect that your work on this issue had on the financial performance of your organization?

Typically, about 60 percent to 75 percent of the initial qualifiers failed to satisfy these requirements and were eliminated at this stage. We then compared the financial performance of their companies against that of competitors. To pass this test companies had to place in the top quartile of their industry. Our demand is that processes and systems that don't affect financial performance cannot be called best practices. Only after a company passed all the objective performance tests was their story published in the annual Best in America Guidebooks. To our knowledge no other publisher applies such a standardized, totally objective set of measures and requires qualifiers to be top financial performers as well as effective human asset managers. Our view is that most, if not all, so-called best practice databases are more interesting than factual.

THE DISCOVERY

The paradoxes arose as we prepared the data for publication the first year and it became clear that there were inconsistent and even contradictory examples from the 22 companies which had qualified. That is, their programmatic responses to their business problems were not similar. For example, one company might have instituted a policy or process related to hiring or paying or employee relations that was diametrically opposed to what others did. Parenthetically, this is when we began to see the problem with reporting programs or projects as examples of best practices. The logical conclusion must be, "If Company A drives a car and Company B rides a bike but both leave from the same point X and arrive at destination Y in the same amount of time, the vehicle cannot be the determining factor."

This led us back into the data for a closer look. We searched for anything that would explain the divergence. Was there something common to most or all of the companies that might account for their excellent performance? After a thorough review of activity it became clear that there were a number of largely unseen drivers behind the visible programs. In time, we uncovered nine factors (later reduced to eight by combining two) that were common to all qualifiers. The reason that the factors had gone unnoticed was that each company played them out in its own way.

What was common was that they *all* exhibited these traits. We then went back to the general population of the report and conducted a random sampling of the better performers who had not qualified. The eight factors were not commonly evident and in some cases were even reversed. From these data we tentatively announced our belief that the eight factors might be the antecedents of exceptional performance. In 1992 and 1993, we repeated our study using the same database with about a 15 percent turnover of participants. Remaining as bias free as we could by employing a largely new part-time research team, we witnessed the same phenomena. This led us to finally conclude that these eight factors are what we mean when we talk about best human asset management practices. Over the three-year period just over 100 companies qualified. We labeled those companies BHAMS or *best human asset managers*. The factors are shown in Table 23.1.

Table 23.1
Eight Best Human Asset Management Practices

Values: A constant focus on adding value in everything rather than simply doing something. In addition, there is a conscious, ongoing and largely successful attempt to balance human and financial values.

Commitment: Dedication to a long-term core strategy: They seem to build an enduring institution while changing methods but avoiding the temptation to chase management fads.

Culture: Proactive application of the corporate culture. Management is aware of how culture and systems can be linked together for consistency and efficiency.

Communication: An extraordinary concern for communicating with all stakeholders. Constant and extensive two-way communication using all media and sharing all types of vital information is the rule.

Partnering: New markets demand new forms of operation. They involve people within and outside the company in many decisions. This includes the design and implementation of new programs.

Collaboration: A high level of cooperation and involvement of all sections *within* functions. They study, redesign, launch, and follow-up new programs in a collective manner enhancing efficiency and cohesiveness.

Risk and Innovation: Innovation is recognized as a necessity. There is a willingness to risk shutting down present systems and structure and restarting in a totally different manner while learning from failure.

Competitive Passion: A constant search for improvement. They set up systems and processes to actively seek feedback and incorporate ideas from all sources.

EXEMPLARS

Across the board the 110 companies that qualified showed consistent evidence of the eight factors. All the companies did not practice all the beliefs, traits, and stratagems all the time; that would be too perfect to believe. Nevertheless, they were very consistent. Some of the standouts are Massachusetts Mutual Life or Iams, the highly successful producer of premium pet foods; both have a deep-set commitment to human and financial values as well as a long-term commitment to their core strategies. AT&T Universal Card Services is an excellent example of a strong culture linked with appropriate reinforcement systems. United Services Automobile Association (USAA), the financial services firm operating out of San Antonio, is the only firm selling insurance in all 50 states. It is one of the most effective communicating companies we've ever seen at Saratoga. Provident Bank of Baltimore has found partnering to be a highly successful management tool. Its employees work very well with community agencies for the benefit of all involved. The all-time best example of collaboration existed at Prudential Property and Casualty (P&C) before the Rock reorganized the division. It is possible that some of Pru's highly publicized recent malpractices came about partly because they didn't learn the lesson from P&C. Memorial Sloan Kettering Cancer Center and Raynet, the fiberoptics division of Raychem, are both long on innovation and risk management. All the qualifiers, from the Boy Scouts of America, Consumer Value Stores, and Ames Rubber Company in New Jersey to regional banks such as First Tennessee, showed a never-ending fascination with improvement.

CORROBORATION

Recently, we have seen instances of studies which found results similar to ours. The closest example is Collins and Porras's (1994) report published in *Built to Last*. Their eight factors map about 75 percent on ours. We found stronger evidence of the effects of extensive communications. We saw collaboration and partnering at which they only hinted. Some of the processes that Peters and Waterman (1982) uncovered in *In Search of Excellence* are also evident in our population. Looking at this from a futures perspective we see relationships with Imparato and Harari's *Jumping the Curve* (1994), and with Hamel and Prahalad's (1994) views underlying strategic architecture. In fact, the more we look into large scale, longitudinal studies the more correlations we find. Many of the traits that Drucker (1954) has championed for the past forty years: value focus, long-term commitment, culture management, prudent risk and innovative drive, are in our list.

THE CENTRAL POINT

The absolutely most critical lesson from this research is that

it isn't what you see, it's why you see it

that makes something a best practice driver. For example, as Peters and Waterman later declared, "managing by walking around" was not the real excellence issue. It's *why* the managers of excellent companies spent a lot of time in direct contact with their people that made them excellent. The fact that we give examples of communicative practices or processes can be a misleading paradox. The point is, the company's belief in the importance of communication is more important than any communicative act itself. The *belief* that drives the process is the real best practice.

RESISTANCE

Some people don't like these results. They still want a programmatic magic wand that they can wave. They like to say, "Company X did this so we should adapt it to our organization." There is nothing wrong with knowing how someone else does something, but usually after a very cursory examination we go way overboard in adopting the benchmark's method.

This is an example of our natural desire for a simple solution to a complex problem. It is the substitution of a visible outcome for the less visible driver. It is the choice of the effect over the cause. Finally, it is the application of yesterday's industrial method to tomorrow's information requirement. For human resources as a profession to endure and contribute, it must avoid quick-fix, surface-coating methods. HR managers have to stop using workload as an excuse. Instead of chasing the program-of-the-month we must persist in developing fundamental, bedrock capabilities that will serve our organizations well into the next millennium.

APPLICATIONS

The BHAM factors can be applied to every restructuring, reengineering, downsizing, outsourcing decision that we as business people face, but they require us to conduct a self-examination. This leads us to search for the answers from within, which is where they always reside. Any time that we want to make a major organizational intervention these eight factors can serve as criteria.

So, before we attack our organizational problem we should ask ourselves, "How do the eight factors work within our organization? Have we ever consciously thought about them? Do we regularly consider one or more of them in our organization design thinking? Specifically, do we have a value orientation that we truly live by? Have we formulated a core strategy and made a long-term commitment to it? Can we describe our cultural style and norms as the base for systems design? What and how do we communicate? Are we open to partnering? Is there evidence of collaboration as our modus operandi within departments? Do we like to innovate, take risks, and learn from our failures? Are we willing to never rest in our search for improvement?" These issues must be dealt with if we want to be world class operators. Our belief is that HR should play the role of provocateur in stimulating management to building enterprises.

Once we have some sense of who we are and how we operate, we can then use that knowledge in specific business opportunities. Figure 23.1 is a short format sample for applying the factors to an intervention. Several of these questions are not easy to answer; they take some thought and often spark serious debate. Many companies do not have clear value visions. Many more do not operate under a long-term core strategy. Culture is seldom given any deep consideration. Communication is an afterthought. Partnering and collaboration require a collective commitment to a superordinate organizational goal. Innovation is often called for, but the personal risk involved is sometimes daunting. Finally, the passion to improve is not evident in many firms. Where these conditions flourish best practices have no chance. But where and when HR can use the eight drivers to help management design, implement, and evaluate its operations it will become a best practice organization.

THE BOTTOM LINE

An examination of the financial records of the BHAM companies showed that they were consistently among the top financial performers in their industry. This lends further support for the common sense idea that good human management positively affects earnings. Saratoga's is one of several studies in the past decade that provide hard data in support of that notion. It is obvious that the behaviors suggested by the eight factors would build trust and loyalty within the workforce. Trust and loyalty increase retention and stimulate motivation and a desire to excel. The work of Huselid, Jackson, and Schuler (1997); Kravetz (1988); Schuster (1986); and Schlesinger and Heskett (1991), among others, suggests that sound human asset management contributes to financial success. Saratoga Institute's study adds one more block to the foundation by clarifying the true nature of best human asset management practices.

Figure 23.1
Application of BHAM Factors

BHAM CHECKLIST

VALUE: How will this intervention support the balanced value ethic?

_____

_____

STRATEGIC COMMITMENT: What resources do we need to make this fit with our long term commitment to our core strategy?

_____

_____

_____

CULTURE: How does this intervention fit with our culture as it is or as we want it to be?

Fits _____

Needs to Change _____

COMMUNICATION: How will we communicate this: who, what media, and methods?

Who (persons)	Media (e-mail, speech, newsletter, etc.)	Method (personal or group)
_____	_____	_____
_____	_____	_____

PARTNERING: Who do we need to involve from outside our unit to help drive this program?

_____

_____

COLLABORATION: What role and responsibility will other persons and units in our department have in designing and supporting this?

Person/Unit	Role
_____	_____
_____	_____
_____	_____

INNOVATION AND RISK: Is this an innovation that will contribute to competitive advantage: What is the risk in this change and how do we reduce it?

_____

_____

COMPETITIVE PASSION: What kind of system will we set up to get constructive feedback to continually improve this?

_____

_____

REFERENCES

Best in America guidebooks. (1991, 1993, 1994). Santa Clara, CA: Saratoga Institute.

Collins, J., & Porras, J. (1994). *Built to last.* New York: Harper-Collins.

Drucker, P.F., (1954). *The practice of management.* New York: Harper and Row.

Hamel, G., & Prahalad, C.K. (1994). *Competing for the future.* Cambridge: Harvard Business School Press.

Human resource financial reports. (1991–1994). Santa Clara, CA: Saratoga Institute.

Huselid, M.A., Jackson, S.E., & Schuler, R.S. (1997). The significance of human resource management effectiveness for corporate financial performance. *Academy of Management Journal, 40,* 171–188.

Imparato, N., & Harari, O. (1994). *Jumping the curve.* San Francisco: Jossey-Bass.

Kravetz, D. (1988). *The human resources revolution.* San Francisco: Jossey-Bass.

Managing in a time of great change. (1995). New York: Truman Talley Books/Dutton.

Peters, T., & Waterman, R. (1982). *In search of excellence,* New York: Harper-Collins.

Schlesinger, L., & Heskett, J. (1991). The service driven service company. *Harvard Business Review,* September-October, 71–81.

Schuster, F. (1986). *The Schuster report.* New York: Wiley.

CHAPTER 24

HUMAN RESOURCES AS A SOURCE OF SHAREHOLDER VALUE: RESEARCH AND RECOMMENDATIONS

BRIAN E. BECKER, MARK A. HUSELID,
PETER S. PICKUS, and MICHAEL F. SPRATT

The role of the human resource management (HRM) function in many organizations is at a crossroads. On one hand, the HRM function is in crisis, increasingly under fire to justify itself (Schuler, 1990; Stewart, 1996) and confronted with the very real prospect that a significant portion of its traditional responsibilities will be outsourced (Corporate Leadership Council, 1995). On the other hand, organizations have an unprecedented opportunity to refocus their HRM systems as strategic assets. Indeed, the same competitive pressures that provide an incentive for firms to outsource costly HRM transactions have dramatically increased the strategic value of a skilled, motivated, adaptable work force, and the HRM system that supports and develops it. Transforming this crisis into an opportunity, however, requires a new organizational perspective on the HRM system, one that is also a perspective *shared* by the CEO and the chief HR officer (CHRO). At its core, this strategic perspective requires that the CHRO be focused on identifying and solving the human capital elements of important business problems (e.g., those problems likely to impede growth, lower profitability, and diminish shareholder value). The tangible evidence of this focus is an internally coherent, externally aligned, and effectively implemented HRM system.

THE NEW STRATEGIC ROLE FOR HRM

Pfeffer (1994) describes how changing market conditions have rendered many of the traditional sources of competitive advantage, such as patents, economies of scale, access to capital, and market regulation, less important in the current economic environment than they have been in the recent past. This is not to argue that such assets are not valuable, but rather in a global economy that demands innovation, speed, adaptability, and low cost, these assets do not differentiate firms the way they once did. Instead, the core competencies (Hamel & Prahalad, 1994) and capabilities (Stalk, Evans, & Schulman, 1992) of employees that help to develop new products, provide world class customer service, and implement organizational strategy are relatively more influential.

Unlike conventional assets, this form of intellectual or organizational capital (Tomer, 1987) is largely invisible (Itami, 1987) and therefore does not appear on the firm's balance sheet.[1] Although organizational and intellectual capital may well be "invisible," the *sources* of this capital are not. They are found in a skilled, motivated, and adaptable work force, and in the HRM system that develops and sustains it. Hamel and Prahalad (1994, p. 232) argue that these "people embodied skills" are directly reflected in conventional measures of firm profitability.[2] Indeed, as intellectual capital has come to represent an increasing fraction of many firm's total assets, the strategic role of the HRM system has also become more critical. Ulrich and Lake (1990) point to such HRM systems as the source of organizational capabilities that allow firms to learn and capitalize on new opportunities. The HRM function that traditionally focused on transactions, practices, and compliance was, and is, appropriately considered a cost center. In contrast, the HRM system that develops and maintains a firm's strategic infrastructure should be considered an investment. It is an essential element of the infrastructure that supports this value creation process and a potential strategic lever for the organization. Moreover, as one of the more malleable and underdeveloped strategic levers available to most CEOs, the HRM system represents a policy option with very substantial and accessible returns.

WHAT IS THE EVIDENCE FOR THE STRATEGIC IMPACT OF HRM?

The strategic HRM literature tends to emphasize the entire HRM *system* as the unit of analysis, in contrast to the traditional focus on individual policies or practices. This systems-level focus is consistent with the conceptual rationale for the presence of a strategic impact and is a significant

departure from traditional work in the field. Such HRM systems, often referred to as *high performance work systems* (HPWS) are generally thought
to include rigorous recruitment and selection procedures, performance-
contingent incentive compensation systems, and management development
and training activities linked to the needs of the business.[3] Specifically, how
does the adoption of an HPWS affect firm value? As Figure 24.1 illustrates,
the essential feature of these strategic HRM systems is that they are linked
to the firm's business and strategic initiatives. The result is an HRM system that produces employee behaviors that are focused on key business priorities, which in turn drive profits, growth, and ultimately market value.[4]

Much of the prior research on this subject has been limited to the intermediate relationships depicted in Figure 24.1. In contrast, Becker, Huselid,
and their colleagues have focused on the strategic impact of the HRM system, namely the ultimate effect of the HRM system on both market-based
and accounting-based measures of firm performance (Delaney & Huselid,
1997; Becker & Huselid, 1996; Huselid, 1995; Huselid & Becker, 1995,
1996; Huselid, Jackson, & Schuler, 1996). The use of market-based measures
of firm performance is particularly appropriate in this line of research because these measures reflect the present value of the firm's future cash flows
and are, therefore, net of any additional costs associated with implementing
these systems. While there is no consensus measure of an HPWS in this
emerging literature, based on responses to more than 30 specific questions
from a sample of 740 firms, Huselid and Becker (1995) created an index of
each firm's HRM system reflecting the degree to which a firm had deployed
an HPWS.[5] Huselid and Becker have consistently found that firms with
higher values on this index, other things equal, have economically and sta-
tistically significant higher levels of firm performance. They further estimate that plausible changes (a one standard deviation improvement) in the
quality of a firm's HPWS are associated with changes in market value of

Figure 24.1
A Model of the HR—Shareholder Value Relationship

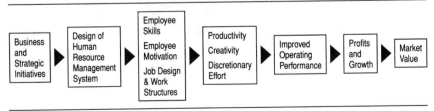

$15,000 to $60,000 per employee. For a firm with 10,000 employees this increase represents more than half a billion dollars in market value.

The work by Huselid and Becker suggests that a properly designed and deployed HRM system represents a significant economic asset for an organization. It does not, however, provide direct evidence of *how* such a system creates that value. To date there is very little research that "peels back the onion" and describes the processes through which HRM systems influence the principal intermediate variables that ultimately affect firm performance as described in Figure 24.1. Based on recent work in the field of competitive strategy (Barney, 1991), however, we would expect that if a firm's HRM system is to be a source of sustained competitive advantage, it must be difficult to imitate (Wright & McMahon, 1992). This suggests that organizational HPWS are highly idiosyncratic and must be tailored carefully to each firm's individual situation to achieve optimum impact. In other words, if a properly configured HPWS could be created by simply benchmarking competitor firms, it could be easily replicated by competitors and therefore not likely to provide a source of sustainable competitive advantage.[6] Cappelli and Crocker-Hefter (1996) state this case very well:

> We believe that a single set of "best" practices may, indeed, be overstated . . . there are examples in virtually every industry of highly successful firms that have very distinct management practices. We argue that these distinctive human resource practices help to create unique competencies that differentiate products and, in turn, drive competitiveness. Indeed, product differentiation is one of the essential functions of strategic management, and distinctive human resource practices shape the core competencies that determine how firms compete. (p. 7)

In short, we believe that both the source of the HRM effect on firm performance *and* its inimitability reflect an "idiosyncratic contingency."[7] Namely, HRM systems only have a systematic impact on the bottom line when they are embedded in the management infrastructure and help the firm achieve important business priorities such as shortening product development cycle times, increasing customer service, lowering turnover among high-quality employees, etc. The particular form of these problems, and more importantly the appropriate design and alignment of the HRM system with business priorities, is highly firm-specific. To the extent that real value creation occurs as part of these firm-specific alignments, benchmarking will play a very limited role in the development of an HPWS. CHROs might profitably look to other firms for best in class practices, but these practices will only have a strategic impact if they are appropriately aligned with the rest of the HRM system and with the firm's broader strategic infrastructure.

Thus, we believe that an inordinate focus on best practices is misguided and may even be counterproductive to the extent it diverts valuable managerial effort from the difficult and time-consuming job of developing an internally coherent and externally aligned HPWS. Competency-building efforts should focus on the firm-specific relationships described in Figure 24.1. Best practices (e.g., investments in training, performance management, and incentive compensation systems) are only a point of departure. In other words, *if* a firm has decided to incent employees with a particular form of team compensation, it should be optimally designed for its intended purposes. Within this context, benchmarking can provide a useful source of ideas; however, while becoming "best in class" may be a necessary condition for ultimately improving firm performance, it is not a sufficient condition. The more crucial strategic decision is how these team incentives align with *other* HRM practices and how the total HRM system is designed such that it supports key business priorities. Without the latter, the HRM system will be just a best in class version of an HRM function in crisis. If the HRM system is not properly aligned, these individual best practices can potentially be in conflict within the HRM system and actually diminish firm value.

As an example of this phenomenon, Huselid and Becker (1995) interpret their empirical evidence of nonlinearities in the HRM-firm performance relationship as an indication of roles played by best practices and the alignment of the broader HRM system with business priorities. Based on their HPWS index, Figure 24.2 describes the relationship between improvements

Figure 24.2
The Impact of HR on Shareholder Value

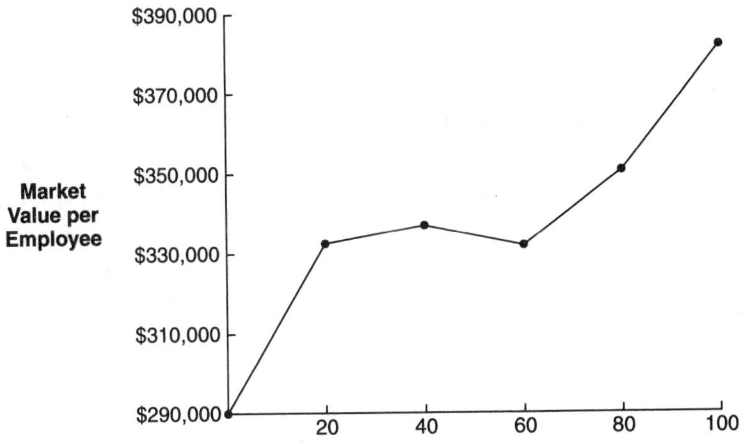

in the relative quality of a firm's HRM system and changes in its market value per employee. A more sophisticated HRM architecture (defined as higher values on the Huselid-Becker scale) reflects the greater deployment of an HPWS.[8] Figure 24.2 illustrates two broad findings. First, the impact of more intensive deployment of a HPWS is associated with substantially greater market value per employee. Second, Figure 24.2 shows that the *returns* from investments in an HPWS are not linear. We believe the nonlinearity in this relationship emphasizes the linkage between best practices and strategic alignments discussed above. As firms make initial steps toward the development of an HPWS (i.e., moving from the lowest firms in the ranking to the 20th percentile) the HRM system moves from an impediment to a neutral strategic influence. Here the HRM system creates value by getting out of the way. For the broad middle range, improving the relative sophistication of the HRM system (adoption of best practices) has little marginal impact on firm performance. This approach does no damage, but HRM is not really a strategic partner. Finally, firms above the 60th percentile arguably have all the appropriate best practices, but more importantly have begun to integrate this system more broadly into the operational fabric of the firm. Here the marginal impact on firm performance is the same as those HRM systems below the 20th percentile but for different reasons. In short, we believe the impact of HRM on firm performance among these better HRM systems is much more than the payoff for the adoption of best practices. It is the reflection of the payoffs to a competitive advantage that combines these best policies into an internally coherent system that is directly aligned with business priorities and operating initiatives most likely to create economic value. In essence, these results point both to the potential returns from effecting very significant changes in a firm's HRM system as well as the potential difficulty of doing so.

WHERE THE RUBBER MEETS THE ROAD: THE SYSTEM IS THE SOLUTION!

To this point we have described the theoretical and empirical support for our contention that a new role for HRM throughout the firm is required and have presented evidence to document the magnitude of economic opportunity associated with the adoption of a *high performance work system*. How do we begin to capture such returns? Where do we start? An important first step is the development of "systems" thinking among line *and* HR managers. In contrast to the functional view of HR, a systems perspective reemphasizes such interrelationships as the recruiting function being linked with the selection system, which in turn provides sensible inputs into the training subsystem. Subsequently, the performance management and incentive compensation system must define desired employee behaviors and reward those behaviors in meaningful ways when goals are achieved. Equally important, the goals and desired employee behaviors developed and rewarded by the HR system are entirely focused on achieving critical business priorities.

For the CHRO and the HR group to genuinely become a source of value creation for the firm, however, requires more than just an occasional reminder of the necessary relationship among the respective functional responsibilities within HR. Quinn, Anderson, and Finkelstein (1996) describe four levels of professional intellect within an organization: cognitive knowledge, advanced skills, systems understanding, and self-motivated creativity. Traditional HR manager competencies include both cognitive knowledge and advanced skills. For a firm's HRM system to have a strategic impact, to be a source of shareholder value, however, it is crucial that HR managers develop the capacity for systems understanding. The systems perspective is essential because it provides a

> deep knowledge of the web of cause-and-effect relationships . . . permit[ing] professionals . . . to solve larger and more complex problems . . . creating extraordinary value . . . [by] anticipat[ing] subtle interactions and unintended consequences. (Quinn et al., 1996, p. 72)

Based on our empirical work and experiences in a wide variety of companies, we believe the failure to appreciate these "subtle interactions and unintended consequences," what we have termed *Deadly Combinations* and *Powerful Connections,* to be the single greatest challenge facing traditional HR managers as they make the transition to becoming true business partners.

Deadly Combinations develop when firms adopt HRM policies and practices that might well make sense in isolation but when evaluated within the context of *other* HRM practices deployed throughout the firm are a recipe for disaster. Simple examples can be found in firms that invest in sophisticated performance management systems only to adopt compensation policies that provide for little meaningful economic distinction between high and low performing employees; or firms that encourage employees to work together in teams, but then provide raises based on individual contributions. Alternatively, *Powerful Connections* reflect the presence of complementarities or synergies that can occur when economic returns from the whole of the HRM system adds up to more than the sum of its parts.

For example, in empirical work in over 1,500 companies we have found that combining above-market pay policies with comprehensive performance management systems has a 50 percent larger effect on firm performance than the effects of the two policies considered in isolation. This finding reflects the synergistic gains of a better applicant pool, more talented hires, and an HRM system that is able to recognize and reward these more talented employees for their superior performance.

A more complex example of this type of synergy, reflecting both *Deadly Combinations* and *Powerful Connections,* is illustrated in Figure 24.3. Based on our empirical work, the downward sloping arrow in Figure 24.3 shows the effects of an organizational policy of promotion from within on firm performance, ignoring any effects of related HRM practices. While promotion from within can, on one hand, serve as an essential foundation for building core competencies, it can also degenerate into a low performance, "civil service" culture when compensation and advancement opportunities are not linked to performance. The latter effect apparently predominates and is reflected in the downward sloping arrow in Figure 24.3. In contrast, the upward sloping arrow shows the effects of a promotion from within policy when it is part of an HRM system that includes extensive training, incentive pay, and relatively greater pay differentials between high and low employee performance. In this case the civil service dimension of promotion from within has been mitigated by other elements of the HRM system that helps to develop a skilled and motivated work force.

Figure 24.3
Deadly Combinations and Powerful Connections

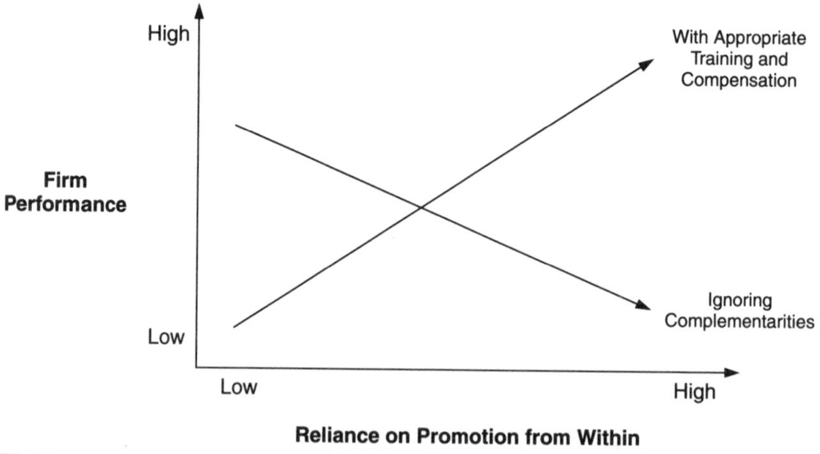

These same *Deadly Combinations* and *Powerful Connections* will probably not be present in every firm, or even most firms. Indeed if these synergies and unintended consequences are idiosyncratic there will be no one common organizational experience, or right answer; however, the only way that any organization can hope to identify the HRM system that is appropriate is to adopt a systems perspective. This means that business priorities drive the development of the HRM system, and the evaluation of any element of that system (recruiting, selection, compensation, etc.) is always considered within the context of *other* elements of the system *and* the business priorities of the organization.

TOWARD HUMAN CAPITAL MANAGEMENT

This chapter outlines both the conceptual and empirical evidence supporting the view that HR can have an important influence on shareholder value. In a departure from the traditional view of HR we argue, and provide strong research support for our contention, that the HR system can potentially represent a strategic asset for the organization. The key to realizing this potential is to think of HR, first and foremost, as a system that is characterized by synergies such as the *Powerful Connections* and *Deadly Combinations* discussed above. To create this value, however, requires a fundamentally different perspective on HR; a perspective probably more accurately described as human capital management than as HRM. The concept of human capital management emphasizes the essential point that a firm's human resources and subsequently its HRM system can be more than a cost to be minimized. A firm's human resources have an asset value that corresponds to the present value of future net cash flows that are derived from the skills, motivation, and adaptability of the firm's workforce. It requires that both the CEO and the CHRO share a focus on one essential question: *How do we architect a human capital strategy that is aligned with business priorities and capable of rapidly adapting to a shifting competitive landscape?*

In the past, market conditions have not required a human capital perspective. The HRM function could focus largely on transactions and compliance with little opportunity cost. If HR managers are going to evolve into human capital managers, however, they will require a dramatically different set of competencies. For example, Ulrich, Brockbank, Yeung, and Lake (1995) argue that HRM competencies fall into three domains: (1) knowledge of the business, (2) HRM functional expertise, and (3) management of change. They show that demonstrated competencies in each of these domains are associated with greater perceived effectiveness of the HRM function. Most HR managers receive high marks in the domain of HRM functional expertise, but their knowledge of the business' sources of competitive advantage, industry dynamics, and the skill sets associated with the management of change are often much less well developed. Yet these are *exactly* the competencies required for human capital management. Similarly, Huselid, Jackson, and Schuler (1997) identified two broad competencies that help HR managers to develop effective HRM systems. (1) *Professional HRM capabilities* were related to the delivery of traditional HRM activities such as recruiting, selection, and compensation. In contrast, (2) *Business-related capabilities* reflected an understanding of the business and the implementation of competitive strategy. Both contributed to HRM effectiveness, which in turn had a substantial positive effect on several measures of firm financial performance. Huselid, Jackson, and Schuler's conclusions emphasize our point: Professional HRM capabilities are a necessary, but not sufficient, condition for better firm performance. More importantly, the business-related capabilities of HR managers (i.e., those linked to human capital management) are not only underdeveloped within most firms, but they also represent the area of greatest economic opportunity.

In the broadest terms these changes require a dramatically different role for the HR function and CHRO. Specifically,

1. *HR Must Focus on Business Level Outcomes Rather than HR Level Inputs.* The number one priority for the value-creating HR function is to develop the perspective and competency to solve business problems. HR matters when it can point to human capital problems that limit the ability of the firm to achieve important business priorities *and* can provide HR solutions to those problems. Adopting the latest appraisal methodology, for example, only creates value when it can be evaluated within this context.

2. *HR Must Become a Strategic Core Competency Rather than a Market Follower.* A *high performance work system* that creates real shareholder value is not a commodity than can be benchmarked from other organizations. Bench-marking might keep the firm in the game, but it will not provide the intellectual capital to create a sustained competitive advantage.

3. *Strategic Competencies Are More Important than Functional Competencies.* The most important value creating HR competency, and the one most underdeveloped in many firms, is the ability to understand the human capital dimension of each of the firm's key business priorities and be

able to communicate how solving these human capital problems will directly affect operating performance.

4. *The Most Important Missing Element in the HR Functional Expertise Is a Systems Perspective.* Functional competencies must blend traditional HR functional expertise with a system perspective to avoid *deadly combinations* and identify *powerful connections.*

Just as we have argued for a systems perspective throughout this paper, these recommendations must also be considered as a system composed of mutually reinforcing elements; they cannot be implemented in isolation.

This brings us back to our initial thesis. We argued that the practice of HRM is in crisis because its traditional role does not create value for the organization. Alternatively, we have described theoretical and empirical evidence suggesting that HRM has the *potential* to have an economically significant effect on firm performance. This transformation from HRM to human capital management will require that *both* the CEO and the CHRO think of the HRM *system,* first and foremost, as a source of strategy implementation and as a means to achieve important business priorities. This shared perspective, and the commitment to developing the competencies in both line and HR managers to effectively implement this perspective, is the key to realizing this potential source of competitive advantage.

Notes

1. Not only are investments in human capital not reflected in a firm's balance sheet, they are expensed in their entirety on an annual basis. Thus, in contrast to capital investments (e.g., the purchase of a building) that are depreciated over their useful lifetimes, investments in people lower accounting earnings (net income and cash flow) by their full amount in the year in which they are incurred. This treatment of human capital provides managers whose compensation is tied to accounting rates of return a significant disincentive to invest in human capital.

2. These human capital based competencies are in part the source of the intangible capital represented by the difference between the book value of a firm's assets (i.e., shareholder's initial investment) and the current market value of those assets. The best known variant of this measure is known as Tobin's q, which is ratio of firm market value to the replacement cost of its assets.

3. See for example Arthur (1994), Huselid (1995), Ichniowski, Shaw, and Prennushi (1995), Jackson and Schuler (1995), and MacDuffie (1995) in references for the most recent research on this subject. For compilations of the most recent empirical research on the subject, the reader should consider recent special issues of the *Academy of Management* and *Industrial Relations.*

4. A more complete description of the processes through which HPWS affect employee behaviors, and subsequently firm performance, is beyond the scope of this paper. Interested readers can see Huselid (1995) for an overview.

5. A single index of the HRM system is used for two reasons. First, it is the entire HRM *system* that is the appropriate level of analysis for reasons described above. Second, information on a particular policy is generally taken to be an indicator of what is going on in that element of the larger HRM system. However, *taken together* these observations can paint a relatively accurate portrait of the entire HRM system. An analogy might be indices of "best places to live." Cities are measured based on health care, schools, climate, crime, recreation, etc. While any one of those measures is a limited indicator of that feature of the community, when taken together they probably describe "life" in that community pretty well. Just as those indices allow some cities to be rated higher than others, so does this HRM index.

6. Note that even in a world where these systems were easily imitated it would still be better to have them than not to have them. In this environment a High Performance Work System would simply become another *sine qua non* for entry in the market much like low cost and quality have become.

7. The strategy literature describes two features of organizational systems that increase their inimitability and would apply to high performance work systems: path dependency and causal ambiguity (Collis & Montgomery, 1995). Path dependency refers to policies that are developed over time and cannot be easily purchased in the market by competitors. Causal ambiguity focuses the numerous and subtle interrelationships in such a system that are not easily observed from outside the firm.

8. A percentile ranking of zero does not imply that firms have no elements of a HPWS, only that they have relatively fewer of these attributes than any other firms in the sample.

REFERENCES

Arthur, J.B. (1994). Effects of human resource systems on manufacturing performance and turnover. *Academy of Management Journal, 37,* 670–687.

Barney, J. (1991). Firm resources and sustained competitive advantage. *Journal of Management, 17,* 99–120.

Becker, B.E., & Huselid, M.A. (1996). Managerial compensation systems and firm performance. Paper presented at the 1996 Academy of Management Annual Meeting, Cincinnati, OH.

Cappelli, P., & Crocker-Hefter, A. (1996). Distinctive human resources *are* firms' core competencies. *Organizational Dynamics, 24,* 7–21.

Collins, D.J., & Montgomery, C.A. (1995). Competing on Resources: Strategy for the 1990's. *Harvard Business Review;* July–August, 118–128.

Corporate Leadership Council. (1995). *Vision of the future: Role of human resources in the new corporate headquarters.* Washington, D.C.: The Advisory Board Company.

Delaney, J.T., & Huselid, M.A. (1996). The impact of human resource management practices on perceptions of performance in for-profit and nonprofit organizations. *Academy of Management Journal, 39,* 949–969.

Hamel, G., & Prahalad, C.K. (1994). *Competing for the future.* Boston, MA: Harvard Business School Press.

Huselid, M.A. (1995). The impact of human resource management practices on turnover, productivity, and corporate financial performance. *Academy of Management Journal, 38,* 635–672.

Huselid, M.A., & Becker, B.E. (1995a). High performance work systems and organizational performance. Paper presented at the 1995 *Academy of Management* annual conference, Vancouver, BC.

Huselid, M.A., & Becker, B.E. (1995b). The strategic impact of high performance work systems. Working Paper, School of Management and Labor Relations, Rutgers University.

Huselid, M.A., & Becker, B.E. (1996). Methodological issues in cross-sectional and panel estimates of the HR-firm performance link. *Industrial Relations, 35,* 400–422.

Huselid, M.A., Jackson, S.E., & Schuler, R.S. (1997). The significance of human resource management effectiveness for corporate financial performance. *Academy of Management Journal, 40,* 171–188.

Ichniowski, C., Shaw, K., & Prennushi, G. (1995). *The effects of human resource management practices on productivity.* Working Paper, Columbia University, Graduate School of Business.

Itami, H. (1987). *Mobilizing invisible assets.* Boston: Harvard University Press.

Jackson, S.E., & Schuler, R.S. (1995). Understanding human resource management in the context of organizations and their environments. *Annual Review of Psychology, 46,* 237–264.

MacDuffie, J.P. (1995). Human resource bundles and manufacturing performance: Organizational logic and flexible production systems in the world auto industry. *Industrial and Labor Relations Review, 48,* 197–221.

Milgrom, P., & Roberts, J. (1995). Complementarities and fit: Strategy, structure, and organizational change in manufacturing. *Journal of Accounting and Economics, 19,* 179–208.

Pfeffer, J. (1994). *Competitive advantage through people.* Boston: Harvard Business School Press.

Quinn, J.B., Anderson, P., & Finkelstein, S. (1996). Managing professional intellect: Making the most of the best. *Harvard Business Review,* March–April, 71–80.

Schuler, R.S. (1990). Repositioning the human resource function: Transformation or demise? *Academy of Management Executive, 4,* 49–60.

Stalk, G., Evans, P., & Shulman, L. (1992). Competing on capabilities: The new rules of corporate strategy. *Harvard Business Review,* March–April, 57–69.

Stewart, T.A. (1996). Taking on the last bureaucracy. *Fortune,* January 15, 1996, 105–107.

Tomer, J.F. (1987). *Organizational capital.* New York: Praeger Publishers.

Ulrich, D., & Lake, D. (1990). *Organizational capability: Competing from the inside out.* New York: Wiley.

Ulrich, D., Brockbank, W., Yeung, A.K., & Lake, D.G. (1995). Human resource competencies: An empirical assessment. *Human Resource Management, 34*(4), 473–495.

Wright, P.M., & McMahan, G.C. (1992). Theoretical perspectives for strategic human resource management. *Journal of Management, 18,* 295–320.

CHAPTER 25

TRANSFORMING THE HUMAN RESOURCE FUNCTION

SUSAN ALBERS MOHRMAN and EDWARD E. LAWLER, III

The emergence of the global economy, over-capacity in many industries, monumental improvements in the power of computer and telecommunication tools, and the emergence of the knowledge economy are among the forces that are resulting in fundamental change in the design of organizations. A whole constellation of organizational features—vertical integration, managerial control, stability, and two-way loyalty between organization and employee—that fit in a benevolent, relatively stable environment are giving way to new organizational designs for competitiveness, flexibility, continuous improvement, and self-management. Organizations are downsizing, reshaping themselves, outsourcing, joint venturing, merging, divesting, and partnering in order to improve their competencies and capabilities.

The preeminent criterion for all organizational design decisions is contribution to the accomplishment of organization strategy. As strategies have become more complex, global, and developed, this criterion has led to the reexamination of organization designs at all organization levels: corporations, business units, work units, work processes that cut across the organization and jobs. Within the same organization, different units are being constructed with very different logics, each optimizing the value that it adds by tailoring its design features to the work it does.

The traditional corporate design has been taken apart and put back together again in many organizations; new organization architectures have resulted (Nadler, Gerstein, & Shaw, 1992; Galbraith, Lawler, & Associates, 1993). In that process, a variety of new organization forms have emerged. Vertically integrated corporations are being transformed by outsourcing and networking. A proliferation of roles and structures designed to integrate laterally across the organization are being developed (Galbraith, 1993). Self-contained teams and business units are being established to facilitate focused cross-functional decision making at lower levels in the organization (Lawler, Mohrman, & Ledford, 1995).

This organization redesign is driving fundamental change in the work lives of people. Lifetime employment is dead. Organizations are using a shifting array of work forces including a core work force, contractors, and contingent, part-time, or temporary workers (Handy, 1991; Rousseau & Wade-Benzoni, 1995; Hall & Mirvis, 1995). As the work force increasingly operates through a series of dynamic structures—work teams, task teams, and projects—the concept of job is being replaced by rapidly shifting work assignments (Mohrman, Cohen, & Mohrman, 1995). Careers are becoming portfolios of experiences that span functions and companies. In short, an organization is created in which the human resource management practices of the past no longer fit. Organizations are faced with a situation that cries out for new solutions to the thorny challenges of integrating business and people needs.

In traditional bureaucratic organizations, human resource professionals have, for decades, created and administered the systems—career development, training, selection, and rewards—that define the key parameters of the stage on which employees have enacted lifelong employment roles and careers. The human resource function added value by creating systems that produced bureaucratically correct behavior as well as the predictable and orderly development of people and their careers. Not surprisingly, it gained a reputation as the bastion of the status quo.

But the era of traditional bureaucratic organizations is over; stability needs to be replaced by change, innovation, and new organizational designs. This fact represents both a major threat and a major opportunity for the human resource function. The human resource function can deliver immense value to corporations and to society by helping them navigate the uncharted waters of the new era. If it can create human resource management systems that fit the new organization designs that are appearing, the function can not only survive, it can thrive because it will make a major contribution to organizational effectiveness. If this does not happen, the function will virtually disappear because the traditional human resource activities that have been its reason for being will be either eliminated or outsourced.

PEOPLE MANAGEMENT CHALLENGES

An important key to successfully creating new human resource systems concerns dealing with the paradox that just as employees can expect less loyalty from companies, companies are more than ever dependent on high-level performance from them. To be effective, companies must have a supply of employees willing and able to play by the new rules of the game. In order to deal with this paradox, we believe the human resources profession must reshape itself, populate itself differently, and blur its mental and organizational boundaries. It must become a true business partner that helps develop new approaches to selection, training, careers, rewards, and information systems so that organizations can create strategically critical competencies and capabilities (Lawler, 1996).

Five interrelated challenges must be met in order for the human resource function to make this contribution; meeting each of them requires blending business and human resource concerns.

1. Organizing for High Performance

Organization restructuring should have as an ultimate outcome the most effective application of human resources to accomplish the mission of the organization. Fashionable changes such as creating small, flexible, cross-functional units, aligning people around value-adding tasks rather than "overhead" tasks, outsourcing, partnering, configuring work around core processes, and creating customer focus can only be successful if the conditions can be created that successfully transition the human resources of the organization and that create high levels of motivation. Legitimate concerns about the condition of the workforce left in place after rounds of downsizing, take aways, and restructuring exist and must be dealt with.

Sustained high performance will result only if new organization forms result from a design process that takes into account the nature of the task and the nature of people. This design process demands deep knowledge of strategy and design as well as the principles of motivation and the use of new and more varied approaches to goal-setting and rewards—approaches that give people a meaningful stake in business performance.

2. People Deployment

The days of an orderly progression of people through a series of jobs in a functional hierarchy are gone. In new organization designs, people are as likely to move through a series of projects and rotational moves as through an orderly progression of jobs. Bosses are likely to have little understanding of the knowledge bases of many of their reports. Much work will be done by a "virtual" organization—assembled from across the organization, often informally, and possibly connected only electronically to complete a task (Savage, 1990). This virtual organization may include part-time and temporary employees as well as partner company employees.

In such an organization, the challenge of deploying people with the right talents to different work opportunities is a daunting one especially when combined with the need to develop people. Much of the development that takes place in an organization will occur through work or task assignments (Hall & Mirvis, 1995). As careers are increasingly enabled by the creation of a portfolio of experiences, people will be competing for work assignments rather than for promotions up a hierarchy. A completely new information infrastructure will be required to make possible the tracking and deploying of the human resources available to the company and the efficient and effective movement of people between assignments (Lawler, 1996). In addition, new reward system approaches will be required in order to attract, develop, and motivate this diverse, ever-changing work force.

3. Managing Organizational Competencies and Capabilities

In the knowledge economy, the management of the competencies of the human resources and the capabilities of the organization are urgent tasks which have survival implications (Ulrich & Lake, 1990). Knowledge and information are increasing exponentially, requiring the nurturing of the deep knowledge bases central to the task of the organization and the development of enhanced analytic capabilities to exploit knowledge at a faster rate than competitors.

Dynamic environments, strategies, designs, and technologies mean that the need for competencies and capabilities changes, with some becoming obsolete, noncritical, or irrelevant. The new organization requires different and often more advanced skills in group process and organizational understanding. Training and other approaches to development, while more important than ever, are only a piece of this puzzle: the strategic "make-buy-partner" decisions will be important in securing human resource talent as in making product and service decisions.

4. Managing Organization Learning

An issue closely related to the management of competencies is the management of organizational knowledge and learning. In the traditional organization, company specific and deep discipline knowledge are carried in people's heads and shared through the interaction of people in discipline-based departments and work groups.

Organizations can no longer function competitively with informal approaches to knowledge and learning. Knowledge is too important an asset not to be actively managed. Increasingly, it is dispersed in cross-functional groupings and needs to be exploited across geographic bounds. People often come in temporarily and need a quick way to gather information and get on board. Finding ways to embed knowledge in organization processes and documents, to distribute information and know-how in readily accessible forms, and to disseminate knowledge and accelerate learning are key challenges facing organizations.

5. Defining the New Psychological Contract

The psychological employment contract reflects the individual's understanding of the employment relationship's terms and the normative beliefs about what organizational members owe and are in return owed (Rousseau & Wade-Benzoni, 1995). Recent changes in organization strategies and designs have resulted in a major disruption of the prevailing psychological contract, but in most organizations, a new one has yet to be established.

Organizations appear to be entering an era of highly differentiated psychological contracts. The contracts with different groups of employees—core workers, contract workers, and temporary and part-time workers—will each have to acknowledge the particular needs and motivation of that group of employees as well as the performance expectations of the organization. It seems clear that if new norms and expectations are not purposefully set, and new ways of contracting for work are not devised, behavior in the new organization may not meet its needs. It also seems clear that if the new contract does not give employees a stake in the performance of the organization, it is unlikely that the organization will achieve the levels of commitment found in the old era of two-way loyalty.

THE NEW ROLE OF THE HUMAN RESOURCE FUNCTION

None of the five challenges that we have identified falls cleanly and solely into the domain of the human resource function. They can only be addressed by dealing with the organization as a system and by generating systemic solutions.

Human resource management practices are an integral part of all organization systems and are integral to organization capability development. For an organization's human resources to contribute to performance, human resource practices must fit with each other and with the strategy and design of the organization. In order for the members of the human resource function to impact performance, they must be knowledgeable about, have influence on, and be closely connected to the other organization systems, as well as have a solid base of knowledge about human resource practices.

The human resource function must be able to operate at multiple levels of analysis: at the individual, work group, business unit, organization, and cross-organizational levels. It cannot work exclusively at the level of the individual performer. It must contribute to the development and performance management of teams, product lines, divisions, joint ventures, consortia, and wherever else performance is strategically important. It also must operate with good understanding of industry trends and other competitive issues so that it can be a contributor to the business.

There is evidence that the evolution of the human resource function toward being a business partner is under way (Mohrman, Lawler, & McMahan, 1996). In some corporations, it is an integral part of the management team, helping to develop strategy, improve organization performance, and develop organization capabilities that focus on speed and quality (Lawler, 1995; Evans, 1994).

Our view of the expanded role of the human resource function argues for it to have a full partnership role in each of the following key business processes:

1. Developing Strategy

The human resource function should contribute to business strategy based on its knowledge of the competencies and capabilities of the organization, its understanding of the organization changes that will be required to support different strategic directions, and its knowledge of the network of human resources available to the company including the opportunities or constraints inherent in that network.

2. Designing the Organization

The human resource function should be a repository of organization design expertise, and its members should play the role of internal consultants to the ongoing designing and redesigning that will characterize organizations and their subunits as they continually modify themselves to achieve shifting strategies, new capabilities, and higher levels of performance.

3. Change Implementation

The human resource function should help the organization develop change management capabilities to weather the ongoing changes that will continue to be part of the environment. It should help with the ongoing learning processes required to assess the impact of change and to enable the organization to make corrections and enhancements to the changes (Mohrman & Cummings, 1989). It should help the organization develop a new psychological contract, new career tracks, and ways to give employees a stake both in the changes that are occurring and in the performance of the organization.

4. Integrating Performance Management Practices

The human resource function should work with line managers to make sure that the performance management practices of the organization (goal-setting, performance appraisal, development practices, and rewards) are integrated with each other and with the business management practices of the organization, and that they fit with the nature of the work. These processes must give individuals a stake in the performance of the business, and they must measure and reward performance that supports the business strategy.

The human resource challenges being faced in today's restructured organizations demand a sophisticated business partner capability on the part of human resource professionals. Business partners need to be able to think systematically and to be part of cross-functional organization leadership teams that plan and manage the complex issues of rapid change. These business partners/human resource professionals are a microcosm of the new organization, an organization in which more and more contributors will have to work cross functionally and will be expected to address business issues as well as their particular discipline's issues.

THE NEW HUMAN RESOURCE ORGANIZATIONS

It is beyond the scope of this chapter to discuss in any detail what the human resource function must look like in order to play the business partner role we have defined. It is important, however, to mention some of the major characteristics which the human resource function must have in order to perform effectively. To be specific, the human resource function needs to:

- Be staffed by individuals who understand the business as well as change strategy.

- Be a valued member of management teams by contributing to business strategy and operations decision making.
- Effectively use outsourcers as a way to reduce the cost of the human resource function and to draw on expertise that is not easily built into the organization.
- Retain control over setting the strategic direction for the organization's human resource systems, while using outsourcers when appropriate.
- Have high levels of competency in designing human resource systems and in managing their implementation.
- Effectively utilize information technology to support the development of organizational capabilities and competencies and of individuals' careers.
- Develop computer-based human resource management systems which free the human resource organization from the day-to-day management and administration of the human resources in the organization.

Finally, we foresee companies increasingly establishing alliances and partnerships with each other, with universities, and with governments for the purpose of providing services such as training and development, career and financial counseling, and for the development of portable benefits and other systems required to create a foundation for the new workforce. We expect that through interorganizational mechanisms a new language will be established for describing careers and competencies, and new resources will become available to a workforce struggling to adapt to the changing employment landscape.

Our studies reveal that human resource departments are moving in these directions, although progress is not as dramatic as is indicated in reports that talk of transformational change and revolutionary change (Mohrman, Lawler, & McMahan, 1996). Strategic redesign of companies is slowly driving change not only in human resource practices and services but also in the way the human resource function is organized. One of the most important challenges every human resource function faces is to reinvent its structure and organization so that it can deliver in the future the kinds of systems and business partnership behavior that will make its organization more effective.

REFERENCES

Evans, P. (1995). Business strategy and human resource management: A four stage framework. Working paper, INSEAD, Fountainbleau.

Galbraith, J.R. (1993). The value-adding corporation: Matching structure with strategy. In J.R. Galbraith, E.E. Lawler III, & Associates (Eds.), *Organizing for the future: The new logic for managing complex organizations.* San Francisco: Jossey-Bass.

Galbraith, J.R., Lawler, E.E. III, & Associates. (1993). *Organizing for the future: The new logic for managing complex organizations.* San Francisco: Jossey-Bass.

Hall, D.T., & Mirvis, P.H. (1995). Careers as lifelong learning. In A. Howard (Ed.), *The changing nature of work.* San Francisco: Jossey-Bass.

Handy, C. (1991). *The age of unreason.* Cambridge, MA: Harvard Business School Press.

Lawler, E.E. III (1995). Strategic human resources management: An idea whose time has come. In B. Downie & M.L. Coates (Eds.), *Managing human resources in the 1990's and beyond: Is the workplace being transformed?* (pp. 46–70). Kingston: IRC Press.

Lawler, E.E. III (1996). *From the ground up.* San Francisco: Jossey-Bass.

Lawler, E.E. III, Mohrman, S.A., & Ledford, G.E., Jr. (1995). *Creating high performance organizations: Practices and results of employee involvement and total quality management in Fortune 1000 companies.* San Francisco: Jossey-Bass.

Mohrman, S.A., Cohen, S.G., & Mohrman, A.M., Jr. (1995). *Designing team based organizations.* San Francisco: Jossey-Bass.

Mohrman, S.A., & Cummings, T.G. (1989). *Self-designing organizations: Learning how to create high performance.* Reading, MA: Addison-Wesley.

Mohrman, S.A., Lawler, E.E. III, & McMahan, G. (1996). *New directions for the human resources organizations: An organization design approach.* Los Angeles: The Center for Effective Organizations.

Nadler, D.A., Gerstein, M.S., & Shaw, R.B. & Associates. (1992). *Organizational architecture: Designs for changing organizations.* San Francisco: Jossey-Bass.

Rousseau, D.M., & Wade-Benzoni, K.A. (1995). Changing individual-organization attachments: A two-way street. In A. Howard (Ed.), *The changing nature of work.* San Francisco: Jossey-Bass.

Savage, C. (1990). *5th generation management: Integrating enterprises through human networking.* Digital Press.

Ulrich, D., & Lake, D. (1990). *Organizational capability.* New York: Wiley.

CHAPTER 26

A FUTURE VISION OF HUMAN RESOURCES

JAMES W. PETERS

Here is Edward Bear, coming down the stairs now, bump, BumP, BUMP-
on the back of his head, behind Christopher Robin. It is as far as he knows,
the only way of coming down the stairs, but sometimes he feels that there
really is another way, if only he could stop bumping for a minute and think
of it.

A.A. Milne, Winnie the Pooh

$\mathbf{F}$or many members of the human re-
source profession, the state of Edward Bear rings true. Fortunately, there are
people who have been giving thought to another way. There are inexorable
changes occurring within the profession transforming the function from
what it looks like today to a future vision. This future vision of the function is a radical departure from what we in the profession know and do in
contemporary organizations. Michael Hammer (1994), of reengineering
fame, called for the profession to "reengineer thyself." We prefer this perspective to that of Thomas Stewart (1996), the noted management writer
from *Fortune,* who has called for the profession to be "nuked." Future
changes should eliminate the contention and criticism of the function of
" . . . there's no clearly articulated vision of what HR should become . . ."
(Brenner, 1966).

This chapter postulates a future vision of human resources with a certain
degree of trepidation, for I recognize "The power of studying the future is
to get ready for it. No one can really predict, control, manage, or fully anticipate the future." Simultaneously we in the profession are encouraged to

recognize the value of studying those forces that are at work that will have the potential to profoundly transform the function (Hamel & Prahalad, 1994).

The future vision of human resources is a calculated target. It is based upon inexorable forces currently working within the world of organization, as well as the function of human resources itself. These forces are the rapid development and adoption of technology dissolving the administrative burden currently placed on the human resource professional; the demand from line executives and managers for human resource professionals to add value to the business; the transformation of the human resource professional from human resource generalist to change master; and the emerging need for the enterprise to focus on human capital planning, knowledge asset management, and the development of intellectual capital.

BUILDING THE FUTURE VISION FROM LESSONS LEARNED

In 1990, the members of the Professional Development Committee for the Human Resource Planning Society thought it would be intellectually stimulating to explore and apply the new management thinking of reengineering to the function of human resources. To this end, an executive laboratory was created and implemented. The reception for this seminal session was overwhelming. Since then, hundreds of companies have launched into HR reengineering/rethinking/reinventing initiatives; countless public workshops have been conducted spreading the word on innovations and management advances; and numerous consulting firms have developed significant business in providing expert consultation and guidance to organizations transforming the nature and the function of human resources. In general, there are four ways in which the work of human resources can be changed: restructuring, automation, outsourcing, and redesign.

Members of the human resource profession are intimately familiar with the *restructuring* approach to changing work. During the past decade, as company after company downsized its organization, the human resource profession became consumed with the notion of HR ratios. How many human resource professionals should an organization have per the number of employees? 1:50 became 1:100, then 1:150 to 1:250, and so on. Downsizing the size of the human resource bureaucracy, however, did not and does not change the nature of human resource work. Instead, *the restructuring of human resources left less people to do the same amount of work.*

The human resource profession has learned that *automation* is not necessarily an answer to enhancing HR performance. Unless the nature of the work is carefully scrutinized, automation may mean bad/wrong work is simply being done faster. One of the most profound findings from human resource reengineering initiatives is that 60 percent to 70 percent of HR work is administrative, and the majority of this administrative work is single transaction in nature: adding someone to payroll, making an address change, changing a beneficiary. Given the technological capabilities currently available, as well as those anticipated to emerge in the future, automation and the application of technology can dissolve the administrative burden placed on the profession, but prior to automating human resource work, the profession needs to challenge if it should be doing the work at all.

The recent and rapid emergence of *outsourcing* has been in response to the question by human resource professionals, "Should we do this work at all?" Should the HR franchise need to be in the benefits administration business? Does HR need to manage an enormous payroll organization confronting 60 or more payroll cycles? Should HR provide staffing services to an organization when stable core/flexible ring is the predominate operating structure? All of these activities, and many more, are being outsourced to providers external to the enterprise. In some cases, with great success, and in others, with questionable benefits to the company. Outsourcing human resource work should be undertaken only if service delivery can be sustained or improved, while cost can be stabilized or reduced. If not, we need to question the integrity of an outsourcing solution.

Redesign requires the intense scrutiny of the existing work of HR. The "as-is," the current nature of HR work, is placed in contrast to a "to-be." Faster-better-cheaper stand behind the redesign of HR work. Why should it take three months to price a new job or role within the organization? Why can't just-in-time staffing occur? Why not be an exporter of talent because the bench is too deep? Why do performance appraisals occur annually, rather than on a real-time basis? Rather than scan in resumes, can we recruit and hire people without paper?

THE NEW HR FRANCHISE

The lessons learned from all of the rethinking/reinventing/reengineering work, as well as the initiatives taken to change the nature of HR work through restructuring, automation, outsourcing, and redesign, are coalescing into major forces, trends, and patterns suggesting a future vision for the function. This future vision is depicted in Figure 26.1.

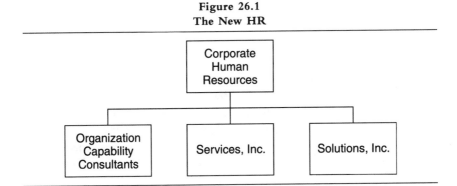

Figure 26.1
The New HR

SERVICES, INC.

All human resource work that is administrative in nature is now located in a repository called Services, Inc. Through the application of technologies such as client server units, data warehousing, the Internet/Intranet, call centers, the administrative burden on the human resource professional is dissolved. Nestled in Services, Inc. is benefits administration, compensation administration, payroll, training and education administration, staffing administration, records management, and other transaction-based human resource work.

Services, Inc. employs a three-tier response capability. Tier One is accessed through the computer or the telephone. Like an ATM dispensing cash, Tier One responds to information changes and requests electronically without the need to speak to a person. This response tier will be the predominant dissolving agent of the administrative burden confronted by the human resource professional. Tier Two directs an administrative request through a call center to a person who can provide interpretation of policy or quickly respond to a unique request for information, explanation, or guidance. Tier Three is a multiple transaction capability staffed by case workers deeply skilled in a given human resource area such as employee relations who are able to provide extended and comprehensive attention to a complex transaction requirement.

The discipline of Services, Inc. is operational excellence.[1] It is driven by the need to be the lowest cost and most efficient provider of services and information for the enterprise. As such, it may or may not report into the corporate human resource function. Given its technological base, it may be better suited as a unit of the Information Services organization. Given its discipline of operational excellence, it may be better reporting into the chief financial officer.

Services, Inc. is a compendium of outsourcing and insourcing solutions to the administrative needs of the enterprise. If there is a lower cost/higher service delivery capability found elsewhere, Services, Inc. will effect an outsourcing partnership with the provider.

Services, Inc. is not dedicated to the human resource function. Instead, it is an enterprisewide service provider addressing the myriad administrative needs of the organization including those of the finance, information services, and legal as well as other business service requirements such as sales, customer service, and security. With extensive centralization of technology and call center capabilities, the enterprise can provide all of the line and staff operating units with the requisite administrative and transaction-based support.

The characterization of Services, Inc. is purposeful. Consider the Lake-Cook Road region in suburban Chicago. Within a short radius, one can find Kraft Inc., Sears, Dean Witter, Allstate Insurance, Baxter International, and other leading large corporations. Given the thousands of employees they have, all will require a service center capability. Today, a number of companies have constructed the technological capabilities to service the sales and marketing needs of large global retailers. The person taking your L.L. Bean catalog order does not work for L.L. Bean, and he or she also responds to the unique customer requirements of numerous other catalog retailers. Instead of duplicating the roles of compensation administration, benefit administration, records management, and other administrative requirements typical of the contemporary organization, why should each of these noncompetitive companies duplicate the creation of a service center? The person responding to your benefits question at Tier Two, may not even work for your company, let alone be based near Lake-Cook Road. A cooperative entity, governed by a board of directors representing all of the participating companies, could manage a cost effective services organization.

SOLUTIONS, INC.

The human resource profession is comprised of subject matter experts (SMEs) with unique skills, a rigorous body of knowledge, and professional credentials. These organizational transformation-based experts include professionals from training and development, communications, union relations, organization design, compensation design, survey specialists, and high-level staffing professionals. These highly skilled and specialized professionals are chartered with the design and development of unique solutions for the enterprise. In most cases, they are currently corporate resources. In the new HR franchise they are part of Solutions, Inc. and are in a separate operating unit.

The hierarchy in Solutions, Inc. is simple and flat: There are partners and associates, akin to other professional service firms such as legal and accounting. Guided by a set of ethical standards, they operate on a for-profit basis. They are not overhead embedded in the infrastructure of the organization and are not designing the HR program of the month. They must sell their services to customers, and therefore, design and develop unique and value-added solutions for their customers. As Tony Rucci of Sears has stated, "If you don't have a customer, you have a problem."[2]

The discipline of Solutions, Inc. is product innovation. These partners and associates are driven by the need of the enterprise to transform the state-of-the-art into the state-of-the-practice. Operating on the cutting edge of their professional expertise, the members of the unit consult with internal customers to design, develop, and implement solutions congruent with the ever-changing strategic and tactical needs of the enterprise and its operating units. Competency-based human resource solutions, reward systems, change management tactics, strategic communication programs, organization design strategies, team-based organizations are their forte and expertise. They deploy their partners and associates on a swat team basis, and craft and contour their solutions to the unique requirements of the business unit/customer. It is a centralized consulting unit, albeit geographically dispersed into centers to address the needs of a global organization.

Solutions, Inc. also serves as the human resource tool room. Similar to the tool room found in manufacturing organizations, Solutions, Inc. is a repository of transformation-based tools and knowledge. Like the wise old sages who manage the tool room in a manufacturing organization, instead of making a new solution/tool they can reach into an old dusty bin and pull out exactly what is needed. They are also world class pracitioners of technology transfer. Instead of being the primary owner of the technology, they transfer their wisdom and tools into the hands of the people who need it—the line management team. Finally, if the solution/tool has enterprisewide application, it is transferred into Services. Inc.

Driven by a profit motive and operating as a highly skilled and disciplined consulting firm, Solution's workers could also sell their services to the vendors and suppliers of the enterprise. Just as Services, Inc. can be cooperatively owned by a number of companies, so can Solutions. In addition, Solutions could be completely outsourced to an existing consulting firm, or the unit could become a freestanding player in the consulting marketplace.

ORGANIZATION CAPABILITY CONSULTANTS

The members of this unit are decentralized and embedded within the operating units of the enterprise. They are not HR generalists. They do not resolve employee relations problems. They do not provide answers to benefit questions. They do not fill out reams of paperwork to enroll a new employee into the company's benefit and 401k programs. Instead of performing these transaction-based activities, they hand out a card with an 800 number on it directing these requests to Services, Inc. When these professionals walk down the halls of the company, line executives, managers, and employees do not see someone representing compliance, policy interpretation, barriers to change, and bureaucracy.

The charter of Organization Capability Consultants is to provide guidance and assistance to the operating unit designed to improve the overall effectiveness of the business. They do so by alignment of human resource strategies, processes, and practices with the particular unique needs of the business. They work with the business unit to build the organizational capabilities, agility, and market response speed through the application of ever-emerging information and digital technologies. They are responsible for driving the reengineering of existing work processes to create better-faster-cheaper approaches, as well as "engineer" new work processes mandated by shifting market and competitive dynamics. They also assist in building the overall capabilities of the business by building the individual capabilities of the operating unit's employees.

The discipline of Organization Capability Consultants is characterized as customer intimacy, both internal and external to the organization. Their superior business acumen allows them to guide, coach, and counsel the senior business team in effecting appropriate strategies for acquiring, developing, and deploying the competency base of the business. They are superior change masters.

If they need a unique human resource solution to a given problem they can contract with Solutions, Inc. or seek out assistance from another consultancy capable of providing a cost competitive and effective solution. All of their transaction-based needs are satisfied through Services, Inc. Their linkage with corporate is cooperative and focused on assisting the enterprise in developing its intellectual capital, knowledge assets, and human capital planning. They ensure every line manager in their business functions as their own human resource manager. Part of their compensation is at risk and is based upon the economic value added to the business. Finally, they are probably *not* human resource people.

CORPORATE HUMAN RESOURCES

The top human resource officer of the enterprise is not an issuer of policy statements, the keeper of information and data, the human resource authority figure, a human resource regulator and compliance auditor, and a manager of the human resource bureaucracy, with a large centralized or decentralized staff support team. The top human resource officer has been transformed into a role akin to Practice Director typically found in large consulting firms. He or she is primarily responsible for developing and coaching the Organization Capability Consultants, and where necessary providing this team with a "peer review." He or she mentors, champions, teaches, cajoles, educates, develops, and influences a specific discipline—removes barriers to change and progress, as evidenced by leadership in creating Services and Solutions.

Top human resource officers work with the senior executive team and the individual business unit leaders to create a shared mindset. They serve as the repository and monitor of the organization's knowledge asset management system and the development of its intellectual capital. They have intimate knowledge of the strengths, weaknesses, and developmental opportunities of the top executive team and the high potential talent pool. Wherever appropriate, they broker this team into developmental experiences to ensure the development of individual agility, and therefore, the collective agility of the executive team. Since the competitive battlefield will be determined by the overall capability of the organization's human resource base, the CEO is responsible for designing, developing, and implementing a human resource strategy. The top human resource officers can serve a useful role in coaching CEOs on this activity, through their superior competency of influencing without authority. They realize they may become extinct.

NOTES

1. Derived from the work of Treacy and Wiersema found in *The Discipline of Market Leaders*. Reading, Mass: Addison-Wesley Publishing Company, (1995). They

have identified three disciplines: operational excellence, product innovation, and customer intimacy.

2. Quoted in Zinno, Vincent, "Eye On The Prize," *Human Resource Executive,* October, 1996, pages 24–25.

REFERENCES

Brenner, L. (1996, March). The disappearing HR department. *CFO: The Magazine for Chief Financial Officers,* 61–64.

Eichinger, R., & Ulrich, D. (1996). *Are you future agile?* The State of the art presentation made at the 1996 Annual Conference of the HR Planning Society. April 2, 1996.

Hamel, G., & Prahahad, C.K., (1994). *Competing for the future.* Boston: Harvard Business School Press.

Hammer, M. (1994). *The Re-engineering transition and changing workforce competencies.* Keynote address at conference on using competency Based Tools and applications to Drive Organizational Performance. Boston, MA. Nov. 2–4.

Stewart, T. (1996, January 15). Taking on the lost bureaucracy. *Fortune,* 105–108.

SECTION V

REMEMBER THE "HUMAN" IN HUMAN RESOURCE

In the quest to make business results happen, sometimes the "human" in human resource seems to have been lost. This part of human resources deals with more than making employees happy; it deals with creating a work environment where they feel commitment to the firm because their needs are being met.

With HR executives striving to become business partners in many companies, the human element of the business has been overlooked. With focus on reengineering HR processes, measuring HR value, and aligning HR practices with business strategies, sometimes HR professionals have ignored the human aspect of business.

The human part deals with understanding and meeting needs of employees. Some of these needs are business-related: the need to have impact, to acquire technical knowledge, to be competent, to be respected. Other human needs are more personal: the need to be valued, to be appreciated, to be part of a team. When these needs go unmet, employees may become less committed. The lack of commitment may lead to lower performance and reduced business results.

In looking to the future, human needs may become an ever more important element of the human resource role. In a work environment where knowledge and intellectual capital are the scarce resources, employees have mobility options. Highly talented employees have the luxury of moving from firm to firm. In Silicon Valley, for example, it is not unusual for talented employees to use firm mobility as a career move, each annual company change increases salary about 15 percent. Paying attention to the human needs means treating these mobile employees as though they were volunteers, because to some extent they are.

Humane treatment of employees should not occur only at the top of the organization. In many operational jobs, employees work for relatively low pay that can be and is matched by other firms. Employees who are not treated in a humane way may move for marginal increases in salary, and the replacement costs become excessive. Employees need to be treated in ways that engender commitment. Human resource professionals concerned about intellectual capital need to create work environments where employee needs are met.

HR professionals working to create work settings that treat employees in more humane ways need to deal with the following questions:

- *How Is Intellectual Capital Operationalized?* Knowing that knowledge and intellectual capital matter and measuring and improving them are two different matters. HR professionals need to derive models and measures to track intellectual capital. These measures need to go beyond current surrogates such as employee satisfaction, retention, or days in training. They need to deal with issues such as competence, commitment, and conviction.
- *How Can HR Practices Be Created that Motivate and Commit Employees?* Treating employees in a more humane way may require innovation in HR practices. Alternative methods of staffing, training, communicating, and rewarding employees may be required.
- *What Is the Impact of Humane Treatment of Employees?* Increasingly, balanced scorecard models are being created that show how the treatment of employees leads to employee satisfaction that leads to customer commitment that leads to financial performance. If this logic is accurate, it is important to identify those practices that impact treatment of employees to begin this flow.

As HR professionals deal with these questions, they may come to realize that the humane treatment of employees is critical to business success. Humane treatment may lead to employees feeling more committed and dedicated to company results. These essays offer insights into how to treat employees more humanely. They suggest that the needs of tomorrow's employees may be somewhat different from today with emphasis on work/life issues, development of competencies, control over work life, and opportunity to have impact on results. With these employee needs in mind, the humane treatment of employees puts the human back into human resource.

CHAPTER 27

THE FUTURE OF HUMAN RESOURCE MANAGEMENT: MARCH AND SIMON (1958) REVISITED

DAVID E. BOWEN and CAREN SIEHL

It has been nearly forty years since March and Simon (1958) so elegantly stated that all employees confront two fundamental decisions in their interactions with organizations.[1] One is the "decision to produce"; the other is the "decision to participate." The decision to *produce* involves whether employees are willing to work as hard and produce as much as the organization demands. The decision to *participate* concerns whether various participants—primarily employees, but March and Simon also discussed customers and investors—choose to remain with the organization or leave. These are substantially different decisions, but both illustrate, as March and Simon emphasized, "the motivational problems involved in using human beings to perform organizational tasks" (p. 110). The management of these motivational problems is a useful way to conceptualize the mission and purpose of human resource management.

In this chapter, we suggest that production concerns have tended to dominate the human resource management (HRM) agenda, but that participation issues have recently emerged as an equally compelling problem. The "decision to produce" has captured the attention of HRM practitioners and researchers since the 1970s, with a focus on models of work motivation, new forms of performance-based reward systems, high-performing teams, reengineering, enriched jobs, and so on. As to the decision to participate, there has been academic and practitioner interest in the issue of turnover, for example, but the main interest has been in how organizational participants

261

actually produce. In recent years, however, the world of work has changed fundamentally due to increasing global competition, a shift to knowledge-based work, enabling information technology, and other related factors. The changing work world has led to basic issues surrounding "who" participates in the organization and "what" participation means coming to the fore in the 1990s as critical challenges for HRM. These issues connect squarely to March and Simon's description of three key variables which must be managed relative to the decision to participate:

- Participants' balance of inducements and contributions.
- Definition of who *are* the organizational participants.
- Desirability and ease of movement in and out of the organization.

We will discuss these key variables in the less-examined decision to participate and their implications for the future of HRM. Our guiding premise is that the basic challenges of organization have not really changed over the 40 or 50 years since March, Simon, and others first presented them. What has changed is how these challenges are now framed and how firms attempt to resolve them.

INDUCEMENTS AND CONTRIBUTIONS: THE "NEW" PSYCHOLOGICAL CONTRACT

An employee's decision to participate is the centerpiece of what has been called "organizational equilibrium" (Barnard, 1938; Simon, 1947). Organizational equilibrium reflects the organization's success in balancing inducements (e.g., compensation to participants) and contributions (e.g., the various inputs that participants make to the organization).

The past decade of restructurings and downsizings has strained traditional approaches to maintaining organizational equilibrium, leading to what has been described as a "new psychological contract" between employees and employers (Rousseau & Geller, 1994; Sims, 1994). A psychological contract is the set of employee expectations that define what the individual and the organization expect to give to and receive from each other during their relationship. As Rousseau and Geller (1994) state, a major function of human resource management is to foster an appropriate psychological contract.

The psychological contract of the past was very straightforward: Both employees and employers saw a cradle-to-grave relationship in which there was a stable, predictable exchange of work for rewards, which included long-term employment (Sims, 1994). There was a paternalistic flavor to this contract. Employers were expected to look out for and protect employees' interests; employees were expected to be dedicated and hard working. This type of psychological contract was intended to demonstrate loyalty between employer and employee. Recently, the old psychological contract has been crushed by the forces discussed above. This change in contract has become particularly visible in recent years because the changes now more than ever before also affect a much larger percentage of the white collar work force.

As we consider the future of HRM, a key challenge will be the ongoing definition and communication of new psychological contracts. For example, the recruitment process can lead to a mismatch between a potential participant's work-related expectations and the expectations of current organizational members which can result in a perceived violation of the psychological contract by either the new employee or by existing organizational members (Sims, 1994). HRM will need to play a role in increasing the likelihood of a mutually satisfying contract through the use of such processes as realistic job previews (RJPs) (Wanous, 1980). We suggest this use be expanded. Firms should not only provide applicants with RJPs, but should also systematically and clearly provide current organizational members with RJPs of their future roles in the organization. Perhaps in the past when the pace of change was slower, firms could assume that incumbents had realistic future expectations and only newcomers needed RJPs. In many of today's firms, however, incumbents' expectations of the future may be no more realistic than those of newcomers.

More broadly, the challenge that organizations face in shaping new psychological contracts affords HRM the opportunity to assume a leadership role relative to an important business issue. This issue is the transformation of the basic nature of "type of company" that the firm represents. "Type of company" is arguably more a source of *sustainable* competitive advantage than type of product, service, or a given quality improvement tool such as TQM (Lawler, 1992).

HRM must first work with senior management to clarify the optimal content of the psychological contract and then should be responsible for making certain that this content "shows," in an internally consistent way to employees in all HR activities, for example, performance appraisal and rewards. HR activities play a critical role as message senders in terms of conveying the psychological contract; a lack of integration across HR activities results in psychological contracts, based on mixed messages, that create problems for both employees and the organization (Rousseau & Geller, 1994).

This lack of integration can certainly undermine the type of company that both insiders and outsiders perceive the organization to be.

Regardless of the particular form the new psychological contracts assume, we agree that they must confront two challenges described by Clifford Ehrlich, Service Vice President of Human Resources for Marriott Corporation. The first challenge involves how to deepen the sense of involvement experienced by now shorter term employees in order that such

> . . . employees will work with the care and interest of people who expect to be there for the duration of their careers. (Ehrlich, 1994: p. 494)

That is, a key challenge for HR is how to create the sense of caring and involvement among possible short-timers that once potentially existed among employees who knew that they and the organization were "in it together" for a lifetime. This issue is strained further by the increasing number of employees who are not only short-term, but part-time as well, as we describe in the next section.

Second, the changing and often less concrete, new psychological contracts pose a significant challenge to the organization's leadership. As the rules of the game change, leaders must work harder on sense-making for employees:

> Leaders have a responsibility to help the people they lead make sense out of what's happening. Their subordinates can't be expected to be "on the bandwagon" unless they understand which bandwagon they're expected to be on and why it's different from the one they used to be on. (Ehrlich, p. 495)

A challenge for HR lies in influencing executive development such that leaders both understand and are equipped to engage in this process. As the set of skills for effective leadership changes, so must HR's role in executive development.

WHO ARE THE ORGANIZATIONAL PARTICIPANTS: THE "BOUNDARYLESS" ORGANIZATION

The organization, as an entity with clearly defined boundaries of who's in and who's out, is becoming an anachronism. Organizational success historically has been based on four critical factors: size, role clarity, specialization, and control (Ashkenas, Ulrich, Jick, & Kerr, 1995). These four factors lead to the need for the establishment of fixed, rigid boundaries for the organization. It was viewed as optimal to have a large dedicated work force, people who were clearly participating in the organization. It was optimal to have everyone know his or her job, accept the boundaries, and perform against specifications. As the world has changed, these historical success factors have become major liabilities, and a new set of success factors has emerged. This set includes speed, flexibility, integration, and innovation (Ashkenas et al., 1995), each of which has implications for the issue of "Who are the participants?" A *focus on speed* forces organizations to respond to customers more quickly, bring products to market more quickly, and to generally be more responsive. *An ability to change* is not positively correlated with fixed organizational size, and hence, there is a shift from a focus on size to a focus on flexible work forces. There is also a move from explicit role clarity to flexibility in job descriptions, work assignments, and shifting roles. *Integration* involves pulling specialists together in order to collaborate and transfer learning regardless of whether the specialists are full-time members of the organization. This, in turn, fosters *innovation,* risk taking, and moving away from rigid, formal control. These factors suggest that the nature of participation will change and will become more fluid. Boundaries will continue to blur between who's in and who's out, for how long, and under what types of relationships.

In the past decade, it has become quite a challenge to inventory, if you will, the organization's set of employees. There are more part-timers, more contingent workers, and more telecommuters who are rarely seen by most of their coworkers and colleagues. As the work world is witnessing the end of the traditional job (Bridges, 1994), it is also witnessing the end of the clearly visible, physically-bounded, work force.

These new developments present HRM with several future challenges including the following:

- Playing a role in building cohesiveness among participants who are physically separate from one another and possibly only "in" the organization for a short time.
- Enhancing the "soft" skills, not just the technical skills, of participants. For example, HRM will need to further develop valid selection techniques and effective training practices for assessing and enhancing employee flexibility.
- Reassessing the importance of widely shared values or strong organizational cultures. In this changing world of work, will such cultures continue to be as important as they have been in the past (Collins &

Porras, 1994)? If so, how can HRM influence the reinforcement or creation of such cultures as organizational boundaries dissolve and the diversity of employment relationships expands?

Participants Other Than Employees

Employees are certainly the focal participants for whom the balance of inducements and contributions determines a decision to remain in, or leave an organization. March and Simon (1958), however, listed *"five* major classes" of participants: employees, investors, suppliers, distributors, and consumers. They argued that the motivation of *all* five of these classes had an impact on the equilibrium of the organization. In other words, they took the decision to participate by parties such as consumers and suppliers seriously, well before recent writings on TQM and "boundaryless organizations" suggested, anew, that these groups should also be viewed essentially as organizational members and drawn within the organization's boundary. Indeed, Tom Peters (1994) has suggested that the best design for contemporary organizational structures is a circle, and all stakeholders belong inside.

Regarding customers, it is now common to hear that they should be drawn in as organizational participants in product/service design and delivery. In the service sector, customer participation has always been present—as customers frequently are physically on-site and help serve themselves, for example, when you go into a branch bank and fill out a deposit slip. Customers in these roles have been termed "partial employees" (Mills & Morris, 1986) and "customers as human resources" (Bowen, 1986) who need to be managed just as employees, themselves, are managed. In addition, customer participation can entail more than customers helping to serve themselves. For example, Southwest Airlines (SWA) uses frequent-flying customers as members of the SWA interviewer panel that screens applicants for flight attendant positions. In other words, customers help SWA administer its HRM practices.

Another example of "boundaryless" participants is the formation by General Electric (GE) of teams, comprised of GE employees and customers, who are then trained (as a team) in change management practices. This hands-on training focuses on a problem that the GE/customer team faces together and provides the team with a set of change tactics to accelerate problem solutions. Clearly, GE sees both its employees and its customers as human resources, deserving of investments, such as training.

A final challenge, or opportunity, for HRM is presented by the research that shows that *employee* perceptions of HRM practices, for example hiring and training, are positively correlated with *customer* perceptions of the service quality they receive (Heskett, Jones, Loveman, Sasser, & Schlesinger, 1994; Schneider & Bowen, 1985). There appears to be a spillover effect from HRM's impact on employees to an impact on customers. That is, the effects of HRM practices *extend beyond* the organization's boundaries. The implication for HRM is that it should validate its practices against not only internal criteria such as employee satisfaction but also against external criteria such as customer satisfaction.

DESIRABILITY AND EASE OF MOVEMENT: THE "LOYALTY EFFECT" ARGUMENT

Whereas March and Simon (1958) focused on the *antecedents of turnover* among organizational participants, a provocative book by Frederick Reichheld (1996), *The Loyalty Effect,* highlights the *consequences of turnover.* From research on companies including State Farm, Toyota/Lexus, John Deere, and the Leo Burnett Advertising Agency, Reichheld concludes that it is impossible to maintain a loyal customer base without a base of loyal employees. An increase in employee turnover tends to be associated with an increase in customer defection data; this squares with other research that has shown a relationship between employee and customer turnover intentions (Schneider & Bowen, 1985). At Sears, in stores with the highest customer satisfaction, service employee turnover was 54 percent; in stores with the lowest customer satisfaction, turnover was 83 percent (Ulrich, Halbrook, Meder, Stuchlik, & Thorpe, 1991). Reichheld's data show that a strong negative relationship exists between customer defections and profitability. For example, a credit card company that could retain another 5 percent of its customers each year could see the total lifetime profits from a typical customer rise, on average, by 75 percent.

Movement rates among employees and customers in most companies, however, make it impossible to realize the gains of the "loyalty effect." Investors are also included in this pool of movement, as Reichheld (1996) summarizes:

> In a typical company today, customers are defecting at the rate of 10 to 30 percent per year; employee turnover rates of 15 to 25 percent are common; and average annual investor turnover now exceeds 50 percent per year. How can any manager be expected to grow a profitable business when 20 to 50 percent of the company's most valuable inventory vanishes without a trace each year? (p. 4)

The consequences of this turnover are that "business is conducted among strangers; trust is low; and energy dissipates rapidly." Related to these consequences is research by Lawler, Mohrman, and Ledford (1995) which demonstrates that employment security is critical in facilitating the trust necessary for successful employee involvement efforts.

Certainly, HRM has a role to play here. Reichheld (1996) adds his voice to others who have previously documented the connections between investing in human resources and satisfying customers (Heskett & Schlesinger, 1991; Schneider & Bowen, 1985). It seems increasingly clear that HRM practices that help a firm to be the preferred employer in the labor market are also associated with more satisfied and more loyal customers in the marketplace. As firms invest in their employees through development and rewards, these employees tend to remain with the organization and to gain in value to that organization as they (the employees) both learn over time more about a variety of roles and gain increased knowledge of preferred customers' needs.

A preferred employer perspective of HRM requires that many employers shed their misconceptions carried over from the "old" psychological contract. As Peter Drucker (1992) notes:

> Most still believe, though perhaps not consciously, what nineteenth century employers believed, that people need us more than we need them. But, in fact, *organizations have to market membership as much as they market products and services—perhaps more.* (p. 100, emphasis added)

In focusing on customers, the key is not just to retain as many customers as possible, but to retain as many of the *right* customers as possible (Schneider & Bowen, 1995). The right customers are those in the firm's targeted market segment, those who fit the firm's product/service concept and production/delivery system. The customer at Motel Six who complains about the unavailability of pure down pillows is not the right customer to invest in retaining. In other words, there can be *functional* customer turnover as is true for employees. From a different angle, Reichheld (1996) even suggests that some customers are *inherently* more loyal than others, that perhaps the "loyalty coefficients" of various types of customers can be measured. He cites the example of an insurer that examined its customer database and discovered that customers in the Midwest and rural areas were very loyal, while Northerners and city dwellers were quick to switch. Might employees also have predictable loyalty coefficients?

Investors, as organizational participants, also tend to come and go. As Reichheld notes, this is ironic because often the senior management team works harder to satisfy investors, than to satisfy employees and customers. Again, the membership issue boils down to selecting the "right" investors, those interested in establishing a long-term relationship with the company, not just those who are short-term traders.

In sum, the loyalty effect argument urges firms to reduce the "churn" among employees, customers, and investors. Reichheld argues that the goal is to forge a strategic alliance among these parties. Others have previously made a similar case by encouraging HRM to focus on forging strategic unity, that is, a shared mindset between employees and customers as key organizational constituents (Ulrich, 1992).

A New Metaphor for the "Decision to Participate": The "Employee as Volunteer"

It has been said that "employee as vendor" is a useful metaphor for employee participation in today's business environment. It is being suggested that employees and organizations connect with one another via a series of "spot contracts" in which employees sell their services to various bidders.

We believe that a metaphor more likely to build effective psychological contracts is the "employee as volunteer." Traditional hierarchical organizations have treated employees like conscripts or children who need to be supervised and controlled—thus, being completely "in" the organization enhanced management's ability to control.

Today, employees, particularly knowledge workers, are becoming more like volunteers or "talent" who *choose* to participate for an undetermined period of time. In addition, even during times of downsizing, the most talented employees act as volunteers in that they can choose to participate in any number of organizations. The relevance of viewing employees as volunteers is reinforced by the fact that by the year 2000, there will be net yearly additions to the work force of only 1 percent, only the third time in 100 years that this figure has been so low.

"Employees as volunteers" can be a useful metaphor for focusing on the need to build *respectful* relationships between participants and organizations. Thinking of "customers as volunteers" is also a more respectful framing of their participation. Such relationships can facilitate the transfer of learning and knowledge as well as contribute to the development of a new form of loyalty.

What should the "employee as volunteer" metaphor suggest to HRM as HRM plays a central role in attracting and retaining a highly skilled work force? Useful direction is provided by Peter Drucker (1989), who encourages businesses to look to America's largest employer—the nonprofit sector—for lessons in how to build the commitment of knowledge workers. Many "real" volunteers can be found here. Drucker argues that organizations such as the Girl Scouts and the Red Cross believe that their best volunteers are engaged through the following keys:

- Have a clear mission that drives everything the organization does. In private sector firms, employees often feel there is no mission, only expediency.
- Offer meaningful work, put people's competence and knowledge to work.
- Provide training, training, and more training, then let veterans train newcomers.
- Allow volunteers high involvement in setting their own performance goals and in decisions that affect their work and the work of the organization as a whole.
- Build in accountability, volunteers prefer to have their performance reviewed against preset objectives.

These insights from nonprofits on how to manage volunteers, literally, could usefully be applied to manage employees as volunteers, figuratively. The fact that nonprofits have had to learn how to build a committed staff of volunteers, without being able to offer the inducement of a paycheck, has forced them to effectively manage the decision to participate with considerable imagination and innovative thinking.

In closing, we believe that March and Simon, more than forty years ago, neatly framed the two main challenges that will forever face organizations in managing human resources. One is managing the "decision to produce"; the other is managing the "decision to participate." As times change, however, so will the factors that influence these two decisions as will the relative difficulty of managing one versus the other. We believe that recent changes affecting the workplace indicate that the "decision to participate" will have increasingly important implications for HRM. The challenge lies in dealing proactively with the changing business world and the resultant issues arising from who's in and who's out, for how long, and under what types of relationships.

NOTES

1. James G. March is the Fred H. Merrill Professor of Management, Graduate School of Business, Stanford University. Herbert A. Simon is the University Professor of Psychology, Carnegie Mellon University. Professor Simon was awarded the Nobel Prize in Economics in 1978. Professors March and Simon are widely regarded as two of the most provocative thinkers of the past fifty years. Their work is among the most widely cited in the organizational theory literature.

We thank Dave Ulrich and Mike Losey for their very useful feedback during the preparation of this chapter.

REFERENCES

Ashkenas, R., Ulrich, D., Jick, T., & Kerr, S. (1995). *The boundaryless organization.* San Francisco: Jossey-Bass.

Barnard, C.I. (1938). *The functions of the Executive.* Cambridge, MA: Harvard University Press.

Bowen, D.E. (1986). Managing customers as human resources in service organizations. *Human Resource Management, 25*(3), 371–383.

Bridges, W. (1994). The end of the job. *Fortune,* September 19, 62–73.

Collins, J.C., & Porras, J.I. (1994). *Built to last.* New York: Harper Business.

Drucker, P.F. (1989). What businesses can learn from non-profits. *Harvard Business Review,* July–August, 88–93.

Drucker, P.F. (1992). The new society of organizations. *Harvard Business Review,* September–October, 100.

Ehrlich, C.J. (1994). Creating an employer-employee relationship for the future. *Human Resource Management, 33*(3), 491–503.

Heskett, J.L., & Schlesinger, L.A. (1991). Breaking the cycle of failure in services. *Sloan Management Review, 32*(3), 17–28.

Heskett, J.L., Jones, T.O., Loveman, G.W., Sasser, W.E., & Schlesinger, L.A. (1994). Putting the service-profit chain to work. *Harvard Business Review,* March–April, 164–174.

Lawler, E.E. (1992). *The ultimate advantage: Creating the high-involvement organization.* San Francisco: Jossey-Bass.

Lawler, E.E., Mohrman, S.A., & Ledford, G.L. (1995). *Creating high performance organizations: Practices and results of employee involvement and total quality management in Fortune 1000 companies.* San Francisco: Jossey-Bass.

March, J.C., & Simon, H.A. (1958). *Organizations.* New York: Wiley.

Mills, P.K., & Morris, J.H. (1986). Clients as partial employees of service organizations: Role development in client participation. *Academy of Management Review, 11,* 726–735.

Peters, T. (1994). *Crazy times call for crazy organizations.* New York: Vintage Books.

Reichheld, F.F. (1996). *The loyalty effect.* Boston: Harvard Business School Press.

Rousseau, D.M., & Geller, M.M. (1994). Human resources practices: Administrative contract makers. *Human Resource Management, 33*(3), 385–403.

Schneider, B., & Bowen, D.E. (1985). Employee and customer perceptions of service in banks: Replication and extension. *Journal of Applied Psychology, 70*(3), 423–433.

Schneider, B., & Bowen, D.E. (1995). *Winning the service game.* Boston: Harvard Business School Press.

Simon, H.A. (1947). *Administrative behavior.* New York: Free Press.

Sims, R.R. (1994). Human resource management's role in clarifying the new psychological contract. *Human Resource Management, 33*(3), 373–382.

Ulrich, D. (1992). Strategic and human resource planning: Linking customers and employees. *Human Resource Planning, 15*(2), 47–62.

Ulrich, D., Halbrook, R., Meder, D., Stuchlik, M., & Thorpe, S. (1991). Employee and customer attachment: Synergies for competitive advantage. *Human Resource Planning, 14*(2), 89–103.

Wanous, J.P. (1980). *Organization entry: Recruitment, selection, and socialization of newcomers.* Reading, MA: Addison-Wesley.

CHAPTER 28

IS THE HUMAN RESOURCE FUNCTION NEGLECTING THE EMPLOYEES?

BRUCE R. ELLIG

$\mathbf{T}$o be optimally effective, the human resource (HR) function must be both an employee advocate and a business partner. The former was viewed by many as synonymous with the title Personnel, as identifying the in-house Socialist focused on feel-good events. Not surprisingly, many moved to the new identifier, human resources, with the emphasis on being a business partner, optimally utilizing these employee assets. Many have gone too far, however, and are in danger of contaminating the HR identifier by excluding the role of employee advocate. In organizations where this has happened it may be appropriate to introduce a new descriptor, "employee resources (ER)." See Table 28.1 for a comparison of these identifiers. For those who prefer to identify employees as associates, partners, or using some other term, a different modifier will be required, but when the responsibilities identified under "employee resources" are being carried out by the HR function it may not be necessary to change the identifier.[1]

THE ISSUE

The HR function is under attack from several perspectives. Some believe the function should be disbanded as it does little more than set up holiday parties and retirement events. Others believe the function should be replaced by outsourced specialists as it is ruled by bureaucrats unable to respond to business needs. Still others believe a major overhaul is required as the

Table 28.1
Respective Functional Responsibilities

Focus	Personnel	Human Resources	Employee Resources
Vision	Employer of choice	Most productive work-force within peer group	Both
Mission	Improve quality of work life	Improve quality and quantity of work output	Both
Role	Address employee needs	Address organization needs	Both
Description	Employee advocate	Business partner	Both
Emphasis	Employee	Organization	Both
Structure	Vertical	Horizontal	Both

function has become so closely aligned with the business that it has deserted the employees of the organization.

How did HR get into this mess? Answer: We did it to ourselves! Some *are still* the in-house socialists focused on "feel good" events. Others *have* carefully constructed a number of policies and procedures which only they can be expected to administer. Still others *are* focused primarily on re-structuring the organization by taking employees out of the organization through layoffs and special opportunity programs. In other words, to some degree there is an element of truth to the charges, and, therefore, it is not surprising that HR is perceived by some as part of the problem rather than part of the solution. Rather than shout angry epithets at those questioning the continued viability of the HR function, one should be quietly thank-ful. For many, it is a wakeup call.

FUNCTIONAL FOCUS

Every HR professional needs to do a self-examination. How is he or she profiled in terms of employee advocate, administrator, and business part-ner? The employee advocate is focused on employees receiving fair treat-ment. The administrator is ensuring policies and procedures are followed. The business partner is attempting to maximize the productivity of the firm's employee resources. The employee advocate is employee-focused to the exclusion of business needs; the business partner is intent on restruc-turing the organization leaving employees to fend for themselves; the ad-ministrator or bureaucrat is focused on compliance, typically viewing employees and the business not as customers but as impediments.

Need for Balance

The above suggests that buying into any one role to the exclusion of others is too narrow and of questionable overall value. *The answer is balance* with emphasis on employee advocate and business partner. The administrative role is a prime candidate for reengineering, downsizing, and outsourcing (employing the power of technology to do it cheaper and better) and will be discussed further with the restructuring of the function. First I'll examine employee advocate and business partner a little closer.

Evolution of Roles

Personnel to many typifies the employee advocate and administrative role. Human resources was coined by those who wished not only to disassociate themselves from the softness of personnel but to also identify a loftier mission, that of business partner.

As stated, however, the function must be more than a business partner, it must also serve as an advocate for employees within the organization. After all, if not HR, then whom?

It is the dual responsibility of business partner and employee advocate that captures the true value added of the function by ensuring both that the organization has the human resources it needs, when and where it needs them; *and* that the organization is a "right fit" for its employees. For this evolutionary reason, it may be appropriate as indicated earlier that a new descriptor be introduced, one that does a better job of describing the function than do either personnel or human resources if it is believed both are limiting. As stated earlier, employee resources may be appropriate for it is friendlier than HR but still conveys the strategic nature of the function.

BUSINESS PARTNER

Being an employee resources business partner means matching the employee resources with business needs. It means putting the right person in the right place at the right time with the right skills.

To do this one must understand the business. What does our firm produce? Who are the suppliers? Who are the customers? What do they want? Who are our competitors? What are the threats and opportunities facing us? One can gain this understanding from within employee resources on an "earn while you learn," that is, you can learn about sales, marketing, and the other functions by serving as their HR contact to meet their needs. Why not start work elsewhere in the organization moving across functions to learn the business? Would not a person who has worked in research, manufacturing, marketing, and sales be more likely to know the business than someone who has only looked at these functions over the organizational wall? Some employee resources skills will also likely have been acquired along the way by having served in other functions especially if some supervisory responsibility was added.

EMPLOYEE ADVOCATE

Being an employee advocate means ensuring employees receive fair treatment. Individuals who believe they are not being treated properly should be able without fear of reprisal to bring this to the attention of their supervisor and/or anyone else in the chain of command as well as the employee resource function. The complaint must be thoroughly investigated, the results reported, and appropriate action taken. There is no place for inappropriate treatment much less harassment, intended or not, in the organization. Conversely, counseling individuals on inadequate work performance is not harassment.

The other major responsibility of employee advocacy is ensuring equal opportunity. This means more than simply not discriminating. It means providing, on company time and at company expense, training and development programs for individuals who wish to raise their skills levels to compete more effectively. Without this proactive effort on the part of the organization, equal opportunity for advancement exists only in theory.

VISION

Inculcating within one's own organization the values of fair treatment and truly equal opportunity goes a long way toward developing the reputation of being an attractive employer. Isn't that a desirable vision, to be recognized as the employer of choice? That is only the enabling part of the vision; the remainder is wanting one's employees to constitute the most productive organization within its peer group.

MISSION

The mission to achieve this vision is threefold. First, every ER professional should achieve the necessary skills to be both an employee advocate and a business partner. Second, the ER professional should assist in the transfer of the employee resource skills to managers, giving them back the responsibility for employees they manage. Finally, the ER professional should assist managers in transferring these skills to employees. Only if these are accomplished will employees be adequately empowered to succeed in the new environment. How can one expect teams to recruit, select, train, and reward their members without the appropriate employee resource skills? With the advances in technology, information can now be made readily available wherever needed. Ensuring that information is accessible to employees is a prerequisite to effective teamwork and productivity growth. Without this change (i.e., accessible information), the mission will be almost impossible to accomplish.

The real value-added of the employee resource function, however, is not in carrying out the tasks on behalf of managers or employees; it is, rather, in coaching and counseling, helping these managers acquire the needed employee resource skills so that they can accomplish these duties, tasks, and responsibilities themselves. In other words, teach them how to fish instead of continuing to give them the fish.

IMPROVEMENT OPPORTUNITY

The two responsibilities, employee advocate and business partner, are not being carried out very well in most organizations for one or more reasons including: management has not endorsed the above detailed role of the function, and too much time is spent on administration.

Management Endorsement

In many organizations, especially large ones, senior management has recognized the role the employee resource function can play to help optimize return on the invested cost of the employees. Typically this is the business partner portion only. Not surprisingly, but regrettably, the HR function in response to the opportunity of helping to restructure the organization has often left employees to fend for themselves.

When the function has not served as a business partner, the personnel function (for it is probably functioning primarily as an employee advocate with a heavy administrative responsibility) should take the initiative. It may be necessary to go to the line managers and have them evaluate the employee resource function for effectiveness (doing the right things) and efficiency (doing things right). Where scores are low examples must be gathered of what could be done to raise the ratings. Additionally, examining published environmental scans of economic indicators and HR issues is useful.

It encourages and aids in the analysis and evaluation of the external and internal data, the identification of the issues likely to affect the organization and the development of a plan of action (including costs and timing) of how to address the concerns. Logically the emphasis should be on low cost and quick implementation. Where possible the changes should be implemented and modified as appropriate. Armed with the above, one can approach his or her manager for further approvals. Assuming it is logical and reasonable it probably will be endorsed. It is hard to believe that the manager would not be impressed both by the initiative and results.

Alternatively one can sit passively on the sidelines, complaining about the lack of attention from management. Not only is this not productive, it is likely to result in the loss of one's job at some time either through reengineering (and loss of responsibility) or by someone more creative in structuring the role (taking one's place).

Administrative Role

Unfortunately many HR and personnel people spend an inordinate amount of time doing administrative work. This was excusable twenty years ago, but not today. Technology has advanced to the point where almost all of this work no longer needs to go through the function. In some situations, the responsibility is removed. Employees are empowered to enter their personal changes (such as marriage or a birth) on an ATM type kiosk or desktop PC and receive a record of the transaction. Entering changes in this way is faster and more accurate. In other situations the responsibility can be outsourced to specialists (e.g., 401k record keeping and compliance). HR and Personnel people should not retard the move in this direction; they should facilitate its speedy adoption. Rather than lament over the loss of their administrative tasks they should rejoice for it enables them to move up to being Employee Resource professionals—employee advocates and business partners.

STRUCTURE

Employee resource organizations should be aligned to focus on the customers they serve. This alignment results in three different centers of service: One for employees and retirees; the second for the board, CEO, and other senior executives; and the third for all other executives and managers who look for products and services.

Each center provides information periodically as well as upon request. The employee service center has a heavy transaction component: paychecks, retirement calculations, and employee data changes to name a few. The executive center concerns itself with company-wide benefit plan design (to the extent appropriate) and executive compensation delivery systems as well as with executive development and succession planning. The other business center deals with customized pay programs and organization development and intervention as well as training in response to manager and employee requests.

The employee service center is staffed either by the company or outsourced to specialists; the other two centers are internal to the organization but most likely are heavily supported by outside services. The determining factor of whether to do specific tasks oneself or to outsource is whether or not each task is a core competency. If it is, retain it; if it is not, outsource it! What are the core competencies of employee resources business partner and employee advocate? One must be sufficiently knowledgeable about the personnel and human resource skills that support these core competencies. It is more cost effective, however, to engage external experts from organizations specializing in such skills and to apply them in the optimum manner to add value based on the specific business partner and employee advocate culture in one's own organization. It is for this reason that the ER function should neither be blown up nor totally outsourced; it should be restructured.

CONCLUSION

In summary, the personnel and HR functions (as narrowly defined) may not have great futures, but the employee resources function certainly does. It is the Phoenix rising from the ashes of its predecessors.

NOTE

1. In the past 36 years while working for Pfizer Inc. (the last eleven as the top "HR" officer) I have had an opportunity to meet with and listen to many of my counterparts from other organizations in various settings. I'm not suggesting that everyone with the HR identifier is only a business partner or that all those who are in Personnel are only employee advocates; however, I see what appears to be an increasing perception of this separation of roles. To reinforce the dual role, Pfizer has chosen "Employee Resources." We did so by moving to it directly from Personnel as we did not want any confusion with the focus of the function.

CHAPTER 29

FUTURE OF HUMAN RESOURCES

FRED K. FOULKES

Before looking ahead, I wish to look back and put in context my thoughts about the future.

HISTORICAL PERSPECTIVE

Over 20 years ago, in an article in the *Harvard Business Review* (HBR) entitled "The Expanding Role of the Personnel Function" (March–April 1975) I recommended, based on new social and individual values in the workplace, that personnel departments needed to be more active, progressive, and worthy of respect. While neither exhaustive nor a checklist, I proposed that personnel functions that were properly integrated within the company consider developing or refining expertise in the following six human resource activities: attitude surveys or other upward communication programs, the changing workday and worklife, job descriptions, career planning and development, pay and benefits, and supplemental uses of the workplace. I also wrote about the importance of active line management support and involvement and, as part of my conclusion, declared that "Personnel has the opportunity to help make the corporation more of a community by assisting in managing human resources in ways that will both increase productivity and enhance the quality of working life."

In a follow-up article, written with Dr. Henry Morgan, published in HBR in 1977 (entitled "Organizing and Staffing the Personnel Function," May–June 1977) we wrote about the need for personnel departments to make their objectives consistent with corporate strategy. We also identified and discussed four distinct aspects of the personnel function:

1. Formulation of personnel policy—a top management responsibility,
2. Implementation of policies by the line manager-the service function,
3. Audit and control—the establishment of standards and procedures to see that organization policies are maintained, and
4. Innovation—research and development of new practices, procedures, and programs.

We, in addition, wrote about staffing and achieving the appropriate balance between generalists and specialists; about competence and the importance that personnel people, if they are to be effective, have a working knowledge of what goes on in a plant or office; and about the importance of measurements and evaluations.

Each article has its controversial points. In the 1975 article, I not only stated that the personnel function, to be effective, had to be at a high level within the organization but also that top human resource people be considered for board membership. With respect to this point, I wrote, "It would be a sign of recovery from both ineffectiveness and prejudice should board members one day be found to come more often from personnel." The editor of HBR did not like this recommendation, for, based on his experience, it reduced the credibility of the article.

The controversial point from the second article was our statement that a danger requiring a strong warning was the "self-appointment by personnel to the role of 'change agent.'" We stated that " . . . self-appointment to a change agent role can be suicidal for the individual and dysfunctional for the organization."

ASSESSMENT

If one examines what has happened during the 1980s and 1990s, one has to note much progress. In large companies today, more and more, the top HR person reports to the CEO, is a member of the management or executive committee, and is a key member of the top management team. There are even a few cases where the salary of the HR person makes the company's proxy, for he or she is in the top five of the company. It is even the case that some HR people have become members of their companies' boards of directors or board members of other companies. The heads of HR at both GTE and Eastman Kodak were board members until both companies joined a trend of reducing the number of insiders on company boards. The strategic nature of HR work has been widely recognized, and it is seen in the caliber of appointments, compensation, and roles and responsibilities. If effective, HR management is a differentiator for sustained competitive advantage. None of these changes are surprising.

What has also happened during the past 20 years is the emergence of so many women in leading HR jobs. While there have always been a good number of well-qualified women doing HR work, it is only in recent years that the glass ceiling has been broken in many large companies. It was time, and one can legitimately ask why it took so long.

The top HR jobs today at Abbot Laboratories, American Express, the Bank of America, the Bank of Boston, Merck, Monsanto, Pitney Bowes, and State Street Boston, to name just a few large companies, are held by women. In most cases, this is not only a company first but also represents the first time a company's executive committee has had a female member. These women serve as important role models not only for women in their companies but also for the many women enrolled in masters degree programs.

While it is still the case, in my judgment, that the self-appointed change agent role is unwise and a mistake, it is true that more and more HR job descriptions include change as a key part of the job. HR has become, in many companies, a key player with respect to change—whether it be strategic change, cultural change, or changing traditional approaches to staffing, career development, and compensation.

Symbolic of so many of the changes that have occurred, the word personnel is hardly used anymore. Human resources has replaced it in titles and department names and, in many cases, it does represent a more strategic and proactive approach.

If one looks to the future, there would seem to be four certainties: (1) the importance of effective human resource management, whether it be for reasons of competitive advantage, cost and/or productivity, (2) the reality of new and very different ways that work will be done—as Pete Peterson, SVP-HR at Hewlett-Packard has said, "Work today gets done in funny places at funny times," (3) the inevitability of a highly-competitive and challenging global business environment and the need for constant change, and (4) the new possibilities for handling many human resource activities, whether they be new organizational arrangements, different roles and responsibilities, outsourcing, or technology deployment.

One does not have to spend much time with this audience discussing the dramatic changes in the pace of business, the speed of change, and the changed nature of work. At one large and well-known high-technology company, over 90 percent of 1996 revenues came from products that did not exist five years ago, and 30 percent came from products that did not exist just 18 months ago. The need for flexibility and speed has never been greater. Starbucks, the successful coffee shop chain, has no site with more than 20 full or part-time employees.

The number of employees who will join a company and then stay for a full career is not high—possibly 10 percent to 15 percent—yet, many company benefits, from vacation policy to defined benefit pension programs, fit better in a prior era.

Given the need for flexibility and need to avoid fixed costs, it is not difficult to understand the growth of the so-called contingent work force and the necessity of replacing the implied employment security contract of the past.

The way in which personnel or human resources work gets done has also changed drastically. In the past, for example, it did not take too much persuasion to see the wisdom of contracting out, say, the employee assistance program or the cafeteria or the conference center to an outside vendor. Today it is possible to contract out much of HR work. The outsourcing of HR has become an important topic at HR conferences and professional meetings. There are both vendors and technologies that make it possible to outsource virtually every facet of HR work, from benefits administration to expatriate compensation and relocation, to training and employee education. For example, the Boston-based Forum Corporation, an international education firm, has essentially taken over the entire training functions of DuPont and Vanguard.

It may be that much of HR's future role will be in the selection and the monitoring of an array of vendors that will have long-term relationships with the company, like those accounting and law firms have long used.

Insourcing, or the centralization of many HR activities helped by advanced technology, makes it possible to improve service and lower costs in many administrative areas of human resources. As an HR director explained it recently to the students in one of my classes: "We now have $35,000 per year people wearing headsets available 12 hours a day answering questions accurately and consistently, replacing $65,000 per year HR people who were hard to find and often gave out inaccurate or inconsistent information." As the HR leader in one large high-technology company put it, "Once you decide the function can be performed a mile away from the employee, then it does not matter if it is 1,000 or 3,000 miles away." With the Internet and a PC available to almost every employee, personnel manuals are becoming electronic.

The combination of technological advances and the emergence of so many well-qualified vendors with deep pockets makes it clear that there are almost endless new possibilities for how and at what cost and service level

HR work can be performed today and tomorrow. Selecting the right vendors or partners will become increasingly important.

FUNDAMENTAL ISSUES

While much has and will continue to change for proper and understandable reasons, there are, nonetheless, three issues that I wish to raise:

1. The need for some personnel presence at sites of a certain size.
2. The need for reinforcement of the traditional employee advocacy role on the part of HR.
3. The need to rethink HR career development, from selection to training to career development.

PERSONNEL PRESENCE

At a recent Human Resources Policy Institute meeting there was a lively debate between the heads of HR at two large organizations. One person, whose company had its headquarters in Boston reported that at a site in Texas with 400 employees there was not a single HR person. He said that if line management was educated and sensitive and if all employees had access to personnel through an 800 toll-free number, there was no need for a personnel person to be at the site. He further argued that if there were any major issues, from sexual harassment to union organization, representatives from Boston could be at the site within 24 hours. The other person, also from a large company, disagreed and said that he saw a need for a personnel presence at the Texas site. This question goes to issues of philosophy, cost, and human resource management effectiveness. While one wants all line managers to be effective people managers, the reality is that many are not. In my view, one has to "kick the tire," or be on site to sense the climate or atmosphere. The real issue a person with a question about overtime pay, for instance, may want to discuss is the autocratic behavior of a supervisor, a subject one would be reluctant to raise to a stranger on an 800 toll-free number. This assumes that the personnel generalist at the site has the appropriate relationship with the managers and the employees, is trusted, and can strike the right balance between the needs of the company and the needs of the employees. Outsourcing and technology have their place, but in the human side of enterprise there is a need for relationships, trust, sensitivity, and compassion. Figuring out how these needs will be met, both organizationally and economically, is, in my opinion, an important question.

Jerry Weisner, former president of MIT, said that in human affairs, as in physics, there is a need for redundancy. That is why he established in the office of the president an ombudsperson, not to replace the HR department, but to supplement or complement it.

EMPLOYEE ADVOCATE ROLE

There is no doubt that, at least in theory and rhetoric, there has been a major shift in HR's role from administration, guardian of the corporate values and development, and developer of programs to the role of business partner and change agent. It is also clear that the HR generalists who have survived downsizings and reorganizations are those who have good technical, change management, political, and, of most importance, business skills. Many of these HR generalists seem, for understandable reasons, to show much more allegiance to their line management bosses than to their weakened HR functional bosses. This seems to have resulted in a substantial reduction in the traditional employee advocate role. When push comes to shove, many HR generalists have gone along with their line management bosses to produce the desired short-term results. Some of these decisions not only threaten the long-term health of the organization but can be quite risky in the short-term as well, whether the risks be legal, employee-based, or public relations.

A very wise personnel person once told me of the body analogy he used to guide his work as well as the work of his staff—namely, that personnel must be both the hand of the employee and the arm of management. While in the past the pendulum may have swung too far to the side of the employee advocate role, today, in too many organizations, it seems to have swung too far to the side of the business partner role. Whether because of values, law suits, attitude survey results, or the use of the company's employee assistance program, more and more CEOs are recognizing this and addressing it. It is unfortunate if the initiative to correct this imbalance has to come from the CEO rather than from the head of HR.

CAREER DEVELOPMENT

Finally, with increased specialization, outsourcing, and automation, what is the appropriate education, training, and career path for future HR leaders. Whether they be HR generalists or specialists, the broadest education possible would seem the wisest approach. This may be a master's degree in human resources with an appropriate number of business courses or an

MBA with a concentration (or at least a good number of courses) in human resources. What is more significant is how one finds the right training and the appropriate career path. While good bosses and challenging work opportunities have been and will continue to be the essential tools of individual development, the issue of career path is not so clear. It used to be that one could start in employment or training and then move to compensation or benefits and then become a specialist or an HR generalist. In today's corporation many developmental job opportunities no longer exist, and HR work that was once done on site is now done by a vendor. The new deal or contract, which should provide opportunities, training, and career development so that the individual remains employable, involves a partnership between the employee and the corporation, with each party having responsibilities and obligations. While it has always been true that real development is self development, in the future the reality is that the individual will have to take much more responsibility for his/her development and career. This new reality means that for most individuals, both training and career development will be in several organizations. After one has had a successful entry level experience, whether it be at a company, consulting firm, or HR vendor, the next job, if a good developmental opportunity is not available at hand, will be in another organization, perhaps in fact in a partner firm.

CONCLUSION

For many years, calls have been made for expanding the role of human resources in the workplace—that based on new social and individual values in the workplace, personnel departments needed to be more active, progressive, and worthy of respect. This essay discusses important changes that have occurred in HR over the past 20 years such as the top HR person reporting directly to the CEO, being a member of the management or executive committee, and a key member of the top management team; salary improvements; the emergence of more women in leading HR jobs.

This essay also projects future directions—the importance of effective human resource management, the reality of new and very different ways that work will be done, the inevitability of a highly competitive and challenging global business environment, the need for and reality of constant change, and the new possibilities for handling many human resource activities.

Three issues are raised and discussed that need to be addressed to continue the growth and development of HR:

1. The need for some personnel presence at sites of certain size.
2. The need for reinforcement of the traditional employee advocacy role on the part of HR.
3. The need to rethink HR career development from selection to training to career development.

Great changes have already occurred in the HR profession. With focused attention, discussion, and action, the wisdom and influence of HR in the business community will continue to increase.

CHAPTER 30

IN PRAISE OF THE "SOFT" STUFF: A VISION FOR HUMAN RESOURCE LEADERSHIP

SHARON A. LOBEL

I recently attended a meeting of individuals from 30 corporations. Peppered throughout the two-and-a-half day meeting were words like "community service," "balance," "respect," "domestic violence," "education," and "children." If you had to make a guess as to the functional background of these individuals, which of the following would you choose?

1. Finance.
2. Marketing.
3. Human resources.
4. Production.
5. Information services.
6. Research and development.
7. All of the above.

I imagine that a random sample of adults working in functionally organized companies would overwhelmingly select number 3, Human resources. Indeed, I would be astonished to find these words circulating in any other meeting of corporate minds. For this reason, I believe that the human resource (HR) function has a very unique role to play, both now and in the future. This role involves making the business case for "soft" issues, namely people issues that do not, on the surface, have much to do with the business. (As used here, "soft" issues are those that are likely to be *perceived* by other organizational members as peripheral to the business, even though this perception is inaccurate. I do not mean to imply that these issues are easy or uncomplicated.)

I will first briefly describe how this employee advocacy role fits within the evolution of the human resource field. Then I will discuss two specific "soft" issues—(1) building partnerships with communities and (2) balancing work and personal life. I will describe how these issues have been "sold" to the rest of the business and present brief case examples of initiatives in these areas.

THE HR FUNCTION IS STILL UNIQUE

For some time, human resource practitioners have attempted to change their image from bureaucrat to strategic partner. To accomplish this objective, they have focused explicitly on integrating business issues with HR solutions. HR managers have learned to listen to internal customers with the goal of understanding how to serve their competitive needs, rather than merely offering packaged products and fads. In organizations where this transition has been most effective, the HR function now commands much more respect than it did 30 years ago. Even where HR activities have become widely decentralized, or outsourced, or absorbed by line managers, there has been a greater recognition of the links between how we manage people and the bottom line.

As a result of reskilling, HR managers recognize that, like line managers, they are accountable for business results. Line managers, in turn, have learned that the process of achieving results can be facilitated through effective management of people with processes such as team building and participative decision making. With the proper training, many line managers can be effective managers of people, performing the essential functions of staffing, development, performance appraisal, and making compensation decisions. As lines blur between line and staff, does this mean that, in an ideal world, HR managers will be out of a job? I believe that the answer is "No"—or at least, not until the ideal world yields "all of the above" as an answer to the quiz at the beginning of this chapter.

We are still a long way from this outcome. Line managers face pressures to meet ever-expanding customer expectations in a shorter time frame with fewer resources and heightened global competition. Even as line managers absorb many human resource functions in the present context, they will undoubtedly need to be duly persuaded to take on HR issues that appear to be quite peripheral to immediate demands and that seem to belong to the world outside of work. It is no surprise, then, that to date, HR managers have an exclusive niche on making the business case for issues such as community service, public schools, domestic violence, and the unique work/life conflicts faced by low-wage workers. It is up to the HR professional to show that the line between the world of work and the world outside work is much more fluid than it may initially seem—indeed, that the distinction between soft stuff and hard stuff is specious. Without the HR function, I don't believe there would be much of an effort to make the business case.

I will focus next on two "soft" issues—building partnerships with communities and balancing work and personal life—in more depth, to show that the business case is more solid than one might initially expect. Indeed, HR managers also face distinct pressures to demonstrate value while reducing staff and budget. Fluff can no longer be afforded, if it ever could. When HR advocates "soft" issues, there *must* be a business link.

BUILDING PARTNERSHIPS WITH COMMUNITIES

Downsizing has had a drastic impact on the nature of organizations and organizational membership—once stable, now fluid and uncertain. Strategic alliances with external stakeholders, such as suppliers, have also challenged the definition of "organizational member." Organizational boundaries are more flexible than in the past.

As organization boundaries change, not once and for all, it has become legitimate to ask, "To what extent does this issue or entity have to do with our business?" The question is phrased as a matter of degree rather than a "True" or "False" statement. Still, organizational decision makers have been quicker to discern that customer and supplier concerns are of direct relevance to the business than to acknowledge that community concerns deserve attention. To some, it seems self-evident that customers and suppliers can affect the bottom line in a way that families and communities cannot. Moreover, historically, these latter domains have been purposely kept separate from work, if only to protect employee privacy.

Corporations are required, via taxes, to invest in the communities they serve, but there is a host of social and economic reasons to support voluntary investments in community development. Organizations suffer from the failures of public education, families, and communities, all of which contribute to a lack of skilled labor; to a decline in individual productivity; and arguably, to collective deficits in character. On the flip side, organizations benefit from efforts to build bridges with communities. It is in their best interest to do something—whether philanthropy, benefits and services that help employees with non-work conflicts and needs, or encouraging volunteerism. For example, researchers have found that stakeholders, such as investors and customers, may use corporate social responsibility as an indicator of management skill (Alexander & Bucholtz, 1978; Bowman & Haire, 1975). Furthermore, lack of social responsibility may make a firm more vulnerable to costly lawsuits and fines (McGuire, Sundgren, & Schneeweis, 1988). Positive relations with communities can enhance a firm's reputation and help the organization become a supplier, investment, or employer of choice (Lobel, 1996). Ultimately, corporations that focus on customer relations cannot divorce themselves from a key source of customers, namely communities.

A completely laissez-faire attitude is no longer appropriate. With the decline in community associations and traditional family structures, processes available in the past to deal with family and social problems have been dramatically altered. Citizens distrust the public sector's ability to address social ills. Recent research shows that people are spending less and less time in community associations because they are spending more and more time in front of the television (Putnam, 1996). Corporations have unique organizing abilities, resources, and skilled labor—how can they not participate to some degree?

These kinds of economic, social, and moral arguments for building partnerships with communities are likely to be made by HR personnel. Although corporate decision makers have a wide array of means available to them, specific initiatives to build bridges with communities, such as the following two examples, are likely to originate within HR.

- The American Business Collaborative, a $25.4 million fund supported by 137 private and public organizations, was designed to increase the supply and quality of dependent care services throughout the country. According to Ted Childs, Director of Workforce Diversity at IBM and one of the founders of the Collaborative, "We have a fundamental focus on the needs of our employees and on the 200 key communities where they live. . . . We see our strategy as 'investing,' not just 'giving.' . . . We are going to help our people come to work. . . . We are also much more attuned to the failing of service organizations to respond to quality issues and to business pressures. We are better equipped to place demands on them to be better managed. . . . I think there may be issues that could be addressed effectively by particular industry sectors. For instance, our country has a homeless problem. It is possible that the aluminum companies and the lumber industry could come together to respond to that" (Googins, Hudson, & Pitt-Catsouphes, 1995).

- Mentor Graphic, of Wilsonville, Oregon employs 2,400 people worldwide who design and distribute electronic design automation software and provide support services. Margaret Browning, Director of Work/Life Programs and Chair of Mentor's Business and Education Council, initiated a domestic K–12 "School to Work" program to promote employee volunteerism. An internal and external web page provides information regarding the various ways employees can get involved in education. The Business and Education Council is processing requests from schools as well as encouraging sites to develop educational partnerships. The Mentor Graphics Foundation pays individual schools $500 for every 100 hours of Mentor Graphics' employee volunteer time per program year. The hours can reflect the combined effort of employees, and service may occur at the worksite or in the school. Says Margaret Browning, "We feel that it is important for us to support our employees in the communities in which they live. And, as good corporate citizens, we recognize the importance of supporting education. These programs are a tangible way for us to demonstrate our company values. We trust that our employees are committed to meeting their business objectives first; and we know they will plan and manage their volunteer hours accordingly."

The concerns of different stakeholders, such as shareholders and communities, may conflict and may be weighted differently by decision makers, but, as these two examples demonstrate, "win-win" scenarios—those that address community and business needs in tandem—are certainly within reach.

BALANCING WORK AND PERSONAL LIFE: EMPLOYEES AS "WHOLE PERSONS"

Within the field of HR, the work/life agenda includes a critical component of managerial effectiveness—promoting a view of the employee as a "whole person" having significant interactions with people and responsibilities outside the traditional domains of work. Along with Employee Assistance Programs (EAP) and diversity, both areas which are sometimes integrated with work/life in one form or another, these are the only structures within the organization that accord non-work roles the attention they deserve.

Several vivid case examples have demonstrated that the work/life arena is an especially powerful avenue for the kinds of organizational changes that have been touted with the lingo of reengineering. This is because almost everyone can identify with the tensions that can arise between work demands and obligations or interests in relation to life outside of work. Especially now that work/life has expanded to address the issue of work and personal lifestyle, rather than simply childcare, it has become a rallying point for all employees.

In recent research conducted at Xerox Corporation by MIT Professor Lotte Bailyn and her colleagues, a small group of engineers responded to a survey question asking them to describe "What is it about the way work gets done around here that makes it difficult for you to integrate your work and personal life?" The respondents expressed a need for more time, quiet time in particular. In order to examine how they used time, participants kept a log of work activities. The log revealed that they were spending 52 percent of their work time meeting with others, formally or informally. The group instituted a "quiet time" period in the morning, banning any form of interruption. As a result, the group achieved the first on-time launch of a new product in the business' history and also reduced absenteeism by 30 percent.

The Xerox example shows reengineering at its finest. Work practices were changed and, as a result, the group became more efficient and effective. What is important about this example, however, is that the effort was driven by work/life concerns, or at least, it was framed as a work/life problem. This lens mobilized people with a zest that a "quest for excellence in customer service" might not have been able to match.

A similar example occurred at Merck's Canadian operations. Managers asked employees about their work–family conflicts. In focus groups, salespeople complained that they spent their evenings and weekends filling out analytical reports. Further investigation by a task force concluded that many of these reports were unnecessary. As a result, fluff was eliminated, and employees gained more personal time. According to Perry Christensen, former Director of Human Resources at Merck, a year later, employees found that the number of required reports had crept up again. The process needs to be continually revisited, but now it is more of a management priority than it might have been in the past.

At Baxter Healthcare, as part of the Work and Life Strategic Initiative, managers and employees participated in interviews, focus groups, and surveys about work and life priorities. The results showed the following four work and life priorities, in order of importance: respect; balance; flexibility; programs, policies, and practices. Respect was defined as "recognition of the whole person and treating others with dignity." Once again, by using the work/life lens, decision makers have been reminded of the basics.

By and large, work/life professionals have been focusing on work/life programs, policies, and practices, assuming that other people are "taking care of the basics," such as creating an atmosphere of trust and respect. In fact in recent years, with downsizing and increasing competitive pressures, other people are not "taking care of the basics." A recent Towers Perrin (1995) survey of 3,300 employees of large corporations confirms this finding. What may surprise some about the Towers Perrin survey is that employees are not content to be disengaged in reaction to the uncertainties they perceive around them. Despite disappointment with management and ineffective downsizing, employees are strongly committed to making a difference. For example, 75 percent of respondents said they were motivated to help their employer be successful. As part of the new deal, Towers Perrin concludes that employees want respect, fairness, and responsiveness to their needs, most significantly their need for flexibility. Employees want stability in terms of commitment to these basic values. Work/life professionals remind other managers that treating employees as "whole persons" is an essential managerial skill.

HR ADVOCACY FOR MANAGERIAL EFFECTIVENESS

Corporate experience with work/life, quality, diversity, and downsizing initiatives has clearly demonstrated the importance of changing organizational culture to achieve goals. Effectiveness in any of these realms depends on intangibles, not simply on designing programs and articulating policies. The human resource function is uniquely suited to serve as a catalyst for the changes necessary to achieve true managerial effectiveness.

By advocating for building partnerships with communities, HR managers remind other decision makers that employees and their organizations are members of communities in need. "Virtual corporations" are uniquely suited to meet these needs. These anytime, anyplace corporations have an ever wider reach and potential for impact. HR managers can champion the case for making apparently peripheral stakeholders, along with customers and suppliers, essential business partners.

By advocating for work/life integration, HR managers demonstrate the value of viewing an employee as a "whole person." This lens can be a very powerful catalyst for dramatic reengineering and can also put often-touted managerial skills, such as results orientation, to the test. The kinds of deficits that managers have been able to "get away with," such as judging performance on "face time" rather than results, will not survive the movement toward flexibility.

I have argued for HR managers not only to preserve but also to energize their role as advocates for "soft" issues. In doing so, HR managers will show that the label "soft" is truly a misnomer, that there is a compelling link between healthy employees and communities and competitive organizations. Ultimately, it is my hope that HR leaders will stimulate managers throughout the organization to think of these issues as part of the natural repertoire of managerial skills for effectiveness.

NOTE

I would like to thank Margaret Browning, Perry Christensen, Mike Losey, Gregory Prussia, and Dave Ulrich for comments on this manuscript.

REFERENCES

Alexander, G., & Bucholtz, R. (1978). Corporate social responsibility and stock market performance. *Academy of Management Journal, 21,* 479–486.

Bowman, E., & Haire, M. (1975). A strategic posture towards CSR. *California Management Review, 18*(2), 49–58.

Googins, B.K., Hudson, R.B., & Pitt-Catsouphes, M. (1995). *Strategic responses: Corporate involvement in family and community issues.* Boston: Boston University, Center on Work and Family.

Lobel, S. (1996). *Work/life and diversity: Perspectives of workplace responses.* Boston: Boston University, Center on Work and Family.

McGuire, J.B., Sundgren, A., & Schneeweis, T. (1988). Corporate social responsibility and firm financial performance. *Academy of Management Journal, 31,* 854–872.

Putnam, R.D. (1996). The strange disappearance of civic America. *The American Prospect,* Winter, 34–48.

Towers Perrin. (1995). *The 1995 Towers Perrin workplace index.* New York: Author.

CHAPTER 31

THE FUTURE HUMAN RESOURCE PROFESSIONAL: COMPETENCY BUTTRESSED BY ADVOCACY AND ETHICS

MICHAEL R. LOSEY, SPHR

. . . friendships that are acquired at a price and not with greatness and nobility of spirit are bought, but they are not owned and when the time comes they cannot be spent.

Machiavelli

My introduction to human resource management began more than 35 years ago at the University of Michigan's Business School. There, I studied under and worked for Dr. George Odiorne, the director for what was once the school's Bureau of Industrial Relations. Dr. Odiorne started what is now the well-respected *Human Resource Management Journal* the year I graduated.

Given my day-to-day accountability for the world's largest professional human resource society, I asked myself what I could contribute to permit those who share my interest in the profession to gain a new perspective? Then, I thought of a January 1996 *Fortune* article by Thomas Stewart urging CEOs to "Blow the sucker (HR) up." In his article, Mr. Stewart suggests that the human resource function provides essentially no added value and that other functions could handle what little HR contributes to the effectiveness of an organization.

Is this true? Should HR folks be updating their resumes? Or should we just shout "unfair, untrue" and be angry and defensive? I believe the truth lies somewhere in between, depending upon the competency and effectiveness of an organization's HR executive and the respect and positioning the organization gives the human resource function.

The suggestion that anyone can do HR work simply is not true. Human resource management is a profession. As with any profession, there is an established body of knowledge. In addition, the HR body of knowledge can be taught, learned, tested. It has its own ethical code of conduct. I believe what we will see in the future of this profession is not necessarily the continued growth in the number of HR professionals, but more competent HR people. There will be no room for the untrained, the unprepared, the uncommitted, or the unprofessional. Simply stated, those who do not stay current and maintain respect as legitimate business partners are at great risk. This is the way it is—and should be—for a demanding profession.

Those with HR accountabilities recognize the increasing demands and the need for higher levels of competence being placed on the profession. These are just a couple of reasons why the Society's membership is the largest ever. It took more than 40 years for the Society for Human Resource Management (SHRM)/(formerly American Society for Personnel Administration) to obtain 40,000 members. In just the last 5 years, the Society has added more than 34,000 members—individuals who wish to keep pace with an increasingly demanding managerial and business environment and to renew their competencies through professional development.

The HR professional's future will consist of more than just knowing and applying the human resource management body of knowledge. I am confident others in this book will write about the importance of being a strategic business partner and "knowing the business." Let me also suggest that regardless of the size of the organization, HR competency must also be buttressed by *advocacy* and *ethics*. Advocacy and ethics are important for any profession, but they are especially significant roles for human resource managers. As my good friend and colleague Dave Ulrich has said more than once: "The HR professional should not be the company stooge."

Today companies are accused of sometimes acting too much out of self-interest and with little regard for employee and community interests. At the same time, every HR professional wants to be a *team player* and a valued member of management. It is customary that the HR executive makes his or her contribution by first and always being a member of management. At the same time, HR executives are paid to understand their communities, workplace, employee attitudes, and government regulations and requirements. It is up to the HR professional to balance and advance the interests of all parties within the business and strategic thrust of the organization.

On occasion, the HR executive may even find it necessary to put him- or herself at risk in order to balance these interests. This is especially the case when situations are not clearcut or where a double standard may appear to exist. Examples are increasing the cost of health insurance for employees while top management seeks to buffer itself from such requirements or applying sexual harassment guidelines to employees but not to top management.

To illustrate the importance of advocacy within the human resource management profession, allow me to take you back to when I was 25 years old. Dr. Odiorne had been consulting for Sperry Corporation and when they needed a personnel manager for a small plant in their New Holland, PA, division, he recommended me. I jumped at the opportunity, leaving my entry-level labor relations post at the Ford Motor Company for my first manager's job. I remember starting my new position two weeks before Labor Day, but, as it turned out, it was much more than a simple holiday.

On Labor Day, the mother of one of our hourly employees died. When I returned to work from the holiday I was approached with one of my first policy questions as the new HR person: "Was Ollie, the employee, going to be paid holiday pay?"

Ollie had worked the prescribed day before the holiday, but he was not able to return immediately to work due to his mother's funeral. The holiday policy required employees to work the day before *and after* the holiday in order to qualify for holiday pay.

Although other employees and his immediate management welcomed my quick and reassuring response that Ollie would be entitled to holiday pay, they suggested I double check with the plant general manager and my new boss. Their understanding was that no exceptions were to be made for fear the policy would be abused.

"No problem," I suggested, and without hesitation promptly went to see my new boss, Frank. I reminded him of Ollie's mother's death and he asked if we were sending flowers and if anyone would attend the funeral. I assured him that those issues had been handled but pointed out the controversy about the holiday pay entitlement. Frank, as others had predicted, regretfully confirmed that Ollie would not be eligible for the holiday pay. He suggested that establishing such a precedent would not be a good idea. For good measure, he added, "After you are here a while, you'll understand."

I immediately appealed to him. I told him that when Ollie's mother died, we didn't expect him to be at work; Ollie was not arbitrarily extending his holiday to the company's disadvantage. He was not only on an excused but a paid absence. In addition I told my new boss that I was confident no other area company would treat an employee this way and, that if we had a union, this issue would be "a loser." Then, for my good measure, I added, "And if we continue to act in this way we surely will get a union." And all to no avail. Frank, however, recognized my disappointment and as though he needed a "clincher" he added, "Well anyway, Bob would never approve of this."

Bob was Frank's boss, the vice president for manufacturing. It did not take me long to meet Bob. He was a self-made man. With a machinist and toolmaker background, his career had grown parallel to the growth of the company. He was well-respected and known as a straight shooter. I was worried a little, however, because it was reported he had no real affection for college graduates and, especially, personnel-trained college graduates.

Frank took me to Bob's office. After Bob's short greeting, which included his opening remark that my 5'7" height made me "too short for the job," he introduced me to the other top management representatives of the firm. One of the managers was the vice president of finance, J. Paul Lyet, destined to later leave our division and become chairman of Sperry Corporation.

Immediately after being introduced, Mr. Lyet asked me what I thought of the organization's personnel policies. Without mentioning the Ollie issue that was still fresh on my mind, I stated the policies should be reviewed. Not leaving it there, Mr. Lyet immediately insisted that I "identify one policy that, if you had the ability to change, you would change."

I paused. I was uncertain about how I should respond with my boss and Bob sitting there. He persisted and opened a door for me to do what I had to do—to right a wrong. As HR professionals, we must never allow the door to shut on doing what's right. We must always be willing to assume the risk of appealing a management position depending solely upon our own competency and ability to make that appeal?

I told Mr. Lyet the story about Ollie. I argued that it was crazy and stupid to treat employees in such a way. Did we want each subsequent Labor Day to serve as a reminder of the company's short-sighted and uncompromising employee relations policies? I closed by highlighting that this was not personnel's bureaucracy, but management's own—and all for one lousy day's pay.

Mr. Lyet appeared as surprised as I was that such a practice existed. He turned and asked Frank and Bob, "Do we do that?" Bob's answer preempted Frank's dilemma of what to do with a new HR manager who did not understand. Bob's answer was immediate and characteristically direct, "Not anymore!"

Later, the ride from the division headquarters to our plant seemed to be taking forever, although it was only a few miles. Frank was driving and nothing had been said. I assumed that he was disturbed about my capturing the opportunity to appeal this issue to his boss and another member of top management. Then as the gentleman and lifelong friend he turned out to be, he said, "Mike, I forgot why we brought you here. I am not saying that I will always agree with you, but I will always listen, and listen a lot closer."

Of course, this minor issue did not go unnoticed at the plant. Soon employees had renewed confidence in this hardly dry-behind-the-ears personnel person. For me, luck and fate had mixed with a dose of minimum competency to enable me to make a difference on a simple issue. It is upon such simple issues, however, that organizational cultures are built. Sometimes it is the decisions on simple issues that determine the difference between good performance and "also rans" in the HR profession.

Recently—hundreds of Ollies later—I had a telephone call from a woman who asked if she could talk to me without identifying herself or her company. After I provided such assurances, she described her problem. She said that she was the human resource director for a company of 700 employees. The firm had been very successful for the first seven years of its existence, but it was now going through some difficulties, and she had been charged to help prepare for the firm's first reduction in force.

She said she had already been working with the various department heads attempting to identify skills needed in the reconfigured organization. She was also attempting to implement some type of voluntary reduction-in-force program and wanted to determine the impact that length of service, performance, and other issues would have on termination decisions. She said she was confident she was doing the right things. However, just as she and the department heads were going to implement the program, she reported that her company president came to her and said, "Make it easy on yourself and lay off the singles first."

Recognizing that laying off the singles first was inappropriate and probably illegal, given the potential for disparate impact, she answered that such an action would not be the right thing to do. As he left her office she told me he responded, "As a personnel person I knew that you would have to say that, but as a team player I know that you can find a way to make it happen."

Her question to me was, "What do I do?"

Her question reminded me that as we discuss and write about the human resource management profession in the midst of change and at a crossroads, much of what made HR valuable 35 years ago is still valuable today and should not change.

In her case, I knew that she had approached the reduction in force professionally, planning all the correct and necessary actions. Quitting in protest was not the answer regardless of her personal circumstances. Besides, she sincerely wanted to do the right thing for herself, the employees, and the organization. She expressed confidence that if she were given the freedom to act that her plan, as developed in conjunction with other management, would work. She did not need to be told what to do. I recognized her attempt as an HR professional to balance the interests of all parties—the organization, top management, peers, and employees. I wanted to tell her to go to her boss and tell him the real meaning of teamwork—not letting your boss make a mistake! I wanted her to tell her boss that she knows her job, is prepared to do it, and is willing to take whatever performance consequences exist if she should fail.

I wanted her to have that opportunity but could not immediately find the right words to encourage and guide her.

Then, the now ancient words of my dear friend Frank came to me. I told her to go to her boss and simply ask, "Have you forgotten why you brought me here?"

REFERENCE

Stewart, T. (1996). Taking on the last bureaucracy. *Fortune,* January 15, 105–108.

SECTION VI

GO GLOBAL

$\mathbf{A}$ few years ago, a survey of U.S. adults found that 9 percent of those over 18 had a valid passport; even fewer used it. Traditionally, geographic boundaries enabled countries to become somewhat inbred and ethnocentric. Adults in the United States did not need a passport because they had no need to travel to another country. English was the only language you would ever need. The cultures of other countries could be seen through movies or videos.

This is no longer true. Technological advances in information, travel, media, and other parts of our lives have made a large world smaller. Changes in one country are quickly understood and/or adapted throughout the world. When an airline crashes off Africa, it headlines in the newspapers in London, Paris, Tokyo, Hong Kong, and Detroit the next day. It is on CNN within the hour. Within 24 hours, five chat-boxes have been created on the Internet with conspiracy theories about the cause.

As information becomes both a differentiator (knowledge is power) and a commodity (we all have access to similar information very quickly), the world gets smaller. Globalization will become critical for HR professionals in the future and with globalization come many traps and challenges not yet fully understood.

Globalization changes discussions of diversity—overlaying the topic of cultural differences onto the agendas of gender, race, and so on. Learning to run an enterprise in countries with different ethnic backgrounds, levels of education, and value systems becomes a challenge for HR professionals. Learning to move intellectual capital from one site to another becomes equally challenging since no one site may have all the answers to business requirements.

- *What Are the HR Implications of a More Global Business?*

  Doing business in different countries means understanding cultural differences and learning to adapt HR practices to those differences. A colleague recently described a situation in which an Indian executive wondered about the Western practice of hiring in which one would advertise in public media, screen hundreds of resumes to select a few who would be interviewed, then select the candidate based on a few hours of interviews. In contrast, the executive from India remarked that their staffing process would depend on knowing the requirements of the job, then sometimes matching those requirements to candidates well known by the hiring executive, for example, a nephew or niece. He rationalized that Western concerns with nepotism were less viable than his ability to ensure commitment from a known employee.

- *How Can HR Practices Help a Business Develop a More Global Outlook?*

  Creating an organization that is able to do business around the world comes from HR practices. For example, understanding how to mobilize talent around the world, through local hiring, expatriate movement, global teams, and temporary assignments becomes critical for HR professionals to build global enterprises.

- *What Are the Competencies of Global Leaders?*

  As business becomes more global, new types of leaders will be required. Leaders who have the ability to move across global boundaries will be difficult to source. They will have to be comfortable dealing with cultural differences, be able to adapt to local conditions, and be energized by creating globally competitive enterprises. Defining and developing these leaders will be central to the global challenge.

In these chapters, authors explore the importance and challenges of becoming more global. They highlight the emergence of the global enterprise and the implications for global HR practices. HR professionals who understand these global issues will be aware of how to create the global enterprise, move talent around the world, share knowledge across country boundaries, and develop global leaders.

CHAPTER 32

GLOBAL WOMEN LEADERS: AN INVISIBLE HISTORY, AN INCREASINGLY IMPORTANT FUTURE

NANCY J. ADLER

> Studies of global leadership . . . have been remarkably nongender specific.
> This is due primarily to a tacit assumption . . . that all leaders are men! His-
> torically, there is of course a good deal of validity to this assumption—
> almost all . . . [global] leaders *have been* men. To refer to a generic . . .
> [global leader] as "him" may thus be understandable, if inaccurate.[1]
>
> *Adapted from Michael Genovese (Ed.)* Women as National Leaders

No one doubts that the world needs wise and insightful leaders to guide the global community into the twenty-first century; that we as world citizens need different approaches than we have used in the twentieth century if the planet and humanity are to survive, let alone prosper.[2] Similarly, everyone agrees that tomorrow's world leaders will need to challenge and to transcend the more parochial and limited leadership styles of the past. Yet while many people continue to review men's historic patterns of success in search of models for twenty-first century global leadership, few have even begun to appreciate the equivalent patterns of historic and potential success in global women leaders. The myth is that there are few, if any, global women leaders and that their assumption of power is not only rare but is also a sporadic occurrence. If people in general observe senior political leaders, however, they find that 27 women have held the positions of president or prime minister of their country, with almost half of them having come to office since 1990.[3] Will women increasingly assume the highest level of global political leadership in the twenty-first century and yet fail to successfully assume leadership in the worlds' major corporations? While the historic answer would appear to be "yes," careful observation strongly suggests otherwise.

WOMEN AND TRANSNATIONAL CORPORATIONS[4]

Counter to many people's assumptions, today's leading transnational corporations include women in ways that domestic, multidomestic, and multinational firms neither could nor would. Five major changes in the competitive environment explain the rationale behind transnationals' increasing and unprecedented promotion of women into the managerial and executive ranks:

1. *Extraordinarily High Opportunity Cost of Prejudice.* Today's extremely competitive business environment forces transnational firms to select only the very best people available. The opportunity cost of prejudice—of rejecting women and limiting selection to men—is much higher than in previous economic environments. As succinctly stated in *Fortune* (September 21, 1992), "The best reason for believing that more women will be in charge before long is that in a ferociously competitive global economy, no company can afford to waste valuable brainpower simply because it's wearing a skirt." (p. 56)[5]

2. *Local Culture Less Limiting for Transnationals.* Whereas domestic and multidomestic companies primarily hire local nationals and, therefore, must closely adhere to local norms on hiring—or not hiring—women managers, transnationals are not similarly limited. Because their corporate culture is not coincident with the local culture of any particular country, transnationals have greater flexibility in defining selection and promotion criteria that best fit the firm's needs rather than those that most closely mimic the historical patterns of a particular country. Said simply, transnationals can and do hire local women managers even in countries in which the local companies rarely do so.

3. *Foreign Women Respected.* Most countries do not hold foreign women to the same professionally limiting roles that restrict local women. Because transnationals use both expatriates and local managers, these companies can benefit from the greater flexibility that many cultures afford foreign women. The outstanding success of women expatriate managers in all areas of the world—Africa, the Americas, Asia, Europe, and the Middle East—encourages firms both

to continue sending women abroad and to begin to promote more local women into management.

4. *Transnational's Organizational Culture Supports Women's Skills.* Whereas domestic, multidomestic, and multinational firms traditionally have been characterized by structural hierarchies, transnationals increasingly organize around networks of equals. Recent research suggests that women work particularly well in such flatter networks. For example, transnational firms find that many women bring needed collaborative and participative skills to the flatter structures of multinational project teams and are particularly good at developing relationships with international clients and suppliers.

5. *Diversity Increases Innovation.* Continuous innovation and learning are key factors in global competitiveness. An inherent source of innovation is well-managed diversity, including, of course, gender diversity. Women bring diversity to transnational corporations that have heretofore been primarily dominated by men (especially in the managerial and executive ranks).

Transnational corporations, faced with the most intense global competition, appear to be leading in hiring and promoting women into significant global management positions. Can they risk not selecting the best person just because her gender does not fit the traditional managerial profile? Needs for competitive advantage, not an all-consuming social conscience, may answer the question, if not, in fact, define it. Successful twenty-first century companies will select both women and men to manage their global operations. The option of limiting global management to men has been reduced to an archaic "luxury" that no company can continue to afford.

Women Managing across Borders[6]

What can companies do to increase their chances for successfully sending women managers abroad? *First,* they need to monitor their assumptions carefully. Unfortunately, many senior executives still believe three erroneous myths about global women managers:

- *Myth 1: Women Do Not Want to Be Global Managers.* Wrong. Research has shown that today women and men are equally interested in accepting international assignments and in pursuing global careers.
- *Myth 2: Dual-Career Marriages Pose Insurmountable Problems.* Wrong. Leading companies successfully expatriate dual-career couples by using

different approaches from those that they traditionally used for male expatriates who were accompanied by unemployed wives and children. For example, they use international executive search firms and design flexible benefits packages to meet the needs of the trailing spouse and family. Whereas it is true that traditional expatriate packages do not solve dual-career concerns, creative packages are highly effective.

- *Myth 3: Foreigners' Prejudice Precludes Women's Effectiveness as Expatriate Managers.* Wrong. Even though many cultures traditionally limit the access of their own women to professional and managerial roles, they rarely limit foreign women in the same ways. Local managers see women expatriates as foreigners who happen to be women, not as women who happen to be foreigners. The difference is crucial. Research to date shows that, counter to many executives' assumptions, women expatriate managers are slightly more effective than their male counterparts.

Second, companies need to follow a few simple recommendations:

- *Do Not Assume That She Doesn't Want to Work Abroad, Ask Her.* Although both single and married women need to balance private and professional life considerations, many are very interested in taking international assignments and pursuing global careers. Research has shown that the best predictor of success on a global assignment is desire to go.
- *Do Not Assume That It Will Not Work.* Do not use the success or failure of local women to predict that of foreign women managers; foreigners do not treat expatriate women managers the same way they treat their own local women.
- *Offer Flexible Benefits Packages.* Given that most expatriate benefits packages have been designed to meet the needs of traditional families (employed husband, unemployed wife, and children), companies must modify their benefits packages to meet the needs of managers who are single (women and men) and in dual-career marriages.
- *Give Women Every Opportunity to Succeed,* including, for example:

    Accord women managers full status from the outset—not that of a temporary or experimental expatriate—with the appropriate title to communicate the company's commitment to her.

    Have the highest ranked person in the region introduce her to new colleagues and clients. Do not be surprised if local colleagues and clients initially direct their comments to male managers rather than to the new woman manager during their first meeting with her. However, do not accept such behavior; redirect discussion, where appropriate, to the woman. Such behavior from international colleagues should not be interpreted as prejudice, but rather as a reaction to a new, ambiguous, and unexpected situation.

Coach her on how to use her novel status as an advantage, rather than attempting to "hide" the fact that she is a woman.

- *Do Not Confuse the Role of the Spouse with That of a Manager.* Although the single most common reason for male expatriates' failure and early return from international assignments is the dissatisfaction of their wives, this does not mean that women cannot cope in a foreign environment. The role of the expatriate manager's spouse (whether male or female) is much more ambiguous and, consequently, the cross-cultural adjustment is much more demanding for the spouse than for the manager. Wives have had trouble adjusting, but their situation is not analogous to that of women managers and, therefore, is not predictive.

CREATING THE FUTURE: GOING BEYOND MYTHS AND INACCURATE ASSUMPTIONS

There are many myths and inaccurate assumptions being made about global women managers and executives. For example, people assume that Japan and Korea are inhospitable to foreign women managers, and yet expatriate women themselves report that they are highly successful in both countries. Similarly, people assume that international management would be too demanding for women managers with young children. The extra household help often available on international assignments, however, makes it possible for women to balance the time consuming roles of mother, wife, and manager in ways that are nearly impossible when they remain based at home. In a few companies, women now actively seek global assignments to coincide with raising a family. Similarly, counter to popular wisdom, global women managers are finding that their role as a mother often enhances business relationships—including improving negotiations and business transactions— rather than detracting from them.

Given the novelty of women in global management, the best advice is to make judgments based on the actual experience of women working abroad, not on the best guesses of men and women who lack direct international experience. Don't become trapped by past patterns of conventional twentieth century companies; encourage managers to create new patterns that will best fit the demands of business success in the twenty-first century.

Notes

1. Adapted from Michael Genovese (Ed.) *Women as National Leaders.* Newbury Park, CA: Sage Publications, 1993, p. ix.

2. See Nancy J. Adler's "Global Leadership and the 21st Century" and the third edition of her book, *International Dimensions of Organizational Behavior.* Cincinnati, OH: South-Western Publishing, 1997.

3. Based on Nancy J. Adler, "Global Women Political Leaders: An Invisible History, An Increasingly Important Future," *Leadership Quarterly,* 7(1), 1996, pp. 133–161.

4. Based on Nancy J. Adler, "Competitive Frontiers: Women Managing Across Borders" in Nancy J. Adler and Dafna N. Izraeli (Eds.), *Competitive Frontiers: Women Managers in a Global Economy.* Cambridge, MA: Blackwell Publishing, 1994, pp. 22–40.

5. Anne B. Fisher, "When Will Women Get to the Top?" *Fortune,* September 21, 1992, p. 56.

6. Based on Nancy J. Adler, "Competitive Frontiers: Women Managing Across Borders," see Note 4.

CHAPTER 33

PERSPECTIVES ON THE FUTURE

LYNDA GRATTON

Our insights and biases about the future are in part a continuation and extrapolation of our own current understanding and our cognitive maps. They are profoundly personal and idiosyncratic. My own view of the future of human resources has been influenced and shaped by a number of experiences, not least by engaging with senior executives from many of Europe's major companies to help them to understand and articulate the scenarios they believe could emerge over the next decade and the impact these scenarios could have on their organizations and the people within them. My perceptions of the future have also been shaped by the experience of working as a member of a research project (called the Leading Edge) which over the last five years has investigated human resource processes and employee perceptions in seven large and successful companies.

THE LEADING EDGE RESEARCH

Since the beginning of the 1990s a multidisciplinary team based at London Business School has studied in seven large, successful companies: BT, Citibank, Glaxo Wellcome, Hewlett Packard, Kraft Jacob Suchard, Lloyds Bank, and WH Smith.[1] These organizations were tracked from 1992 to the present. Employees at all levels were included in structured interviews, questionnaire surveys, focus groups, and ethnographic interviews. The aim of this research is to understand the human resource processes and outcomes at a deep level, uncovering the reality rather than simply the management rhetoric—the theory enacted as well as the theory espoused. Senior managers from these companies met frequently, together with the research team, to debate the results and to create a dialogue about their meaning, helping to understand how these issues were unfolding. This glimpse into the meaning of human resource management highlighted some of the profound challenges facing these companies as they prepared for the next century. As a community of researchers and managers we sought to understand the broad trends for the future, and the ways in which these would impact upon the management of people.

Human Resource Scenarios

Concurrently I worked with teams of European senior managers in over 20 multinational organizations creating a framework within which a focused dialogue about the future can take place.[2] The process I developed begins with the team of senior managers imagining that it is now the year 2005 and describing and discussing their own cognitive maps of how the organization will be structured, what the key elements of the culture will be, how leaders will behave, what form the human resource architecture will take, and the key attributes and skills of the work force. During these lively dialogues, the assumptions and boundaries of each member of the team emerge and are discussed. The teams consider all the factors and select the 10 with the most significant impact on the future. The current alignment of these 10 factors of strategic impact is then debated. At this stage, a Risk Matrix is created with axes representing strategic impact and alignment. This enables the team to focus on those factors that they believe will have a high strategic impact on the future but where current alignment is low. These factors should be uppermost in their long-term strategy.

Over the years, these debates have brought real insight into the way senior executives consider the future and the impact this may have on people and the role of human resources.[3] Over 20 teams in over 20 large, international companies have focused on the year 2005 and identified the areas they believe should be at the top of the agenda for change. The most frequently discussed factors are:

Creating Horizontal Teamworking: Integrating these highly decentralized organizational structures through horizontal teamworking across regions, functions, and businesses.

Decentralized Decision Making: Forming simpler, flatter, more transparent structures and decision-making processes.

Facilitating Communication and Learning: Creating an organization where learning takes place rapidly across the business and associated partners and joint ventures.

Managing for High Performance: Linking the stretching and ambitious goals of the organization with the performance of individuals. A particular challenge is the creation of performance metrics capable of assessing not only the hard but also the softer performance outcomes, such as team management or innovation.

Recruiting and Retaining Key Talent: Balancing the need to be an employer of choice for those with key talents, with the need to renegotiate the employment and psychological contract with other members of the company.

Creating Global Training and Development: Meeting the global growth plans through developing both internationally experienced management cadres and cost-effective local country training.

My research with the Leading Edge team and my scenario planning activities have brought many insights into the current reality of human resource management and the challenges for the future. These six factors of strategic impact described by teams of senior executives set a broad agenda for the next decade. They address the content of the challenge, identifying where leverage could potentially be gained. I believe, however, that the challenge we face in human resources is not one of content—the *what,* but rather of process—*how* can we create horizontal teamwork, *how* can we manage for high performance? The challenges described in this chapter concern process. The challenge is to create a real understanding of how human resource systems function as a totality rather than as discrete interventions and to build and embed processes capable of supporting and enriching longer term thinking.

FUTURE TRENDS FOR HUMAN RESOURCES: FROM DISCRETE INTERVENTIONS TO TOTAL SYSTEMS

The challenge of creating horizontal teamwork (the most frequently discussed strategic factor for 2005) provides an illustration of the necessity of considering the total system rather than working with discrete interventions.

During the scenario work, the teams of senior managers described their companies in 2005 as operating globally. Their business scenarios created a vision of a movement of markets from Europe to Asia Pacific, with a significant proportion of the work force operating in Asia. For many this process of globalization has been taking place over the last decade, and the international career paths and local recruitment practices are in place to support this growth. The issue that was central to their perceptions of the human resource scenario was how globalization could be underpinned with information and organization structures capable of creating networks of learning and of rapid and transparent decision making. A team from the telecommunications company, Nortel, spoke of "a structure that no longer reflects separate functions, but reflects the needs of the market place and has fewer layers." To quote a team from the pharmaceutical company, Sandox, with a vision focused on product innovation and speed of development, "Potential synergies between functions and territories can only be realized through an organizational structure which is team-based, matrixed, and networked, where the sharing of knowledge and information occurs across functions and divisions."

Speaking of the present, the teams identified many blocks to change: functions speaking different professional languages; rigid structures making horizontal working difficult; functional "barons" failing to release their best people for project teams; the lack of cross-functional or cross-business career paths; appraisal and reward processes that focus on a single function and boss and thus undermine horizontal working. To bridge the gap, the teams realized that leveraging for horizontal working would require a complex, interrelated set of actions. Senior managers must support horizontal mobility by releasing and parenting people and facilitating discussions between staff. Greater numbers of horizontal project teams must be created at all levels in a company, and change agents must be developed who are capable of supporting and facilitating rapid team formation and high performance. The impact on people processes that they identified included creating horizontal career planning, refocusing the performance management processes to encourage and reward teamwork, and establishing training in project management.

The results of the scenario—work focusing on horizontal working—illustrate a fundamental challenge for the human resource function as we prepare for the next decade. The challenges organizations face cannot be just described or addressed by individual techniques. They cannot be solved simply through team-based rewards, 360-degree appraisal, or horizontal career development. These challenges are illustrative of aspects of dynamic, complex, integrated systems. Within each system a number of key linkages must exist, both vertical linkages from business strategy to human resource processes, and horizontal linkages between the human resource processes. To create change within these systems requires an understanding of the dynamic nature of these linkages and an awareness of those points of leverage from which maximum effect can be gained.

This point is well illustrated by the experiences of the human resource team at the pharmaceutical company, Glaxo Wellcome, one of the companies we studied in the Leading Edge research project. In the initial discussions in 1991, senior executives talked at length about the increasingly competitive forces in the marketplace, about the need to get products to market as quickly as possible, and to create a new wave of products. In discussions with their human resource colleagues, it became clear that horizontal teamwork could play a key role, through creating closer collaboration between research and marketing and sales, by increasing the speed of response, and by ensuring the customer's voice was heard deep within the organization. In 1992, the human resource team began to formulate an approach. The team members were aware of the complexity of the system and identified key points of leverage that would really make a difference. Of all the possible points of leverage, they agreed to focus on horizontal working and management. Between 1993 and 1996, significant numbers of people were trained to facilitate and support the creation of high-performing teams; an increasing amount of work was structured across rather than within functions; and a series of programs encouraged and supported managers in acting as coaches and mentors. At the same time team-based rewards and multiple feedback systems were piloted and rolled out.

In 1993 and again in 1996, we surveyed over 200 people and interviewed 30 from board level to sales representatives. At both times we asked about teamwork, about the role of the manager, and about work structures. We found significant changes between these two periods. In 1996, 73 percent of the employees we surveyed said teamwork had increased. We asked employees to rate the significance of a range of developmental activities. In 1993, 13 percent reported mentoring had played a significant role, and 22 percent said teamwork was a significant part of their development. By 1996, these percentages had increased to 27 percent and 42 percent. How had these results been achieved? I believe they indicate a team of human resource people who understood the nature of the challenge faced, who saw these interventions as part of a large and complex system, who identified a number of points of leverage, and who managed to focus enormous amounts of the organization's energy and resources on these leverage points.

In other companies, we observed weak links between the business strategy and human resource processes and poor horizontal linkage across the human resource processes. One of the consequences of this weak linkage was that corporate plans and mission statements remained simply that, senior executive rhetoric that had little meaning to those people tasked with delivering customer delight or bringing complex products rapidly to market.

Exhortations to "move closer to the customer" were accompanied by task objectives that limited the amount of time individuals spent with customers, while those to "become more international" were juxtaposed with career systems that reduced opportunities for cross-country posting and created senior executive cadres dominated by home country nationals. Mission statements to "solve problems through teams" were undermined by appraisal and reward systems that remained resolutely individualistic and tournament-based promotions that encouraged competition between team members. Faced with this plethora of contradictory messages, the "unwritten rules of the game" described a reality that was far from management rhetoric.[4]

FUTURE TRENDS FOR HUMAN RESOURCES: FROM SHORT-TERM TACTICS TO LONG-TERM VISIONS

The timeframe for human resources is significantly longer than for almost any other resources. For example, it took one day for Glaxo Wellcome to raise a million dollars from the financial markets but 10 years to create an international management cadre. In one week, we observed Citibank making profound changes to its financial offerings yet to develop, pilot, roll-out, and gain commitment to team-based rewards took many years.

Because the timeframe for human resources reaches right into the next decade, we must be thinking and visualizing now for what may come in the new millennium. Yet, like many other commentators, I have been struck by the lack of long-term thinking in most Western companies. In the scenario planning sessions, the teams engaged with enormous enthusiasm and creativity in the task of creating and describing their company in the year 2005. What was most striking was the novelty of this experience for them. For many, it was the first time they had set aside two days in their busy schedules to debate the future. Our research in the Leading Edge has brought clear insights into why this was so. Many managers are under enormous pressure to deliver short-term results; planning horizons are six months at the longest; and short-term employment contracts reduce a manager's long-term commitment.[5]

It is the responsibility of the human resource function to challenge this short-term thinking, to facilitate and support, and to create ongoing forums and processes in which a vision for the future is actively and cogently debated. This vision of the future then becomes part of the dynamic system that creates (1) vertical linkage between strategy and human resource

Figure 33.1
The People Process Model: Embedding Transformational Change

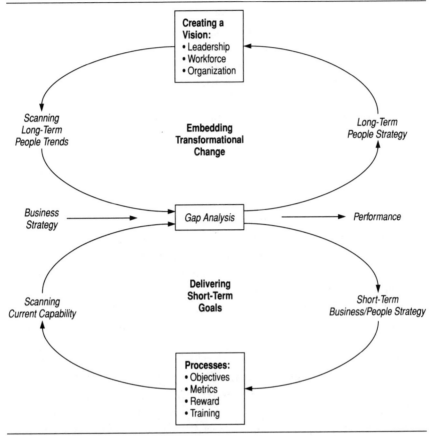

processes, (2) horizontal linkage between processes, and (3) temporal linkage between current reality and future visions. The dynamic nature of this system is illustrated in Figure 33.1, which captures some of the dynamics in the total human resource system.

There are four interlinked clusters of processes that bring adaptation and change into the dynamics of the model. They serve to create a shared understanding of the future, to translate this into the human resource implications, and to create awareness and action around the gap between the needs of the future and the current state of the system. In summary, they help to create the feedback loops crucial to organizational learning and fundamental to the ability to embed the capability of adaptation and transformation:

1. *Creating a Vision:* Dialogues and debates which create a shared understanding of the potential futures for the business and how these scenarios can be sustained through people, organizational structures, culture, and human resource processes.

2. *People Strategy:* Developing a human resource function capable of fully participating as an active member in the vision and strategy creating forum; a human resource strategy that captures the broad future trends.

3. *Long-Term Scanning:* Systematic scanning and integrating of long-term external trends, including demographic, aspirational, contractual, and skill-based trends.

4. *Gap Analysis:* Understanding the current state of the system and the gap between current capability and the needs of the future.

In the Leading Edge research over the last five years, we have examined the processes and procedures supporting each of these clusters and spoken extensively to senior managers and those in human resource functions about their perceptions of the strengths of these systems. For most of these companies, those processes that focus on the short-term business strategy are relatively well-developed. Senior members of the human resource team play an active part in debating the short-term business strategies and developing an awareness of the people implications. At Hewlett Packard, this is particularly well articulated through the Hoshin system which links business goals with a set of agreed upon corporate actions for the year. At Kraft Jacob Suchard, the MAP process links business objectives to the performance of every employee.

We have also seen significant developments in the ability to understand the current data regarding the system. Over the five-year period we have studied these companies, both the use of employee surveys and skill audits has significantly increased. This has brought deeper understanding to executives about the state of the human resource processes and the commitment and satisfaction of the work force. We are beginning to see some of these "soft" quantitative metrics appearing alongside the "hard" financial metrics in appraisal systems. At Glaxo Wellcome, Citibank, and Hewlett Packard, these measures expressed in the *Balanced Scorecard* are increasingly seen as key variables in the business metrics. Those parts of the systems that focus on the short-term are relatively well-developed across the companies in the sample.

When we turn to the longer term processes, those that create a long-term vision, and scan for long-term trends and articulate the gap between current capability and future needs, the picture is less clear. We found very few examples of the people implications of longer term business strategy being debated in a systematic way or in a way that involved a wider audience. Interestingly, the scenario planning described by Shell executives appears not to have been adopted in other multinational companies. Where there are formal visioning processes in place, they have been created and supported by a far-sighted individual rather than through organizationwide initiatives. Scanning processes are internal and short-term, not external and long-term. The majority of the companies engaged in ad hoc information gathering about particular areas of concern—for example, the impact of the European directives on Works Councils and the Social Chapter—but these were primarily tactical responses to immediate concerns.

Why have the longer term processes been less well-developed? These processes are more complex and the current understanding of how longer term human resource strategies can be created and implemented is not well articulated. Moreover, these longer term perspectives run counter to the prevailing drive for short-term results. This places immense pressure on managers in all functions to behave in a focused, tactical way rather than the rather ambiguous way demanded of the visioning process. This thinking, however, is critical and already plays a significant part of the role of senior managers in Japanese and Korean companies. I believe it is the role of the human resource function to make the case for long-term thinking, to support the development of scenarios, to create visionary strategic processes, to confront the undiscussible. Without this, the function sinks to a "clerk of works" role, and human resource processes remain tactical and incremental.

NOTES

1. The Leading Edge research team includes Lynda Gratton, Veronica Hope-Hailey, Patrick McGovern, Philip Stiles, and Katherine Truss.

2. I have described my human resource scenario methodology in "Implementing Strategic Intent: Human Resource Processes as a Force for Change," *Business Strategy Review*, 1994, vol. 5, no. 1, pp. 47–66.

3. A detailed description of these strategic factors and their relationship to the strategic vision of the companies is presented in "Implementing a Strategic Vision: Key Factors for Success," *Long Range Planning*, 1966, vol. 29, no. 3, pp. 290–303.

4. The analysis of the subtext in these organizations, using the "Unwritten Rules of the Game," played a central part in our methodology. The concept is described by Peter Scott Morgan in *The Unwritten Rules of the Game* (New York: McGraw-Hill, 1994).

5. Some of these dilemmas and the pressures on managers in the companies in the Leading Edge are described in a paper about the role of line managers in supporting human resource processes. McGovern, Gratton, et al., "Tilting at Windmills: HRM Practices Among Line Management," *Human Resource Management Journal*, (in press).

CHAPTER 34

HUMAN RESOURCES IN THE FUTURE: AN OBSTACLE OR A CHAMPION OF GLOBALIZATION?

VLADIMIR PUCIK

There seems to be a wide-ranging agreement among human resource (HR) scholars and practitioners alike that HR in the future will be increasingly global. Virtually no firms, large or small, irrespective of industries, are today shielded from the impact of globalization. Competitive threats and, in particular, opportunities are more and more global. The ever-expanding scope of global competition is forcing a continuous reexamination of how human resources can best support the rapid pace of business globalization.

Firms competing in the global environment are facing a multitude of new demands on their organizations and people, often being pushed simultaneously in several contradictory directions. In response, the new global organizing paradigm is centered on complementarities, not on trade-offs; on management process, not on organizational structure and procedures. This paradigm symbolizes a shift away from traditional and static structural solutions to global business challenges, towards an acceptance of the global organization as a fluid and evolving dynamic network.

In order to survive and prosper in the new global competition, companies are embracing global integration and coordination, but at the same time they must push for local flexibility and speed. Global companies have to nurture global organizational learning by stimulating creativity, innovation, and the free-flow of ideas across boundaries, but also advocate a disciplined and methodical approach to global continuous improvement. To succeed in global competition requires an open and empowered organizational climate, but also a tightly focused global competitive culture.

In a global competitive arena, the sustainable competitive advantage will depend less on the strategic planning debates inside the corporate headquarters and more on the behavior of employees across all regions of the world. When the handful of proven competitive recipes is well-known, the key to success is the organizational capability to execute. If global organizational capability, intrinsically linked to people issues, is the principal tool of competition, it is only natural that HR in the future should become the pivotal partner in the globalization process.

HUMAN RESOURCES: AN OBSTACLE TO GLOBALIZATION?

Paradoxically, in spite of the value-adding opportunities for HR contributions to competitive advantage driven by the demands of business globalization, in many companies today the HR function is still perceived not as a full partner in the globalization process, but perhaps even as its principal obstacle. The ethnocentric and parochial HR systems and policies inherited from the past and focused on a single country or a select group of employees, are all too often the most common barriers to the implementation of effective global organizational processes.

What are the most frequent causes of parochial behavior in human resources? First of all, compared to most other business functions, many current HR leaders have not yet had much direct exposure to issues spanning national boundaries. In a typical corporation today, be it American, European, or Japanese, the careers of most HR managers evolve primarily within their own native countries or perhaps within a small region. Only in exceptional cases would a HR executive career involve multicountry experiences. International issues are the domains of HR specialists focused on expatriate compensation and benefit issues and on operational firefighting.

In parallel, most operational HR activities are decentralized into individual country organizations. While such a decentralized approach is, in principle, logical (after all, the vast majority of employees are and always will be "local," embedded in the local culture and impacted by the local legal and regulatory environment), when HR localization is taken to an extreme and everyone is treated as local, who is "global"? A natural outcome of this well-intentioned, but ultimately destructive, localization bias is that HQ nationals are considered implicitly "global," and all others are local. That's why the top HR leadership group is generally not very representative of the employee population at large.

Another factor limiting HR effectiveness as a partner in the globalization process is the traditional focus of international HR on selecting and supporting expatriates rather than on serving the global employee population. In many corporations worldwide, the operational needs of the expatriate management system, much of it centered around compensation and benefit issues, still dominate the international HR agenda of the corporate HR.

Finally, the HR function is often satisfied with just being an innocent bystander to the ongoing globalization. There seems to be little desire to get involved and influence its direction, measure its progress and its impact on business performance, as well as to define where and how HR can make a difference. Without a willingness to become accountable for the outcome of the globalization process, it is not very likely that in the current era of downsizing and outsourcing, there will be many resources left for HR to impact the globalization process, besides an occasional global HR conference and a few bows toward cultural diversity in company newsletters.

Developing a Global Mindset in Human Resources

The challenges facing the global human resource function are formidable, but so are the opportunities to make a difference. The cornerstone for HR leadership in the globalization process, however, is its capacity to become a global role-model. Unless the HR function is seen as a living example of, for example, how a global organization recruits, develops, and rewards people; how it stimulates and supports global networks; and how it makes decisions that integrate global and local perspectives, it may be difficult to gain the credibility to influence others.

There are also a number of fundamental issues that may need to be addressed within the HR function before HR can assume its legitimate and necessary role as the champion of globalization. Among those issues, those linked to the influence of national cultures on human resource practices are perhaps the ones where a deeper understanding of challenges ahead may be essential.

First of all, having a global HR mindset implies a recognition of benefits that can flow to the whole organization from encouraging and valuing cultural diversity in people, not just as members of distinct cultural groups but as individuals. Success in building cross-border networks of relationships that are the core veins of effective global organizations is dependent on understanding and valuing cultural diversity. Yet valuing diversity must go well beyond the traditional emphasis on bridging the distance between the clusters of national cultures by focusing on average national characteristics.

Cultural knowledge in human resources implies knowledge of differences within a culture as well as across cultures. The barrier that hinders effective cross-cultural interactions is not just the average distance between national cultures, but also the lack of comprehension about diversity within a given culture by outsiders who do not understand the historical, political, and social context of within-culture differences and thus have to rely on often misleading general assumptions and stereotypes. Now that we in human resources have stopped stereotyping about gender and race, perhaps we should tackle culture with the same determination.

At the same time, how unique can the basic philosophy of human resources in a global firm be? Maintaining a healthy differentiation that creates competitive advantage while responding to local cultural characteristics is a major obstacle facing global HR. Within their home culture, few HR professionals would question the benefits of differentiation. Leading-edge companies are seldom scolded by the business press for being different in management style from their competitors. Rather, their idiosyncratic cultures and values are celebrated and often sought out to be emulated.

Being different in a foreign culture, however, is considered by many HR professionals as somewhat rude and arrogant, if not fundamentally wrong and improper. Yet, in the process of balancing global business needs with multiple cultures, the role of HR should not be just to defend cultural traditions in the name of cultural diversity but to implement the necessary organizational strategies with sensitivity to specific cultural influences. Unfortunately, where and how to "push," and where and how to "give" in to cultural differences, are the kinds of specific global knowledge that not many HR leaders today have had the opportunity to develop.

GLOBALIZING HR PROCESSES

With cultural foundations for the global HR mindset in place, the next challenge is to implement a set of comprehensive HR processes to speed up the globalization process; foster global competitive capabilities; and support the selection, retention, and motivation of future global leaders. In this context, *global staffing* and *global leadership development* are perhaps the two components of global human resources with the greatest potential for powerful leverage that global firms such as Citicorp, Procter & Gamble, Motorola, Shell, and Unilever have already recognized. In both of these areas, however, the deepening emphasis on globalization requires a major paradigm shift in HR orientation in comparison with the traditional perspective.

It is critical to recognize the differences between global and expatriate managers. The former are defined, in a broad sense, as executives who perceive global competition as an opportunity; have a hands-on understanding of global business and an ability to work across organizational, functional, and cross-cultural boundaries; and are able to balance the simultaneous demands of global integration and local responsiveness. In short, global managers are defined by their *state of mind,* in contrast to expatriate managers who are identified *by location* as executives in leadership positions that involve cross-border assignments.

Global HR should be focused on present and future global leaders, not just on current expatriate managers. Where will the future global leaders come from? Will global opportunities be available to employees all over the world, or only for those located in one or a few key countries? From a long-term perspective, a truly global organization must satisfy a simple but demanding test: "It does not matter where one enters." Worldwide, probably very few companies today can meet this ambitious target.

In addition, the expectations regarding expatriate roles are also going to be substantially changed. Today, most international assignments are still demand-driven, filling positions where sufficient know-how is not available locally, or when the authority of headquarters needs to be upheld in a more direct fashion. In other words, expatriates are *teachers,* transferring new capabilities and maintaining order. Given the expense, the emphasis on limiting the number of "teaching" expatriates is only natural.

In the future, however, the role of expatriates will change dramatically. With less need for knowledge transfer from headquarters, most expatriates will be *students,* not teachers, learning through experience about market and cultural differences, while developing long-lasting networks of relationships. In this case, the more, the better. The HR support system will have to adjust to this redefinition of expatriate roles by linking policies and practices more tightly to the purpose of the assignment.

GLOBAL STAFFING

While it may seem intuitively obvious that global firms will need more and more employees with "global brains," translating this attractive vision into operational reality is not simple. Does every employee need to be global? Who really needs global brains? Most managers are not born global; they acquire global brains through a series of experiences, many of them at a substantial cost to the organization. What is the return on investing in developing people with global brains? Making a rational business case concerning the future need and use of global managers is one of the critical strategic decisions the global HR function and business leaders must make together.

Once the demand parameter is set, a corresponding long-term supply strategy needs to be put in place. Should future global managers be developed on the inside "bench" or is it better to recruit them from the outside labor market when the actual need arises? Insiders benefit from the knowledge of the business and the organization; outsiders often bring in ready-made global skills. What would be the cost and benefits of the two approaches, given firm-specific technology, organizational processes, and culture? Also, if global skills are critical for future leaders, to what degree should the entry-level selection process focus on an employee's potential to acquire global skills, expressed, for example, as the willingness to move across borders?

There is some empirical evidence that global mobility enhances the opportunities to develop a global mindset (although not everyone who frequently moves across country boundaries necessarily fits the characteristics of a global manager). At the same time, the socioeconomic and cultural trends around the world point to increasing barriers to employee mobility. Dual-career families, parental care needs, children's education constraints due to the competitiveness of the home-country education systems, the equalization of economic opportunities lessening the incentives to move—all are factors that may diminish the desire of employees to actively seek out international assignments.

In response, global organizations will have to become more and more creative in finding suitable alternatives to mobility. Given the need to flatten the organizational hierarchy supported by advances in modern communication technology, the traditional country-based job boundaries will begin to disappear, stimulating demand for positions with multicountry responsibilities. Again, weighing and managing the cost and benefit tradeoffs of alternative global staffing strategies is a major challenge facing the global HR.

GLOBAL LEADERSHIP DEVELOPMENT

A global mindset is one of the key characteristics of future global leaders, and one of the principal tasks of global leadership development should be to create and support an environment where global mindsets can flourish. Global leadership development in the future will focus on providing a broad spectrum of employees with opportunities to acquire and enhance their global leadership skills and capabilities, often using nontraditional developmental techniques such as cross-border job swaps or assignments to multicultural task forces and project teams.

Internal education programs in global organizations are likely to emphasize the acquisition of global experience. As learning by doing is the best, if not the only, effective method to develop global skills, and given the high cost involved in most global training programs, a tighter linkage of leadership development with global business needs through a variety of action learning approaches will be necessary (e.g., GE's Crotonville model). In turn, this implies that development professionals themselves have to significantly upgrade their understanding of globalization issues.

Future global organizations are going to rely increasingly on flexible networks of relationships to foster global integration and coordination, therefore, a significant component of developmental activities should focus on the socialization aspects of leadership development. The purpose should be to create and enhance the relationship networks and to support the sense of common purpose, trust, and cooperation among employees across the whole global organization. Again, facilitated joint projects are probably the best tools to accomplish this objective.

Finally, in spite of the increasing barriers to mobility cited earlier, international mobility is likely to remain the critical building block for enhancing the awareness of global issues and for the development of global leadership skills. Global assignments should, therefore, become an integrated part of the career planning and development process. In contrast to the past patterns of expatriation, the learning-driven global assignments are likely to occur relatively early in an employee's professional career and may involve rotations across the whole global network, not just the traditional exchanges between home country and country affiliates.

In this broader context, and in order to move the organization forward to its ideal transnational state, the key task of those responsible for implementing global leadership development activities is to secure equitable access for talented employees worldwide to take advantage of available opportunities.

HUMAN RESOURCES AS A CHAMPION OF GLOBALIZATION

What are the next concrete steps that HR can take today to launch its globalization journey?

The challenges facing human resources in the future as the function strives to become the champion of globalization can be generalized under three broad problem areas: (1) developing a global mindset inside the HR organization, including a deep understanding of the new global competitive environment and the impact it has on the management of people worldwide; (2) aligning core human resource processes and activities with the new requirements of competing globally while simultaneously responding to local issues and requirements; and (3) enhancing global competencies and capabilities within the HR function so it can become a borderless business partner in rapidly exploiting business opportunities worldwide.

Probably the first step that should be taken is to globalize the core HR leadership group so that it is more closely aligned with business opportunities worldwide as well as with the cultural diversity of the organization. This may involve global rotation and assignments, a redefinition of roles and responsibilities, and global development programs targeted at HR.

The second complementary step should take aim at enhancing and extending the formal and informal coordinating mechanisms linking HR professionals in the worldwide organization. Here, information technology, global task forces and project teams, short-term developmental assignments, and global training are the key instruments of change.

In order to accomplish the globalization objective in the longer run, it will be necessary to increase dramatically the rotations and exchanges of high-potential HR professionals across countries early in their careers, including more international HR internships for students, so they can assimilate the hands-on skills of managing people issues in a multicultural environment. This may also require changing the traditional criteria for selecting the entry-level HR professionals worldwide with a new emphasis on cross-cultural and language skills.

Human resources in the future will be much more diverse than today and for all of us in the HR field who enjoy diversity, it will be great fun.

CHAPTER 35

HUMAN RESOURCES MANAGEMENT AND THE ASIAN AFFIRMATION

GORDON REDDING

Three features of the international managerial scene are especially relevant for understanding the future shape of human resource management from a comparative standpoint. *First,* distinct business systems have crystallized out of the history of attempts by various societies to modernize and develop to high levels of economic activity and wealth. *Second,* these systems contain distinct ways whereby organizations hold people in and keep their co-operation and commitment. *Third,* these formulae, once stabilized, tend to replicate themselves and to absorb new influences without losing their integral characteristics. Japanese management remains in some deep sense Japanese, so too Korean, and so too that typical in Chinese capitalism. Moreover, they all remain different in significant ways from the forms that have evolved in the Western world and that so pervade the textbooks, the world of consultancy, and the blizzard of advice visible in airport bookshops.

This is not to deny that cross-fertilization does not occur between the systems. The "art" of Japanese management, and its encapsulation in books such as *"Theory Z"* had a major impact on HRM systems in many Western companies in the 1980s, in both the management of people and of production systems. Much earlier, in the 1950s and 1960s and not forgetting either the 1880s and 1890s, the flow of influence from Western manufacturing practices was also strong in the other direction toward Japan. Similarly the incursion of Western multinationals into many Asian business environments has brought with it the demonstration of forms of professionalism in people management that tend to be more structured, more clear, and more engaging of individual ambition than the surrounding local systems. They are thus commonly looked to as ideals despite their deracination. Their openness and attempted fairness can be seductive for people accustomed to the less neutral, more personalized, obligation-saturated social contexts of much local management practice.

Borrowing flows both ways, but in doing so continues to demonstrate that systems of organization in a particular country are embedded so deeply in the local context that change is evolutionary and rarely revolutionary. And change is controlled, filtered, reinterpreted until it fits and allows the re-assertion of core local values surrounding the two main issues in organizing people: What kind of authority is legitimate; what are the ground rules and structures used by this society in horizontal co-operation? These also happen to be governed by the two most powerful of the features which distinguish any one culture from another: power distance and individualism—collectivism. The West, by and large, is egalitarian and individualist. The Asian tendency is to be hierarchical and collectivist. Much follows from these ancient invisible rules of conduct.

The way in which such influences work is indirect and not easily traceable. This is because the influences work historically to establish a societal fabric of institutions that reflects the cultural ideals. Such institutions include legal systems, educational systems, traditions of labor relations, forms of professionalism, government structures and policies, and the practical workings of a society's philosophies of welfare and responsibility. It is this set of institutions that is embedded in the culture. The organizations are embedded in the institutional fabric that represents the culture in action.

THE MANAGEMENTS OF PACIFIC ASIA

The most striking thing about the management systems of Pacific Asia is their variety and range. At the top end is the large, highly complex Japanese *Keiretsu* arguably as sophisticated an organization as the world has produced. At the other end are the small family organizations operating in developing world contexts of deep poverty. So too is there an immense variety of political structures ranging from the crudest forms of totalitarianism in Myanmar and North Korea to the forms of democracy seen in Thailand and Japan. In this context, the notion "Asian" has no sensible meaning. Within the variety, however, it is possible to identify three dominant and successful managerial forms, each able to compete in world markets: the Japanese, South Korean, and regional ethnic Chinese. Over the past 30 years, the world has come to appreciate that the organizations emerging in these three forms are not just on a learning path trying to become classic textbook multinationals but are creating new organizational forms for tackling global markets, forms that are still evolving, and forms that show a remarkable capacity for organizational learning and for the relentless pursuit of their aims. In particular, their systems for managing people are able to coordinate and release talent in ways not conceived of in the twentieth-century Western world.

The Japanese

The primary purpose, the essential reason for existence, of the Japanese firm is to employ people and to keep them employed. Contrast this with the Anglo-Saxon capitalist obsession with return to shareholders as the firm's core rationale and you begin to see what lies beneath the contrast between the Western job slaughterhouse of the past 10 years and the Japanese struggle to cope with recession without such betrayals of perceived trust.

There is in the Japanese case a series of moral contracts running vertically through the society that are based on ethics of reciprocity. In exchange for being looked after by a boss or a firm, the employee feels obliged to offer loyalty in exchange. This vertically structured organizational glue has two important outcomes in the workplace. First, the employee, given a sense of security, can take a long-term view of his or her position and can see benefits in thinking on behalf of the firm and acting with it in mind. Second, the firm can demand more of the employee in areas such as job mobility, acquisition of new skills, compliance with systems, and general discipline. This is not to say that Japanese workers are any more satisfied than workers in advanced economies elsewhere, but simply that the balance of components in the human resource system is distinctly Japanese. The determinants of this go back a long way, particularly into the social structures of Tokugawa, Japan, but they are also visible in the surrounding institutions of modern society such as the labor laws, the company based unions, the way status is ascribed, and systems for acquiring education and skills.

Japan constantly re-invents itself and a series of large influences is now forcing Japanese companies to rethink their employment systems. First, much labor-intensive industry has been moved to other parts of the region. Second, production technology has continued to replace human skills with machine skills. Third, the number of aged people in the population is rising rapidly and challenging those in employment to find even better means of enhancing productivity. Fourth, the pressures to rationalize the use of skill in the interests of productivity are causing a constant experimentation with less structured, more individual-driven, and more "Western" employment practices, all of which tend to destructure the comfort of lifetime employment and promotion based on length of service. Last, the slow opening of the economy to outside competition and the release of strategy making from the great ministries into the private sector, is causing more volatility, more experimentation, and more managerial innovation.

The questions surrounding future HRM practices in Japan are: Will the average Japanese employee come to re-assess the bargain struck with his society that requires him to live in cramped conditions, work long hours if one includes travelling time and (for managers) evening duties, and remain heavily dependent on his employer for much welfare provision? Will he re-assess the bargain struck with his firm that he remain patient for promotion until old enough, that he commit for a lifetime of duty, and that he make the firm part of his own identity?

For the HRM executive the questions are: How can loyalty and commitment be maintained if the established traditions of dependence break down and the labor market instead of being handled internally to the firm moves more to being an external one? Can there be a continuation of the inventiveness which allowed Japanese firms to be competitive when the yen was 250 to the dollar to still be so at 100 to the dollar?

I do not know the answers to such questions, but it is possible to argue for certain conditions within which managerial coping with their effects will be conducted and thus for certain ground rules to apply to the adjustments that will ensue.

Dependency will remain central to the Japanese psyche. It is too deeply embedded, backed by too long a series of social traditions and structures, to change in any radical way. The employee will continue to look upwards for protection, is likely to receive it, and to pay for it in loyalty. Collectivism and the sense of belonging to a group, the importance of *wa* or group spirit, and the easy acceptance of the workplace as an alternative psychological home, additional to the nuclear family, is unlikely to change. The moral contract of those in authority to behave paternalistically to subordinates will remain the prime source of legitimacy for their dominance, and that is so deeply embedded in the Japanese interpretation of the Confucian ethic, that it too is likely to remain robust.

All of which is to say that Japanese management, grounded as it is in Japanese culture and institutions will change on the surface undoubtedly, but not below the surface. New techniques will be Japanized in their application, as always. New balances will be struck in the proportions of permanent, temporary, and part-time employees. New incentives for innovation and creativity will appear. Reward systems will move more to recognize individual qualities in pay and promotion. Inequities in benefits between large and small companies may lessen. Unions may make more quality of life demands. But all the time the deepest formulae for governing co-operation vertically and horizontally will remain distinctive, nonreplicable, and unexportable except in heavily modified form. Japanese management is a child of Japanese social history and will remain so.

South Korea

The Korean miracle began in the 1950s as a totally devastated country, having lost its industrial base to the north, began to reconstruct itself. In doing so, it espoused two principles: First, to join the major league of wealthy countries; second, never again to be subjugated by Japanese power. The coming together of these two principles led to the creation of the *chaebol,* large industrial conglomerates able to take on and beat the Japanese, and also willing to act as instruments of government policy in directing the economy, at least in the early decades of export-led growth. In exchange, they received strong government support in finance, licensing, technical training, and research and development.

It has worked. Korea is now a major industrial power, but the balance of elements in the formula is changing. Government is no longer so clearly in the driving seat on strategy as many companies have weaned themselves from financial dependence on it. Labor relations are a field of challenge as labor costs rise, in recent years at 16 percent annually. Growth for the *chaebol* now means dealing with the organizational challenges of globalization, something the Koreans are now handling with formidable application to detail, concentration, and intensity. So far they have tended to succeed well in third-world markets. Now they are attacking directly the markets of the first world.

The *chaebol* is unusual in that it is essentially huge family business, and the main ones are still dominated by the *hoejang,* or founding president. Family control remains strong in most cases, and this differentiates the company from the large Japanese equivalent. As a result, the organizational psychology is much more personalistic, more meaningfully familistic, than in other organizations of this scale and complexity internationally.

To understand the future of human resources in the Korean case requires a coming to terms with the patrimonial nature of Korean (and also Chinese) society so as to answer the prior questions: Will patrimonalism change? First, what is it?

There are two structure types in East Asian societies, the *patrimonial*, typical of China and Korea, and the *feudal*, typical of Japan. They contrast with each other in the way vertical coordination is organized. In the patrimonial case, power in society traditionally rests with an elite civil bureaucracy to which subordinates have open-ended obligations and superiors do not normally offer in exchange, reciprocal rights, or privileges. In the feudal case, by contrast, there is an exchange of rights, duties, and privileges in the hierarchy. In the patrimonial case also, the rewards for service that are offered downwards are entirely at the discretion and the grace of the superiors. In feudal society, by contrast, such rewards are more normally stipulated and of substantial benefit, such as land ownership in the traditional case.

When one sees descriptions of Korean organizations being disciplined, hierarchical, militaristic, centralized, it is possible to see echoes of the ancient understanding of how power is legitimized in Korea. To make the point more tangibly, when the chairman of Samsung suddenly announced his interpretation of the new Samsung man as starting work at 7 AM, and finishing at 4 PM to spend the rest of the day improving himself, compliance was immediate and total by tens of thousands of people.

Descriptions of human resource management in Korea speak of nepotism, personalism, a focus on vertical connections, emotional humanism, authoritarianism, status sensitivity, family-centered collectivism, and thus individualism in the workplace, respect for seniority, and the constraint on autocracy imposed by the leader's responsibility for harmony.

These features are deeply grounded. The rise of the Korean *chaebols* so far suggests that this social psychology can be incorporated into modern economic structures and not inhibit efficiency. We have a vision of an alternative route to modernization to contrast with that of the West which will adapt as it goes along, and borrow from other systems, but it is likely to remain essentially true to itself as the system gathers strength.

The Ethnic Chinese

People of ethnic Chinese descent in the rest of Pacific Asia outside of China itself have achieved in the last 40 years one of the world's greatest economic performances historically. Their great citadels of Hong Kong, Taiwan, and Singapore together have foreign reserves of $250 billion and per capita income in Hong Kong and Singapore is now within the world's top five in purchasing power parity terms. Their cousins in Indonesia, Malaysia, Thailand, and the Philippines dominate the private sectors of those economics and do so with respectively 4 percent, 37 percent, 8 percent, and 1 percent of the populations. They are formidable businesspeople locked into the modern world economy as suppliers and service providers, but making the Pacific Asian region, including China, their own and using alliances to assist in their mastery of its unlevel playing fields.

Their economic instrument is the family business, another version of the patrimonialism mentioned earlier and based on the same underlying principles, but different from the Korean by virtue of the differences in societal and government contexts in which the Chinese operate.

The typical Chinese family business is small, although large versions now exist. It is characterized by having an elite group of power holders, usually but not always entirely family, which retains a monopoly on strategy making, finance, and personnel decisions. Surrounding them is a circle of trusted senior employees treated in many ways as honorary family, looked after and bonded to the paterfamilias by ties of obligation. These two groups form the core of the organization's working. Where the organization has split into several divisions, these executives will be spread throughout the key decision-making bodies to achieve coordination.

Down through the organization go various re-interpretations of patrimonialism. Personalistic ties to key superiors are important both ways. Subgroups form based on such affiliations. Dependency is high and exacerbated by a lack of rationality, openness, and neutrality in fields such as performance assessment, reward, and promotion decisions.

At the same time, given leadership by the owner in creating a familistic organizational climate and given the traditional Confucian concerns for civility and harmony, it is possible to achieve high levels of motivation and cooperation. These in turn are fostered by the psychology of the individual worker which supports work diligence in the interest of obligation strongly felt toward his or her own family and its financial stability. One of the more distinct and interesting aspects of the scene is the close sharing of ideals and values between bosses and workers, the consequent lack of hierarchical resentment, and the safety value of entrepreneurial employees going out on their own. This creates a constant stream of new small companies in which patrimonialism reasserts itself in miniature and Confucian values serve to stabilize hierarchy and sponsor cooperation and work diligence.

The intensity of managerial commitment by owners, using their own money as working capital, is one of the main sources of the system's energy. This is helped by two other features: the flexibility and reduction of risk brought by networking and the ability to transcend the limitations of small scale by the same means. In turn, this leads to the efficiencies of concentration. The whole structure thrives on the agility possible when single individuals can commit organizational resources instantaneously as owners, in network links that are based on strong ethics of interpersonal trust and thus low costs of transaction.

Such a form of Chinese capitalism has now begun to filter into China and re-establish itself as a natural expression of Chinese commercial instincts. Arguably 25 percent of the Chinese economy will be private by the year 2000 and will resemble the above description. At the same time, in China there will be two other forms of organization: the state-owned enterprises and the collective sector or town and village enterprises.

The state-owned enterprises are expressions of communist welfare ideals and carry heavy burdens of welfare responsibility that make them uncompetitive in an economy increasingly open to the outside world. The agonizing process of dismantling these old structures will continue as China slowly removes its support and finds other means of managing those industries.

The collective sector is much more vibrant and decidedly more efficient. It grew out of the communes and collectives of an earlier period, all of which had produced goods locally. Indications are that this hybrid form of organization, in which local officials (often outside joint venture partners) have autonomy to run things will behave increasingly in imitation of the paternalistic capitalism so natural to Chinese economic culture. This sector is likely to account for 50 percent of the value of production in China by the year 2000. Together with the private sector, making up 75 percent of the total, a new form of performance-driven, market-sensitive enterprise will emerge. It will be manifest in several forms and may well vary geographically with more small-scale entrepreneurialism in the south, with large-scale industrial conglomerations in the north, and perhaps more cosmopolitan sophistication around Shanghai.

Regardless of the shape of the organizational envelope, the social psychology of the Chinese organization will see a reversion to traditional Chinese values governing co-operation: paternalism in the interpretation of a patrimonial distribution of power, personalism in cementing co-operation horizontally and vertically, the rule of ethics governing harmony and civility, and the persistence of insecurity as a guarantor of the work ethic.

THE ASIAN AFFIRMATION

Samuel Huntington's clash of civilizations argument is based on (1) the salience of religion-based culture as a defining feature of a set of people, (2) the constant need for a sense of identity, and (3) the inevitable search for identity to be based on a definition of separateness. Whom are we different from defines who we are.

In this context, the recent affirmations of "Asianness" follow naturally from decades of increasing economic strength, and they presage a new period of cross-cultural contest. In this, the societies that derive their organizational structures and rules of internal conduct from ancient and robust understandings of how civilized people handle vertical and horizontal order are unlikely to see more borrowing as justified.

There is a belief in the region that East Asia will surpass the West in economic power and also that this success is based in Asian cultural norms that compare with Western decadent norms. There is acceptance that across the variety of Asian success stories a common denominator is the Confucian order, albeit in different manifestations. Finally, among such beliefs is the idea that the West should now learn from Asia and not vice-versa.

This idea would still be hard to sustain as an argument in the field of technology, and in the field of human resources it remains as naive as the Western assumption that preceded it: namely that textbook managerial professionalism has universal relevance. If the systems are grounded in local cultures, by definition they cannot be transferred. Even so, the mindset is becoming clearer and firmer, and the middle ground for experimentation more interesting and worthy of entering.

One final observation on Western ethnocentrism. Managerial behavior uses knowledge that can be codified (e.g., put in a textbook) and knowledge that is tacit and uncodifiable, the latter especially in the arena of managing people. This tacit knowledge, this understanding of organizational process, continues to be either ignored or pointlessly codified to foster the professionalization of Western managers and understanding gets no further. Asians never theorize about this; they just do it, and they appear to do it very well.

CHAPTER 36

THE HUMAN RESOURCE CHALLENGE IN CHINA: THE IMPORTANCE OF GUANXI

ANNE S. TSUI

THE IMPORTANCE OF *GUANXI* IN CONTEMPORARY CHINA

Any businessperson who has had some experience in the Far East, especially in societies with a strong traditional Confucian culture such as China or Taiwan knows that one cannot be successful without good personal relationships, or *guanxi*. This popular poem from Taiwan captures the essence of *guanxi*, "Youth is treasure, degree is a necessity, knowledge is considered a reference, the most important of all is *guanxi*." A comprehensive survey conducted in and near Shanghai in 1988 clearly shows that people perceive *guanxi* to be essential to social-economic life in China (Chu & Ju, 1990). When asked to rate the importance of *guanxi* connections in Chinese society, an overwhelming majority of the respondents said that *guanxi* connections are very important (42.7%) or important (26.9%). Only 4.9 percent said that they are not very important at all. Furthermore, 71.7 percent of the respondents said that they should try to go through connections to solve a problem rather than follow normal channels. The same survey also showed that younger people seemed to attach greater importance to *guanxi* than did older people. The report concluded that the practice of *guanxi* has now reached almost epidemic proportions. Scientific research has confirmed the importance of using connections to obtain jobs for young people in China (Bian, 1994, 1996). *Guanxi* is a form of social capital (Coleman, 1988) for an individual. Through *guanxi,* an individual can gain information or influence—both are important for attaining goals.

The importance of personal relationships or connections in developing countries such as mainland China has been widely discussed in popular writing for managers (e.g., *Asian Advertising and Marketing,* 1989; Fox, 1987). As United States (U.S.) companies expand their involvement in China, knowledge of what *guanxi* is, how it works, and how to cultivate it will be critical for business success. HR professionals who are knowledgeable about this complex issue will be better able to help their foreign national firms gain a competitive advantage through utilizing *guanxi* in the recruitment, selection, evaluation, and development of their local human resources. For example, HR can play a critical role in selecting local managers who have good connections or extensive personal relationships in the local business networks as well as to train their expatriate managers in the skills to develop and maintain important personal relationships.

THE MEANING, BASES, AND HISTORICAL ROOTS OF *GUANXI* IN THE CHINESE CONTEXT

Guanxi refers to the existence of particularistic ties between people, that is, they share some common background. This term is also used to refer to the existence of a connection through particularistic ties to a third party. For example, you and I do not share any common background but we have a common friend with whom we each share some kind of particularistic ties, therefore, our *guanxi* is based on an indirect tie. Direct ties in general lead to a stronger and more dependable relationship than do indirect ties. Particularistic ties can be based on kinship, locality (native place) or provincial origin, coworker (past or present), classmate, or teacher-student. There are multiple bases of *guanxi,* and relationships may vary in strength or intimacy depending on the form of ties that connects two or more individuals. *Guanxi* is so pervasive in the Chinese society today that the term is used commonly to refer to the existence of a relationship with or without particularistic ties. *Guanxi* and good relationship are interchangeable terms. *Guanxi* is not just any kind of relationship but a particular kind that develops due to the existence of particularistic ties, either directly or indirectly. The common bond based on particularistic ties is the distinguishing characteristic of the relationship.

While use of connections to facilitate business activities may be seen negatively in Western culture, *guanxi* does not carry a negative connotation in the East. *Guanxi* is an important and needed substitute for institutional stability that is normally provided by a reliable government and established rule of law (Xin & Pearce, 1996). *Guanxi* is important for the regulation of transactions in the absence of institutional or structural support. In developing economies, which usually also imply weak and unstable institutional structures, personal relationships are a better source of reliable information and resources. The idea of *guanxi* is certainly not unique to China. *Blat* in Russia and *pratik* in Haiti refer to the same type of instrumental-personal ties (Walder, 1986).

In China, *guanxi* has its roots in Confucian ideology (Tsui & Farh, 1996). According to Confucianism, an individual is fundamentally a social or relational being. Social order and stability depend on properly differentiated role relationships between particular individuals (King, 1991). Confucius defined five highly differentiated dyadic roles: emperor-subject, father-son, husband-wife, older-younger brothers, and friend-friend. This is a highly formalistic system in which each actor performs his or her role in the precise manner as specified. The individual's self is defined in relation to others. For example, an otherwise successful business executive is often introduced as someone's son rather than be accorded his own independent identity. As part of this emphasis on differentiated relationships, attention to others is highly selective and the tendency to divide people into categories is strong. This tendency to treat people differently depending on one's relationship with them constitutes the basic reason why *guanxi* is of such importance in Chinese societies.

The formalistic dyadic roles defined by Confucianism and the definition of self in relation to others form the cultural root for three basic categories of interpersonal relations in China (Yang, 1993); *chia-jen* (immediate family members), *shou-jen* (familiar persons such as distant relatives, neighbors, friends, colleagues, or classmates), and *sheng-jen* (mere acquaintances or strangers). These three categories of relationship have completely different social and psychological meaning to the parties involved and are governed by different sets of interpersonal rules. The *chia-jen* relationship is characterized by relatively permanent, stable, expressive relationship in which the welfare of the other is part of one's duty. Interactions with people in the *sheng-jen* category, at the other extreme, are superficial and temporary, and are dominated by concerns for personal gains or losses. The relationship with *shou-jen* is a mixture of that with *chia-jen* and *sheng-jen,* and one which takes on both utilitarian and expressive forms. Relationship with *shou-jen* must be nurtured and maintained by reciprocal exchanges of interpersonal favors, referred to as *renqing*. The strongest (and most positive) relationship is that with *chia-jen,* followed by that with *shou-jen* and weakest with *sheng-jen.* Those *shou-jen* who have achieved a certain level of intimacy are treated more

or less like family. These close friends would be granted special consideration and privilege in the relationship.

The art of building connections through discovering common particularistic ties and developing intimacy with the connection through *renqing* (or reciprocal obligations) is referred to as *guanxixue*—the science of *guanxi* (Yang,
1994). The ultimate purpose of *guanxixue* is to move the relationship from
the *sheng-jen* category through the *shou-jen* category into the *chia-jen* category.
As *chia-jen,* it is our obligation to help each other. To refuse help to *chia-jen*
is a culturally unacceptable behavior. In general, fulfilling one's obligation
to one's relatives and friends is expected culturally and still pervades in contemporary China (Yang, 1994; Wand, 1994). If one denies one's obligations,
one not only would lose face, one might also pay the ultimate price of
losing one's *guanxi* networks and the social resources embedded in them
(Hwang, 1987; Smart, 1993).

THE PRACTICE OF *GUANXI*

Guanxi practice includes the building and maintaining of relationships between two or more individuals through (1) the discovery of common direct particularistic ties, (2) the use of intermediaries to build a connection
with someone with whom one does not share any direct particularistic tie,
and (3) participation in *renqing,* that is, extending and receiving help or reciprocal exchange of obligations. Cultivating *renqing* is a prerequisite to
sustaining a *guanxi.* To engage in *renqing* or to establish a *guanxi* with others usually incurs heavy social investment. In the *guanxi* "*wang*" (net or a
web of interconnected relationships), there is a high degree of interdependence. Each member in the *guanxi* net is obliged to respond to any request
for help from others. Individuals in a dense *guanxi* network actually lose autonomy and freedom. This is the cost of building and using *guanxi.* One
must be willing to incur the social investment and to fulfill the social obligation of reciprocal assistance. Gifts, favors, and banquets are all different
ways to maintain and repay *renqing.* It was observed that the practice of gift
giving has increased greatly in the 1980s and 1990s in China (Yang, 1994).
This is further proof that the practice of *guanxi* dominates the contemporary social relationship in China.

The larger one's *guanxi* network, and the more diverse one's *guanxi* connections (i.e., with people of different occupations and positions), the better will be an individual's ability to obtain resources and opportunities.
New *guanxi* can be established by self-initiation or by going through an intermediary. The latter is generally more effective because the intermediary

can vouch for one's character, integrity, and understanding of *renqing*. Another way to enlarge a *guanxi* network is to use one's existing *guanxi* as a resource to attract and maintain more guanxi connections. One's ability to help someone attracts other people who may provide a different kind of resource that one may need now or later. A manager's *guanxi* net is his or her social capital which is as important as, if not more important than, personal capital (e.g., education, talent) or financial and physical capital (e.g., technology) that his or her organization or business may possess. It is common knowledge in China that a business, even with money, cannot guarantee that they can get the raw materials or move goods to another location for distribution. *Guanxi* is a necessity to get things done in China today.

IMPLICATIONS OF *GUANXI* FOR HUMAN RESOURCE MANAGEMENT

The challenge for the foreign company in China or Taiwan is to understand how the practice of *guanxi* can hinder or facilitate human resource management. *Guanxi* can play an important role in at least four HR areas: recruiting and selection, performance evaluation, interpersonal relations, and management development.

Recruiting

Just as job seekers can use *guanxi* to obtain a desired position, so can companies use *guanxi* to gain access to high quality applicants. University professors and placement officers have information about the quality of their graduates. Developing and cultivating relationships with university professors and placement officers can have handsome payoffs in terms of attracting or having access to high-quality job applicants. Current employees can also serve as intermediaries to potential applicants in a highly fragmented labor market. HR managers who understand the inner workings of the *guanxi* network and are skilled in building and expanding *guanxi* nets can be more effective in expanding the applicant pool and discovering talents than can HR managers who are oblivious to these processes. It is known that most employees for factories in special economic zones such as *Sheng-zhen* are friends, relatives, or people from the same remote province. *Guanxi* provides people in remote regions with employment opportunities in other parts of China. Employers gain access to labor pools that are not otherwise available without the *guanxi* connections of their current employees.

Selection of managerial personnel can especially benefit from knowledge about *guanxi* and the *guanxi* network of the applicant. *Guanxi* can lead to good referrals. Through the referring connection, more can be known about the background of the applicant. By knowing the *guanxi* networks of the candidate and his or her *guanxi* building and maintenance skills, the potential for future job effectiveness can be estimated. In China, it is often said that who the person knows is more important than what the person knows, therefore, selection criteria for important management positions might have to reflect the important role that *guanxi* can play in an enterprise's success.

Performance Evaluation

Guanxi can also influence objectivity in performance assessment. It might, therefore, be useful to know which employee may share particularistic ties with their supervisors. Preliminary research using 530 supervisor-subordinate dyads (Farh, Tsui, Xin, & Cheng, 1996) in Taiwan, however, did not find any relationship between the existence of particularistic tie and performance evaluation of the subordinate by the supervisor. In the same study, it was found that *guanxi* was associated with increased trust by the subordinate toward the supervisor. Another study (Xin & Pearce, 1996) found *guanxi* to also be important for trust in lateral relations. A business leader reported a higher level of trust in a connection who shared one or more particularistic ties. In this study, there was no measure on performance. Until further evidence is available, it is advisable that an independent evaluation be obtained when one or more particularistic tie exists between a supervisor and his or her subordinates.

Interpersonal Relations

The essence of *guanxi* is in the cultivation and maintenance of interpersonal relations. Here, the principle of *renqing* applies. HR managers can capitalize on the social facilitation effect of *guanxi* by systematically uncovering the type and extent of particularistic ties among the employees. Chinese New Year bonuses and gifts further solidify the relationship between the employees and the employer. Social competition could be created among groups of employees who share common background within the group but different backgrounds between the groups. For example, in an office in Taiwan, the Shanghai contingency and Fuzhou group competed to be the 100 percent club winner (i.e., meeting or exceeding sales quota). Conversely social relations were strained because these two groups did not share any common ties. In this case, special efforts could be made to discover other *guanxi* bases that members of the otherwise distinct groups may share (e.g., past schools, neighborhood, religion). Managing social relations among employees who do not share common background is not too dissimilar from managing social relations in an ethnically diverse organization in the United States.

Management Development

Not all Chinese are equally good at *guanxixue,* therefore, providing knowledge on the importance of *guanxi* and skills to develop and nurture *guanxi* relationships seem like sensible management development agenda items. Expatriate managers, especially, are least likely to have connections who share direct particularistic ties. Identifying and cultivating intermediaries are necessities if expatriate managers want to develop this particular form of social capital. The principle of *renqing,* when and how to give gifts, or hosting banquets are all etiquette associated with *guanxixue.*

SUMMARY

Guanxi is part of the stock knowledge of Chinese adults in their management of daily life (King, 1991). Knowledge and practice of *guanxi* is necessary for success in many spheres of life. Guanxi building is the Chinese version of network building, but it is a different kind of network. The members are not anyone but ones with whom an individual must share some direct particularistic ties. *Guanxi* building is based on shared attributes such as kinship, locality, surname, and so on and thus this social cultural activity precludes the involvement of those who are not Chinese. This is not because they are not Chinese by nationality or race, but because they do not share the cultural heritage of understanding *guanxi,* the lack of common attributes that are important in the Chinese culture. These attributes refer to background and experience, and not to the physical or biological characteristics of the individuals. The cultural dynamic of *guanxi* is a source of vitality for China (King, 1991); it is through *guanxi* that things get done in the absence of stable or reliable institutional rules. *Guanxi* building is a cultural strategy to mobilize social resources. Gaining knowledge of *guanxi* and learning how to use it can be a competitive advantage for foreign firms in cultures such as China where *guanxi* practice is pervasive and ingrained in the social fabric of interpersonal relationships.

REFERENCES

Bian, Y. (1994). Guanxi and the allocation of jobs in urban China. *China Quarterly, 140,* 971–999.

Bian, Y. (1996). Getting a job through a web of guanxi. In B. Wellman (Ed.), *Networks in the Global Village.* Boulder, CO: Westview.

Chu, G., & Ju, Y. (1990). *The great wall in ruins: Cultural change in China.* Honolulu: East-West Center.

Coleman, J.S. (1988). Social capital in the creation of human capital. *American Journal of Sociology,* 94: S95–S120.

Farh, J.L., Tsui, A.S., Xin, K.R., & Cheng, B.S. (1996). The influence of relational demography and g*uanxi:* The Chinese case. *Organization Science,* in press.

Fox, M. (1987). In China, *"guanxi"* is everything. *Advertising Age,* No. 2: 5–12, S14.

Graft: An ugly fact of life in China. (1989, January 28). *Asian Advertising and Marketing.*

Hwang, K.K. (1987). Face and favor: The Chinese power game. *American Journal of Sociology, 92,* 944–974.

King, A.Y. (1991). *Kuan-Hsi* and network building: A sociological interpretation. *Daldalus, 120*(2), 63–84.

Smart, A. (1993). Gifts, bribes, and *guanxi:* A reconsideration of Bourdieu's social capital. *Cultural Anthropology, 8,* 388–408.

Tsui, A.S., & Farh, J.L. (1996). Where *guanxi* matters: Relational demography and guanxi in the Chinese context. *Work and Occupations.*

Walder, A. (1986). *Communist neo-traditionalism: Work and authority in Chinese industry.* Berkeley: University of California Press.

Wand, D.L. (1994). *The institutional culture of capitalism: Social relations and private enterprise in a Chinese city.* Paper presented at the annual meeting of the Association for Asian Studies. Boston, March 23–27.

Xin, K.R., & Pearce, J.L. (1996). *Guanxi:* Connections as substitutes for structural support. *Academy of Management Journal.*

Yang, K.S. (1993). Chinese social orientation: An integrative analysis. In L.Y. Cheng, F.M.C. Cheung, & C.N. Chen (Eds.), *Psychotherapy for the Chinese: Selected papers from the first international conference* (pp. 19–56). Hong Kong: The Chinese University of Hong Kong.

Yang, M.M. (1994). *Gifts, favors and banquets: The art of social relationships in China.* Ithaca, NY: Cornell University Press.

CHAPTER 37

ORGANIZATIONAL PRESENCE, NOT JUST ORGANIZATIONAL CAPABILITY: HUMAN RESOURCES' AGENDA IN DEVELOPING ASIAN COUNTRIES

ARTHUR K. YEUNG and KENNETH J. DeWOSKIN

During the last decade, North American human resource (HR) academicians and practitioners have realized the importance of using HR practices to build organizational capability (Ulrich & Lake, 1990). While this remains an important way for HR to add value to business competitiveness in many developing Asian countries (such as China and Vietnam),[1] we believe the HR function has another strategic, but often neglected, role to play in these countries: establishing an effective organizational presence. Organizational presence refers to the perceived prestige and power of a company. This chapter discusses why organizational presence is critical in developing Asian countries, suggests how corporations can create an effective organizational presence through HR, and explores cross-cultural challenges for HR professionals.

Like intellectual capital, organizational presence is an intangible asset for corporations doing business in Asia. While organizational presence may also be important for corporations in North America and Europe, it is much more important in countries where (1) the demand for critical resources (such as talented work force, competent strategic alliance partners, high-quality raw materials) far exceeds the supply, (2) relationships between government and businesses are complex and not clearly defined, (3) the perceived role of the producing entity (i.e., enterprise or corporation) is more broadly and directly related to social goals, and (4) business

345

competition is driven not only by economic concerns but also by political, social, and personal considerations. In Asia's highest potential markets, regulatory and tax practices are neither transparent nor uniformly implemented; often the most valuable business development opportunities are shaped on a case-by-case basis. In these business contexts, effective organizational presence can offer enormous benefits.

The effective organizational presence of a corporation is determined by at least six factors:

1. The perceived political clout of the corporation, as measured by the strength and extent of the personal network between its top executives and senior government officials at different levels.
2. The perceived economic strength of the corporation, as determined by the total investment of the corporation in a country.
3. The perceived competency of the organization to execute its goals and to advance the interests of its employees.
4. The perceived community contribution and managerial progressiveness of the company.
5. The global brand recognition and reputation of products and services.
6. The perceived quality of its products and/or services domestically.

In many developing Asian countries, strong organizational presence is an asset because it gives senior management access to government officials who can help shape business opportunities. It also enhances the corporation's image as a partner and employer of choice. Corporations that have developed a solid organizational presence in a country (as have Siemens, Motorola, Volkswagen, and Hewlett-Packard in China) enjoy a unique competitive edge over other companies in many areas of business operations: influencing regulators, winning sales contracts, negotiating better terms of cooperation with local strategic alliance partners, recruiting top talent, insuring the procurement of needed raw materials, and establishing new business operations.

Organizational Presence as It Relates to Asia's Business Environment

First, there is a potential contribution to market development. Major customers in many Asian countries are not individual consumers but rather are government ministries and quasi-government corporations. Because many of these countries are still developing their economies, the most important industries requiring foreign investment and assistance are related to the countries' basic infrastructures, such as telecommunications, transportation, power generation, and aerospace (*Business Week,* 1993). Most of these industries are managed either by government ministries or quasi-government corporations. The buying criteria of these major customers are not rooted purely in economic concerns of product and service quality, instead, they also offer business opportunities to companies on the basis of the degree to which these companies have contributed to the economy and community of their host countries. Thus, there is a spirit of reciprocity, a sense of repaying contributions made.

Second, there is the basic issue of defining and establishing commercially feasible businesses. Doing business in developing Asian countries entails complex and vague relationships with a plethora of government agencies. A telling example focuses on AlliedSignal which recently established its wholly-owned turbocharger subsidiary in a special economic zone in Shanghai. By its very nature—being in a special economic zone and set up as a wholly-owned subsidiary—this represented a significant simplification of what would otherwise be a very difficult and protracted process; it streamlined many government controls and simplified the negotiation process. Yet, despite this, the initiative still required no less than 140 approvals from various government agencies.

Foreign investors must deal with complex Asian regulatory practices. The policies and regulations in developing Asian countries are often so general and broad that a wide latitude of interpretation is possible on the part of the government officials in charge. If a corporation is well-respected and well-connected to powerful government officials, these relationships can expedite laborious approval processes. The logistics of setting the business plan into motion can be simplified. By circumventing a potential morass, these key contacts can reduce costly delays that could jeopardize a company's economic strength and erode its business opportunities. Seen positively, strong organizational presence helps create opportunities at the "experimental" edge of what is permissible, offering significant market entry advantages over international competitors.

The supplier infrastructure in many developing Asian countries is weak and underdeveloped. Good suppliers of critical raw materials are hard to identify and are in great demand. In order to increase the percentage of local components in their products and to reduce production costs, importing raw materials from elsewhere is not in the long run economically feasible. Many corporations, therefore, find themselves competing for raw materials from good local suppliers. Again, effective organizational presence helps a corporation develop better relationships with local suppliers and enjoy a higher priority to procure the suppliers' products.

Finally, strong organizational presence helps address the most intractable problems of business development in Asia: localization of management. So often in Asian countries, the critical resource is not money but talent. Many investment projects in China and other parts of Asia fail not because of inadequate strategic planning, but because of poor execution. These failures—common among foreign companies doing business in Asia—almost always occur in the areas of management and human resource development. Managerial talent—individuals who can function effectively in the local business environment—is desperately needed to fuel the rapid growth in Asia.

Seen from the standpoint of high potential local talent, the job transition from state-owned enterprise to private or joint venture enterprise offers a paradoxical combination of huge financial reward and personal risk. While substantial financial rewards are common throughout the foreign-invested sector, only companies with an exemplary organizational presence can ameliorate the risk of leaving the security and sanctuary of a state-owned enterprise. They emerge from the crowd of foreign-invested enterprises by offering the appearance of greater stability and durability and better future career prospects for local hires. As a result companies enjoying higher levels of organizational presence are more capable of attracting and retaining scarce local talent.

STRATEGIES FOR BUILDING AN EFFECTIVE ORGANIZATIONAL PRESENCE

The development of organizational presence requires both a long-term and well-orchestrated strategy on the part of corporations. In particular, the HR function can contribute substantially to building a strong presence through the following efforts:

1. *Educate and Encourage Senior Executives in Building High Visibility Personal Relationships with Top Government Officials.* In North America, customers and shareholders are the key stakeholders. As a result, senior executives are willing to invest time in developing relationships with them. In developing countries, however, senior executives need to appreciate the strategic importance of establishing a network of contacts with senior government officials at various levels in different ministries and cultivating close relationships with them. The rationale is that this group of powerful officials exerts a major influence over the company's customers, suppliers, employees, and

regulators. The map of useful relationships is neither simple nor clear. It extends beyond the ministries directly regulating a particular industry and includes other ministries and bureaus of external and internal trade, finance, labor, education, and health. HR professionals can take primary responsibility for educating senior executives (especially expatriates) to understand why and how to build such relationships. They can also assist in mapping relationships that are useful to business development goals.

HR professionals can help orchestrate occasions of high visibility, for example, by inviting top government officials to attend the opening ceremony of the company's facility or to visit the corporation on special occasions. At such occasions, it is vital to take photos that can then be published in newspapers, newsletters, and/or annual reports, as well as placed in senior executives' offices, in lobbies, and so forth. Organizations with strong presence in Asia are careful to attach "faces" to public and private representations of their activities. HR professionals can significantly assist in creating strong executives' personae and strong "face" for the organization in the marketplace. All these efforts enhance the prestige and influence of the company.

2. *Demonstrate a Strong, Long-Term Commitment of the Corporation in the Country.* For many emerging countries in Asia, their scarcest resources are not raw materials, capital, or labor but rather technical and managerial know-how. HR professionals can help the corporation to understand that investment in training and development can serve to create a solid organizational presence in a country. Corporations that invest heavily in these activities are favorably regarded by the nation's businesses and governmental communities. Such efforts reflect the long-term commitment of a corporation to building up the talent base in a country. A striking example is that of Motorola which, before it even launched its operations in China, set up the Motorola University in Beijing in 1987—the purpose: to train more than 10,000 managers in the telecommunications industry. While some of these participants may be their potential customers or employees, Motorola University did not specify that as admission criteria. As a result, this initiative not only laid the groundwork for Motorola's presence in China but also opened up tremendous business opportunities that were not available to potential competitors.

Similarly, for several consecutive years in the late 1980s, General Electric (GE) sponsored a three-month program called China Management Training Program that enabled groups of Chinese managers from different industries throughout China to receive training both at Crotonville and in GE businesses. Again, the costs to these participants were nominal, but the payoffs to GE were tremendous. While GE may use these training programs to build up personal relationships with key potential customers in China, these programs also sent powerful messages to the Chinese government: (1) GE is willing to contribute to the development of Chinese economy; and (2) GE is interested in long-term investment in China, not just short-term benefits. Similarly ambitious programs were undertaken by AT&T, Coca-Cola, Holiday Inn, and many of the successful entrants into the Chinese market.

Without question, the investment in training and development activities by Motorola and GE are astute business strategies. They helped the companies enter the Chinese market, nurture critical business relationships, and build up their progressive image on human resource development. The benefits are both short- and long-term. These examples illustrate how the intangible benefits of organizational presence should be taken into account in any cost-benefit analyses of human resource investment. A comprehensive training and development program in Asian countries is strategically powerful as it serves the country in both symbolic (i.e., organizational presence) and substantial (i.e., organizational capability) ways.

3. *Adopt Progressive Management Practices and Aggressive Localization.* In order to become an employer and partner of choice, corporations need to create a work environment that fosters employees' contributions and commitment. While foreign–invested companies are all notable for better working conditions, benefits, and salaries, loyalty of high potential employees to foreign-invested companies is notably low. Aggressive head-hunting from other companies has created an alerting level of turnover in most businesses. Companies must strive to stabilize their human resources and gain the benefits from their investments in training by means other than competitive salary programs alone. Localization of senior management positions is an essential component to develop an enduring and progressive company.

There are three interlocking forces that drive the need to localize. *First,* in a talent market in which demand greatly exceeds supply, salary and benefits are insufficient to retain high quality employees unless corporations are willing to open up career opportunities for local talent at the very top levels (Yeung, 1996). If the local management staff members feel that all senior positions will inevitably be filled by expatriates, they will view their current jobs as springboards for the next higher paying jobs in other companies. As a result, they cannot be expected to give any long-term commitment to their jobs and companies. A high turnover rate among local talent would create instability and discontinuity for the corporation, especially when overseas assignments for senior expatriate executives are generally short-term (2–3 years). The whole issue becomes a syndrome, a self-fulfilling situation in which the high turnover of local talent further reduces the prospects of localizing the top and second-tier management positions.

Second, expatriates are too expensive to maintain as the business environment becomes more competitive and operating efficiency becomes increasingly critical to market success.

Last but not least, corporations bear the substantial cultural risk that is associated with large expatriate management corps without at least one local face among their senior executives. Localization sends an important message to key stakeholders that the company intends to operate as a local company and is pursuing a development trajectory that not only localizes top management but contributes to the development of locally sourced talent. It demonstrates that the company is fully responsive to the wide range of development priorities of the host country.

4. *Show One Strong Face in the Host Country.* Over the years, business units of multinational corporations may have individually pursued economic cooperation with numerous local partners. As a result, a large number of economic entities were formed without leveraging the synergy across multiple operating units. To increase their perceived economic strength as a corporation, a corporation should form a holding company or some other mechanism to centralize an array of core services and focus on the shared need to develop strong organizational presence. In addition to taxation benefits and greater administrative control, a holding company can increase the organizational presence of a corporation within a country, achieve efficiencies in various business and human resource development functions, and control the substantial risk of uncoordinated corporate activity in the new market.

PRESENT AND FUTURE CHALLENGES: RETHINKING HR IN A CROSS-CULTURAL CONTEXT OF HR PROFESSIONALS

This chapter builds on one underlying premise: that knowledge and practices of HR professionals are developed out of a specific context. As HR professionals look at the evolution of HR roles in the United States, they can see the roles have changed over the years. In the 1960s and 1970s, HR practices tended to be very operationally oriented, then, in the 1980s and 1990s, competition intensified, customer expectation increased, and technological changes accelerated. Western academicians and practitioners have started to develop the notion of strategic human resource management in which organizational capability is a key concept.

As HR professionals in the United States transfer their body of professional knowledge in the 1990s to the starkly different settings of developing countries, they need to re-examine how and why the context, too, has changed. In many developing countries in Asia, the business environments are quite different: competition is quasi-market; customer expectations (especially those of major institutional customers) are not purely economically driven; regulatory changes exert a strong impact on market developments; and many different economic infrastructures are being developed. While the formulation of strategic plans presents great challenges, the execution of such plans is even more demanding. Strong organizational presence becomes extremely valuable in the execution of these business plans.

Among other important implications, this analysis suggests that the HR role for foreign investors in Asia has strategic demands associated with it that are somewhat novel to the Asian environment. With a change in the business context, HR professionals need to be aware of their revised strategic roles and the contributions they can make in developing countries such as China and Vietnam. HR can become a strategic business partner but in a different way. Given the dual agendas of organizational presence and organizational capability, many HR practices may need to be re-examined and re-evaluated according to different perspectives. For instance, one of the new roles for HR professionals is not only to develop the leadership competencies of senior executives, but also to develop their *relationship equity* (i.e., the intangible asset value of having a network of personal relationships). HR professionals design and deliver training programs to build the talent base, but also to enhance organizational presence. Given this new consideration, HR professionals are required to rethink the design of their training programs, asking themselves: What are the purposes of the programs? What is the curriculum? Who should attend? Who should teach? Where and when should the programs be offered? How can the programs' visibility be increased? Similarly, HR professionals need to reinvent their roles in the strategic stages of business development and play a larger role in business structure design, partnering, and organization design.

Asia has become the number one investment target for many corporations, with China leading planned investment among the world's one thousand largest companies by three to one. HR professionals must prepare themselves for new business opportunities and challenges in that part of the world. These opportunities and challenges require that HR professionals understand their unique contributions in that business environment and assert themselves aggressively in strategic roles during strategic planning stages of new market entry. HR researchers and scholars must also re-examine the extent to which they can readily transfer their existing body of knowledge to other countries which have contrasting stakeholders, business environments, and challenges.

We have offered only one alternative perspective for exploring how HR can add value to business success. Looking ahead, we believe Asian-based or Latin American-based HR theories and practices will proliferate as these regions receive more attention from scholars and practitioners alike.

NOTE

1. While the issues discussed in this article are generally relevant to most developing Asian countries, they are especially relevant to China and Vietnam due to the politico-economic systems of these nations.

REFERENCES

China: The emerging economic powerhouse of the 21st century. (1993, May 17). *BusinessWeek,* 54–69.

Ulrich, D., & Lake, D. (1990). *Organizational capability: Competing from the inside out.* New York: Wiley.

Yeung, A. (1996). *Becoming the employer of choice in China.* Viewpoint Series 8, published by International Consortium for Executive Development Research.

CHAPTER 38

HUMAN RESOURCES OF THE FUTURE: CONCLUSIONS AND OBSERVATIONS

DAVE ULRICH

These chapters represent a cross section of thinking about the future of HR. They are from academics, HR executives, and consultants who spend much of their professional lives thinking about HR issues. Having read the essays, some consensus emerges around several themes:

- HR is under scrutiny, and this scrutiny is a good thing.
- HR as we have known it needs to change.
- Changing HR will represent important challenges and will require new competencies.
- If HR does not meet the challenge of change, it is at risk of being disbanded.

While some answers concerning the future of HR seem to be known and shared, there is more that is unknown. In these cases, the questions are more compelling than answers.

THINGS KNOWN

The authors agree to the inevitability of ongoing change. They suggest that the pace and unpredictability of change will increase. Pace means that whatever will happen will happen faster than anticipated. Once the Internet becomes standard, for example, literally millions of people can sign on overnight to learn new ideas for work and personal lives. What took months to share (e.g., printing and marketing a book, sharing the best practice from within a firm, or publishing research findings) may be disseminated in days or hours. Unpredictability of change means that we cannot fully predict what will happen and as pace and unpredictability increase, questions which took a long time to answer need to be answered more quickly. Which organizational forms will become the norm? Which leaders who are deified today will be disparaged tomorrow? Which companies with great reputations today will lose them quickly?

Most authors agree on the drivers for change. *Globalization* will require seeing and acting beyond local boundaries. *Technology* will make information more accessible and join people together electronically in ways that can impact organizations and work relationships. A more *knowledge-based work force* will make many employees into volunteers because they could choose to work elsewhere for equal or more money, so they work in an organization by choice, not by obligation. Turning worker knowledge into productivity and leveraging *intellectual capital* will become work force challenges of the future. *Redefining firm performance* away from merely cutting cost to profitable growth also will require change.

Knowing the pace and unpredictability of change does not mean that firms have learned to manage change. Change redefines risk. In a low-change world, reducing risk means getting more of the right answer before taking action. In a world of high amounts of change, reducing risk means acting without full answers but having the capacity to adjust midstream. Agility becomes more important than accuracy in reducing risk. HR professionals cannot assume that they will design the "perfect" program. They must learn to quickly design thoughtful programs, to act on those programs, then to learn and adjust.

Change comes at two levels. First, fundamental change means changing culture or identity. Firms which have for decades had an identity may find that their traditional culture fails to create current customer value; for example, Sears, IBM, and General Motors are in the midst of fundamental culture or identity change. Fundamental culture change will probably affect almost every firm from government agencies learning to become more responsive and service oriented to universities learning to serve students of all ages and across many geographies to airlines mastering customer loyalty.

Second, capacity for change means responding quickly to that which is occurring around us. Reducing the cycle time for completion of business initiatives becomes the requirement and demand for HR professionals. A firm recently went from the concept of an HR competency model to delivery in 10 weeks, and the leader of the HR function then asked that a similar process be applied to other staff functions in 6 weeks. Making things happen more quickly, but still better, is an outcome of change.

From these essays we can conclude that the workplace and work force of tomorrow will be different from that of today, that change outside HR will require change within HR, and that HR is at a crossroads in its ability to deal with this change.

THINGS UNKNOWN

These chapters show that we know more about the context for HR in the future than about the content. The content deals with issues of role, focus, practices, and governance of HR in the future. For each of these areas, we see questions which should elicit debate, dialogue, and experimentation over the next few years.

Role of HR: What Is the Future Role of HR?

A number of continua can be used to describe what the future role of HR might be; each offers an array of choices for roles HR can and should play.

- *Administrative vs. Strategic:* The evolution of the function has been from administrative to strategic. There are arguments, however, that if the administrative work is not done efficiently, accurately, and timely, HR professionals cannot play strategic roles. How to balance and be dualistic in these roles will be an ongoing challenge for the profession.
- *HR Departments:* Existing vs. transformed vs. disappeared. Some argue HR should rediscover its past (paying attention to employee unrest, unions, firm values, and administrative processes). Others argue that HR should be transformed into an elite strategic corps of business partners which creates globally competitive organizations. Others argue that HR departments should disappear and be outsourced. These debates will continue as will the debates as to what to name the HR department (human relations, human resources, employee resources, organizational capability, human capital management, etc.).
- *Doing HR Work:* HR professional vs. line manager vs. staff—who does HR work? What part of HR work is done by HR professionals, line managers, or other staff groups? In a focus group of line managers talking about the HR department, participants uniformly stated that as HR was becoming "more strategic" most of the traditional HR work fell to them, the line managers and that they did not want to do it. They

wanted HR to return to doing HR work (meaning, let them as managers be freed up to manage). How to clearly define roles and accountabilities will be discussed for the next few years.

- *Metaphors for HR Professionals:* Leaders, architects, stewards, partners, or players? Image and identity are important because they shape behavior. HR professionals know many of the images they want to shed, for example, policy police, bureaucrats, administrators, regulators, etc. It is less clear what the future identity of HR should be. In all probability, multiple roles will be played by HR professionals depending on the business context and the proclivity of the HR professional but knowing alternative metaphors increases the debate.
- *Aggressiveness of HR:* Advocacy vs. acquiescence, proactive vs. reactive? Under what circumstances should HR professionals become more assertive and take a stand? Learning when to have a unique point of view, which should be articulated and advocated, and when to enlist as part of the team will be ongoing concerns for HR professionals.

Arguments have been well made in these essays for multiple points of view about the future role of HR.

Focus of HR: What Should Be the Focus of HR?

The focus of HR describes more where the work is done. Again, a number of continua highlight questions about the setting for HR.

- *Target Audience:* Work force vs. customer vs. investor vs. government? Investments in HR practices may be focused on improving the work force (ensuring more competent, committed, and dedicated employees), serving external customers (creating organizational capabilities that customers value and pay for), investors (reducing cost, which leads to profitability), and/or government (crafting policies with national interest). Each audience has merit; balancing the needs of multiple audiences raises questions about the focus of HR.
- *HR Work:* Domestic vs. global? Globalization has moved from a buzzword to a reality; however, crafting HR work so that local organization needs are served along with global requirements will force rethinking of many HR tasks.
- *HR Constituents:* Within firm vs. across alliances? A number of the essays point out that future HR work will be housed in organizations that differ greatly from what we have today. As organizations become

more an assortment of alliances and relationships, HR practices will also need to cross boundaries. Legal definitions of firm boundaries cannot be constraints for HR practices. We need to learn how to leverage HR work both within the firm and across firm alliances.

The setting for HR will change in response to new organizational arrangements and agreements. These settings will require more flexible, dynamic, and responsive HR professionals.

Practices of HR: What Are the Emerging HR Practices?

The essays point to a number of emerging HR practice areas. They are areas that will require investments of time, talent, and resources to turn a set of ideas into tools. Some of these areas include:

- *Building Leadership Bench:* What are the competencies for the leader of the future, both at the top and the middle of the organization? How can HR practices be crafted to develop leaders who meet tomorrow's needs today? These essays contain wonderful examples of how leaders will need to lead in the future and what the subsequent HR implications are supporting the development of such leaders.
- *Creating Organizational Capabilities (Knowledge-Based Organization/High Capability Organization):* Organizations often take on lives of their own characterized by personalities, traits, and habits. HR professionals will need to learn how to codify and create aligned organizational capabilities in addition to individual competencies by addressing such questions as: What are critical organizational capabilities? How are they created? How are they changed?
- *Enhancing Knowledge Transfer:* Knowledge transfer means that best practices are shared within a firm, among firms, and between firms and government. HR professionals must master tools of learning such as knowledge generation (e.g., experimentation, benchmarking, continuous improvement, competence acquisition) and knowledge generalization (e.g., moving information, skills, decision making, and rewards across boundaries). As knowledge-based organizations proliferate, HR professionals play different roles.
- *Leveraging Technology:* Technology will change how work is done in general and how HR is practiced in particular. A sample of HR-related technology questions include: How will technology connect employees without face-to-face contact? How will technology change

communication patterns (e.g., electronic all-hands meetings)? How will technology change specific HR practices (e.g., resumes through the Internet, distance learning for training, automated performance reviews, tailored benefit programs)?

The traditional HR practices of staffing, training, performance management, benefits, regulation, labor relations, and so forth will not go away, but they will become the table stakes for HR, with new practices emerging constantly.

Governance of HR: How Do We Get HR Work Done?

The practical act of doing HR work will change. Several themes emerge from these essays as to how HR work will be governed.

- *Deliverables More than Doables:* For decades HR has focused on doing good work through the design of programs which affect people and processes. Increasingly, the emphasis must be more on deliverables. Deliverables represent the results or outcomes of doing good HR work. What happens because we have crafted innovative staffing, training, or high-performing team programs? What are the organizational implications? These essays point to a number of possible deliverables: making employees volunteers, implementing strategy, creating economic value, ensuring cultural heritage, managing employee work/life needs, globalization, etc.
- *Benchmarking:* Institutionalization theory reviews the process of sharing ideas across boundaries. In the HR world, this has been operationalized as benchmarking and best practices. Conferences, publications, consultants, and other forums exist where ideas are quickly shared from one unit to another. HR professionals must become masters of benchmarking by not falling into the "if they did it, so must we" trap.
- *Measuring More and More Accurately:* Too often, HR works at the personal whim of a CEO. When the CEO "takes a liking" to HR issues, HR gets attention; when he or she does not, it does not. These essays call for and predict a more rigorous and demanding measurement process for HR in the future. How do we know when HR works? How do we tie HR work to business results? In the next few years, we will see more precise, valid, and reliable measures of HR effectiveness.
- *Theory Based vs. Haphazard:* From their roots in these essays a wonderful mosaic of theories of HR emerges. Some of these theories focus

on individual development (e.g., HR's role in developing leaders and nurturing employee well-being). Some theories focus on organizations (e.g., HR's role in coordinating work across flexible and alliance organizations).

- *Change and Continuity:* In the midst of predicting a dramatically different future for HR, some of the essays thoughtfully demonstrate that much of what HR has done, it must continue to do. Employees have always been hired, developed, and paid; and organizations have always had to have processes to take care of employees. Much of the past will be found in the future, but learning what of the past to keep and what to change may be an ongoing governance issue.

At minimum, some HR work will be done differently. If an HR professional from a previous decade arrives in the year 2000, expectations, skills, and outcomes will be different.

FINAL THOUGHTS

If our purpose is to propose a debate about the future, it is better to end with questions than with answers. Questions elicit new frameworks, approaches, and alternatives, so, the final two questions we would ask (with our answer) are:

Do you want to play in this always changing and at times unclear future?

Are you having fun?

Without a doubt, all the authors in this volume and many others of the best HR professionals we know answer with a resounding "yes."

About the Authors

Nancy J. Adler is a professor of management at McGill University in Montreal, Canada. She received her B.A. in economics, M.B.A. and Ph.D. in management at UCLA. Dr. Adler conducts research and consults on strategic international human resource management, cross-cultural management, and global women leaders. She has authored numerous articles, produced the film, *A Portable Life,* and published the books, *International Dimensions of Organizational Behavior, Women in Management Worldwide,* and *Competitive Frontiers: Women Managers in a Global Economy.* Her work on multinational teams is featured in the BBC program, *A Survival Guide.*

Kenneth M. Alvares is vice president of human resources and a corporate executive officer with Sun Microsystems, Inc. Dr. Alvares holds a B.S. in psychology from Indiana University, an M.A. and Ph.D. in industrial/organizational psychology from the University of Illinois. Previously Dr. Alvares was vice president of personnel for Frito-Lay, a \$3 billion, 26,000 employee division of PepsiCo. He also founded and managed Personnel Development Inc., a management consulting firm specializing in organizational/individual assessment and development. Prior to joining Sun, Dr. Alvares served as vice president of human resources for Nichols Institute, a medical diagnostics laboratory located in San Juan Capistrano, California.

R. Wayne Anderson oversees worldwide human resource functions for Amoco Corporation. Mr. Anderson has a B.A. in psychology from Southern Methodist University and an M.A. in labor and industrial relations from the University of Illinois. He completed the Executive Management Program at the University of Chicago in 1979. He is a member of the corporate strategic planning, human resources, and investment committees. In addition, he serves on the Metropolitan Life Insurance Customer Advisory Board, the National Council of LaRaza Corporate Board of Advisors, and the Board of Directors for the Atlanta-based American Institute for Managing Diversity.

Homa Bahrami is a senior lecturer at the Haas School of Business, University of California, Berkeley. Her research focuses on global organizational trends, managing knowledge workers, and emerging professional roles and competencies. She is the coauthor (with Harold Leavitt) of *Managerial Psychology: Managing Behavior in Organizations*. Her research findings in the high technology sector have been published in leading journals. She is active in consulting, designing, and teaching executive development programs in the United States, Europe, and Asia-Pacific.

Richard (Dick) W. Beatty is a professor of human resource management in the School of Management and Labor Relations at Rutgers University. He is the recipient of Human Resource Planning Society's Research Award and also has served on the editorial boards of the *Academy of Management Review, Journal of High Technology Management, Human Resource Planning,* and is an associate editor of *Human Resource Management*. He received his B.A. from Hanover College (in biology and genetics), his M.B.A. from Emory University, and his Ph.D. (in human resources and organizational behavior) from Washington University.

Brian E. Becker is professor of human resources and chairman of the department of organization and human resources in the School of Management at the State University of New York at Buffalo. Professor Becker has published widely on the financial effects of employment systems, in both union and non-union organizations. His current research and consulting interests focus on the relationship between human resource systems and firm performance.

Michael Beer is professor of business administration at the Harvard Business School, where his research and teaching have been in the areas of organization effectiveness, human resource management, and organization change. He received a Ph.D. in organizational psychology and business from Ohio State University. Prior to joining the Harvard faculty, he was director of organization research and development at Corning Glass Works. Dr. Beer has authored or co-authored several books and many articles. He has consulted with numerous *Fortune* 500 companies.

David E. Bowen is a professor of management in the School of Management at Arizona State University-West. His research, teaching, and consulting interests focus on the organizational dynamics of delivering service quality, and the effectiveness of HRM departments. His articles have appeared in numerous professional journals. Dr. Bowen co-edited *Academy of Management Review's* 1994 special issue on "Total Quality

Management." He has published six books on service management, including *Winning the Service Game,* co-authored with Ben Schneider and published by Harvard Business School Press in 1995. Dr. Bowen serves on the editorial review boards of the *Journal of Management Inquiry, Human Resource Management, Journal of Quality Management,* and *International Journal of Service Industry Management.*

Wayne Brockbank is a clinical professor of business administration at the University of Michigan Business School. He is the faculty director or co-director of the three HR executive programs which were recently rated as the best HR executive programs in the United States and Europe by the *Wall Street Journal* and *BusinessWeek.* His current research and publishing focus on (1) conceptual and process linkages between human resource practices and business strategy and (2) creating customer-focused organizational cultures. Professor Brockbank has consulted in these areas with many private corporations including Texas Instruments, Hewlett-Packard, General Motors, Citibank, Motorola, and Cathay Pacific Airways.

W. Warner Burke became chair, in 1996, of *Organization and Leadership,* a new department consisting of more than 25 faculty members at the Teachers College of Columbia University. He has also served as the executive director of the Organization Development Network, Board of Governors of the Academy of Management, and is a Diplomate in the American Board of Professional Psychology. Dr. Burke has written extensively on organization development, training, and social and organizational psychology—and has been either the author or co-author of more than 13 books. He has received the Public Service Medal from NASA and the Lippitt Memorial Award from the American Society of Training and Development. Dr. Burke has consulted with a wide variety of organizations in business-industry, education, government, religion, and medical systems.

Ralph N. Christensen is vice president of human resources at Hallmark Cards, Inc., the world's largest publisher of greeting cards and related products. Mr. Christensen is responsible for ensuring that Hallmark has the people and organization to successfully pursue its corporate and financial objectives. He directs the company's various corporate human resources functions which include employee relations, compensation and benefits, organization and human resource planning, education and training, staffing, diversity planning and employee services. Mr. Christensen earned both a B.S. in business finance and an M.A. in organizational behavior from Brigham Young University.

Kenneth J. DeWoskin is professor of international business and Chinese studies at the University of Michigan in Ann Arbor. A former chair of Michigan's Department of Asian Languages and Cultures, he has been directly involved in Asian business since 1971 and actively engaged in public and private sector activities with the People's Republic of China since the early 1980s. Dr. DeWoskin works with both Michigan and Wharton in executive education and international conference programs, and he consults with a number of *Fortune 200* companies on their China market entry and business development initiatives. Author of numerous books and articles on China, he has recently co-edited a comprehensive volume on contemporary China entitled, *The Chinese: Adapting the Past, Facing the Future,* 2nd ed. (Ann Arbor, 1992).

Clifford J. Ehrlich is senior vice president, human resources of Marriott International. A graduate of Brown University and Boston College Law School, his involvement in professional organizations has included the following leadership roles: chairman of the Employee Relations Committee of the Business Round Table, chairman of the Employment Policy Foundation, chairman of the Personnel Round Table, and vice chairman of the Labor Policy Association. He has testified before Congressional Committees and Executive Branch Commissions on a variety of employment and employee relations matters. In 1993, Mr. Ehrlich was elected a fellow of the National Academy of Human Resources.

Robert W. Eichinger has 35 years of experience teaching at the University of Minnesota and The Center for Creative Leadership, consulting, and working in corporations, and is now running Lominger Limited, Inc. He spent ten years consulting in Texas, eight years with PepsiCo, two years with Pillsbury in executive development, and seven years and counting in Executive Success, his own consulting practice. He has co-authored a number of articles on executive development with Michael Lombardo and with him co-designed The LEADERSHIP ARCHITECT® Suite of executive and management development tools used at over 500 companies worldwide.

Bruce R. Ellig graduated Phi Beta Kappa with a B.B.A. and M.B.A. from the University of Wisconsin. Before his retirement he served as corporate vice president in charge of worldwide human relations for Pfizer. He has held leadership positions in many professional HR organizations, is a prominent author, has been interviewed on national radio and television programs, and has been widely quoted. He has received numerous awards including election to the National Academy of Human Resources.

Stuart Evans is a senior associate at the Centre for International Business and Management, the Judge Institute of Management Studies, University of Cambridge, England, and chairman of Pedagogy, Inc.—an educational software company—in Menlo Park, California. He was previously with SRI International, Bain and Company, Sand Hill Venture Group, and was a visiting scholar at the Graduate School of Business, Stanford University. His research, teaching, and writing focus on strategic flexibility in knowledge-based companies and high-tech entrepreneurship.

Jac Fitz-enz, founder-president, Saratoga Institute. In the 1970s, Dr. Fitz-enz was the first to publish quantitative data demonstrating the financial value of the human resource function. He is the father of HR benchmarking and performance evaluation. Under his direction, Saratoga Institute annually publishes benchmarks on human financial performance, best practices, and HR customer satisfaction in 20 countries. Dr. Fitz-enz has published nearly 100 articles and three books on HR performance measurement. His *Human Value Management* won the 1991 SHRM Book of the Year Award. His fourth book, *The Eight Practices of Effective Companies* (March, 1997) expands on this article.

Fred K. Foulkes received his B.A. degree from Princeton University and his M.B.A. and D.B.A. degrees from Harvard. He was a member of the Harvard Business School faculty before coming to Boston University where he is a professor in human resources management and strategic management. He has written several books and articles and has developed over 150 case studies. Professor Foulkes is a fellow of the National Academy of Human Resources. He is a consultant to several large companies and participates in corporate executive development programs.

Marshall Goldsmith is a founding director of Keilty, Goldsmith & Company (KGC) and a board member of the Peter Drucker Foundation. Leadership feedback processes that KGC has helped to develop have been used by more than one million people in leading organizations around the world. He has received national recognition for co-designing one of America's innovative leadership development programs. He is co-editor of the best-selling books, *The Leader of the Future* and *The Organization of the Future*. Mr. Goldsmith was ranked in the *Wall Street Journal* as one of the top ten consultants in the field of executive development.

Lynda Gratton is associate professor of organizational behavior at the London Business School. Over her twenty years in the field she has worked as a practitioner and a consultant. She now balances academic study with advising large complex companies. She is regarded as one of Europe's leading authorities on human resource management and for the last 6 years has directed the major research consortium, The Leading Edge. The findings from the study are described in *Human Resource Management and Organizational Transformation* published by Oxford University Press.

James L. Heskett is the UPS professor of business logistics and **Leonard A. Schlesinger** is the George F. Baker Jr. professor of business administration at the Harvard Business School where their teaching and research focus in the areas of general management, organizational adaptation, and service management. Their chapter draws on a broader research effort reported in *Out in Front: Building High Capability Service Organizations* (Boston: Harvard Business School Press, forthcoming).

Gordon Hewitt has been visiting professor of international business and corporate strategy at the University of Michigan Business School since 1994; he is on the core faculty for the senior executive programs. He also holds academic appointments at the University of Glasgow, Scotland, where he is the honorary professor at the Faculty of Social Sciences, and at the Manchester Business School, England, where he holds a chair of business strategy. He is a regular keynote speaker at executive conferences worldwide on global competition and corporate competitiveness, and is a consultant to many leading *Fortune* International 500 corporations.

Mark A. Huselid is an assistant professor in the School of Management and Labor Relations (SMLR) at Rutgers University. He holds a Ph.D. in Human Resource Management, an M.A. in Industrial Psychology, and an M.B.A. His current academic research and consulting activities focus on the linkages between human resource management systems, corporate strategy, and firm performance and has published numerous articles on these topics. Dr. Huselid was the recipient of the SHRM'S Yoder-Heneman Scholarly Achievement Award for 1993, the *Academy of Management Journal's* Best Paper Award for 1995, and the Academy of Management's Scholarly Achievement Award in Human Resource Management for 1996.

Harold E. Johnson has been an executive search consultant since 1989, serving with both Korn/Ferry International and Norman Broadbent International. From 1985–1988, he was senior vice president, human resources and corporate administration, for The Travelers Companies, Inc. Previously, Mr. Johnson was senior vice president, human resources, for Federated Department Stores, Inc., and before that, senior vice president,

Human Resources for INA (CIGNA) Corporation. He has also worked for Kennecott Copper Corporation and began his career with American Can Company. He graduated from the University of Nebraska.

Steven Kerr is vice president and chief learning officer for General Electric, including responsibility for GE's renowned leadership education center at Crotonville. He was previously on the faculties of Ohio State University, the University of Southern California, and the University of Michigan, and was dean of the faculty of the USC business school from 1985–1989. He has also been a consultant at the CEO and EVP levels to many *Fortune* 500 corporations. Dr. Kerr was 1989–1990 President of the Academy of Management. He has been featured in *Fortune, Forbes,* the *New York Times* and other publications, and on network and public television.

Howard V. Knicely is executive vice president, human resource and communications for TRW Inc. Mr. Knicely's human resource responsibilities include employee and labor relations, organization planning and management development, training, equal opportunity programs, compensation and benefits. In communications, he is responsible for corporate advertising, public relations, employee communications and community relations. In 1992, Mr. Knicely received the Society for Human Resource Management's Award of Professional Excellence as the outstanding human resource executive of the year. Also in 1992, Mr. Knicely was one of 12 fellows inducted into the inaugural class of the National Academy of Human Resources and now serves as chairman of the academy. In 1996 he was named Human Resource Executive of the Year by *Human Resource Executive* magazine.

Thomas A. Kochan is the George M. Bunker professor of management at M.I.T.'s Sloan School of Management. He came to M.I.T. in 1980 as a professor of industrial relations. From 1988 to 1991, he served as head of the behavioral and policy sciences area in the Sloan School. He also served as a member on the M.I.T. Commission on Industrial Productivity. He received his Ph.D. in industrial relations from the University of Wisconsin in 1973. Since then he has served as a third-party mediator, factfinder, and arbitrator and consultant to a variety of organizations. He has done research and authored numerous books on a variety of topics related to industrial relations and human resource management in the public and private sector.

Dale G. Lake has served as consultant and workshop leader to more than one hundred organizations including General Electric, HUD, MasterCard International, NASA, University of Michigan, Amoco, Harley-Davidson,

Sony, Northern Telecom, and British Airways. He has written numerous books and articles in the areas of leadership and management, strategic implementation, accelerating change, competitive advantage, global team development, sourcing, and human resource development. Dr. Lake is currently a member of the Management Executive Committee at Conagra where he serves as lead consultant on competitive advantage. He received his doctorate in social psychology from Columbia University.

Gerry Lake is Managing Editor of the *Human Resource Management Journal,* which presents research on cutting edge HR topics and is affiliated with the University of Michigan Business School. Dr. Lake has designed, managed, and made presentations in workshops around the world for clients such as Amoco, Digital Equipment, Federal Aviation Administration, Chubb Insurance, Columbia University, and the University of Michigan. She has published in the areas of adult transitions and human resources. Dr. Lake's current research interests are on the effects on women of going through life crises without support systems and on the changing ethics in Unites States' culture.

Edward E. Lawler III is a professor of management and organization in the business school at the University of Southern California. He has been honored as a top contributor to the fields of organizational development, organizational behavior, and compensation. He is the author of over 200 articles and 25 books. His most recent books include *Strategic Pay* (Jossey-Bass, 1990), *The Ultimate Advantage* (Jossey-Bass, 1992), *Organizing for the Future* (Jossey-Bass, 1993), *Creating High Performance Organizations* (Jossey-Bass, 1995), and *From the Ground Up: Six Principles for Creating the New Logic Corporation* (Jossey-Bass, 1996).

Sharon A. Lobel is an associate professor of management at Seattle University. She received her Ph.D. from Harvard University. She is an associate editor of *Human Resource Management* and is on the editorial board of *Academy of Management Journal*. She is a research fellow at the Work and Family Roundtable established by the Center on Work and Family at Boston University and is a member of the Wharton/Merck Work/Life Roundtable. Her research on managing diversity and work/life has appeared in numerous journals. Her publications include a co-edited book, *Managing Diversity: Human Resource Strategies for Transforming the Workplace.*

Michael M. Lombardo is co-founder of Lominger Ltd., Inc., a leadership development products firm that created the LEADERSHIP ARCHITECT® Suite of products. Mr. Lombardo spent 15 years at the Center for Creative

Leadership, primarily in research positions. While there, he focused on executive development and effectiveness and is co-author of a book, *The Lessons of Experience*. He is an author of the 360° feedback instrument, *Benchmarks*®, and of *Looking Glass, Inc.*®, a widely used behavioral simulation. He is the recipient of three national awards for research in the field of executive development.

Michael R. Losey, SPHR, is president and CEO of the Society for Human Resource Management (SHRM). With 35 years of HR experience, he is a frequent author and spokesperson on human resource management issues; a fellow and director of the National Academy of Human Resources; and serves as Secretary General of the World Federation of Personnel Management Associations (WFPMA), a worldwide coalition of human resource professional organizations representing more than 55 countries. Mr. Losey holds both a B.A. and an M.B.A. in industrial relations from the University of Michigan.

Kathryn D. McKee, SPHR, CCP, is senior vice president, compensation practice area for Marshall Group, Incorporated. Prior assignments include senior vice president and regional HR director for Standard Chartered Bank; senior vice president of HR and compensation and benefits for First Interstate Bancorp, and independent consulting. She graduated from the University of California, Santa Barbara where she received Senior Honor Key and Outstanding Senior Woman awards. She wrote "New Compensation Strategies for Emerging Career Patterns" published by *HR Magazine* which won the William Winter Award from the American Compensation Association. Other honors include IAPW's 1986 Member of the Year, PIHRA's 1990 Award for Professional Excellence, SHRM's 1991 Award for Professional Excellence.

Susan A. Mohrman is a senior research scientist at the Center for Effective Organizations in the School of Business Administration at the University of Southern California. Her research and publications focus on management and human resource innovations including employee involvement and total quality management, organizational change, organizational learning, organizational design processes, and team design and the lateral organization. She is co-author of *Self-Designing Organizations: Learning How to Create High Performance* (Addison-Wesley, 1989), *Designing Team-Based Organizations* (Jossey-Bass, 1995), and *Creating High Performance Organizations: Practices and Results of Employee Involvement and Total Quality Management in Fortune 1000 Companies* (Jossey-Bass, 1995).

James W. Peters is a practice director in the human resource strategy and information technologies practice of AON Consulting Group. In addition, he is the owner/editor of *HR Strategies & Tactics,* a widely read newsletter currently running a series on "Rethinking Human Resources." He received his B.A. and M.A. from the University of Wisconsin.

Jeffrey Pfeffer is Thomas D. Dee professor of organizational behavior at the Graduate School of Business, Stanford University. He previously taught at the business schools at the University of Illinois and the University of California, Berkeley, and served as a visiting professor at the Harvard Business School. Mr. Pfeffer has authored seven books including *Managing with Power* and *Competitive Advantage Through People* as well as more than 90 articles and book chapters. He has served as director of executive education at Stanford and has presented executive seminars in 19 countries and to numerous companies and associations in the United States.

Peter S. Pickus is a senior consultant in the Chicago office of the Organization Effectiveness and Development Division of the Human Resource Advisory Group of Coopers & Lybrand L.L.P. He is a leading member of the human capital effectiveness practice and is dedicated to the development of the Human Advantage: ValuMetrics, C&L's systemic methodology for evaluating a firm's human capital. He has an M.B.A. from the University of Michigan where he graduated with High Distinction.

Vladimir Pucik is associate professor and academic director of international programs at The Center for Advanced Human Resource Studies at the ILR School, Cornell University. His research interests include management practices in global firms, transnational human resource policies, international alliance strategies, and comparative management with a particular emphasis on the Far East and Europe. He has published extensively in academic and professional journals. Dr. Pucik's most recent major work is *"Globalizing Management: Creating and Leading the Competitive Organization."* He has consulted and conducted workshops for major corporations worldwide. Dr. Pucik also teaches regularly in a number of executive programs.

Gordon Redding is Poon Kam Kai professor of management studies at the University of Hong Kong and also director of the Poon Kam Kai Institute of Management which conducts executive and corporate development work. In Hong Kong since 1973, he was founding director of the University of Hong Kong Business School. He also holds a visiting professorship at INSEAD and works there in the Euro-Asia Centre. His research field is comparative management with an emphasis on Pacific Asia and a specialism in forms of Chinese capitalism. He is currently working on explanations of alternative systems of capitalism and their implications for processes of globalization by both Asian and non-Asian firms.

Anthony J. Rucci was elected executive vice president, administration, of Sears, Roebuck and Co. in November 1993. He is responsible for the human resources, quality improvement, ethics, strategic sourcing, diversity, aviation and facilities management functions of Sears. He also is chairman of the board of directors for Sears de Mexico and serves on the boards of Sears Canada and the Western Auto subsidiary of Sears. He holds a Ph.D. in industrial/organizational psychology from Bowling Green State University.

Craig Eric Schneier heads his own management consulting firm in Princeton, NJ. The firm specializes in assisting organizations execute strategy and change culture, as well as enhance the effectiveness of the HR systems. Dr. Schneier has held consulting positions with Ernst and Young, Booz-Allen, ODI, and Sibson. He has been on the faculty of the University of Maryland, University of Colorado, and Columbia University. Dr. Schneier has been co-author or co-editor of over 100 articles and several books, including *Managing Strategic and Cultural Change* and has won the SHRM best book award and the HRPS best research paper award twice. He has consulted with over half of the *Fortune* 100 companies.

Caren Siehl is associate professor of management at The American Graduate School of International Management. She had prior appointments at INSEAD in France and the University of Southern California. She earned her undergraduate degree in French and Linguistics at the University of California at Los Angeles and holds a Ph.D. from Stanford University's Graduate School of Business. Dr. Siehl's field of concentration is organizational behavior where she works with issues of culture, human resource management, and leadership styles in changing work environments. Dr. Siehl has been a consultant and an executive development specialist for numerous companies. She has published articles in a wide variety of academic journals. She has served on the Editorial Review Board of *Administrative Science Quarterly* and is currently the program chair for the Organization Development and Change Division of the Academy of Management.

Michael F. Spratt is a principal and managing director in the San Francisco office of Coopers & Lybrand, L.L.P. He leads the human capital effectiveness practice, and he provides strategic advisory services on accelerating business transitions. He has 18 years of consulting experience and 9 years of management experience in high technology industry. He holds a Ph.D. in psychology from the University of California and has published and spoken on a wide variety of business, organization, and human resource topics. He is co-authoring a book on *The Accelerated Transition* to be published in 1997.

Anne S. Tsui is professor and head of the department of management of organizations at the School of Business Management, Hong Kong University of Science and Technology. She is also a faculty member in the Graduate School of Management, University of California, Irvine. She received her Ph.D. from the University of California, Los Angeles. Dr. Tsui has a variety of research interests with current focus on managerial self-regulation and effectiveness, effectiveness of human resource departments in complex organizations, employee-organization relationship, and analyses of demographic effects on work outcomes.

Dave Ulrich is professor of business administration at the University of Michigan Business School. He is on the core faculty of the Michigan Executive Program, co-director of Michigan's Human Resource Executive Program, and the Advanced Human Resource Executive Program. He studies how organizations change, build capabilities, learn, remove boundaries, and leverage human resource activities. He has generated multiple award winning national databases on organizations which assess alignment between strategies and human resource practices and HR competencies. He has published over 80 articles and book chapters. He is editor of *Human Resource Management,* serves on the editorial board of five other journals, and writes a monthly column for *Human Resource Executive.* He is a fellow in the National Academy of Human Resources; co-founder of the Michigan Human Resource Partnership; been listed by *BusinessWeek* as one of the world's "top ten educators" in management and the top educator in human resources; and received the Pericles Property Meritus Award for outstanding contribution to the field of HR. He has consulted and done research with over half of the *Fortune* 200.

Mary Ann Von Glinow is an expert in global HR best practices, having worked extensively in China and many other parts of Asia, and most recently Latin America. She also specializes in technology transfer to China and doing business in Vietnam. She has a B.A. in international relations/political science from Bradley University, and her M.B.A., M.P.A. and Ph.D. in management science from the Ohio State University. Dr. Von Glinow was the 1994–1995 president of the Academy of Management and serves as Professor of Management and International Business at Florida International University. Previously on the faculty of the University of Southern California, she has authored over 100 journal articles and six books.

Arthur K. Yeung is the executive director (Asia-Pacific) of the University of Michigan Business School, a faculty member at the Michigan Executive Education Center, and a professor at the China Europe International Business School (Shanghai). Dr. Yeung's areas of specialization include Asia-Pacific management practices, HR process redesign/reengineering, strategic human resource management, and organizational learning. He is an associate editor of *Human Resource Management Journal* and published more than 15 articles in leading HR journals. Dr. Yeung is involved in leadership development programs for numerous corporations in Asia, including Philips, Carrier, Hewlett-Packard, ICI, and AlliedSignal Inc.

INDEX